Warfare, State and Society on the Black Sea Steppe, 1500–1700

In the sixteenth and seventeenth centuries Muscovy waged a costly struggle against the Crimean Khanate, the Ottoman Empire, and the Polish-Lithuanian Commonwealth for control of the fertile steppe above the Black Sea. This was a region of great strategic and economic importance – arguably the pivot of Eurasia at the time. Yet, this crucial period in Russia's history has, up until now, been neglected by historians. Brian L. Davies's study provides an essential insight into the emergence of Russia as a great power.

The long campaign took a great toll upon Russia's population, economy, and institutions, and repeatedly frustrated or redefined Russian military and diplomatic projects in the West. The struggle was every bit as important as Russia's wars in northern and central Europe for driving the Russian state-building process, forcing military reform and shaping Russia's visions of Empire.

Warfare, State and Society on the Black Sea Steppe, 1500–1700 examines the course of this struggle and explains how Russia's ultimate prevalence resulted from new strategies of military colonization in addition to improvements in army command-and-control, logistics, and tactics.

Brian L. Davies is Associate Professor of History at the University of Texas at San Antonio. His publications include *State Power and Community in Early Modern Russia: The Case of Kozlov, 1635–1649* (2004).

Warfare and History
General Editor Jeremy Black
Professor of History, University of Exeter

Air Power in the Age of Total War
John Buckley

*The Armies of the Caliphs:
Military and Society in the
Early Islamic State*
Hugh Kennedy

*The Balkan Wars, 1912–1913:
Prelude to the First World War*
Richard C. Hall

English Warfare, 1511–1642
Mark Charles Fissel

*European and Native American
Warfare, 1675–1815*
Armstrong Starkey

European Warfare, 1660–1815
Jeremy Black

European Warfare, 1494–1660
Jeremy Black

The First Punic War
J.F. Lazenby

*Frontiersmen: Warfare in Africa
Since 1950*
Anthony Clayton

*German Armies: War and German
Politics, 1648–1806*
Peter H. Wilson

The Great War 1914–1918
Spencer C. Tucker

*The Irish and British Wars,
1637–1654. Triumph, Tragedy,
and Failure*
James Scott Wheeler

Israel's Wars, 1947–1993
Ahron Bregman

*The Korean War: No Victors,
No Vanquished*
Stanley Sandler

*Medieval Chinese Warfare,
300–900*
David A. Graff

*Medieval Naval Warfare,
1000–1500*
Susan Rose

*Modern Chinese Warfare,
1795–1989*
Bruce A. Elleman

*Modern Insurgencies and
Counter-insurgencies: Guerrillas
and their Opponents since 1750*
Ian F.W. Beckett

*Mughal Warfare: Imperial Frontiers
and Highroads to Empire
1500–1700*
Jos Gommans

Naval Warfare, 1815–1914
Lawrence Sondhaus

Ottoman Warfare, 1500–1700
Rhoads Murphey

*The Peloponnesian War: A Military
Study*
J.F. Lazenby

*Samurai, Warfare and the State in
Early Medieval Japan*
Karl F. Friday

*Seapower and Naval Warfare,
1650–1830*
Richard Harding

The Soviet Military Experience
Roger R. Reese

Vietnam
Spencer C. Tucker

*The War for Independence and the
Transformation of American Society*
Harry M. Ward

*War and the State in Early Modern
Europe: Spain, the Dutch Republic
and Sweden as Fiscal–military
States, 1500–1660*
Jan Glete

*Warfare and Society in Europe,
1792–1914*
Geoffrey Wawro

*Warfare and Society in Europe,
1898 to the Present*
Michael S. Neiberg

Warfare at Sea, 1500–1650
Jan Glete

*Warfare in Atlantic Africa, 1500–
1800: Maritime Conflicts and the
Transformation of Europe*
John K. Thornton

*Warfare, State and Society in the
Byzantine World, 565–1204*
John Haldon

*War in the Early Modern World,
1450–1815*
edited by Jeremy Black

*Wars of Imperial Conquest in Africa,
1830–1914*
Bruce Vandervort

*Western Warfare in the Age of
the Crusades, 1000–1300*
John France

*War and Society in Imperial Rome,
31 BC–AD 284*
Brian Campbell

*Warfare and Society in the
Barbarian West*
Guy Halsall

*War in the Modern World since
1815*
edited by Jeremy Black

*World War Two: A Military
History*
Jeremy Black

*War, Politics and Society in Early
Modern China, 900–1795*
Peter Lorge

*Warfare in the Ancient Near East,
to c. 1600 BC*
William J. Hamblin

*The Wars of the French Revolution
and Napoleon, 1792–1815*
Owen Connelly

*Indian Wars of Canada, Mexico and
the United States, 1812–1900*
Bruce Vandervort

*Warfare, State and Society on the
Black Sea Steppe, 1500–1700*
Brian L. Davies

Warfare, State and Society on the Black Sea Steppe, 1500–1700

Brian L. Davies

Routledge
Taylor & Francis Group
LONDON AND NEW YORK

First published 2007
by Routledge
2 Park Square, Milton Park, Abingdon, Oxon OX14 4RN

Simultaneously published in the USA and Canada
by Routledge
270 Madison Ave, New York, NY 10016

Routledge is an imprint of the Taylor & Francis Group, an informa business

© 2007 Brian L. Davies

Typeset in Bembo by
Book Now Ltd, London
Printed and bound in Great Britain by
Antony Rowe Ltd, Chippenham, Wiltshire

All rights reserved. No part of this book may be reprinted or
reproduced or utilised in any form or by any electronic,
mechanical, or other means, now known or hereafter
invented, including photocopying and recording, or in any
information storage or retrieval system, without permission in
writing from the publishers.

British Library Cataloguing in Publication Data
A catalogue record for this book is available from the British Library

Library of Congress Cataloging in Publication Data
Davies, Brian L., 1953–
Warfare, state and society on the Black Sea steppe, 1500–1700/Brian L. Davies.
    p. cm. – (Warfare and history)
Includes bibliographical references and index.
1. Crimean Khanate–History, Military. 2. Ukraine–History–1648-1775.
3. Ukraine–Relations–Crimean Khanate. 4. Crimean Khanate–
Relations–Ukraine. 5. Russia–Relations–Crimean Khanate.
6. Crimean Khanate–Relations–Russia. I. Title.
DK508.9.K78D38 2007
947.7′04–dc22   2006034953

ISBN10 0–415–23985–0 (hbk)
ISBN10 0–415–23986–9 (pbk)
ISBN10 0–203–96176–5 (ebk)

ISBN13 978–0–415–23985–1 (hbk)
ISBN13 978–0–415–23986–8 (pbk)
ISBN13 978–0–203–96176–5 (ebk)

Contents

Acknowledgments vii
List of archival sources viii
List of abbreviations ix
Frontispiece Map I xii–xiii
Frontispiece Map II xiv–xv

1 Colonization, war, and slaveraiding on the Black Sea steppe in the sixteenth century 1

Early Polish-Lithuanian and Muscovite expansion towards the Black Sea 1
The Crimean Khanate and the Ottoman Empire 6
Poland-Lithuania and the Ottoman–Tatar alliance 9
Muscovy and the Ottoman–Tatar alliance 11
Crimean Tatar invasions 17
Crimean Tatar slaveraiding 23
The Nogais and Kalmyks 27
The formation of the cossack Hosts 29
Poland-Lithuania's southern frontier defense system 33
Southern frontier security: the Muscovite approach 39

2 Muscovy's southern borderland defense strategy, 1500–1635 41

The Bank Array 42
The Abatis Line 44
Command-and-control 47
Mobilizations and logistics 49
Tactics 52
Combined operations 56
Town garrisons 59
Reconnaissance, sorties, and sieges 61
The changing social profile of military colonization 64
Borderland defenses after the Troubles 66

CONTENTS

Military reform for the Smolensk campaign 70
The Smolensk War and its impact on southern Muscovy 73

3   The Belgorod Line   78

New danger from the Khanate 78
Refortifying the Abatis Line 79
New methods of military colonization 81
The odnodvortsy *85*
The Azov crisis and the founding of the Belgorod Line 88
The first Don expeditions by Muscovite forces 95
Cossack unrest in Commonwealth Ukraine 97
Impact on Muscovy 100
Bohdan Khmel'nyts'kyi's revolt 103
The decision to intervene 106
The consequences of the Pereiaslav Agreement 111

4   The Ukrainian quagmire   115

The Thirteen Years' War: the first phase, 1654–1657 115
The revolt of Hetman Vyhovs'kyi, 1657–1659 125
Expanding the foreign formations 132
From Chudnovo to Glukhov, 1659–1664 142
Stalemate 148
The Andrusovo Armistice and the new Ottoman threat 150

5   The Chyhyryn campaigns and the wars of the Holy League   155

Ottoman military intervention in Ukraine, 1669–1676 155
The First Russo-Turkish War, 1676–1681 159
Improving logistics and command-and-control 172
Muscovy in the Holy League 175
The Azov campaigns of Peter I 183

6   The balance of power at century's end   188

The Polish-Lithuanian Commonwealth 188
The Crimean Khanate 190
Ottoman power on the northern Black Sea coast 193
The cossack polities 198
Muscovy 201

Notes   208
Bibliography   223
Index   249

Acknowledgments

My first debt of thanks is to Jeremy Black, for inviting me to contribute to Routledge's *Warfare and History* series, and to Emma Langley and Philippa Grant, my patient editors at Routledge. I also wish to thank the staffs of the Lenin State Library, the Russian State Archive of Ancient Acts, Joseph Regenstein Library at the University of Chicago, the British Library, the Library of the School of Slavonic and East European Studies at the University of London, and the Summer Research Laboratory at the University of Illinois at Champaign-Urbana for access to their collections. Opportunities to conduct research in Moscow were made possible by the International Research and Exchanges Board. The Military History Summer Seminar at the US Army Academy, West Point, provided an introductory overview on how to write military operational history. The University of Texas at San Antonio provided a semester's leave from teaching.

I am forever grateful for the encouragement and insights offered by my friends and colleagues Richard Hellie, Daniel Kaiser, Carol Belkin Stevens, Philip Uninsky, Robert Frost, Janet Martin, Wing chung Ng, Beverly Davis, Kolleen Guy, and William Bishel. My greatest gratitude is, of course, to my wife Paula for her love and her unfailing ability to brighten my life.

I dedicate this book to the memory of my parents, Bruce Karl Davies (1923–1965) and Jeanne Kay Starnes (1929–2006).

Archival sources

RGADA (Rossiiskii Gosudarstvennyi Arkhiv Drevnikh Aktov, Moscow)
   F. 210, Razriadnyi prikaz
   Prikaznyi stol stolbets no. 385.
   Sevskii stol stolbets no. 223.
   Belgorodskii stol stolbtsy nos. 92, 176, 201, 210, 223, 385, 921, 994, 1301.

Abbreviations

AAE	Akty, sobrannye v bibliotekakh i arkhivakh Rossiiskoi imperii arkheograficheskoiu ekspeditsieiu imperatorskoi akademiia nauk 4 vols. + index. St. Petersburg, 1836, 1858.
AI	Akty, istoricheskie, sobrannyia i izdannyia arkheograficheskoiu kommissieiu 5 vols. + index. St. Petersburg, 1841–1843.
AIuB	Akty, otnosiashchiesia do iuridicheskago byta drevnei Rossii, izdannyia arkheograficheskoiu kommissieiu 3 vols. + index. St. Petersburg, 1857, 1864, 1884, 1901.
AIuZR	Akty, otnosiashchiesia k istorii iuzhnoi i zapadnoi Rossii, sobrannye i izdannye arkheograficheskoiu kommissieiu 15 vols. + supplements. St. Petersburg, 1846–1892.
AMG	Akty Moskovskago gosudarstva, izdannye imperatorskoiu akademieiu nauk, ed. N. A. Popov 3 vols. St. Petersburg, 1890–1901.
ChOIDR	Chteniia v obshchestve istorii i drevnostei rossiiskikh pri Moskovskom universitete. Sbornik 264 vols. Moscow, 1845–1918.
Chuvash	Dmitriev, V. D. "'Tsarskie' nakazy kazanskim voevodam XVII veka," *Nauchno-issledovatel'skii institute pri sovete ministrov Chuvashskoi ASSR. Sbornik statei* 3 (1974): 285–419.
DAI	Dopolneniia k aktam istoricheskim, sobrannyia i izdannyia arkheograficheskoiu kommissieiu 12 vols. + index. St. Petersburg, 1846–1875.
DR	Dvortsovye razriady, izdannye II-m otdeleniem sobstvennoi ego imp. velichestva kantseliarii 4 vols. St. Petersburg, 1850–1855.
Kotoshikhin	Uroff, Benjamin P. "Grigorii Karpovich Kotoshikhin, *On Russia in the Reign of Alexis Mikhailovich:* An Annotated Translation," Ph.D. dissertation, Columbia University, 1970.
OMAMIu	Opisanie dokumentov i bumag, khraniashchikhsia v Moskovskom arkhive ministerstva iustitsii 21 vols. St. Petersburg, 1869–1921.

ABBREVIATIONS

PSZ	Polnoe sobranie zakonov Rossiiskoi imperii. Sobranie pervoe 45 vols. St. Petersburg, 1830–1843.
RIB	Russkaia istoricheskaia biblioteka, izdavaemaia arkheograficheskoiu kommissieiu ministerstva narodnago prosveshcheniia 39 vols. Moscow, Leningrad, 1872–1927.
SGGD	Sobranie gosudarstvennykh gramot i dogovorov 5 vols. St. Petersburg, 1813–1894.
Solov'ev	Solov'ev. S. M. *Istoriia Rossii s drevneishikh vremen* 15 vols. Moscow, Leningrad: Sotsekgiz-Mysl, 1959–1966.
Uchenye zapiski RANION	Uchenye zapiski Rossiskoi assotsiatsii nauchno-issledovatel'skikh institutov obshchestvennykh nauk 7 vols. Moscow, 1926–1929.
Ulozhenie	Hellie, Richard, trans. and ed. *The Muscovite Law Code (Ulozhenie) of 1649, Part One: Text and Translation (The Laws of Russia. Series I, Medieval Russia, Vol. 3).* Irvine, CA: Charles Schlacks Jr., 1988.
Vremennik	Vremennik imperatorskago Moskovskago obshchestva istorii i drevnostei rossiiskikh 25 vols. Moscow, 1849–1857.
ZARG Kommentarii	Akademiia Nauk SSSR. Institut istorii SSSR. Leningradskoe otdelenie *Zakonodatel'nye akty Russkogo gosudarstva vtoroi poloviny XVI-pervoi poloviny XVII veka. Kommentarii.* Leningrad: Nauka, 1987.
ZARG Teksty	Akademiia Nauk SSSR. Institut istorii SSSR. Leningradskoe otdelenie *Zakonodatel'nye akty Russkogo gosudarstva vtoroi poloviny XVI-pervoi poloviny XVII veka. Teksty.* Leningrad: Nauka, 1986.
ZhMNP	Zhurnal ministerstva narodnago prosveshcheniia 434 vols. in 2 series. St. Petersburg, 1834–1917.

"What has made it impossible for us to live in time like fish in water, birds in air, like children? It is the fault of Empire! Empire has created the time of history. Empire has located its existence not in the smooth recurring time of the seasons but in the jagged time of rise and fall, of beginning and end, of catastrophe. Empire dooms itself to live in history and plot against history. One thought alone preoccupies the submerged mind of Empire: how not to end, how not to die, how to prolong its era. By day it pursues its enemies. It is cunning and ruthless, it sends its bloodhounds everywhere. By night it feeds on images of disaster: the sack of cities, the rape of populations, pyramids of bones, acres of desolation."

J. M. Coetzee, *Waiting for the Barbarians*

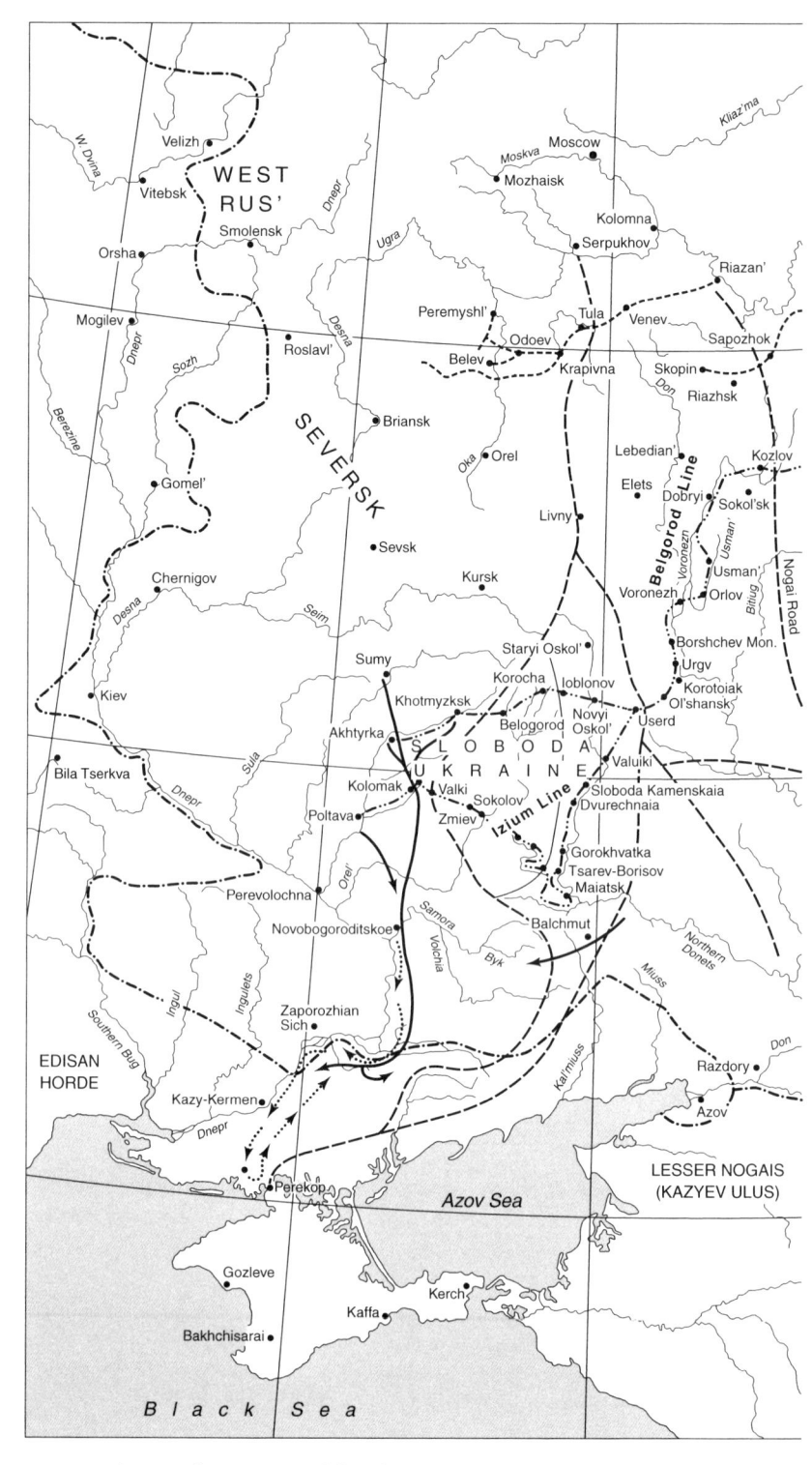

Map I Military colonization and fortified line construction on Muscovy's southern frontier by 1699.

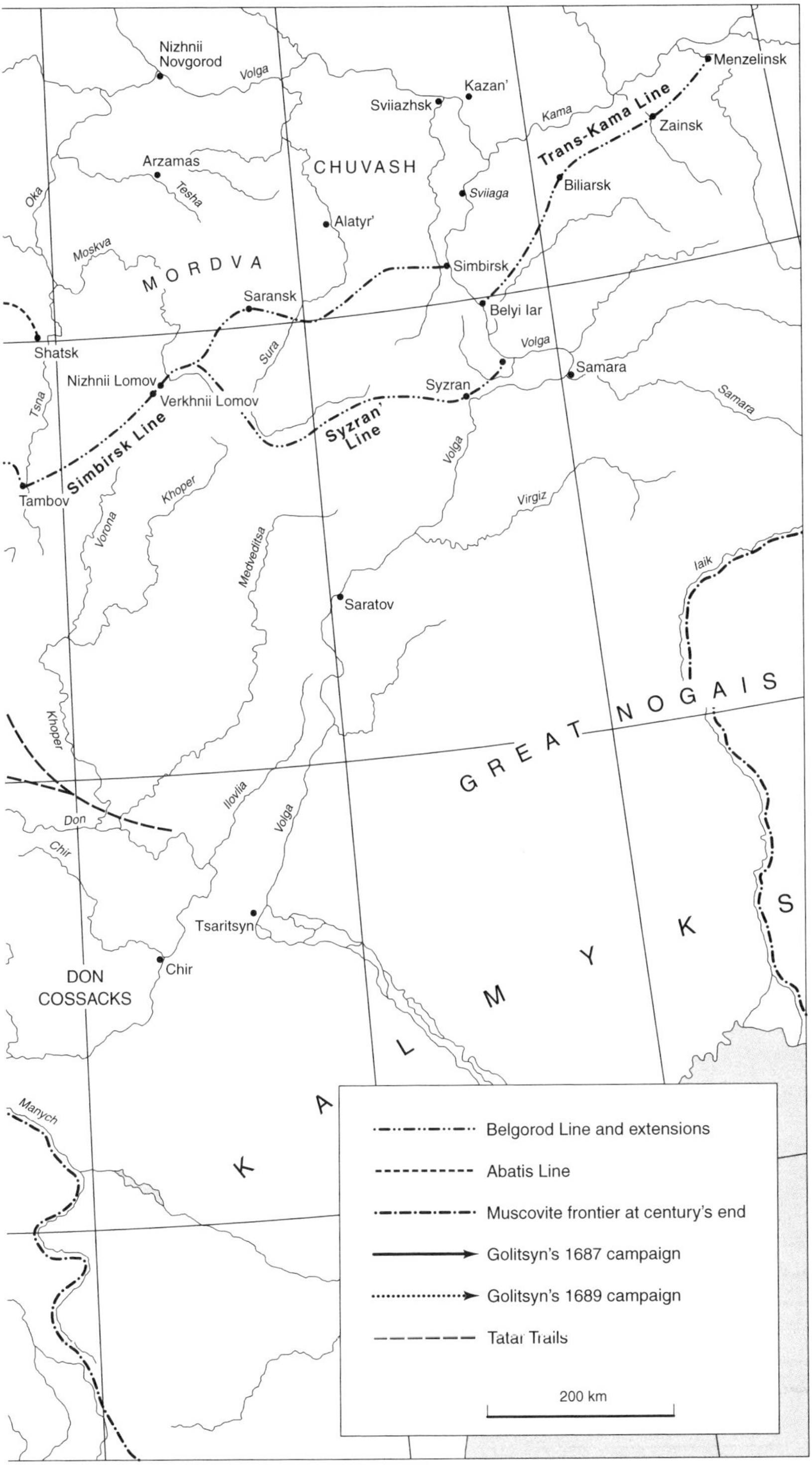

Nizhnii Novgorod
Volga
Kazan'
Sviiazhsk
Menzelinsk
Kama
Trans-Kama Line
Zainsk
Arzamas
Tesha
CHUVASH
Biliarsk
Oka
Sviiaga
Alatyr'
Moskva
MORDVA
Simbirsk
Saransk
Belyi Iar
Shatsk
Sura
Volga
Samara
Nizhnii Lomov
Syzran
Verkhnii Lomov
Tsna
Samara
Syzran' Line
Simbirsk Line
Volga
Tambov
Khoper
Virgiz
Vorona
Medveditsa
Iaik
Saratov
GREAT NOGAIS
Khoper
Ilovlia
Don
Volga
Chir
Tsaritsyn
KALMYKS
Chir
DON COSSACKS
Manych
Belgorod Line and extensions
Abatis Line
Muscovite frontier at century's end
Golitsyn's 1687 campaign
Golitsyn's 1689 campaign
Tatar Trails
200 km

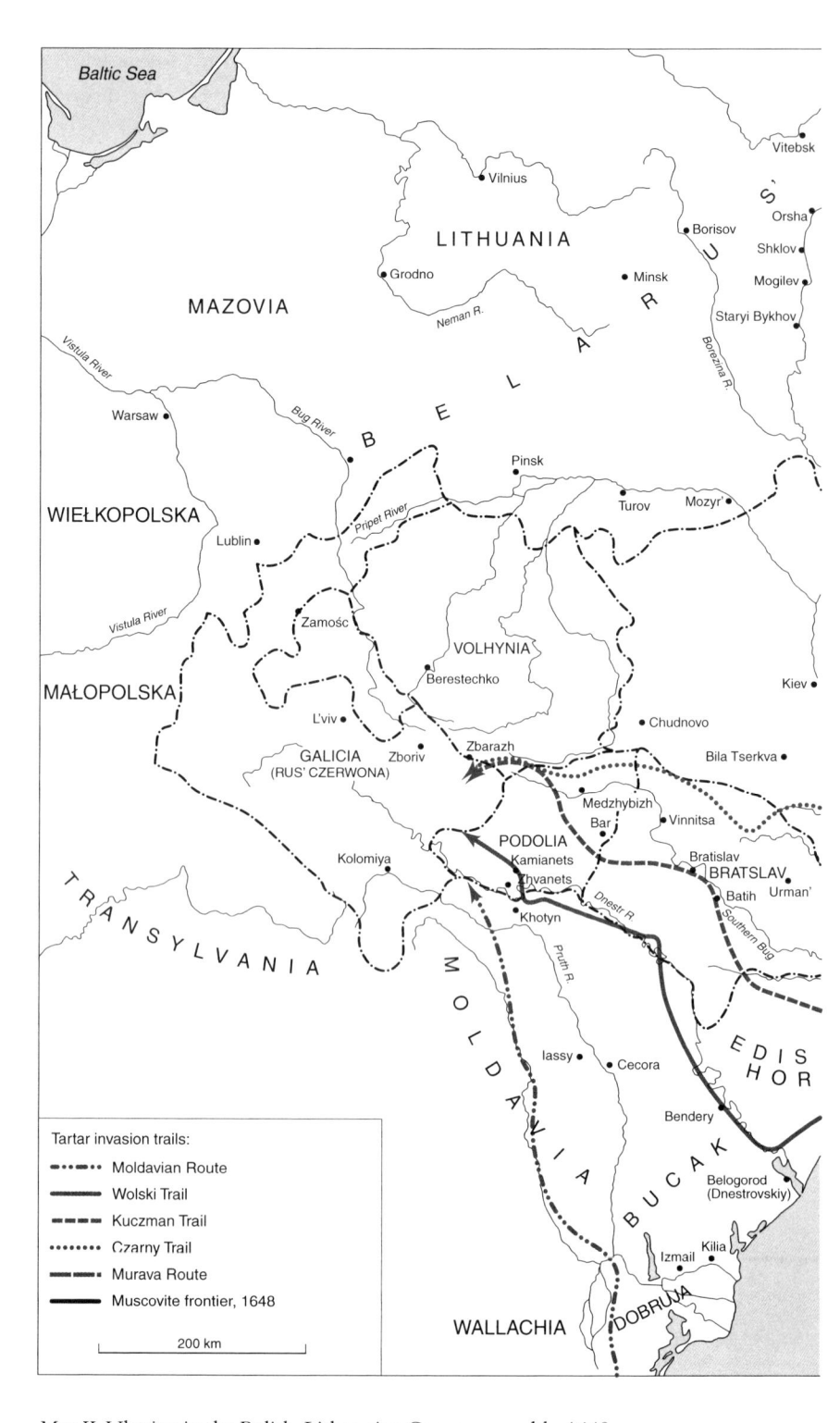

Map II Ukraine in the Polish-Lithuanian Commonwealth, 1648.

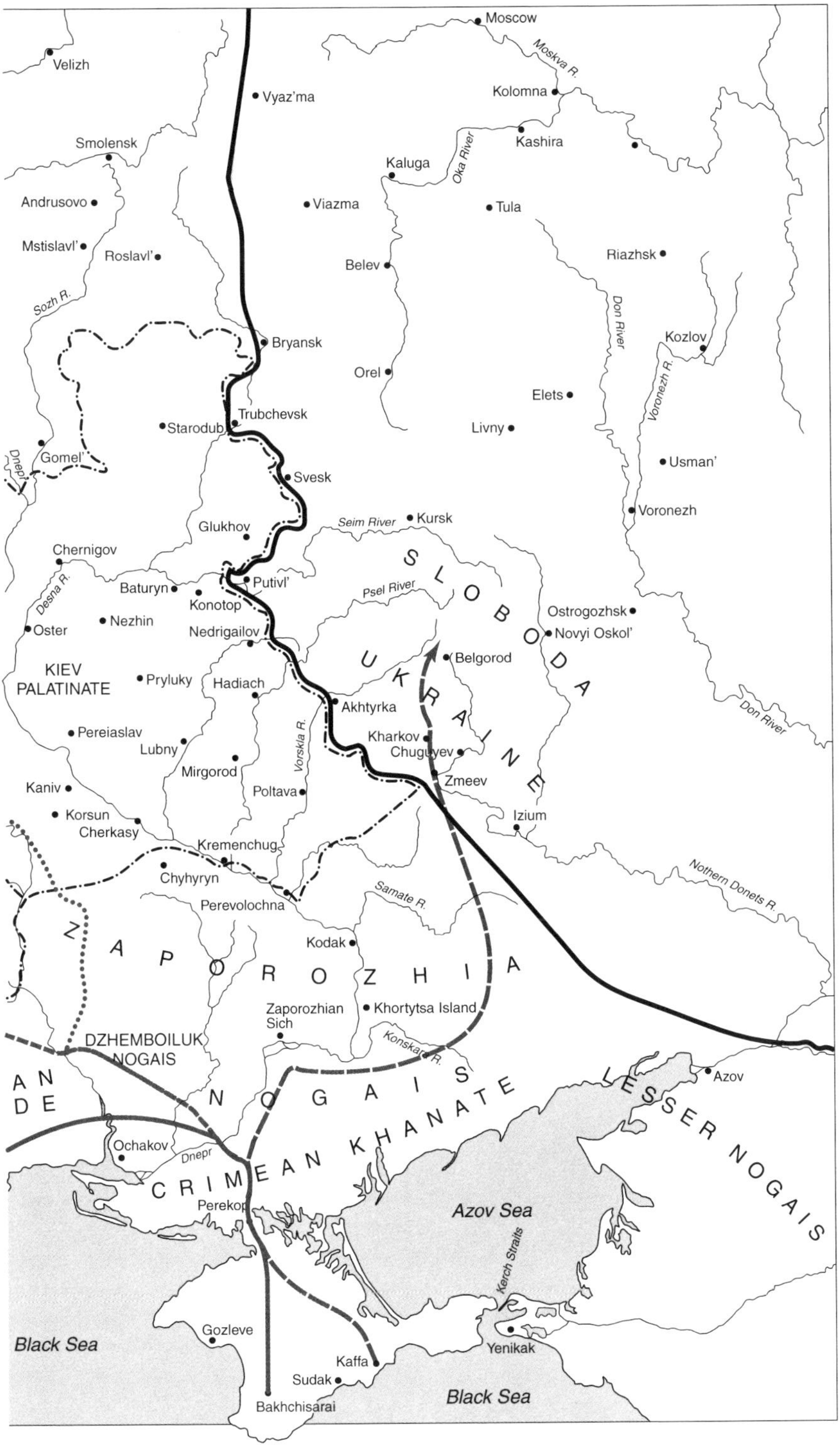
Moscow
Moskva R.
Velizh
Vyaz'ma
Kolomna
Kashira
Smolensk
Kaluga
Oka River
Andrusovo
Viazma
Tula
Mstislavl'
Roslavl'
Riazhsk
Belev
Sozh R.
Don River
Kozlov
Bryansk
Orel
Voronezh R.
Elets
Trubchevsk
Starodub
Livny
Dnepr
Gomel'
Usman'
Svesk
Voronezh
Seim River
Kursk
Glukhov
Chernigov
SLOBODA UKRAINE
Desna R.
Baturyn
Putivl'
Psel River
Konotop
Nezhin
Ostrogozhsk
Oster
Nedrigailov
Novyi Oskol'
KIEV PALATINATE
Belgorod
Pryluky
Hadiach
Akhtyrka
Don River
Pereiaslav
Vorskla R.
Kharkov
Lubny
Chuguyev
Mirgorod
Zmeev
Kaniv
Poltava
Korsun
Izium
Cherkasy
Kremenchug
Nothern Donets R.
Chyhyryn
Samate R.
Perevolochna
ZAPOROZHIA
Kodak
Zaporozhian Sich
Khortytsa Island
DZHEMBOILUK NOGAIS
Konskaia R.
Azov
NOGAIS
LESSER NOGAIS
Ochakov
Dnepr
CRIMEAN KHANATE
Perekop
Azov Sea
Kerch Straits
Gozleve
Black Sea
Yenikak
Kaffa
Sudak
Black Sea
Bakhchisarai

CHAPTER ONE

Colonization, war, and slaveraiding on the Black Sea steppe in the sixteenth century

For nearly four centuries – from the reign of Moscow Grand Prince Vasilii III through the reign of Russian Empress Catherine the Great – the Russian government, army, and people confronted the threats of Crimean Tatar invasion and raiding on their southern frontier. Russia's military conflict with the Crimean Khanate had a profound impact on the course of Russian colonization of the black soil forest-steppe and steppe above the Black Sea; it often frustrated Russian military and diplomatic efforts in the Baltic and central Europe; and it exerted as much impact on Russian military reform as the empire's wars with Poland-Lithuania, Livonia, and Sweden. It is especially the connection between the threat from the Crimean Khanate and Russian efforts to improve military organization, command-and-control, logistics, and tactics that is the focus of this study.

This book examines the first phase of the Russo-Crimean struggle, from the early sixteenth century down to the fall of Azov to the army and fleet of Peter the Great. In this phase the theater of war gradually shifted from east to west, from the Volga towards the Dnepr and beyond, and eventually embroiled the Muscovite state in war with the Polish-Lithuanian Commonwealth, the hetmans of Ukraine, and the Ottoman Turks. At the end of this phase the threat from the Crimean Khanate had been significantly reduced; Poland-Lithuania had been rendered a second-rate power; and Russia was in control of most of the Pontic steppe east of the Crimean peninsula. But her further advance southwest towards the Danube was still blocked by the Ottomans, against whom the Russians would have to wage four more wars in the eighteenth century.

Early Polish-Lithuanian and Muscovite expansion towards the Black Sea

In the middle of the fourteenth century Mongol power on the steppe above the Black Sea and Caspian began to weaken, creating a political vacuum that Muscovy and especially Lithuania and Poland scrambled to fill.

There were several reasons for the declining power of the Mongol Kipchak Horde (Golden Horde) after 1350: depopulation and the disruption of trade resulting from the Black Death; dynastic crisis within the Juchid house, leading to the concentration of power in the hands of a non-Juchid emir, Mamai, in turn provoking revolt against Mamai by Tokhtamysh, at the time supported by Timur Leng; a subsequent savage war between Tokhtamysh and Timur on the lower Volga, in the Caucasus and Transoxiana; and finally, the failure of Khan Edigei's last-ditch attempt to recentralize the Horde (1411). By the 1420s, Crimea had broken away from the Kipchak Horde; by the 1440s, so had Kazan' on the upper Volga. What remained to the Kipchak khans was the lower Volga and the old capital of Sarai. As they no longer controlled all of the Tatar tribes of the Kipchak steppe, their domain was increasingly referred to simply as the Great Horde.

The succession wars and the war with Timur had been waged mostly in the eastern reaches of the Kipchak Horde. But these wars had also weakened the hold of the Kipchak khans on their lands in the west: Crimea, the trading cities of the northern Black Sea coast, and the steppe hinterland from the Danube to the Don. The important Venetian-controlled port of Tana (Azov) had been seized by Timur, and the Genoese, in return for military assistance against Mamai, had extorted from Tokhtamysh recognition of their own sovereignty over Kaffa and the other port cities of Crimea and the northwestern Black Sea coast. The Kipchak Horde's trade routes to Persia and Transoxiana had been cut by Timur, and now its Great Horde remnant had less control over the Black Sea trade with Constantinople and Trebizond. The Genoese were able to draw more Black Sea commerce to their ports at Licostomo and Maurocastro, which stepped up their trade along the Danube into Hungary and across the Dnestr into Poland.[1] This further eroded the Great Horde's position in the Danubian region by promoting the formation of new states – Wallachia shook off Hungarian rule and Moldavia became an independent principality – and then setting Hungary, Poland, and the Ottoman Turks in competition to vassalize them. The new opportunities for territorial aggrandizement in the Danube region in turn produced greater enthusiasm in Poland, Hungary, Bohemia, and Austria for crusade coalition, first against the Tatars, and by the end of the century, against the Ottoman Turks.

Above all the declining power of the Great Horde encouraged the Grand Duchy of Lithuania, the Kingdom of Poland, and the Grand Principality of Moscow to begin expanding their territory southward towards the Black Sea.

In 1362 the Lithuanian Grand Duke Algirdas had defeated the Kipchak khan near the mouth of the Bug and annexed Chernigov, Novgorod-Severskii, Kiev, Pereiaslav, and Podolia. The incorporation of Podolia extended Lithuanian territory all the way to the coast of the Black Sea. Meanwhile the Polish kings were working to annex Galicia and the Chelm-Belz region and extend their power over the trade routes leading from the Black Sea into central Europe.

Algirdas' heir Jogaila had to resume paying tribute to the khan but was left in de facto control of eastern Ukraine, where he allowed Lithuanian nobles to establish new estates. The conversion of many of these Lithuanian landlords to Orthodoxy, their support for the establishment of an Orthodox metropolitanate at Kiev, and their acceptance of Ruthenian (Ukrainian) legal traditions and local institutions helped them legitimate their authority over the Orthodox majority. It also promoted the Ruthenization of Lithuanian administration in the original core of the Grand Duchy. In 1386 Jogaila, facing a revolt by his cousin supported by the Teutonic Order, accepted the offer of the Polish nobility and converted to the Roman rite, married Jadwiga, the daughter of the late King Kazimierz III, and took the throne of Poland as King Władysław II Jagiełło (r. 1386–1434). The Kingdom of Poland and the Grand Duchy of Lithuania were henceforth in dynastic union. Lithuania preserved its autonomy within this union and its nobles were soon admitted into the same noble estate (*szlachta*) with the privileges and rights enjoyed by the Polish nobility, with whom they now shared responsibility for electing Lithuania's Grand Duke and regulating union relations.

The union of Poland and Lithuania under a Jagiełłonian dynasty expanded the Polish sphere of influence in central Europe, making it possible to vassalize Moldavia for a time and, in the 1440s, place Jagiełłonians on the thrones of Hungary and Bohemia. It strengthened Polish-Lithuanian military and administrative power in Ukraine. But it also had the longer-term effect of aggravating social and religious tensions in Ukraine by introducing Polish royal castles and royal officials and allowing Catholic Polish magnates to obtain vast estates there, often at the expense of the Orthodox Lithuanian and Ruthenian nobles and gentry. After Poland recovered the port of Danzig from the Teutonic Order (1455) it was able to participate in the Baltic trade – particularly the grain trade – on a much larger scale. With capital investment from Western European merchants Polish nobles were able to establish vast latifundia in western Ukraine (Rus' Czerwona, western Volhynia) to produce grain for shipment down the Vistula to Danzig. This was followed by the gradual enserfment of the peasantry, a process culminating in the 1588 Third Lithuanian Statute, which abolished peasant tenants' right to transfer residence.

The spread of manorial economy also affected eastern Ukraine, although in a different fashion. The sparser population here made it harder to impose serfdom and the greater distance from the Vistula made it more rational for landlords to specialize in cattle ranching, supplemented by revenue from taverns and mills, tolls, and duties on hunting and fishing. The tendency in the east, therefore, was towards smaller *folwark* manor farms. But the landlords' dependence on excise dues, tolls, and fees had its own feudalizing effect on their relations with the peasantry and lesser gentry, especially as these same landlords often received life appointments as crown officials. The availability of uncolonized virgin land enabled a few magnates to establish latifundia of enormous size by winning vast grants of crown land in return for pledges to settle and defend them. In the 1590s the Palatine of Kiev, Kostiantyn Ostroz'kyi, won title to lands in Volhynia,

Galicia, and Kiev holding about 1,300 villages, 100 towns, and 40 castles. He defended these lands with a private army of 2,000 retainers, about the number of troops in the Crown army in Ukraine.[2]

In the early sixteenth century the Muscovite grand princes Ivan III and Vasilii III succeeded in wresting from Lithuania much of western Rus' – Novgorod-Severskii, Starodub, part of Chernigov, and the strategically crucial fortress of Smolensk. In the 1560s the Muscovite tsar Ivan IV invaded Lithuania and seized Polotsk and the districts just north of the Western Dvina River. This finally pressed the Lithuanian nobility to renegotiate terms of union with Poland and accept the new Union of Lublin (1569), which joined Poland and Lithuania in a federal Commonwealth (*Rzecz Pospolita*) under one Diet (*Sejm*) and a Polish King confirmed (and from 1573, elected) by both realms. The Union of Lublin had important consequences for Ukraine. Before 1569 the Polish Crown had directly administered only the western Ukrainian palatinates of Rus' Czerwona, Belz, and Podolia, holding about 570,000 subjects; now it assumed responsibility for the defense and administration of the eastern Ukrainian palatinates as well (Bratslav, Volhynia, and Kiev, with about 930,000 subjects). Polish royal castles and Quarter Army deployments held a southern Ukrainian frontier running from Kamianets in Podolia through Bar, Vinnitsa, and Bila Tserkva to Cherkasy.[3]

The southward expansion of the Grand Principality of Moscow was a slower process and did not begin in earnest until the last decade of the fifteenth century. Part of the reason it was comparatively delayed was Muscovy's remoteness from the Baltic trade and the Black Sea trade with central Europe, which reduced the economic stimulus for southward economic expansion and left security concerns the most important interest driving Muscovite southward expansion. Another reason was Muscovy's proximity to the Great Horde, rendering Muscovy more vulnerable to entanglement in Horde civil wars and wars with other steppe polities. Thus Moscow's Grand Prince Dmitrii Donskoi had sided with Tokhtamysh against the usurper Mamai and helped defeat Mamai at Kulikovo in 1380; but two years later Tokhtamysh had in turn besieged Moscow in order to reimpose Moscow's tribute obligations to the Great Horde. After Timur Leng's destruction of Tokhtamysh, Timur's emir Edigei, Nogai Khan and de facto Khan of the Great Horde, attacked Moscow yet again, taking thousands of prisoners (1408).[4] The Lithuanian grand dukes also strove to weaken Moscow by supporting Tver', Moscow's principal rival in the race to unify northeast Rus'. In 1425–1453 succession conflict within the Grand Principality of Moscow escalated into civil war and nearly resulted in the disintegration of the principality and its hegemony over northeastern Rus'.

On balance the period 1380–1480 did see significant Muscovite territorial expansion, but it was mostly to the north, at the expense of Novgorod, and to the northeast, to secure the lower Oka and push across the upper Volga. The most assertive Muscovite operation to alter the balance of power on the steppe in this period occurred along the Volga: the establishment in the 1450s of a vassal khanate at Kasimov, to shield central Muscovy against raids out of the new Kazan' Khanate.

Three developments permitted and encouraged Grand Prince Ivan III to turn his attention to the forest-steppe and steppe south of the Oka after 1480. The first of these was his annexation of Novgorod in 1478, which deprived Kazimierz IV, Grand Duke of Lithuania and King of Poland, of one of his most coveted prizes and so pushed Kazimierz into alliance with Khan Akhmet of the Great Horde. To counter this Ivan III negotiated his own alliance with Crimean Khan Mengli Girei, thereby strengthening Mengli Girei in his struggle to overthrow Akhmet and "reunite" the Kipchak Khanate under his own sovereignty. In 1480 Khan Akhmet marched on central Muscovy but was blocked by Muscovite forces deployed along the Ugra River and forced to withdraw. Akhmet had expected Lithuanian reinforcements, but diversionary attacks upon Lithuanian Ukraine by the Crimean Tatars had prevented them from arriving.[5]

The second development was the escalating conflict between Muscovy and Lithuania, which proceeded from the Muscovite annexation of Tver' and Novgorod (1478–1485) and culminated in Moscow's conquest of much of the western Rus' lands incorporated into Lithuania a century before. The Muscovite-Lithuanian War of 1494 gave Ivan III control of the Viaz'ma road to Moscow, the towns of Velizh, Belyi, and Toropets, and forced Lithuania to renounce its claims to Novgorod and Pskov. It also placed Kozel'sk, Novosil', Vorotynsk, Peremyshl', and Belev under Muscovite control, thereby extending Muscovy's southwestern frontier closer to the Starodub and Chernigov domains on the upper Dnepr. A second war in 1503–1505 resulted in the Muscovite annexation of the basins of the Seim and Desna rivers with the towns of Ryl'sk, Putivl', Briansk, Novgorod-Severskii, Trubchevsk, Chernigov, and Starodub (the Seversk region). Most of western Rus' had come under the sovereignty of the Grand Prince of Moscow. "It needed only the cities of Smolensk and Kiev to complete the picture; but Ivan had little reason to complain. Smolensk was under forty miles from the Muscovite frontier; Kiev was within easy reach both of Chernigov and Lyubech on the Dnepr."[6] The Lithuanians were defeated in their attempt to retake these territories in the war of 1507–1508. In 1514 Moscow Grand Prince Vasilii III finally seized Smolensk.

The third development occurred at the eastern end of Muscovy's Oka frontier, just to the southwest from Kasimov and the Volga. The old frontier principality of Riazan', the "trampled land" traditionally most exposed to Tatar attack, had been transformed into an appanage within the principality of Moscow upon the death of Prince Ivan Fedorovich in 1456. In 1521 Grand Prince Vasilii III annexed Riazan' outright by deposing its last prince for allegedly conspiring with the Crimean Khan. This moved Muscovy's defense perimeter far to the south, to the upper reaches of the Voronezh, Tsna, and Moksha rivers. The annexation of Riazan' had great economic consequences as well. It reconnected the Oka-Volga trade route to the old southern trade route descending the Don to Azov and the Black Sea, and it opened to Muscovite colonization and cultivation much of the vast belt of fertile black soil (*chernozem*) running along the Pontic forest-steppe and steppe from Moldavia to the Volga. Yields for wheat and rye were higher on Riazan's black soil than in central Muscovy. A century later the Dutch envoy Adam Olearius judged that Riazan' "surpassed all the neighboring provinces in grain growing, livestock raising, and abundance of grain."[7] Riazan' quickly became the primary provisioner of central Muscovy. Settlement of its once-sparsely populated southern reaches encouraged further colonization to its west, towards the Volga, and to its southwest, towards the newly annexed Seversk lands.

The Crimean Khanate and the Ottoman Empire

The emergence of the Crimean Khanate in the 1440s was further sign of the disintegration of the Great Horde. By the 1480s the Crimean Khanate had acquired, through strategic partnership with the Ottoman Empire, enough military power to constitute its own threat to Polish-Lithuanian colonization of the Black Sea steppe, and after 1509, to Muscovite colonization as well.

The Crimean Khanate was formed in the course of the civil war attending the succession struggles within the Great Horde nomadizing on the lower Volga. The founder of its ruling dynasty, Khan Haji Girei, was a Chingisid prince forced into exile in Lithuania and invited to rule in Crimea by certain aristocratic Tatar clans – the Shirins, Barins, Argins, and Kipchaks – that had likewise broken from the Great Horde. Haji Girei established his capital at Bakhchisarai on the Crimean peninsula but continued to lay claim to the title of "Great Khan of the Great Horde, of the Crimean Throne, and of the Kipchak Steppe," thereby asssserting his sovereignty over the Pontic steppe and forest-steppe from Moldavia to the Volga and as far north as Seversk and the upper Don. The four clans who had invited him to rule over them nomadized across the southern edge of the steppe, just above Perekop and the Black Sea and Azov coasts. By the end of the century there were about 200,000 souls in their domains (*ulusy*), rising to 500,000 by 1550. A smaller Tatar population sedentarized in the towns and villages of the Crimean peninsula. Large numbers of Genoese, Greeks, Armenians, Georgians, and Karaim Jews resided in the largest Crimean towns (Kaffa, Evpatoriya, Azov) as subject millets and paid the *çizje* capitation tax into the khan's treasury; taxes and duties on their trade yielded even greater revenue.[8]

Haji Girei had relied alternately upon alliances with the Poles and Lithuanians or with Muscovy to win and preserve his khanate's independence from the Golden Horde. But the fall of Constantinople in 1453 changed the balance of power in the Black Sea region. Sultan Mehmet II now embarked on a campaign to establish Ottoman hegemony over all the coastal trading towns of the Black Sea. This included the towns of the Crimean coast, the Genoese merchant colonies that had been so important for the commerce of the Byzantine empire and promised comparable benefit for the commercial development of Ottoman Rumelia. After their Byzantine patrons had passed from the stage the Crimean

Genoese had placed themselves under the protection of the king of Poland (1462), had begun hiring Polish mercenaries, and had interfered in factional conflicts within the Muslim Crimean Khanate. This raised the danger that the Genoese might bring all of Crimea under Polish hegemony and extend Polish power along the Black Sea coast as far as the Danube. To prevent this Sultans Mehmet II and Bayezit II moved to vassalize the Crimean Genoese and Crimean khan. This served his additional goal of weakening independent Moldavia, the final obstacle to Ottoman domination of the entire Black Sea coast, by starving Stefan the Great's treasury of the Crimean trade revenues Stefan received through the fortress ports of Kilia and Akkerman he had recently seized.

By 1475 the Turks had seized control of Kaffa, imposed tribute on the Genoese merchants, and annexed most of the Crimean coast and foothills between Inkerman and Kaffa – about a tenth of the Crimean peninsula. They achieved this by recruiting the support of the Shirin clan, whose *bey* held the rights to a share of Kaffa's tolls, and by pitting the Shirins, the khan Haji Girei, and the Genoese against each other. Khan Mengli Girei was spared his life and restored to his throne after pledging vassalage to the sultan. In 1484 he led Crimean Tatar forces in their first joint operation with an Ottoman army – to retake the fortresses of Kilia and Akkerman from the Moldavians. The recapture of Kilia and Akkerman reestablished Ottoman control over the western coast of the Black Sea as far north as the Dnestr – and bounded the Khanate on the west with the Ottoman *pashalik* of Silistria. An Ottoman garrison was also founded at Azov (old Tana), near the Don's mouth at the Sea of Azov – thereby bounding the Khanate on the east. Ottoman garrisons were established within the Khanate at Perekop, Gozlev, Arabat, and Yenikale.

The Black Sea had been transformed into the "Ottoman lake" and the vassalage imposed upon Mengli Girei and his successors assured that Ottoman sultans could make use of Crimean Tatar cavalry in their campaigns in Moldavia, Bessarabia, and Ukraine and generally rely upon the Khanate to deter the Poles and Muscovites from entering anti-Ottoman coalitions or carrying their colonization of the steppe too close to the Turkish garrisons along the Black Sea coast. Meanwhile Crimea provided Istanbul, Rumelia, and northern Anatolia with slaves, grain, salt, fish, meat, and lumber.

In principle the khans' vassalage was of the kind the sultans were imposing upon the hospodarates of the Danube. The khan was under obligation to the sultan to be "the enemy of thy enemy, the friend of thy friend," to contribute troops when the sultan called for them, and pay tribute gifts to the sultan; otherwise the khan remained sovereign over his own domains, minting his own coins, and collecting his own tribute from the Poles, Muscovites, and the other nomadic peoples of the Kipchak steppe. He frequently received Ottoman subsidies as well.

In practice this vassalage did not fully constrain the khan's diplomatic and military power. In some periods – during the reign of Sultan Selim II, and the first decade of Suleiman I's rule – the Porte closely controlled the foreign policy of the Khanate, directing Crimean Tatar military power against its primary enemy of the moment and preventing Crimean raiding against neutral or potentially friendly powers. In other periods the Crimean khans ignored or openly defied the sultans because they needed war plunder to pacify their own restless nobles or because the Ottomans had taken actions (annexing Bucak, attempting to establish an Ottoman military presence on the lower Volga) that threatened to reduce their sovereignty over their own domains. On several occasions the Ottomans found it necessary to depose troublesome khans and exile them to Rhodes. Over time the weakening of the khans' authority over their *beys* and mirzas encouraged the growth of a separatist spirit in the khanate.[9] For most of the sixteenth century, however, the khans strove to serve their Ottoman suzerains. The sultan's protectorate was still of great strategic advantage to them. Although the Turkish garrisons founded at Azov and on the lower Dnepr served first of all to maintain Ottoman control over the termini of the Dnepr and Don river trades, they also stood as reminders to the khans' enemies that the might of the Ottoman Empire protected the Crimean Khanate. This put Poland-Lithuania and Muscovy on warning that cossack raids upon the khanate or the Turkish tripwire garrisons along the northern Black Sea coast could provoke retaliation by Ottoman armies.

The khans' alliance with the Porte also enabled them to draw other nomadic peoples of the western Kipchak steppe into military confederation. In the sixteenth century part of the Nogai Horde abandoned the steppes along the Volga between Kazan' and Astrakhan' to relocate farther west on the grasslands between the Kuban River and the Don; these Nogai émigrés were called the Lesser Nogais or the Kazyev *ulus*, to distinguish them from the Great Nogais who continued to roam east of the Volga. The Lesser Nogais recognized the suzerainty of the Crimean khan and the sultan, and because they preserved their nomadic way of life they came to comprise a large part of the khan's army, replacing the increasingly sedentarized Crimean peninsula farmers who had been allowed to purchase exemptions from military service. Other fragments of the Nogai Horde resettled on the steppes between the Dnestr and Bug as the Edisan Tatars, and in Bessarabia as the Bucak or Belgorod Tatars.[10] In this manner the Pontic steppes between the Danube and the Kuban came under the control of a new Tatar confederation.

Poland and Muscovy had to come to terms with the enhanced power of the Crimean Khanate. Both courted the khans' neutrality with payments of tribute, part of which was sent on to Istanbul. On several occasions each bid to enlist Crimean military assistance against the other. The khans often switched alliances between Poland and Muscovy in the fifteenth and early sixteenth centuries according to which bid higher in tribute. From the 1520s large-scale Crimean operations in the north (as opposed to smaller-scale raids for captives) were more often directed against the Muscovites, and the Khanate and Polish-Lithuanian Commonwealth acted in close concert against Muscovy in 1607–1617.

Poland-Lithuania and the Ottoman–Tatar alliance

The foreign policy pursued by Poland's Jagiełłonian kings in the late fifteenth and early sixteenth centuries placed them in frequent military conflict with the Crimean Khanate and at risk of war with the Ottomans as well. From the 1460s the Crimean khans had been locked in struggle with the khans of the Great Horde for mastery of the Kipchak steppe as far as the Volga, so King Kazimierz IV's 1470 decision to ally with Great Horde Khan Akhmet against Ivan III of Moscow drove Crimean Khan Mengli Girei into a thirty-seven-year alliance with Muscovy and subjected Poland-Lithuania to a series of reprisal raids. Almost every year saw a Crimean Tatar incursion into Podolia, Volhynia, Małopolska, Rus' Czerwona, or Lithuanian Belarus'.[11] Jagiełłonian intervention in the affairs of the Danubian principalities was frustrating Ottoman plans, too: they had allied with Stefan the Great of Moldavia in 1484–1487, in unsuccessful efforts to recover Kilia and Cetatea Alba from the Turks; had subsequently turned upon Stefan and invaded Moldavia in 1497, to try to install Zygmunt Jagiełło on the Moldavian throne; and with Władysław II, son of Kazimierz IV, occupying the thrones of Bohemia (1471–1516) and Hungary (1490–1516) they had appeared poised to complete the formal dynastic union of Poland, Hungary, and Bohemia.

Such provocations gave the Ottomans reason to further encourage Mengli Girei to raid Poland-Lithuania and to prepare their own retaliation. In 1498 an Ottoman army of 40–60,000 men under Bali Pasha, *beylerbey* of Silistria, invaded Poland, striking deep into Małopolska and Mazovia and taking perhaps 10,000 prisoners.[12] A second Ottoman expedition later that year was supposed to join with Tatar forces and attack Cracow or Vilnius; sudden cold weather forced its early withdrawal, but the Poles had been put on warning. Subsequent territorial losses in Lithuania to the armies of Ivan III provided further reason for King Aleksander to seek rapprochement with the Ottomans and the Khanate. In 1503 he signed a five-year peace with Sultan Bayezit II. After losing Smolensk to the Muscovites (1514) King Zygmunt I signed an alliance with the Crimean Khanate (1516) and a peace treaty with Sultan Selim I (1519). An "eternal peace" between the Porte and Poland-Lithuania was signed in 1533 and renewed in 1547.

These treaties, along with annual payments of tribute "gifts" (*pominki*) to the khan amounting to about 15,000 złoties, did not entirely spare Poland-Lithuania from Tatar raiding. Polish and Lithuanian magnates holding estates in Podolia sometimes conducted their own expeditions across the border, provoking Tatar retaliation; and the khans treated as pretext for war any overt move by the Polish crown threatening Ottoman interests in the Danubian region. In 1519 Tatar forces ravaged the Kiev and Volhynian palatinates and even struck Lublin. Podolia and Galicia were invaded in 1526. Invariably the khan and sultan offered plausible denials of responsibility for these attacks. These attacks succeeded in discouraging Zygmunt I from further involvement in the affairs of the Danubian principalities, which fell under more direct Ottoman domination. Louis II, the Jagiellonian King of Hungary and Bohemia, was left isolated; he and his army were destroyed by the Turks at Mohacs in 1526, and Hungary was divided among the Ottomans, the Habsburgs, and the Magyar nobles supporting Transylvanian *voivode* Janos Zapolyai, who soon offered his vassalage to Suleiman I. The expansion of Ottoman hegemony in Hungary in turn undermined Moldavia's independence, whose *voivode*, Petru Rares, was overthrown in 1538. Moldavia was fully vassalized; its southeastern corner, between the Dnestr and the Pruth, was annexed to the Ottoman *pashalik* of Silistria.

Zygmunt I and the last Jagiellonian king of Poland, Zygmunt II Avgust (r. 1548–1572), were both strong proponents of strengthening royal authority and military power by courting the support of the lesser nobility against the senatorial oligarchy and expanding the crowns' fiscal machinery. But neither dared risk returning to a more assertive foreign policy in the southwest lest this provoke Tatar or Ottoman retaliation. They had to content themselves with the gradual strengthening of their small border defense army in Ukraine and concentrating their military resources in the northwest against Muscovite threats to Lithuania and Livonia.

The shadow of the Ottoman–Tatar alliance even influenced the royal succession. Upon the death of the intestate Zygmunt II in 1572, the French candidate Henri de Valois was elected in part because this promised less provocation to the Turks than the election of either of the Habsburg candidates, archdukes Ernst and Maximilian, who appeared to expect Poland-Lithuania to support the Habsburg reconquest of Hungary in exchange for Habsburg permission for the Polish conquest of Moldavia. When Henri abandoned the Polish throne in 1575 the Polish nobility again rejected the Habsburg candidate, Maximilian, for Istvan (Stefan) Bathory, Prince of Transylvania. Bathory had won the Transylvanian throne in 1571 with Ottoman assistance; he was fervently anti-Habsburg, and intended to use the resources of the Polish monarchy to press his own claim to the Hungarian throne. Eventually this project would have set the Ottomans against him as well, but it remained unattempted at the end of his life in 1586.

It was only in the 1590s that the "eternal peace" with the Ottoman Empire began to unravel. Initially this was due more to Zaporozhian raids upon Crimea and the Ottoman fortresses at Kilia and Bendery than to any provocation presented by the Polish crown, despite King Zygmunt III Waza's obvious Habsburg sympathies and his impatience with the *Sejm*'s restraints upon his ability to raise revenue and wage war. Over the longer term the Polish–Ottoman peace was undermined by new Polish adventurism in Moldavia. But this was not the work of the king but of his Chancellor and Grand Hetman Jan Zamoyski, and it was motivated by Zamoyski's hostility towards the Habsburgs rather than defiance of the Ottomans. Zamoyski invaded Moldavia with 9,000 men in 1595 to take advantage of the Habsburg–Ottoman war in Hungary and install his own puppet hospodar, Ieremiia Movila, to preempt Habsburg vassalization of Moldavia. Although this led to brief conflict with Crimean Tatar forces,

Sultan Mehmet III soon agreed to recognize Movila as hospodar provided he accept Polish–Ottoman condominium over Moldavia. By 1600, however, Movila had been overthrown by Mihai Viteazul, hospodar of Wallachia, who aimed at uniting the Danubian principalities under Habsburg protection. This sparked the Magnate Wars, a long and confusing series of interventions by Polish hetmans using private armies, cossacks, and Moldavian allies to try to restore the rule of the Movila family. During it all direct conflict with Ottoman forces was avoided, but there was fighting with the Crimean Tatars on Moldavian and Polish territory. Upon the end of the Habsburg–Ottoman war the Ottomans had reason to view the Polish magnates as the most immediate obstacle to reconsolidating their control over the Danubian provinces. The treaty of Jaruga (1617) therefore required that the Polish-Lithuanian Commonwealth restrain cossack raiders, restore Khotin to the Turks, and refrain from further interference in the Danubian principalities.

Muscovy and the Ottoman–Tatar alliance

Healthy respect for Ottoman military power likewise inclined the Muscovite grand princes and tsars to a Pontic steppe policy that tried to avoid provoking the Porte. For the most part they were successful in this. In the sixteenth century there was only one brief and limited military conflict between Muscovite and Ottoman forces, on the lower Volga in 1569. The more imposing and immediate threat Muscovy faced was the Crimean Khanate, the khans having their own conflicts of interest with Moscow not bearing directly on the sultans' interests.

The breakdown of the Muscovite–Crimean alliance against Poland-Lithuania and the Great Horde had not immediately affected Ottoman–Muscovite relations. Up to 1512 Muscovy's conflict with the Crimean Khanate mattered far less to Ottoman ruling circles than the civil war to reunify their Empire or the threats from Venice and Persia; and under Sultan Selim I (r. 1512–1522) the Muscovite–Crimean conflict did not warrant Ottoman intervention because Muscovy was valued as a counterweight to Poland-Lithuania. The flashpoint of the Muscovite–Crimean conflict lay far to the east, in Kazan', and affected Ottoman security much less than Polish adventurism in Moldavia. Selim I therefore encouraged Muscovite diplomats to discuss friendship and even alliance, and the Ottoman governors of Azov and Kaffa even shared with Moscow intelligence of Khan Mehmet Girei's preparations to invade Muscovy.

The deterioration of Muscovite–Ottoman relations began only in Suleiman I's reign, in 1523, and derived from conflict between obligations to client polities rather than from any direct clash of Muscovite and Ottoman interests. The death of Khan Mehmet Girei I had set off a succession struggle in Crimea and led to the Shirin clan asking Suleiman I to intervene. Suleiman I had settled Saadet Girei I (r. 1524–1532) on the Crimean throne, and to keep him in power had given him an infantry bodyguard of Ottoman *kapikulu* and expanded the Ottoman garrisons in Crimea. Henceforth Ottoman units were expected to play a larger role in supporting the khan's military operations, and this involved them in the power struggle in Kazan' and in attacks on Muscovy. In 1541, for example, Khan Sahib Girei was able to take his army across the Oka on rafts under covering fire from Ottoman gunners.[13] The Ottoman–Muscovite peace was also periodically endangered by the actions of Moscow's clients on the steppe. The Don Cossacks raided the Turkish fortress town of Azov with greater frequency and tenacity after 1550. Ivan IV's success in coopting Ismail and Tinekhmat (Din-Akhmet), mirzas of the Great Nogai Horde, made it possible for the tsar to rely on Nogai support to conquer and annex the khanates of Kazan' (October 1552) and Astrakhan' (1554–1556).

As Great Khan of the Great Horde, Crimean Khan Devlet Girei had claimed sovereignty over Kazan' and Astrakhan' and had long struggled to place his kinsmen on their thrones. Ivan IV's subjugation of the two Volga khanates was therefore an intolerable act of aggression in his eyes. Istanbul had no interest in using Ottoman forces to help him drive the Muscovites from Kazan', but a campaign to recover Astrakhan' was another matter. Muscovite control of Astrakhan' more directly endangered lines of communication between Ottoman Azov and the Empire's Sunni coreligionists and trade partners in the Uzbek khanates beyond the Caspian; in fact the Khan of Khiva was already complaining the Muscovite garrison at Astrakhan' was harassing merchants and pilgrims traveling between Khiva and Azov. The Lesser Nogais, who had split off from the Great Nogai Horde in protest against its alliance with Muscovy, were clamoring for an Ottoman–Crimean campaign to retake Astrakhan', as was the last Astrakhan' khan, then living in exile in Anatolia. But Istanbul's greatest concern was that Ivan IV would use Astrakhan' as a base for Muscovite intervention in the northern Caucasus. In 1567 Ivan IV had a fortress built on the Terek River to establish his protectorate over the Kabardan Circassians. This blocked Azov's line of communication with Derbent, the Ottoman fortress on the Caspian, and thereby threatened to upset the Ottoman–Safavid balance of power in the Caucasus and northern Iran.

The armistice signed with the Habsburgs in 1568 finally freed Sultan Selim II to take action against the Muscovite garrison at Astrakhan'. In 1569 Kasim Pasha, *beylerbey* of Kaffa, led a flotilla out of Azov carrying 3,000 janissaries, 7,000 other troops, and 5,000 laborers. Their mission was to join with Crimean Tatar cavalry and ascend the Don to Perevolok, where it bent eastward towards the Volga; to dig a great canal linking these rivers; and to establish a base there, to liberate Astrakhan' and support future Ottoman expeditionary forces using the canal to descend the Volga, sail across the Caspian, and reconquer Shirwan in northern Iran.

Kasim Pasha's expedition reached Perevolok but found the canal project technically impossible. The evidence is unclear as to whether they came under attack by Muscovite forces under Prince Petr Serebrianyi, sent down the Volga to reinforce Astrakhan', or whether Kassim Pasha made a real effort to besiege Astrakhan'. In late September Kasim Pasha made a difficult withdrawal across the North Caucasus steppe to Azov, losing many men and horses on the march. His Crimean allies do not seem to have given him much support. The Muscovite diplomat Mal'tsev, in detention in Kasim Pasha's train, thought the Tatars deliberately led them across waterless wastes to discourage them from ever returning. Devlet Girei may have decided to let the operation fail lest the Turks cheat him of his Astrakhan' *yurt* and incorporate Astrakhan' into some Ottoman *eyalet*. According to some reports only a third of Kasim Pasha's force survived to reach Azov alive, and all but 700 of them subsequently perished in a storm while sailing back to Istanbul.[14]

The Perevolok episode did not lead to further conflict between Muscovy and the Porte. Ivan IV could not afford to divert resources from his war in Livonia and therefore sent reassurances he wanted to remain in friendship with the sultan and intended no harm to Muslim merchants and pilgrims. In 1571 or 1572 he dismantled his fortress on the Terek, after which the Crimean Tatars drove the remaining Muscovites from Kabarda. Sultan Selim II, now occupied with war with Venice, accepted these developments as grounds to disengage from the Volga problem; he made no further claims to protectorate over Astrakhan', indicating he chose not to contest the tsar's annexation of that region. On the whole Ottoman interests had received no serious setback, for they were again able to move Turkish and Crimean Tatar troops out of Azov across the Kuban and Terek steppe to Derbent to complete their conquest of Shirwan and Azerbaijan.[15]

With the exception of Muscovite encroachment on the Ottoman sphere of influence in the Caucasus, Muscovy's southern steppe policy before the 1650s presented less challenge than Poland-Lithuania's to Ottoman strategic interests. There was therefore no strategic pretext for significant direct military conflict as opposed to proxy conflict involving Tatar and cossack client polities. Nor did religion militate against coexistence. The Muscovite government and Orthodox church sometimes invoked religion in the struggle against the Kazan', Astrakhan', and Crimean khanates, characterizing military campaigns and the founding of new frontier towns as measures to "free the Orthodox peasants from the clutches of the *busurmany* [Muslims]."[16] But a coherent pan-Slavist and anti-Islamic *reconquista* propaganda linking the war against the Tatars to the larger struggle of Christian Europe against the Turk would not emerge until the 1670s, when Muscovy and the Ottoman Empire finally came into direct conflict over control of Ukraine.

It was therefore the Crimean Khanate, not the Ottoman Empire, that presented the greater threat to Muscovite frontier security in the sixteenth century.

The long alliance between Muscovy and the Crimean Khanate (1470–1509) had enabled Ivan III to secure central Muscovy against attack by the Great Horde and gain territory in the west at the expense of Lithuania; it had enabled Mengli Girei to conquer the Great Horde and extort heavy tribute from Poland-Lithuania. But by 1509 Muscovy and the Crimean Khanate no longer had sufficient shared interests to preserve the alliance. The differences now dividing them were in fact sharper than those dividing the Khanate from Poland-Lithuania. It was strategic calculation, not just King Zygmunt I's offer of new tribute gifts, that convinced Khan Mengli Girei to abandon alliance with the Muscovites that year.

The territories Ivan III and Vasilii III had wrested from Lithuania by 1508 – Chernigov, Starodub, Bel'sk, Seversk – gave Muscovite armies a stronger position from which to resume war against Lithuania for mastery of Smolensk and the other west Rus' districts just south of the Western Dvina. Muscovite annexation of these territories also raised for Mengli Girei the specter of eventual Muscovite expansion down the Dnepr into the Kipchak steppe. Mengli Girei therefore realigned the khanate with Poland-Lithuania and pledged to reward Zygmunt I with the patent (*iarlyk*) to the lands Muscovy had seized from Lithuania, as well as Tula and Riazan' and other districts along the Oka, the patent the khan's to award because these districts had formerly paid tribute to the Great Horde. For the time being Mengli Girei remained officially at peace with the Muscovites – he left the leadership of the 1507 and 1512 raids into Muscovy to the *kalga-sultan* and his nobles so he could disavow responsibility for them. But the fall of Smolensk to the Muscovites in 1514 forced Mengli Girei to issue a final ultimatum: Smolensk, a tributary of the Great Horde, must be returned to Zygmunt I on the grounds the khan had awarded the king the patent to this town, while the districts of Briansk, Starodub, Novgorod-Severskii, Ryl'sk, Putivl', and Karachev must be "restored" to the khan. These districts were attacked by Tatar forces in the winter of 1514–1515, probably not to seize and hold them but to extort further tribute from them and press Vasilii III to abandon Smolensk. Mengli Girei's successor Khan Muhammad Girei (r. 1515–1523) continued to demand the restoration of these districts as his pretext for more punitive raiding into Muscovy. A 1517 incursion involved more than 20,000 Tatars. In July 1521 the khan himself led an army reportedly exceeding 50,000 men up the Murava trail, crossed the Oka near Kolomna, and ravaged the southern environs of Moscow for two weeks, forcing Vasilii III to evacuate his court to Volokolamsk.[17]

A second reason for the breakdown of Muscovite–Crimean cooperation had been the attempts of Ivan III and Vasilii III to tighten their protectorate over the Kazan' Khanate. This was intolerable to Mengli Girei and Muhammad Girei in that it repudiated their own claims of sovereignty over Kazan' as Great Khans of the Great Horde, and because it weakened their suzerainty over the Nogais, who depended heavily on Kazan' as a trading partner. Intervening in Kazan' succession politics in fact proved a dangerous game for the Muscovites to play, for they overestimated the strength of the pro-Moscow faction among the Kazan' nobility. In late 1518 Kazan's khan Muhammad-emin died without an heir. Muscovite troops under Podzhogin helped install on the Kazan' throne the thirteen-year-old Shah Ali, tsarevich of the Muscovite vassal khanate of Kasimov. But a revolt by Kazan' nobles supported by Crimean Tatar forces drove Shah Ali from Kazan' in 1521 and enthroned Sahib Girei, the son of

Mengli Girei. Sahib Girei's army then advanced on Moscow from the Volga, raiding Nizhnii Novgorod and Vladimir en route, while Crimean Khan Muhammad Girei's army marched on Moscow from the south. Thousands of Russians were taken captive and Vasilii III was forced to recognize the Girei dynastic reunification of the Kazan' and Crimean khanates.[18]

Fortunately for the Muscovites, Khan Muhammad Girei soon overreached. He led his army against Astrakhan' to overthrow its pro-Moscow khan and complete the reunification of the Great Horde, but the Nogais defeated him and killed him and both of his sons in 1523. The next three Crimean khans (Gazy Girei I, r. 1523–1524; Saadet Girei I, r. 1524–1532; and Islam Girei I, r. 1532) were unwilling to provide enough direct support to keep Sahib Girei secure on the throne of Kazan' and firmly in control of the Nogai Horde; their own power in Crimea was limited, too, for some of their *beys* intrigued against them. Sahib Girei therefore turned to Sultan Suleiman I for assistance. In 1524 Sahib Girei abdicated the throne of Kazan' for his nephew Safa Girei and placed Kazan' under de facto Ottoman protection; then, with Ottoman support, he began to struggle for the throne of Crimea. Fear of Ottoman retaliation soon forced the usurper Islam Girei I to abdicate, and the Turks helped install Sahib Girei I as khan in 1532.

For most of the reign of Sahib Girei I (1532–1551) the Crimean Khanate was in its closest strategic partnership with the Ottoman Empire. Istanbul monitored and partly directed Sahib Girei by surrounding him with a large entourage of Ottoman *kapikulu* officials and guards. This provided Sahib Girei with a counterweight to his *karachi beys* and encouraged him to assert a more autocratic style of rule; he enlarged the army, claimed more sources of regular revenue, and even began styling himself as padishah. It allowed Istanbul to rely on him to maintain the balance of power between Poland-Lithuania and Muscovy to Ottoman benefit, instructing him to attack whichever seemed in ascendance at the moment, but on grounds that allowed the sultan to disavow any responsibility. The Ottoman writer Evliya Çelebi called this the Stratagem of Selim I.[19] The Crimean Tatars therefore raided Volhynia in 1549 even though Poland-Lithuania was still formally at peace with the Khanate. Crimean attacks on Muscovy, especially on the Muscovite districts nearest the Volga, were more frequent and larger in scale because the khan had his own interest in keeping a Girei on Kazan's throne and denying Kazan' to the Muscovites. Moscow's attempts to vassalize the Nogais gave Sahib Girei I further reason to wage war on Muscovy. In 1541 Sahib Girei I attempted an invasion of central Muscovy, and he supported Kazan' Khan Safa Girei's 1536–1537 and 1545 campaigns against the Muscovites.

The Kazan' campaigns greatly escalated the Crimean–Muscovite conflict by showing Ivan IV that central Muscovy's security demanded a final resolution of the problem of Kazan'. When Safa Girei died in 1549 Ivan IV moved to reinstall his puppet Shah Ali on the Kazan' throne. This ignited a new war with the pro-Crimean party in Kazan' (1549–1552). Ultimately the escalating Kazan' crisis alarmed the Ottoman authorities in Kaffa, who reported to Suleiman I their concern that Sahib Girei I was pursuing too independent a policy in the northeast.

> The khan now has too powerful an army and has become too ambitious. He thinks he is better than you in every way. The proof of it is that he now dares to oppose your orders and to make excuses for not sending auxiliary forces [into Iran]. The moment you pass away he thinks he will gain possession of all the Ottoman territories in the Crimea. He does not show the slightest respect to the envoys sent from the Porte. If he unites his forces with the Nogais no one can be a match for him and resist.[20]

Istanbul therefore threw its support to the *beys* chafing under Sahib Girei's autocratic rule. Sahib Girei I was overthrown and executed along with his infant sons and grandsons. Devlet Girei I (r. 1551–1577) took the throne of Crimea with the approval of the sultan.

Khan Devlet Girei I led a large army into southern Muscovy in spring 1552 and managed to place Tula under bombardment by his Ottoman guns. But the approach of Muscovite corps from Kashira and Kolomna forced him to withdraw down the Murava Trail. This freed Ivan IV to concentrate his forces against Kazan', which fell on 2 October 1552. A Muscovite vicegerent was installed in Kazan'. The fall of Kazan' in turn brought the *beys* of the larger Nogai tribes into closer dependency on Moscow and helped the tsar isolate and conquer the Khanate of Astrakhan' (1554–1556). But the *beys* of the Kazyev *ulus* (Lesser Nogais) refused to accept vassalage to the tsar and migrated to the Azov steppe to place themselves under the protection of Devlet Girei.

Although Devlet Girei made attacks on Poland-Lithuania in 1557–1558 his primary concern of the next several years was punishing Muscovy. He led large Crimean Tatar armies into Muscovy in 1555, 1562, 1564, 1565, 1571, and 1572; he provided some support for the Ottoman expedition against Astrakhan' in 1569; and his sons commanded campaigns into Muscovy in 1558, 1563, 1568, 1570, and 1571. These incursions caused great destruction – especially the 1571 invasion, which resulted in the burning of Moscow, the abduction of several thousand captives, and Ivan IV's pledge (soon reneged upon) to abandon Astrakhan'. But the last of Devlet Girei's major incursions into Muscovy, in 1572, ended in his decisive defeat at Molodi. Thereafter Devlet Girei persisted in demanding the restoration of Kazan' and Astrakhan' but had to limit himself to diplomatic means to pursue these goals.

His sons Muhammad Girei II (r. 1577–1584) and Islam Girei II largely kept to the same policy because they lacked the power to mobilize military resources on the scale their father had commanded. Muhammad Girei was eventually deposed for turning upon the Ottoman governor of Kaffa, who had intervened in the selection of the khan's heir apparent; Islam Girei II strove to be the faithful servant of the sultan but provoked an uprising by the Lesser Nogais. The Muscovite government took advantage of this breathing spell to pursue detente with sultans Murat III and Mehmet III. Istanbul indicated it was prepared to maintain peace if the tsar would rein in the Don Cossacks and prevent them from raiding Ottoman territory. Moscow then cited its commitment to curb the Don Cossacks to justify its construction of new garrison towns on the Voronezh and Don rivers. In 1589 the Muscovites built a major new garrison town, Tsaritsyn, on the Volga near Perevolok to connect their Voronezh and Don colonies to Astrakhan' and the Volga garrison network and secure them against Tatar attack from the east.

It was not until the reign of Khan Gazy Girei II (1588–1597, 1597–1607) that the Khanate resumed large-scale military operations: against Poland in 1589, Muscovy in 1591, and in support of the Ottoman army in Hungary in 1592–1606. Smaller raids along the Oka River also kept Muscovite forces busy in 1592–1593, and there was a major invasion alert in 1598. Gazy Girei continued to justify his operations against the Muscovites partly on his claims to Kazan' and Astrakhan', but the likelihood he could actually recover them was quickly receding, so the actual motives for his attacks on Muscovy were to extort more tribute gifts, take prisoners for sale in the slavemarkets of Kaffa, and discourage Muscovite military colonization of the forest-steppe and steppe. He told Moscow's envoy he considered the tsar's founding of new garrison towns on the frontier a threat to the Crimean Khanate:

> Your ruler thus wishes to do as he did with Kazan': at first he established a town close by, then afterwards seized Kazan'; but the Crimea is not Kazan', in the Crimea there are many hands and eyes; it will be necessary for your ruler to go beyond the towns to the very heart (of Crimea).[21]

Crimean Tatar invasions

There were forty-three major Crimean and Nogai attacks on Muscovite territory just in the first half of the sixteenth century; Lithuania and Poland experienced seventy-five incursions over the period 1474–1569.[22] Large Tatar forces were able to penetrate into the heartland of Muscovy even in years when truce with the Commonwealth had allowed the Russians to increase regimental strengths along their southern frontier. In 1571 Khan Devlet Girei invaded with an army of 40,000 Crimeans, Nogais, and Circassians and burned much of Moscow, allegedly killing 80,000 and carrying off 150,000 captives. The Tatars burned the suburbs of Moscow again in 1592 while the bulk of Russian forces were busy fighting the Swedes on the northwestern frontier. In 1633, while the tsar's army was preoccupied in a western campaign to recover Smolensk from the Poles, the Crimeans and Nogais launched devastating attacks upon the interior districts of Kashira and Serpukhov.

The Crimean Tatar armies invading Poland-Lithuania in the early sixteenth century usually numbered 10–20,000 warriors at most, but by mid-century the khan was assembling invasion forces of 30,000, according to Mikhalon Litvin. In the 1630s Guillaume Le Vasseur, Sieur de Beauplan, a French engineer stationed with the Polish army in Ukraine, estimated the maximum size of these invasion armies at about 80,000 if the khan took the field himself and enjoyed the full support of his Nogai confederates. Khan Dzhanibek Girei led 50,000 men to reinforce the 250,000 Turks marching on Khotyn in Polish Ukraine in 1621. Major invasions personally led by the khan were less frequent after the reign of Devlet Girei I, however, for his successors had less power over their *beys* and mirzas, who were now more likely to undertake campaigns on their own initiative, sometimes even in defiance of the khan, to obtain slaves and livestock or because they had been suborned by Polish or Muscovite bribes.[23]

Map I shows the seven main invasion trails (*shliakhi*) into Muscovy and Poland-Lithuania the Crimean Tatars and Great and Lesser Nogais followed in the sixteenth and early seventeenth centuries.

The westernmost road into Muscovy was the Murava Trail, which began at the narrow fortified isthmus of Perekop, where the Crimean peninsula joins the mainland. From Perekop it made a sharp turn to the east, running between the Konskaia and Kalchik rivers. Then it moved north, skirting to the west of the Northern Donets River and the Russian steppe towns of Tsarev-Borisov and Belgorod. From Oskol' the road ran due north, crossing the Bystraia Sosna River at Livny and passing between the towns of Novosil' and Dankov to hit Tula and the other towns of the Borderland Front (the districts just below the Oka, east of the Zhizdra, and west of the Osetr). Tula overlooked the Kostomarov ford of the Upa River, which led invading armies on to Serpukhov and Moscow. Near Oskol' smaller tributary roads ran westward from the main Murava road, allowing raiders to attack the Seversk Front towns of Putivl', Ryl'sk, Sevsk, and Kromy and the Trans-Oka Front towns of the Briansk forest massif to their north.

An Iziuma Trail branched off from the Murava Trail near the Kalicha and Kal'miuss rivers in the steppes above the Sea of Azov. It crossed the Northern Donets much nearer Tsarev-Borisov, ran between Valuiki and Belgorod, and rejoined the Murava Trail at Oskol'.

The third road, the Kal'miuss Trail, also left the Murava road in the Azov steppes near the Kal'miuss River, but then swung farther east, crossing the Northern Donets east of Tsarev-Borisov. It passed east of Valuiki, crossed the Tikhaia Sosna River, and then rejoined the Murava Trail just south of Livny on the Bystraia Sosna. A later branch of this Kal'miuss Trail, used by the Lesser Nogais, started in the steppes just north of the Turkish fortress of Azov and merged with the main Kal'miuss road at the Tikhaia Sosna River.

East of the Kal'miuss Trail Road lay the Nogai Road (*Nogaiskaia doroga*), used most frequently by the Lesser Nogais, or by those Great Nogais roaming the steppes west of the Volga. It started from the southern Don River, at a point halfway between the Azov fortress and the Russian town of Tsaritsyn' on the lower Volga. It ran along the eastern branch of the Khoper River and passed between the sources of the Bitiug and Tsna rivers. At the confluence of the Lesnoi Voronezh and Pol'noi Voronezh rivers it forked – due north towards the towns of Shatsk and Riazan', and northwest towards the towns of Riazhsk, Lebedian', and Dankov.

The Great Nogais and later the Kalmyks and Bashkirs could also advance up the Volga to raid the Russian towns of Tetiushi, Kazan', Sviiazhsk, and Cheboksarai, then drop south through the villages of the Chuvashi and Mordva to blockade the Russian garrisons at Alatyr', Temnikov, Kadom, and Mokshansk or push farther west against Shatsk and the Riazan' region.

The Muscovite territory endangered by these invasion roads thus stretched from Putivl' in the west to the Volga in the east, a front over 1,000 km long at its broadest point, the eastward bend of the Volga at Samara. The southernmost points of Russian military colonization before 1635 were at Putivl', Belgorod, Tsarev-Borisov, Valuiki, Voronezh, and Tsaritsyn and Astrakhan' on the lower Volga. Tsarev-Borisov and Valuiki lay the closest to the border of the Crimean Khanate, standing 150 and 300 km from the juncture of the Murava, Iziuma and Kal'miuss roads. But both towns were too small and isolated from other garrisons to permit further colonization of their environs. Tsarev-Borisov, for example, stood about 150 km from Belgorod and 300 km from Voronezh, and these were its closest neighbors. During the Polish intervention of 1617–1618 it proved too difficult to reinforce Tsarev-Borisov and the town had to be abandoned. As for Valuiki, its population in the 1620s was still huddling behind its walls, unable to safely cultivate their outlying service lands.[24] Thus the territory actually under Russian control could be said to arc from Belgorod through Oskol' to Livny and Elets on the Bystraia Sosna, retreating northward in the face of the wedge formed by the union of the Iziuma and Kal'miuss roads, before dipping south again along the edge of the Voronezh River. And from the town of Voronezh the frontier veered north again, forming a vast indentation of steppeland between the Voronezh and Tsna rivers all the way up to Dankov and Riazhsk, from where dense forests running eastward along the Alatyr' to Tetiushi on the upper Volga finally provided some protective cover for Muscovite colonization.[25]

Three invasion roads also led from Perekop into Ukraine and Poland-Lithuania. The easternmost of these, the Czarny Trail, crossed the Bug and headed due north between Bratslav and Chyhyryn, then forked – one branch continuing northward against Kiev, the other branch turning west into Rus' Czerwona north of Bar.

A Kuczman Trail kept to the south of the Bug and came out into Rus' Czerwona near Bar.

A Woloski Trail ran along the coast of the Black Sea, crossed the Dnestr into Moldavia, ran along the Pruth River, and entered Rus' Czerwona near Kolomyja, then turned north in the direction of Pamosc, Chelm, and Lublin.

The Polish-Lithuanian territory vulnerable to Tatar attack thus ran from the Putivl' border in the east to Małopolska and the approaches to Cracow in the west. Some Tatar incursions reached as far north as Vilnius and Vitebsk in Lithuania.[26]

The Crimean Tatars preferred to invade Poland-Lithuania and Muscovy around harvest time so as to forage and plunder for several weeks. Shorter incursions were often planned for early winter, when the rivers had frozen over and there was sufficient snow on the ground to keep their horses' unshod hooves from cracking from the frost. The most disciplined core of the Crimean Khan's army was a small personal guard of 200–1,000 musketeer foot (*tufenkçi*), organized along janissary lines and supported by some light field guns (*zarbuzan*). The bulk of the army comprised several thousand light mounted archers – the nomadic tribal cavalry mobilized by the *karachi beys*, the chiefs of the four nomadic tribes residing on the steppe above Perekop. Although gunpowder was produced at Kaffa and firearms manufactured at Bakchisarai, they were expensive and wheellocks were very rare, so the Tatar cavalry relied primarily on their short reflex bows, easily fired from horseback and having a longer range and much faster rate of fire than muskets. Tatar horsemen also carried sabers and lances for close combat. The more prosperous of them might wear chain mail hauberks and iron helmets. Their stirrups were set high; they urged on their horses with whips rather than spurs.

In principle, the khan could order total mobilization of all able-bodied males age 15–70 under the *karachi beys*:

> No one is to remain in the land, the entire people or army is to go on war footing, and if there is anyone who is not at the khan's side after Or Agzi [the Ditch at Perekop, where the army usually assembled], his property is to be raided and his head struck down.[27]

In periods when the khan was well in control of his nobles he could expect a good response to his summons to war within just two to four weeks: his invocation of *ghaza* (the duty of religious war), combined with the promise of plunder, helped in this, and every Crimean and Nogai village and tribe was supposedly decimally organized and their units recorded in registers. After the army had assembled at Perekop it rode north, where it might be joined by several thousand Nogai allies. To maximize mobility each warrior took two or three mounts and traveled lightly equipped, taking just a few pounds of roasted millet, bread, or cooked meat and resorting to foraging and raiding to meet the rest of their needs on the fifty-five-day journey to the outskirts of Moscow. If the army did carry additional provisions and arms, it was usually by horse or camel pack train rather than by carts; the exception to this was the khan's infantry guard and artillery, which circled their carts in *wagenburg* in battle.

The Crimean Tatar army traveled in columns several riders in breadth, spaced at greater intervals in hot weather. Beauplan estimated the front of each column at 800 to 1,000 paces across; extended, a column might be ten leagues in length, compacting to three to four leagues in length when tightly massed. "It is an amazing sight, since 80,000 Tatars are accompanied by more than 200,000 horses. Trees are not thicker in a forest than hoses are at such times on the plain." Ahead of them rode an advance guard of about 100 warriors, each leading two mounts for use as relays. Sometimes they encountered difficulties crossing ice or rocky terrain, but snow gave them no trouble – their horses often wore leather stockings in winter – and they could cross all but the deepest and most violent rivers. They avoided marshes and dense forests and tended to keep to the shelter of those valleys with which they were familiar from previous raids. Every hour they halted to rest their horses for a few minutes.

Some three or four leagues short of the edge of enemy territory they camped for two or three days, lighting no fires and maintaining many mounted sentinels; once reassured there were no large enemy forces in the area they resumed their advance, at greater speed, in one large mass if they were intent on penetrating far into the interior, or in several independent groups if intent upon raiding across a broad front. They surrounded and blockaded towns, capturing the inhabitants of outlying villages for sale as slaves and rustling cattle and horses, but because they usually lacked artillery and sappers they did not attempt to take towns by siege. They avoided pitched battles with the enemy unless forced to defend their camps or their columns of prisoners and livestock. When confronted with large Polish or Muscovite forces, the Tatars tried to split them by attacking at several points simultaneously, resorting to their reserve mounts so as to be able to keep up such skirmishing for an entire day if necessary. "When charging the enemy," L. J. D. Collins writes, "the Tatars would take up a formation in the shape of a half moon about forty men broad, 'their leaders placed at the front, rear, and flanks'; the men would scream and ululate." Sometimes they fired their arrows in devastating arcade, and by the seventeenth century the Crimean Tatars (although apparently not the Nogais) were less likely to be broken by enemy artillery or musketfire, as they had come to recognize its inaccuracy.[28]

Even the largest incursions aimed more at raiding villages for captives and livestock rather than at routing enemy armies. Beauplan has decribed the tactics of such raiding. Upon entering hostile territory, the Tatar army split into three corps, two of which rode together in close parallel while the third divided further into left and right wings of 8–10,000 men each. After they had advanced some sixty to eighty leagues into enemy territory, the wings separated to roam ten or twelve leagues from each flank of the main corps. The wings swept across the enemy's villages,

> placing four groups of guards around each village and burning great bonfires all night long, for fear lest even one peasant should escape them. Then they sack and burn it, killing all those inhabitants who resist, and taking away all those who yield, not only men, women, and

children at their mother's breast, but also livestock such as, horses, oxen, cattle sheep, goats, etc.[29]

When the wings returned to the main corps with their slaves and booty two more wings were dispatched in the same manner so as not to diminish the strength of the main corps. After "harvesting" the region to their satisfaction they withdrew along a different route to escape interception and then reassembled at camp to divide up their spoils, a fifth or tenth of which accrued to the commander. This was the point at which they were most vulnerable to surprise attack by the Poles or Muscovites, who tried to separate them from their horses and liberate their prisoners. In 1672 King Jan Sobieski allegedly freed 44,000 captives from one routed Tatar army.

In the summer and autumn individual mirzas led smaller expeditions for slaves and livestock, which penetrated less deeply into enemy territory and withdrew after a few days. The order of battle followed on the great winter campaigns was impractical for such operations; instead, the Crimeans and Nogais entered hostile territory in ten or twelve detachments of one thousand men deployed across the plain like a great net ten or twelve leagues across, with scouts riding a league ahead to take prisoners for interrogation and look for approaching enemy forces. Such an array made it easier to sweep up captives along a broad front while circumventing enemy patrols. Each evening they rendezvoused at a prearranged campsite near the border or in a protected area. If the enemy caught sight of them – usually by spotting the smoke from burning villages – and gave pursuit, the Tatars divided again, riding off in all four directions in small bands (*chambuly*) of 100 men. These bands in turn divided into thirds, and again into parties of ten or twelve men; after scattering for a dozen leagues or so, they reassembled to resume their raiding. Their hardier mounts usually allowed them to outrun their Polish or Muscovite pursuers.

While major Crimean invasions like those of 1571 and 1633 may not by themselves have altered the course of the Livonian and Smolensk Wars, the prospect of Tatar invasion restricted Muscovy's freedom of diplomatic and military action on other fronts. The threat to the Muscovite interior was sufficient to require vast expenditures to refortify the Abatis Line (1638) and to station larger field regiments along it. This in turn limited the manpower and cash and grain resources available for campaigns against Poland-Lithuania on the western front, and on top of that Moscow had to pay some 7–12,000 rubles annually in tribute to the Crimean khans over the years 1613–1650.[30] The logistical problems involved in sending a Muscovite army across the steppes to invade the Khanate were considerable, and the Crimean peninsula was fortified across the isthmus of Perekop. It would therefore take until 1774 for Russia to finally eliminate the military threat posed by the Crimean Khanate.

Crimean Tatar slaveraiding

Even if Muscovy had not provoked the Crimean khans by seizing the Volga khanates and the Ottoman grand strategy had not required the khans to periodically invade Muscovy to restore the balance of power, Muscovy would still have suffered frequent Crimean and Nogai raids for slaves because slaveraiding was essential to the economy of the Crimean Khanate. And if Tatar slaveraiding was a lower-intensity threat than invasion, it was also a nearly constant threat and inflicted heavy costs. It was not enough to maintain defenses capable of keeping the khan's army from crossing the Oka. Tatar attacks harvesting slaves from frontier communities south of the Oka humiliated the government, drained even more state revenue into ransom payments, and above all confined Russian colonization to the forest and forest-steppe zones. While small Russian settlements of hunters, beekeepers, and fishermen could survive under shelter of the wildwoods along the Voronezh and upper Don, larger communities required outlying plowlands, where their cultivators were exposed to attack; and Tatar slavers raided the southernmost Muscovite colonies almost every summer, capturing servicemen and peasants working in their fields, driving off herds of livestock, burning villages and town suburbs, and ambushing patrols and merchant caravans. Most of these raids were undertaken by *chambuly* of a few hundred men yet were able to do a great deal of damage. In the summer of 1643, for example, 600 Tatars and 200 Zaporozhian Cossacks attacked the villages of Iarok and Krivets just west of Kozlov. They killed 19 Russians, all males, and abducted 262 others (almost all women and children) as captives for sale in the Crimean slave markets.[31]

Ironically, such slaveraiding resulted from the weakness of the khans vis-à-vis their tribal aristocracy and from the costs to the Crimean economy of its partnership with the Ottoman Empire. The Crimean khan could not act without the cooperation of the *beys* and mirzas of the great clans, which controlled most of the productive land and tenant labor on the Crimean peninsula and could field larger client forces than the khan. The khan had to offer them frequent opportunities to raid for prisoners to ransom, sell at the Kaffa slave market, or resettle on Crimean lands as agriculturalists. Otherwise the *beys* and mirzas would undertake raids for slaves on their own initiative, without the khan's approval, thereby undermining his efforts to improve relations with Muscovy or Poland-Lithuania.

Before Mengli Girei had become the vassal of the Ottoman sultan, the khan's wealth and power had derived chiefly from the protection money he extorted from merchant caravans and flotillas and the taxes he collected from the Genoese towns along the coast. The feeding of the coastal towns had also encouraged many Crimean Tatar commoners to abandon pastoral nomadism for agriculture in the hills above the coast. But once the Turks took the merchant colonies for themselves in 1475, occupying Kaffa, Akkerman, Bendery, Kilburun, Kerch, and Azov, and governing them directly as the *eyalet* of Kaffa, the khan lost much of his revenue from these towns and the Tatar grain trade with the coastal towns began to decline. Istanbul had

> converted the entire Pontic coastland into a vast and valuable hinterland. Correspondingly, the slender but vigorous urban fringe in the Crimea and near the mouths of the principal rivers that flowed into the Black Sea lost its earlier independent entrepreneurial function vis-à-vis the upcountry.

For the Ottomans, the decline of the Crimean grain trade was easily offset by the grain imports now received from Dobruja and the lower Danube, but the Crimean market had to cast around for a new specialization – and found it in the revival of the Black Sea slave trade originally organized by Italian merchants in the Middle Ages. The core of the Ottoman Empire could now benefit from the new "division of labor between the two portions of ... [its] Pontic hinterland ... drawing grain from the closer region and human livestock from the further parts of Pontic Europe," while the Crimean Tatars had found an easy way to reintegrate into the Black Sea economy, as slavers, by returning to their traditions of nomadic predation on agricultural communities and cooperation with the middlemen in the coastal merchant communities.[32]

The dependence of the Ottoman economy, army, and administration on slave manpower in the sixteenth and seventeenth centuries is well known. The *devshirme* levies continued to be an important source of elite *kapikulu* slave manpower down to the 1630s, but the Empire also depended on common slavery, which required the capture of prisoners in war and on slaving expeditions beyond its frontiers. After 1550 the prisoners taken by the Crimean Tatars in Ukraine, Muscovy, and the Caucasus probably accounted for the larger part of this human booty (*iasyri*).

It is difficult to quantify the yield of the Crimean slave trade. Alan Fisher has tried, by tabulating the figures reported or estimated for the number of Polish, Ukrainian, and Muscovite captives taken on sixty-five major raids and invasions between 1468 and 1694. But some of the numbers offered by contemporary sources – European travelers and Polish and Muscovite annalists – were probably exaggerated for purposes of religious propaganda. For example, Isaak Massa claimed 200,000 Russians were carried off just in 1555. This was unlikely because the need to guard and escort captives usually kept the ratio of war captives to raiders to 1:3; an invading force of 30,000 Tatars would therefore have found it difficult to abduct more than 10,000 captives.[33] There was consensus among contemporary observers that the cumulative effect of Tatar slaveraiding was considerable, however. Giovanni Botero speculated that Muscovy's sparse population must be due to Crimean slavers, while the Lithuanian Mikhalon Litvin (*c.* 1550), watching the procession of captives past Perekop, recalled being asked by a customs collector whether Crimean raids had left any living inhabitants in his country. Litvin wrote of Kaffa, the principal Crimean slave market, that it was "not a town, but an abyss into which our blood is pouring." A century later the Ottoman writer Evlyia Çelebi estimated that Crimea contained about 400,000 slaves but only 187,000 free Muslims.[34]

Muscovy's Military Chancellery kept records of losses from Crimean and Nogai attacks, and these records suggest that Russian losses to the Crimean slave trade were very heavy. Between 150,000 and 200,000 Muscovites were captured by Tatar slavers in the period 1600–1650. This was a large proportion of the Muscovite population settled in the central black soil region, which approached 850,000 by the time of the 1678 census.[35] In Kursk district alone 15,115 Russians were killed or captured by Tatars in the years 1633–1646, and most of those lost were probably captured rather than killed, as it was in the Tatars' interests to avoid battles and the slaughter of potential human booty. For example, total Russian losses to Tatar raids in 1637 were 2,280, of whom only 37 were killed; in 1645 they totalled 5,750, of whom 20 were killed.[36]

The human toll may have been much heavier in Poland and Ukraine. The Crimeans reportedly took 40,000 captives in Volhynia, Podolia, and Galicia in 1676, and Bohdan Baranowski has estimated that an average of 20,000 Poles were captured each year, with total losses for the period 1500–1644 numbering about a million.[37]

A fifth of the prisoners taken on Crimean military expeditions may have been turned over to the sultan as tribute. Other captives were distributed to the khan's court officials, and the tribal aristocrats and Crimean and Nogai warriors kept some as herdsmen, field laborers, and domestics. The rest were sold at the slave markets of Bakhchisarai, Karaseibazar, Evpatoria, and especially Kaffa, where Mikhalon Litvin claimed that at least 30,000 slaves could always be found. Muslim merchants supplanted the Italians as the principal dealers after 1475. Judging from Muscovite diplomatic records and the testimonies of European travelers, the price of a healthy male Russian slave ranged from ten to one hundred rubles and averaged fifty rubles. From their sale the khan took duties of 10 percent. Poles and Ukrainians allegedly fetched higher prices "because they hold cheaper the Muscovite nation, as perfidious and deceptive."[38]

Some Slavic slaves were exported from the Crimean markets to distant regions of the Dar-al-Islam; the archimandrite of a Sinai monastery purchased on the Alexandria market a serviceman from the southern Muscovite town of Kozlov, for example. Many Russian and Polish slaves became rowers on Ottoman galleys. In 1646 Sultan Ibrahim allegedly authorized Crimean raids upon Poland and Muscovy so as to requisition rowers for 100 galleys then under construction. Of 280 rowers freed during a mutiny aboard a Turkish galley in 1642, 207 were Ukrainians and 20 were Muscovites; some of them had spent as much as forty years in captivity. Other slaves exported from the Crimea were used as construction laborers, agriculturalists, and domestic servants. Those remaining in the Crimea, neither sold abroad nor ransomed, were usually manumitted after six years but without the right to return home. They became factors, craftsmen, or farmers. Some converted to Islam to enhance their upward social mobility and may even have found brighter opportunities in the Crimea than awaited them at home, like the former bondsman of boyar V. B. Sheremetev, who chose to convert to Islam so as to serve as an interpreter at the khan's court. The *Chronicle of Samuil Velichko* (1675) relates that the Zaporozhian ataman Sirko freed 3,000 Ukrainians during one of his raids on Crimea but had to put them to the sword when they opted to return to Crimea.[39]

Ransoms were a lucrative supplement to revenues from the sale of slaves, especially as a prisoner of prominence might command a much higher ransom than a sale price. Privately arranged ransoms of servicemen could exceed 100 rubles apiece; a Voronezh gunner who had accumulated considerable wealth as a merchant fetched a ransom of 700 rubles. In 1551, upon the urging of the Orthodox clergy, Ivan IV had instituted a special tax to ransom captives brought to Moscow by Ottoman, Greek, and Armenian merchants and captives brought to Muscovite envoys at the Crimean towns, Kazan', Astrakhan', and Istanbul, but the ransom rates it authorized tended to fall considerably below going market price; the 1649 *Ulozhenie* code, for example, provided for no more than twenty-five rubles towards the ransom of a captured musketeer or garrison cossack, the treasury sometimes refused to ransom subjects captured through their own fault after refusing to repair to the town citadel during a siege alert. The treasury paid out just 8,500 rubles for ransoms in 1644, and 7,337 rubles in 1645, so there may have been more ransoming through private channels – particularly through the Don Cossacks – than through the government's authority.[40]

Crimean specialization in the slave trade discouraged peaceful trade between Muscovy and the Ottoman Empire and thereby limited opportunities for closer political cooperation between the two powers. In 1488 and again in 1496 Sultan Bayezit II informed Grand Prince Ivan III that he desired friendship and would be pleased to see Muscovite merchants bring their wares to Crimean markets. Muscovite merchants were indeed journeying to Kaffa, and especially to Azov, to trade furs, leather goods, salt, and linen for silks, spices, carpets, and precious stones. But their trade never reached significant proportions because it could not compete with Tatar slaveraiding in terms of profitability and advantage to the Ottoman economy. The subsequent Ottoman annexation of Kaffa and the other Crimean coastal towns, the imposition of new customs duties and tolls at these towns, and the establishment of the sultan's monopoly over fur imports further limited Muscovite commercial opportunities at Kaffa and Azov and forced Muscovite merchants to reroute their trade with the Ottomans through Poland and Moldavia. Muscovite–Ottoman trade appears to have declined further after 1580, perhaps due to the heightened tension in Russo–Ottoman relations after the annexation of Astrakhan' and the Perevolok expedition or because of Don Cossack attacks on Ottoman merchants and Tatar raids on Muscovite caravans. In 1593 an Ottoman official, Hussein Çelebi, complained to Moscow that the Don Cossacks had destroyed Azov's commerce, from which the sultan's treasury had used to receive 80,000 pieces of gold; by 1630 the only goods reportedly being traded at Azov were wares the cossacks had plundered along the Black Sea coast and now offered for redemption.[41]

The Nogais and Kalmyks

Since its appeals to the sultan to restrain his Crimean Tatar vassals were usually futile it made sense for Moscow to try to weaken the Khanate militarily by suborning its nomadic allies, particularly the Great Nogais. Ismail and Ishterek, *beys* of the Great Nogai Horde, gave oaths of fealty (*shert'*) to the tsar; they may not have understood that Moscow treated these as pledges of vassalage, but they generally refrained from aggression against Muscovy in 1557–1563 and 1616–1630. Moscow had various tactics at its disposal to obtain the loyalty of the Nogai *beys*, including bribes (Ishterek received 1,064 rubles) and occasional military intervention to guarantee their victory in succession struggles within their Horde. The lesser Nogai nobles were also coopted or coerced by gift plying, registration in the tsar's service from estates in Kasimov and Romanov (worked by Christian Finnic and Russian peasants), or by treaty requiring them to turn over kinsmen as elite hostages to be housed under close surveillance at Moscow or Astrakhan'. The Russian town governors at Astrakhan' were instructed to protect the Nogais from violence and enslavement by Russians, to respect their rights to roam their traditional grazing lands on the eastern Volga steppes, and to defend them from attacks by the Kalmyks and by the Volga and Don Cossacks.

The main problem in managing the Nogais was not that of finding a *bey* ready to be suborned but finding a *bey* to back who had real control over most of the Nogai Horde. The gifts sent to Ismail, and after him to Tinakhmet and Urus', could have helped them consolidate their control over the lesser *beys* and mirzas if shared among the latter as bounty accessible only through the power of the supreme *bey*, who alone could treat with the tsar; but Ismail and his successors never got the opportunity to establish their monopoly over the flow of bounty because the lesser *beys* and mirzas from the start demanded their own gifts from Moscow in proportion to their genealogical status within the Horde.[42] Moscow tried to play it safe by paying them off as well. Over the longer term this tamed the Nogai Horde, but at the cost of its unity; the danger it presented to Muscovy declined with the Horde's political disintegration, but this also meant the Horde was of declining military value as a counterweight to the Crimean Khanate.

On the whole it was the Great Nogais' own strategic vulnerability that held them to vassalage to the tsar. Periodically Don Cossack or Kalmyk pressure had forced the Great Nogais to abandon the lower Volga steppe and cross the Don onto the Crimean steppes, only to be repulsed by Crimeans or Lesser Nogais unwilling to share these grasslands with them (1574). In 1588–1590 the Crimean khan incited the Nogais to attack Russian towns but then refused to support them. In 1646 one Nogai mirza even asked the tsar to establish three new forts in the steppe to defend his *ulus* against the Crimeans, Kalmyks, and Lesser

Nogais. Under such circumstances the Great Nogais felt the limits of Muslim solidarity and the necessity of peaceful relations with Muscovy, which had firmly established its presence at Astrakhan', in the middle of their traditional grazing lands, and was sending them talented diplomats like the Mal'tsevs, fluent in Tatar and untiring in arguing that Muscovy was the true successor to the Golden Horde. There was not much risk that Muscovite diplomacy wooing the Nogais away from the Crimean Khanate would antagonize the Ottomans as the Ottomans had their own concerns that too close a Crimean–Nogai rapprochement might make the Crimean khans less dependent on Ottoman protection and more willing to lay claim to the Ottoman *eyalet* in the Crimea.[43]

Ivan IV's conquest of Astrakhan' and the formation of the Don Cossack Host assisted in the pacification of the Great Nogais by demonstrating militarily the growing risks and declining profitability of Great Nogai involvement in the Crimean slave trade, and over time the expanding scale of Nogai trade with Muscovy presented a more attractive alternative to selling slaves to the Crimean Tatars. Nogai livestock was in great demand in Moscow; in some years Nogai traders accompanying envoys to Moscow brought as many as 27,000 horses and 4,000 sheep for sale.

> Generally speaking, Muscovite merchants, dealing in metalwares, firearms, cloth, and grain, had more to offer the steppe-dwellers than did the Crimean Tatars. ... An agrarian economy possessing skilled, town-dwelling craftsmen and a society based on a pastoral economy could work out in the short run a symbiotic relationship profitable to both. ... Ottoman traders could have filled the economic gap, but the Crimean Tatars, by continuing the fiction of the Golden Horde prerogatives and by putting obstacles in the way of smooth relations with the Ottomans, may have alienated the steppe market and also the Ottoman traders.[44]

Some obstacles to further Muscovite–Nogai rapprochement remained, however. As long as Muscovy's southern frontier remained vulnerable to Tatar *chambuly* it would be impossible to entirely suppress Nogai slaveraiding; Moscow still needed to find ways to keep a closer eye on the governors of Astrakhan' lest they oppress the Nogais and provoke them to break their *shert'*. Above all there was the growing danger from the Kalmyk hordes, who had abandoned their grazing lands in Dzhungaria to trek westward towards the Iaik, where they began to hammer at the Great Nogais, sometimes pushing them across the Volga into Muscovite territory. The early Kalmyk incursions had been sporadic and brief, so that the Great Nogais had eventually been able to return to their reservation on the eastern side of the Volga. But the Kalmyks made a more concerted push under *Taishi* Daichin in 1634, driving the Great Nogais across the Volga and Don en masse to fall upon the Don Cossacks, unite with the Lesser Nogais from the eastern wing of the Crimean Khanate, and begin pushing up the Don, Khoper, and Medveditsa to find themselves new grazing lands. This brought them into conflict with the Muscovite frontier towns. Meanwhile the Kalmyks had become the dominant nomadic power east of the Volga and would eventually follow the Great Nogais in making their own raids on Russian towns.

The formation of the cossack Hosts

Above all Moscow had to rein in the Don Cossacks, who often raided the Nogais, the Crimean Tatars, and even the Turkish garrisons and towns on their own initiative, provoking retaliations against Muscovite border towns.

The relationship between Muscovy and the Don Cossacks mirrored the relationship between the Ottoman Empire and the Crimean Tatars. The Don Cossacks were a client polity which often performed great military services for their patron as a buffer and gatherer of intelligence; and when it was too dangerous for Muscovy to undertake its own aggressive or punitive attacks on the other great powers of the region, the Don Cossacks did so as proxies whose actions the tsar could disavow as the work of brigands. Although they were heavily dependent on Muscovite subsidies of cash, grain, powder, and shot, until 1671 they maintained formal independence from Muscovy (reflected in the fact that the Ambassadors' Chancellery treated with them as with a foreign power), and they periodically demonstrated their "sovereignty" by taking military action on their own initiative, against Moscow's wishes and interests. Survival impelled them to this: like the Crimean Khanate, their economic specialization was raiding for plunder (in their case mostly for livestock and trade goods, but they also sold some Muslim captives to the Muscovites).

The first Don *kazaki* were not Slavs but Tatars whose original tribal affiliations had been broken during the disintegration of the Kipchak Khanate and who survived by turning to independent freebooters. By the early sixteenth century there was a sparse Russian population on the steppe with which they could fuse, for the Mongol invasions had not rolled back all Russian colonization along the Voronezh and northern Don; a few small scattered settlements of Russian hunters, fishermen, and bee-keepers had survived, and some of these settlers had adopted the cossack way of life, supplementing their hunting and gathering with raiding and mercenary activity. They were subsequently joined by fugitives from the north – baptized "service Tatars" from the Volga, runaway peasants and slaves from central Muscovy, and Riazan' servicemen displaced by such conflicts as the civil war in Vasilii II's reign – so that the Slavic element prevailed among the cossacks by the beginning of the sixteenth century and conversion to Orthodoxy had become required for acceptance in their communities. In calling themselves "free cossacks" they saw themselves as standing outside the Muscovite sociopolitical system: they were neither the Sovereign's servicemen (*sluzhilye liudi*) nor his taxbearing "men of draft" (*tiaglye liudi*), but reserved for themselves the right to choose their own masters.[45]

29

By the 1580s the core of the cossack population had shifted southward down the Don towards the Donets River and Azov. The smaller cossack population remaining in the Upper Reaches – the northern Don – was less stable because this region tended to be a waystation rather than final destination for fugitives and because the proximity of the tsar's new borderland garrison towns provided an alternative calling to free cossackizing here, the opportunity to register as garrison servicemen and receive the tsar's bounty in land and grain. Larger, more permanent cossack communities and more formal independent cossack political organization had a better chance of developing farther beyond the Muscovite frontier, on the Don's Lower Reaches, where there was greater opportunity for marauding into Tatar and Ottoman territory. By the early seventeenth century some of the temporary cossack encampments on the Lower Reaches had grown into permanent fortified settlements (Manych, Monastyrskii gorodok, Cherkassk, Razdory). These settlements were of modest size, usually holding no more than a few hundred cossacks each, but they were enough to serve as the nucleus of a self-governing cossack polity – the Don Host (*Donskoe voisko*) – which by the 1620s would claim authority over all Lower Reaches cossacks as well as those Upper Reaches cossacks who had not yet been absorbed into the Muscovite army (about 5,000 men altogether).[46]

Unlike the Crimean Khanate, cossack society on the lower Don lacked the division of labor necessary for the construction of a true state. The Host was a loose military union built from below by the detachments (*stanitsy*) operating out of the scattered camps and fortified settlements; perhaps modeled partly upon Russian peasant communal organization as well as upon traditional nomadic military organization. The *stanitsy*, which varied in size, met in assembly (*krug*) to elect a commander (ataman) and lieutenant (*esaul*) for such tasks as conflict resolution, the division of booty, and military leadership. Sometimes a separate campaign ataman was chosen, and on occasion *stanitsy* joined together on campaign under a single ataman or a team of them. Although a Muscovite document of 1593 speaks of one Don Host, this was wishful thinking on Moscow's part – it wanted a unified Host under a single permanent commander, ideally one that Moscow appointed. But a permanent union of all the *stanitsy* had not yet been achieved, and the *stanitsy* had repudiated Petr Khruschev, Moscow's choice for Host Captain (*golova*), so that the Ambassadors' Chancellery had to continue addressing multiple atamans and dealing separately with different *stanitsy*.

A more formal and centralized Host administration finally emerged in the 1620s. Representatives from both the Upper and Lower Reaches were now periodically summoned into general *krug* council at Razdory to elect a *voiskovyi* ataman, *voiskovyi esaul*, and *d'iak* (secretary); and Moscow began recognizing this *voiskovyi* ataman, headquartered at this time at Monastyrskii gorodok, as commander of all the Don Cossacks.[47] Although the unification of the Host detachments strengthened the Don Host as a Pontic steppe power, it also heralded the erosion of the Host's independence, for the process of Host unification was welcomed and probably encouraged by Moscow, which had grown alarmed at the growing power of the cossack detachments since the turn of the century. During the Troubles free cossack detachments had intervened militarily and politically at several crucial junctures, throwing their support to the Pretenders, withdrawing their support, and finally endorsing the enthronement of a Romanov tsar; thereafter the Muscovite government had been required to devote considerable resources to suppressing cossack "brigandage" in the interior and to registering the cossack population of the Upper Reaches in the tsar's service; and meanwhile the escalating conflict between the Polish-Lithuanian Commonwealth and the Ottomans, provoked in part by Zaporozhian Cossack raids on Tatar and Ottoman lands, had convinced Moscow its own security called for reining in Don Cossack raiding. Host unification therefore promised to make the Host more amenable to Muscovite control.

On the one hand, the unification of the Host through *krug* "democracy" enabled the Host to represent itself as a regime of liberty antithetical to Muscovite authoritarianism, a refuge to runaway serfs and ruined servicemen, and a brotherhood of equals ("they have no 'best men' among them, they are all equal to each other"). In reality there were from the start powerful restraints upon the fuller development of cossack democracy. The cossacks of the Lower Reaches practiced patriarchal slavery, deprived their bondsmen "apprentices" (*chury*) of the right to vote in the *krug* assembly, and permitted the formation of a cossack elite (*starshina*) consisting of the more militarily experienced men likely to monopolize elected office and the subsidies sent from Moscow, which they used to expand their own trading and animal husbandry. The *starshina* bought up forests, fishing sites, and pastures and in some instances turned poorer cossacks into their debtors and dependent laborers. The principle of *krug* deliberation declined in importance as the *voiskovyi* ataman and *starshina* increasingly decided important issues on their own and as less prosperous cossacks and representatives of the smaller settlements were excluded from the *voiskovyi krug*. According to a 1689 report from the governor of Astrakhan', rank-and-file Don Cossacks had come to refer to their elite with contempt as "the boyars and *voevody* of the *stanitsy*."[48]

What the Host lacked in numbers (most of its operations on land involved no more than 500 or 600 men) it made up for in strategic location. The ataman's headquarters at Monastyrskii gorodok was only 60 km from the Ottoman fortress of Azov, which the cossacks attacked in 1574, 1593, 1620, and 1625; the Host was well-positioned to intercept and repulse smaller Crimean and Nogai war parties moving up the Kal'miuss and Nogai trails, and therefore to police these trails on the tsar's request, to protect his borderland towns; and the Host could undertake its own raids upon the camps of the Lesser Nogai Horde, just across the Manych River, or attack them for the tsar, to bring the Lesser Nogais back under fealty to him (as in 1623, when they struck the encampment of mirza Sultan Murat on the Ei River, killing his family and taking some

700 prisoners). The Great Nogai Horde could be more easily controlled when caught between the Don Host to the west and the Astrakhan' governors or Iaik cossacks to the east. As long as the Zaporozhian Cossacks of the lower Dnepr were faithful subjects of the Polish-Lithuanian Commonwealth the Don Host had a role to play in blocking Zaporozhian raids on southern Muscovy. The Don Host was also capable of mounting naval expeditions (sometimes of 2–6,000 men when acting in concert with the Zaporozhians), raiding not only the towns of the Crimean coast but Trebizond and Sinope, which they even briefly held in 1625. Six thousand cossacks landed by longboat to plunder the outskirts of Istanbul itself in 1623. These naval raids threatened to embroil Muscovy in war with the Khanate and Porte and therefore showed Moscow the need for tighter control over the Host.[49]

In Lithuanian Ukraine the cossack way of life began to appear in the late fifteenth century, about the same time as on the Upper Reaches of the Don and Voronezh. Ukrainian townsmen and petty gentry from Cherkasy, Kiev, Kanev, and the Seversk towns had been engaging in seasonal foraging on the steppeland to the south, turning to hunting, fishing, horsetrading, and some small-scale farming to supplement their livings in the "Settled Lands." Of course this put them in conflict with nomadizing or raiding Tatars and forced them to form armed bands (*vatagî*) for their steppe undertakings. These bands soon turned to their own marauding, attacking Tatar villages and herds on the lower Dnepr, and even striking near Ochakov (1528), forcing the Turks to strengthen their garrison there. The greater their profit from these raids, the more quickly they put aside steppe foraging for the warrior trade; and this in turn made the cossack calling more attractive to the Ukrainian gentry, who made themselves captains (atamans) of cossack bands. The Lithuanian border officials, the palatines and *starostas*, began building retinues of hired cossacks and using them to run reconnaissance patrols, hunt down Tatar *chambuly*, defend castles, and raid the Tatars so they could levy duties on the plunder they brought back. The border officials' profiteering from these raids thereby encouraged the spread and militarization of cossack activity. The royal government viewed this process with some ambivalence, welcoming the strengthening of frontier defenses but worrying that cossack raiding would provoke Tatar retaliation.[50]

A turning point in the formation of Ukrainian cossackdom came in the 1550s when the marchlord Dymitro Vyshnevets'kyi (in Polish, Wiśniowiecki) assembled a cossack force and established a permanent camp (*kosh*) on Khortytsa island on the lower Dnepr. This camp remained in use after Vyshnevets'kyi perished in Moldavia, and by the reign of Stefan Bathory there were some 3,000 cossacks residing in winter settlements connected by palisade and blockhouse to the *kosh*. They abandoned informal *vataga* association for more uniform organization in decuries (*desiatki*), centuries (*sotni*), and corps (*polki*) of three to five centuries, and they came together periodically to deliberate on campaign plans and elect their own supreme commander, the *koshevoi* ataman. The emergence of this new organization in the 1580s–1590s was accompanied by a change of name: henceforth they called themselves the Zaporozhian Sich. In the seventeenth century their numbers increased significantly. By the 1670s *koshevoi* ataman Ivan Sirko was able to mobilize up to 15,000 Zaporozhian cossacks for major campaigns.

The emergence of this Zaporozhian Host, free and beyond the reach of Crown authority, eroded Crown control over the Settled Lands in several ways. It offered a refuge for fugitives from manorial exploitation and political oppression. It accelerated the colonization of eastern (Left Bank) Ukraine by better shielding that region from Tatar raiding, and it encouraged subaltern elements on the Left Bank to aspire to cossack status on a scale the government simply could not accommodate. It presented an additional problem for state authority by endangering the Pontic peace through its raids on Crimea and on Ottoman domains.

Poland-Lithuania's southern frontier defense system

Polish-Lithuanian Ukraine had been settled earlier than southern Muscovy and was more densely populated, especially west of the Dnepr. But its defense system was remarkably thin throughout the sixteenth century.

In theory the king's *levee en masse* of the nobility and gentry (*pospolite ruszenie*) could have mobilized up to 50,000 men at mid-century. But there were restrictions on how the *pospolite ruszenie* militia could be used. It was forbidden to take it abroad – say, into Moldavia – unless the *Sejm* gave its consent, and then only for defensive purposes, and for no more than three months. When used within the borders of the realm it could be kept in the field for no more than two weeks and it could not be divided into separate forces. Because it took so long to mobilize it could not provide a very proactive defense against Tatar incursions. Therefore it was used only on a few emergency occasions after 1454. Its rout at Pyliavtsi in 1648 revealed how tactically obsolete it had become.

In the 1490s Tatar raiding became a chronic problem and made it necessary to entrust the defense of the southern frontier to a more regular, if smaller, professional force under tighter Crown control. A new border defense army of 2–4,000 men called the General Defense (*Obrona potoczna*), annually recruited and paid out of the Royal Treasury, was therefore established. This was a permanent but not a standing force, since it served in four seasonal shifts per year and the majority of its troops enrolled for just one or two quarters' active duty. Most of its recruits were gentry from Rus' Czerwona or Podolia, or magnates' sons interested in starting military careers – the *Obrona potoczna* now offering more opportunity for this than the largely defunct *pospolite ruszenie*.

Zygmunt I had tried to make the nobility fund the *Obrona potoczna* by offering to accept cash payments in place of their obligation to serve in the *pospolite ruszenie*, but the nobility had rejected this. In the 1520s the *Sejm* finally agreed to recognize the king's right to devote certain categories of royal revenue to the upkeep of the *Obrona potoczna*, but royal expenditure on the force was still usually capped at 150,000 złoties a year. It was therefore difficult to expand the *Obrona potoczna* beyond 4,000 men. In emergencies the *Sejm* might agree to vote special funds to hire more recruits for a quarter or two, or frontier defense could be reinforced temporarily by summoning the *pospolite ruszenie*, militias raised *ad hoc* by the provincial dietines, and magnates' private armies. In 1563 the *Obrona potoczna* was renamed the Quarter Army (*Wojsko kwarciane*), reflecting the fact that it was now paid from one-quarter of the annual revenues from Crown properties, collected into a special *Rawa* treasury under the joint supervision of the Crown and the *Sejm*.[51] The reign of Stefan Bathory (r. 1576–1586) saw improvements in the equipment of the Quarter Army and some expansion of its infantry contingent. This was possible because of the increased revenue made available to the Crown through the federal union of Lithuania and Poland and the shifting of responsibility for the defense of Ukraine from the Grand Duchy of Lithuania to the Polish Crown. Military buildup had Bathory's unwavering support because of his ultimate goal of winning for himself the Hungarian crown; and it also owed something to the considerable political influence of Grand Crown Hetman Jan Zamoyski, who cultivated the support of the *szlachta* and reconciled them to greater investment in formations other than the old *pospolite ruszenie*.

The main shortcoming of the Quarter Army was that it was no larger than the *Obrona potoczna* yet was responsible for holding a frontier almost 1,000 km long. It stood some chance of intercepting Tatar forces while they were still moving up the invasion roads into Podolia but it was not of much use against *chambuly* that had already penetrated deep into the interior and scattered across a broad front to raid. Its tactics "finally boiled down to endless movement in an endless circle."[52] In 1577 the main body of the Quarter Army, stationed in Podolia, numbered just 2,009 horse and 850 foot, the latter garrisoning frontier fortresses in small detachments of 50–200 men. In 1582 the Quarter Army's field force consisted of 1,200 horse and 530 registered cossacks, with another 500 infantrymen distributed among the major castles, and it became necessary to reinforce it with another 2,100 horse transferred out of the Livonian theater, the *pospolite ruszenie*, and some of the private forces of the magnates.[53]

Once the Quarter Army had intercepted the enemy, however, it usually displayed a tactical effectiveness out of all proportion to its size. The restraints upon its size had encouraged compensatory tactical experimentation.

Perhaps inspired by the recommendation of Konstantin Mihailovic, a Serb émigré who had served in the Ottoman janissaries, the commanders of the *Obrona potoczna* had ceased relying on heavy armored cavalry in the 1490s in favor of *racowie*, an unarmored light cavalry of Serbian model equipped with 3 m lances, small wooden shields, and Turkish curved sabers. In the early sixteenth century their preference shifted to *husarze*, Hungarian-style hussars wearing light *sziszak* helmets and breastplates and armed with 5 m lances and long straight-bladed *koncerz* swords of the type used by Ottoman *deli* cavalry. By 1550 the *husarze* comprised about half the *Obrona potoczna* and established a fearsome reputation for their ability to break and rout much larger masses of cavalry or infantry. They had became the favored formation for magnates' sons and had taken to sumptuous caparison – leopardskin pelisses and, attached to their backplates, light wooden-frame "wings" sporting eagle feathers. Their armament also diversified: they added light sabers, warhammers, bows, and, from 1576, a brace of pistols.

For reconnaissance and support on the flanks the Quarter Army came to rely as well upon *pancerni*, chain-mailed cavalry in *misiurka* skullcap helmets and chain-mail hoods. In the sixteenth century the *pancerni* carried short lances or boarspears and round wooden shields, and by the seventeenth century they were equipped with wheellock carbines. *Pancerni* comprised about a tenth of the Quarter Army in the sixteenth century and about half the force by the 1650s because of their usefulness in patrolling the steppe. Most were recruited from the Ukrainian cossacks. The Quarter Army also continued to use some German mounted pistoleers (*reitary*) and Lithuanian service Tatar archers.[54]

One-third to one-quarter of the *Obrona potoczna* and Quarter Army consisted of infantry. Infantry were needed to garrison the main fortresses along the steppe frontier (Kiev, Bila Tserkva, Kanev, Cherkasy, Bratslav, Oster, Kamianets) and were also tactically useful in the field when the Quarter Army deployed behind earthworks or *wagenburg* athwart an invasion road to intercept the Crimean Tatar army returning from the interior laden with *iasyri*. Commissioning officers to hire volunteers, very effective in forming companies of horse, was of limited utility to forming companies of foot because of the gentry's distaste for infantry duty; so in 1575 King Stefan Bathory proposed a national levy to raise one foot soldier and one mounted soldier from every sixteen commoners. The *Sejm* rejected this but did approve in 1578 the establishment of a Select Infantry (*Wybraniecka piechota*) for the Quarter Army and for service in Livonia, to be levied largely from royal estates at the rate of one soldier from every 320–500 hectares. The most successful of these levies, the levy of 1590, brought in 2,306 recruits. Those taken into the Select Infantry were exempted from taxes but required to train three months per year.[55]

The royal castles could not play an important role in frontier defense strategy. There were too few of them, especially in the eastern half of Ukraine. This left the inhabitants of many eastern districts with no refuge in time of attack other than crude fortifications they built for themselves or the private fortifications of the magnates. Royal castles in the more densely populated western half of Ukraine were often of stone, but those in eastern Ukraine were usually wooden – built of earth-filled oaken cradles in the style known in Muscovy as *po gorodovomu* – and quite small, about the size of a manor courtyard; often they had no more than two or three guns. They provided some ability to monitor enemy movements and give refuge to the inhabitants of the town and a few of the nearest villages, but they could not "dominate the territory to any extent."[56] The burden of frontier defense therefore fell primarily upon the mobile element of the small Quarter Army.

Although the infantry element of the Quarter Army was conscripted, its cavalry element was mobilized by combining royal commission recruiting and feudal retinue obligation. The captains (*rotmistrzy*) commanding the companies (*chorągiew*) of the Quarter Army recruited only part of their commands on their own, on royal commission; typically they aimed at recruiting a limited number of noblemen as their own comrades in arms (*towarzysze*), counting on the *towarzysze* in turn to bring into service their own retinues (*poczty*) of two to six cavalrymen at their own expense. By passing some of the cost of equipping and paying cavalrymen down to the *towarzysze* this saved on expenditure out of the *Rawa* treasury; and the *towarzysze* were willing to shoulder these costs because bringing *poczet* retinues into service gave them the opportunity to build their own political clienteles among the gentry and display their own wealth and social power, thereby recommending themselves to the patronage of loftier nobles higher in the army command. Thus the elite *husarz* lancers could afford firearms as well as ostentatious panoply.

The *towarzysz* system of mobilization improved morale and unit cohesion. A typical cavalry company of 150 to 300 horse would have a solid core of 50 to 80 *towarzysz* knights sharing responsibility with the captain in *koła* (circle) military council and exercising social as well as tactical authority over the *poczet* squires comprising the rest of the company. Robert Frost considers that this

> ensured that units were able to carry out the rapid manuevers and swift regrouping that was the key to battlefield success. It was a structure ideally suited to the requirements of warfare in eastern Europe, which consisted largely of scouting, raiding, and actions by small mobile units, often operating far from their bases.[57]

The Quarter Army also relied upon *towarzysz* solidarity in developing effective tactics against large masses of enemy troops. Its infantry companies and field guns would take shelter behind a *tabor* (a wagon-circle, or, if time allowed, rough earthworks, or both in combination), with the *husarze* and *pancerni* cavalry on its wings or hidden behind the *tabor*. The *pancerni* would advance on the wings to protect against outflanking while the main blow against the weakest part of the enemy's line was dealt by the *husarze*. The *husarze* charged in two to four echelons, the front rank comprising the elite *towarzysze* and the ranks behind them comprising their squires. On the walk, trot, and canter they kept enough space among themselves so that they could react quickly and change course. As the front rank came within 30 m of the enemy's line they increased their speed from fast canter to gallop, closing up until they were almost knee-to-knee, in order to present a front outnumbering the targeted section of enemy infantry line by 2:1. Because of the limited accuracy of unrifled musket fire the front rank of *husarze* were generally exposed to just one volley between the moment they came into musket range and the moment they struck the enemy line; and enemy pikes were of limited effectiveness against them because the *husarz* lances were a good 2 m longer. If they failed to break through the enemy line, the front rank of *husarze* would fall away and regroup just as the second rank of *husarze* – their squires – were hitting the enemy line. A fallen lancer could usually be confident his squires would come to his aid and help him remount.[58]

Against highly mobile Tatar mounted archers riding in loose or no formation the *husarz* echelon charge with lance was less effective. The Quarter Army cavalry would have to rely more on their pistols and carbines and attack in smaller clusters of a few *poczty* to try to drive the Tatars into denser formations more vulnerable to infantry and artillery fire or lance charge; and they would have to be ready to fall back to the cover of the *tabor* if counterattacked by too large a mass of the enemy. A *tabor* of *wagenburg* type was especially useful to the Quarter Army because it could be formed quickly in response to a surprise attack.

Wagenburg tactics were ideally suited to the demands of steppe warfare and could be traced back at least as far as the Pechenegs and Mongols.[59] Prince Mstislav Romanich of Kiev had used them against the Mongols at Kalka in 1223; and Jan Zizka's Hussite army pioneered in combining wagon defense with firearm and artillery firepower in the 1430s. The designation of a fortified wagon-circle as a *tabor* probably began with the Hussites, who invoked the image of Mt. Tabor as a metaphor for their insurgency. Hussite *wagenburg* tactics quickly spread across Hungary and Moldavia and were then adopted by the Polish, Muscovite, Ottoman, and even Crimean Tatar commanders.

Because the Quarter Army was too small to patrol the frontier alone the defense of Ukraine required coordination with cossack forces. Zygmunt I had tried to form a standing cossack militia of 1–2,000 men for frontier defense in 1523–1524 but the Council of the Grand Duchy of Lithuania had refused to vote the funds. In 1541 Zygmunt I ordered a general inspection and the compilation of a register of all local cossacks so that his *starostas* could arrest cossacks making unauthorized raids upon the Tatars that might disrupt the peace; this of course failed because the cossack social condition was fluid, the cossack population uncountable, and the *starostas* unable to maintain effective surveillance. More concerted efforts to integrate the cossack population into the Crown's southern frontier defense system were made in the 1560s following Vyshnevets'kyi's founding of a base for cossack mercenaries on Khortytsa island.

The emergence of an independent Zaporozhian Sich inclined to unauthorized raiding, endangering the Commonwealth's peace with the Khanate and the Porte, pushed the royal government to revive the idea of a cossack register for purposes of control. In 1568 Zygmunt II Avgust ordered the cossacks of the Sich to abandon their raiding, return to the towns of the settled districts, and take royal service on the king's stipend. Cossacks registered in royal service would receive special rights, including exemption from the judicial authority of the hated palatines and *starostas*; they would instead be under the direct authority of a *starshyi* appointed by the king. This amounted to the establishment of a privileged cossack estate, which appealed strongly to cossacks in the settled districts seeking regular pay, elevated status, and protection from enserfment and oppression at the hands of royal officials. It did much to develop a cossack ethos of frontier defense service. It did not, however, guarantee royal control over cossackdom. Quite the opposite: "By introducing cossack immunity ... it created a vacuum within the framework of the Polish state, a sphere free from the laws of the Polish lords, in which the Ukrainian element could again take shape according to its traditional, almost immanent features."[60] To make matters worse the register was unable to accommodate all those striving to obtain cossack privileges, because the *Sejm* denied the Crown the funds to pay more than a few hundred men. In 1572 the register was set at just 300 men; 3,000 were enrolled in the early 1590s, during the breakdown of relations with the Ottomans, but most were dismissed when the crisis passed; the register was expanded to 6,000 in 1625, but only after cossack militias had saved the Crown army from the Turks at Khotyn. The register thereby became a source of cossack conflict with the government rather than an effective instrument for cooptation and control. Henceforth the cossacks of the settled districts demanded that cossack privileges be expanded to all those "living the cossack way" regardless of whether they had been put on the register.

It was not through the register but through independent action that the Ukrainian cossack population made its most significant contributions to frontier defense. By the reign of Stefan Bathory the Zaporozhian Sich was playing the kind of tripwire/forward defense function the Don Host was performing for Muscovy. Zaporozhian infantry in small boats patrolled the lower reaches of the Dnepr and maintained pickets at river crossings; Zaporozhian cavalry patrolled the steppe and pursued Tatar *chambuly* along the invasion trails; and the rapid expansion of the cossack population in the Settled Lands by century's end provided a large manpower pool for volunteer militias supporting Crown and magnate forces for campaigns in the field, including campaigns abroad in Moldavia and Muscovy. By the 1620s the cossacks of the Settled districts of Bila Tserkva, Kanev, Korsun, Cherkasy, Pereiaslav, Chyhyryn, and Lubny had formed their own standing territorial corps (*polki*) with a total strength of 10,000 men. By the middle of the seventeenth century there were by Beauplan's estimate 120,000 cossacks, "all ready for war, and ready to answer in less than a week the slightest command to serve the king."[61]

Beauplan considered cossack infantry to be of higher tactical value than cossack cavalry.

> They show the most fighting skill and competence when they are sheltered in a *tabor* (for they are excellent shots with firearms, their usual weapons), and when they are defending their positions. ... On horseback they are not the best. I remember having seen only two hundred Polish horse rout 2,000 of their best men. It is true that one hundred of these cossacks, protected by their *tabor*, have no fear of a thousand Poles, nor even of a like number of Tatars.[62]

The Zaporozhian Sich also developed the means to strike by sea against Crimean and Ottoman territory. Their small single-mast *chaika* or *baidak* vessels, propelled by twenty or thirty oarsmen, with additional crew of twenty or so and three or four falconets, were able to slip past the Ottoman garrisons on the Dnepr estuary and reach the Anatolian coast in just thirty-six to forty hours, land, plunder and burn, and rush back out to sea. They attacked the towns along the Crimean coast, the Dobruja coast, and occasionally raided the environs of Istanbul. Because their boats sat so low in the water their crews could usually spot Ottoman galleys before they themselves were sighted; and they could attack and board Ottoman galleys by approaching on oar, with mast down, in the darkness of night.[63]

On occasion the Crown might turn a blind eye to Zaporozhian piracy or even secretly encourage it, to throw the Crimean Tatars or the Ottomans on the defensive; it would then deny responsibility for deeds committed by "licentious Cossacks" defying their king. But the Zaporozhian Sich, like the Crimean Khanate, lived partly off freebooting and therefore often raided on its own, in genuine defiance of the Crown, endangering its peace treaties and provoking military retaliation by the Tatars and the Turks. Through most of the sixteenth century Poland-Lithuania was anxious to preserve peace with the Ottomans, so on balance Zaporozhian naval raids created more security problems for the Crown than they resolved. There was no easy solution to this, either: moving to suppress the Sich threatened to provoke armed resistance by its supporters among the larger cossack population of the settled districts, while redirecting Zaporozhian raiding against Muscovy and other powers risked broadening the conflict in Pontic Europe and encouraging anti-Polish coalition. Meanwhile the unregistered cossacks of the Settled Lands were increasingly angry at the Crown's inability to expand the cossack register or extend register privileges to the rest of cossackdom. The cossack rebellions led by Kryshtof Kosynskyi and Severyn Nalyvaiko in the 1590s were partly driven by this anger, and over the next few decades the spread of Polish manorial authority into eastern Ukraine and the perception that Orthodoxy was in danger from the Trojan horse of the new Uniate Church would provide cossackdom with additional grievances. The defense of Ukraine was increasingly dependent upon unregistered cossack elements estranged from the Polish nobility and from royal officialdom, if not from the person of the king.[64]

Southern frontier security: the Muscovite approach

The Ukrainian historian Mykhailo Hrushevsky, comparing the Polish-Lithuanian defense system in Ukraine with the security system developing in southern Muscovy over the sixteenth and early seventeenth centuries, concluded:

> What was conducted weakly and fitfully and came out chaotically and illogically in the Polish-Lithuanian state, given its disorganization, with

its chronic lack of funds and feeble executive, the Muscovite state, with its infinitely well-developed bureaucratism, carried out systematically and according to plan, and executed quite precisely and accurately.[65]

Hrushevsky overstates the efficiency of Muscovy's southern frontier strategy, but over the longer term it did provide better security against Tatar raids, and in the second half of the seventeenth century it made it possible to mobilize manpower and other military resources on such a scale as to enable the tsars to occupy and hold Left Bank Ukraine and eliminate the Polish-Lithuanian Commonwealth as a serious competitor for hegemony on the Pontic steppe.

Hrushevsky was also correct to identify "lack of funds and a feeble executive" as a principal reason for the comparative weakness of the Commonwealth's southern frontier defense system. There were no Henrician Articles limiting the Moscow tsars' powers of resource mobilization for war; there was no Muscovite equivalent to the Ukrainian marchlords, palatines for life, and Senatorial oligarchy commanding private armies larger than the Crown's and sometimes taking up arms against the sovereign *in confederatio*; there was no chance in Muscovy that the private economic interests of magnates would prevail for long against purely strategic considerations in regard to the geographic patterning and pace of frontier colonization.

Instead of relying upon a small mobile field army placed near the edge of a fixed frontier for early interception of the enemy, augmented in times of crisis by cossack militias of increasingly doubtful loyalty, the Muscovite government pursued a strategy of planned military colonization coordinated across a broad front – establishing good-sized garrisons ever farther south, then linking them together along fortified lines, and finally, moving the corps of the frontier defense army down to the new perimeter formed by the fortified line. This process was then repeated – the founding of more garrison towns deeper in the steppe, the construction of an outer fortified line, the redeployment of the field army farther south. This was a long and expensive project, but the principle of universal obligation for service and draft (*sluzhba i tiaglo*) allowed the government to substitute corvée and cheap service-land-based military duty for tax revenue. Central chancellery control over the town governors (*gorodovye voevody*) made it possible to subject the frontier lands enclosed behind the advancing outer perimeter to heavy exploitation to support continued forward expansion. The Commonwealth's cossack problem was largely avoided, too; there was no limit on the size of the cossack register, so Ivan IV, Fedor Ivanovich, and Boris Godunov were able to offer registration on the tsar's bounty to thousands of cossacks on the Upper Reaches of the Don and Voronezh, and the *voevoda* remilitarization of local government after the Troubles made it possible by the 1620s to break the spirit of cossack insurgency within the borders of the Muscovite state.

CHAPTER TWO

Muscovy's southern borderland defense strategy, 1500–1635

In the late fifteenth century Muscovy's first and last line of defense against Tatar invasion had been along the Oka River and its tributary the Ugra. It was somewhere along their banks that the grand prince's field army made its stand in defense of Moscow, taking the field in either a Small or Large Array of three or five corps (*polki*, often mistranslated as "regiments"). The grand prince's court retinue turned out as the Great or Sovereign's Corps, while the *pomest'e*-based middle service class cavalry formed Advance, Rear Guard, Left Wing, and Right Wing corps commanded by the leading service princes and boyars. In the event of an especially grave invasion threat the grand prince might also call up service Tatars and free cossacks as cavalry auxiliaries and press peasant militias into service as irregular infantry, sappers, and transport personnel. The earliest surviving Muscovite deployment records do not report corps strengths, but even when the auxiliaries and the slaves and peasants protecting the baggage train are counted it is unlikely the largest of these arrays in the sixteenth century exceeded 35,000 men, the maximum Muscovite logistics of the time could support in the field.[1]

The array order of center, vanguard, rear, and wings usually served as order of battle when the corps massed on one field. Any infantry and artillery were placed in the center, which tried to stand its ground receiving the enemy's attack while the cavalry on the wings rushed out to strike the enemy's flanks or rear and break up his attack; this had to be done quickly, as the center, if unprotected by earthworks or *wagenburg*, could not be expected to hold for very long once the enemy closed within bowshot. By the 1530s most of the Muscovite cavalry consisted of lightly armed archers clad in thickly padded hemp *tegilai* coats, sitting in short stirrups on small Nogai horses; only the more prosperous cavalrymen had mail or mail-and-plate hauberks. The armored lancer had been largely phased out because steppe warfare favored mobility and preponderance in archer fire and because preference to light mounted archer formations was the more cost-effective means of pursuing numerical superiority given the modest income of most *pomest'e*-based middle service class cavalrymen.

The Bank Array

Beginning in 1512 the rising danger of Crimean or Kazan' Tatar invasion forced Grand Prince Vasilii III to station several thousand troops every spring and midsummer along the Bank (*Bereg*), a 250 km stretch of the Oka between the towns of Kolomna and Kaluga. The purpose of the Bank deployments was to concentrate field army forces to defend central Muscovy – the capital standing only 100–170 km north of this line – so only a few small additional detachments stood beyond the Bank to defend the towns of the forest-steppe zone. The Bank provided more forward defense, however, in that the Array commanders were now expected to advance to intercept before the enemy could reach the Oka. Furthermore, the next several years saw the enlargement of the Bank army and the extension of bank deployments farther west and east. Additional smaller units were stationed south of the Bank near Tula, to the west along the Ugra and farther east near the Meshchera forests, at Riazan', Murom, and Nizhnii Novgorod on the Volga. By 1521 the Bank army had seventy-two commanders and captains in charge of a line of force running from the Seversk region eastward into Meshchera to the upper Volga Front.

In 1522 Vasilii III further centralized command authority by making Kolomna his fixed headquarters for spring and autumn Bank operations and routinizing corps command appointments and corps stations. Certain of his secretaries were now made responsible for compiling biannual deployment lists (*razriady*) recording command appointments, listing towns contributing troops, and describing mobilization plans, march routes, and the appointments to garrison towns of "annual commanders" (*godovye voevody*, the forerunners of the *gorodovye voevody* or town governors).[2] This was an important precedent for the eventual emergence of a central Military Chancellery, and it also encouraged more coordinated and aggressive operation by the Bank Array corps and the smaller field units and garrison forces south of the Bank, especially as it was accompanied by greater investment in the founding of new garrison towns.

The Bank corps were initially exclusively cavalry forces, comprised of provincial middle service class cavalrymen serving from *pomest'ia* and formed on a largely *ad hoc* basis: during mobilization the district's cavalrymen were decimally organized into decuries, quinquagenies, and centuries and allowed to elect their own centurions. Previously centuries might be posted to different corps for each campaign; but now that there was regular biannual defense duty along the Bank and more sophisticated recordkeeping a more regular force structure with greater continuity of command at the century level had become possible. By the early 1550s centurions were more likely to be appointed by Moscow than locally elected and centuries more likely to be assigned permanently to particular corps.

Bank corps mobilizations were further rationalized by Tsar Ivan IV's 1556 Decree on Service. This ordinance systematized the relationship between landholding entitlements and military service obligations for all members of the upper and middle service classes, and it introduced an elaborate system for the differentiation of middle service class military duties on the basis of fitness — defined broadly to include material resources and experience as well as age and physical condition. If pre-mobilization inspection determined that a servitor was old or infirm or possessed fewer than twenty inhabited quarters of land per field he was recorded in the district service list as assigned to "town service" (*gorodovaia sluzhba*, that is, local siege duty), which was considered less onerous because it did not require him to keep a mount or absent himself from his plowlands for any extended period. The physically fit holding more than twenty quarters of land were deemed capable of performing "corps service" (*polkovaia sluzhba*); for some this meant regional defense duty in the armies of the Bank or the newer Abatis Line (*beregovaia sluzhba* or *ukrainnaia sluzhba*), while those of even higher service capacity were liable for campaign duty in more distant theaters (*pokhodnaia sluzhba*). Every holder of a *pomest'e* or *votchina* had to provide one mounted man in full kit (with an extra mount, if assigned to distant campaign duty) from every 100 quarters of land he held. Unlike those relegated to town service, the men assigned to the different forms of corps service were entitled to cash compensation from the tsar, and these cash bounties (*zhalovan'ia*) were further increased if the servitor provided retainers or substitutes over and above the norm. Only those who continued to meet these norms were entitled to receive the Sovereign's cash bounty, to retain right to their *pomest'ia*, and to hope for eventual promotion with a higher *pomest'e* entitlement rate. By the end of the century even the allodial lands of the upper service class theoretically became subject to confiscation in part or full for nonperformance of military duty. This completed the process of binding the metropolitan nobility to compulsory state service alongside the provincial petty nobility.[3]

The 1556 Decree on Service enhanced military planning on the southern frontier by making it possible to project in advance how many cavalrymen and their slave and peasant retainers would be available for mobilization into different forms of service and to calculate the costs of their deployment (in this regard it functioned somewhat like the Ottoman *timar* system, which established the ratio between *çift* allotments and the number of *sipahi* cavalrymen and the *cebeli* retainers they were to support). The additional recordkeeping involved in inspections, promotions, and setting new cash and land entitlement rates also stimulated further bureaucratization of the central military secretariat. By 1566 the secretaries for military affairs had their own office, the *Razriadnaia izba*, which was expanded and renamed the *Razriadnyi prikaz* (Military Chancellery) over the next decades.

The forces on the southern frontier also increased in size and structural complexity as a consequence of Muscovite mastery of gunpowder technology. Improvements in cannoncasting and the adoption of the horsedrawn wheeled guncarriage finally made it practical to equip the Bank army with field artillery in the 1520s, and within another forty years the field artillery had become a distinct tactical unit with its own officers. In 1577 we already find a central Artillery Chancellery in existence. The first significant use of firearms by infantry along the Bank dated from 1522, when Vasilii III deployed 1,500 Lithuanian and German mercenary arquebusiers, but it was under Tsar Ivan IV that firearm-bearing infantry finally became a regular and sizeable contingent within the campaign army as well as the provincial garrisons. In 1550 a 3,000-man standing palace guard of Select Musketeers (*vybornye strel'tsy*) was created; this was soon followed by the formation of musketeer units in the provincial towns for policing and for call-up into the campaign army. Several thousand musketeers participated in the Kazan' and Polotsk campaigns (1552, 1563). They too were organized decimally, but with the difference that every five centuries comprised a command (*prikaz*) under a captain appointed by the tsar. The musketeer commands were assigned to the corps alongside the middle service class cavalry centuries, although the majority were deployed in the center of the array, in the Great Corps. A Musketeer Chancellery was formed by 1577.

The creation of the *strel'tsy* was apparently not a response to the military challenge presented by European infantries, for it predated by a few years the formation of musketeer contingents in the Lithuanian and Polish armies and *strel'tsy* organization, equipment, and tactics owed less to European infantry models than to the example of the Ottoman janissaries. The mission first envisioned for the *strel'tsy* was on the Tatar frontier rather than on the western front, judging from Ivan Peresvetov's 1549 memorandum urging Ivan IV to create a salaried 20,000-man infantry force to man the southern defense lines.[4]

The Abatis Line

Along much of the Bank, from Kozel'sk eastward to Nizhnii Novgorod, several stretches of forest and marshland blocked Tatar penetration into central Muscovy; but there were also portals through this natural barrier, like the Shatsk Gates, a strip of open land cutting through the Riazan' and Meshchera woods; the Russians therefore had to fill in these gaps with earthworks, palisades, ditches, and wolf-traps. Thinner forest was rendered less penetrable by sending work parties into the forest depths, out of sight from the open plain, and having them fell a belt of trees, leaving stumps as high as 1.5 to 2.8 m, the felled trunks pointing out towards the invader to form a kind of rampart or abatis barrier (*lesnoi zaval*) 20 to 130 m deep; a few other trees were left standing at certain intervals as observation and signalling platforms. Wooden blockhouses or earthen forts with towers and artillery, fronted and flanked with wide ditches, pits, and anti-cavalry fences, were built along river fords, gaps in the forest, and strategically located bluffs, while sparsely wooded stretches through which smaller raiding parties might infiltrate were fenced off with oak palisades and earthen walls.[5]

Construction of these defense works had begun on some parts of the southern frontier in the late fifteenth century. By 1533 about 250 km of the length of the Bank had been fortified – predominantly on the western end, between the Zhizdra and the Ugra. The next few decades saw fortification activity shift to the south of the Bank. In the 1550s another segment of fortified line began taking shape to the southeast, linking the new town of Shatsk with Alatyr' on the Volga. By 1600 the Bank had been joined to a newer, longer, and more imposing bulwark – actually a network of fortified lines and forest – called the Abatis Line (*zasechnaia cherta*), most of which lay 100 km or less south of the Bank. The main course of the Abatis Line stretched about 600 km from the Zhizdra River through Tula to Riazan', with another 400 km of defense line linking Belev to Krapivna and joining Skopin, Riazhsk, and Sapozhok to Shatsk.[6]

The direction of corvée and defense operations along the new Abatis Line was initially concentrated in the Gunners' Chancellery at Moscow, which processed inspection reports from the governors of the districts along the lines to decide where to authorize new segments, deploy new forces, or order repairs. Each governor was responsible for maintaining and manning a particular segment of fortified line. He had to expel unauthorized settlers from his abatis zone and use fines, knoutings, or even the death penalty to uphold bans on any traveling, roadlaying, or woodcutting that might damage the forest barrier; he organized peasant corvée for repairs and new fortifications; come spring, his workmen shoveled away the snow so that melting snowbanks would not erode earthworks; and come summer, with the greater risk that brushfires might spread to wooden fortifications, he had work parties mow the grass and cut the brush around them and burn out firebreaks. In late autumn the patrol riders burned large expanses of steppegrass beyond the defense lines, along the Tatar trails, in order to deny the enemy cover and fodder.

There were twenty-seven abatis captains, thirteen abatis stewards, and one hundred and forty abatis guards supervising labor and defense duty on the Abatis Line in 1631. The corvée and guarding of line segments was performed by newly enrolled military colonists given allotments of service land just behind the line, and by detachments of local peasant laborers and militiamen (*podymovnye liudi*) rendering such service as part of their fiscal obligation to the state. On the Krasnosel'skii segment near Riazan' it was practice to levy peasant guards and laborers at the rate of one man from every three households from every village within 15 km of the line, or one man from every five households within 16–25 km. Moscow recognized that these levies were unpopular because line duty disrupted peasants' agricultural work – they were required to stand guard on day and night shifts from early spring until winter – so it required segment commanders to submit to the Gunners' Chancellery rolls and reports on line guard and labor deployments and punished commanders who ordered levies without military need in order to extort bribes from the villages. The working orders of segment commanders indicate they were expected to use their troops and militia not only to repulse attacking Tatars but to pursue smaller *chambuly* back onto the plain (to seize prisoners for interrogation) and to send part of their forces to reinforce endangered neighboring line segments.[7]

In districts with few peasant taxpayers corvée and guard duty fell entirely upon the service community. This did not necessarily result in better performance, however, as it tended to be foisted upon the more impoverished servicemen already overburdened by patrol and sortie duty – their more prosperous comrades having already been assigned to corps service. When the government ordered a major reconstruction of the entire Abatis Line in 1638, servicemen deserting from abatis duty were as much a problem as peasant taxpayer flight.[8]

Moscow had never intended the Abatis Line forests and fortifications to be impermeable. The Abatis Line was first and foremost a platform for observation and signalling, which might also be able to slow the enemy advance a little while the corps of the field army moved up to engage the Tatars. The corps were all the more crucial – really the only line of force capable of repulsing Tatar invasions of central Muscovy – given the weakness of the southern town garrison network before 1635. The real tactical significance of the new Abatis Line, therefore, was as the new line of deployment of the Bank corps. Starting in the 1550s Moscow began setting new muster points south of the Bank along the emerging Abatis Line perimeter: corps now assembled at Pronsk, Mikhailov, Tula, Dedilov, Mtsensk, Karachev, Putivl', and Shatsk each 25 March, with a second shift stationed each September at these points as well as at Briansk, Starodub, and several other southwestern border towns. This meant the Bank now served as the line of deployment only for reduced reserve forces for a brief part of the summer at the height of the invasion season. On occasion the tsar even deployed small forces on the steppe near Livny, Elets, and Kursk.

Eventually it would become possible to field a maximum of three discrete army groups or "arrays," called *razriady* after the deployment lists. The first was the Bank Array, consisting of the Great (or Center) Corps at Serpukhov, the Right Flank Corps at Tarusa (or at Myshega or Aleksin), the Vanguard Corps at Kaluga, the Rear Guard Corps at Kashira (or at Krapivna or Kolomna), and the Left Flank Corps at Kashira or Lopasnia. A second array, a Borderland Array consisting of corps at Tula, Dedilov, and Riazan' or Mikhailov, was added by 1582; and towards century's end a third array emerged, a Riazan' Array consisting of corps at Pereiaslavl'-Riazan', Pronsk, and Mikhailov. These arrays permitted the Military Chancellery to work out an elaborate routine of troop mobilization venues and reinforcement march routes in closer relation to considerations of terrain, the Tatar invasion roads, and the courses of the Bank and Abatis Line. Such an imposing and solid line of force was erected along the Bank in 1598, for example, that the invading Crimean Tatars had to withdraw and sue for peace. The following year it seemed warranted to discontinue the Bank Array altogether, and for the next six years the corps stood only in the Borderland and Riazan' arrays, testifying to the fact that Muscovy's inner perimeter defense had shifted southward by about 100 km by taking advantage of the new garrison towns and the completion of the Abatis Line.

This southward shift had taken fifty years to accomplish not only because it had required massive investments in both defense line construction and military colonization. An expanded defense perimeter extending farther south necessitated improved patrolling and intelligence-gathering if the corps were to be effective in intercepting the enemy south of the Bank, and this in turn required the establishment of more town garrisons along and below the new Abatis Line.

It had also been delayed because of the long Livonian War (1558–1582) and the tsar's *oprichnina*. The scale of military operations in Livonia and Lithuania had by the early 1560s drained manpower from the southern front and required that some corps from the Abatis Line be pulled back to the western half of the Bank to support operations against the Lithuanians. This left Muscovy's eastern forest-steppe more vulnerable to the Tatars, who even burned Riazan's *posad* in 1564. The Ottoman expedition against Astrakhan' in 1569 finally shocked Moscow into restoring deployments across the entire southern front, using 50,000 men recently made available by the stalemate on the Lithuanian front: five corps were now stationed along the Bank, with three on the central part of the Abatis Line and another three smaller corps in the Riazan' region. But the corps were not authorized to march south of the defense lines to provide a more preemptive defense, and their flexibility of response was hampered by the discord the *oprichnina* provoked among Ivan IV's generals. As a result the Crimean Tatars slipped past them in 1571 and crossed the Oka, burning Moscow and raiding dozens of other towns.[9]

Command-and-control

The Bank and Abatis Line corps remained roughly the size of the southern frontier corps fielded in the first half of the century, the Great Corps consisting of a few thousand men and the lesser corps ranging down to 500 or so. But they were no longer exclusively cavalry forces; the proportion of artillery, musketeers, and cossack infantry had increased, particularly in the Great Corps. The proportion of service Tatar auxiliaries had also increased.

Deployment in partial or full five-corps array, depending upon the gravity of the situation, continued as before, except that a special light cavalry Reconnaissance Corps (*ertaul'nyi polk*) occasionally preceded the Vanguard Corps. The order of battle also remained largely unchanged: if it became necessary for the corps to converge into one mass or column to meet the main force of the enemy it was with the Reconnaissance and Vanguard corps taking the front, followed by the Right Flank, then the Great Corps, the Left Flank, and the Rear Guard.

But from mid-century much greater emphasis was given to centralizing command authority and strengthening coordination across the array. Moscow gave the senior commander of the Great Corps more detailed instructions and the authority and staff to more actively direct operations by other corps. It became more common to decree certain command positions or even entire operations exempt from precedence challenge, and, when necessary, to divide the respective authorities of a corps' senior and junior "associate" (*tovarishch*) commanders by giving the former exclusive authority over two-thirds of the corps.[10] An especially important development for command-and-control was the emergence of a field headquarters staff: the Military Chancellery began placing some of its secretaries and clerks on special field assignment to the senior commander of the Great Corps for the duration of the campaign, to serve in his Array Pavilion (*razriadnyi shater*). Structurally the Array Pavilion resembled the office (*s"ezzhaia izba*) of a town governor, though one that was mobile and temporary; the staff of the Array Pavilion compiled and maintained the corps rolls, supply inventories, cash accounts, and records of salary distributions; they served as a judicial board hearing the suits of mobilized servicemen; and above all they communicated with the other corps commanders, the neighboring town governors, and the Military Chancellery in Moscow. Array Pavilion staff remained small even up to the 1650s (just one secretary and two or three clerks) but would expand during the long Thirteen Years' War, providing a precedent for more ramified regimental and army group administration. By the end of the seventeenth century we find Array Pavilion staffs as large as two to three secretaries and nine to fourteen clerks.

The introduction of Array Pavilions aimed at improving coordination of array forces by the senior commander of the Great Corps but also at enhancing control of the senior commander from Moscow, for the Military Chancellery at Moscow, by detailing some of its secretaries and clerks to the Pavilion, gradually acquired more direct experience of field operations so it could take on more of the functions of a kind of General Staff.[11]

To this end the Military Chancellery was now placing greater emphasis on its written communications with commanders in the field. Its working orders to commanders were becoming more explicit and comprehensive and were followed up more frequently by decree rescripts clarifying or altering instructions in response to changes at the front; in return the Military Chancellery expected more regular and careful reports from commanders in the field so that all operations could be "executed according to those current decree articles and in reference to previous decree articles, with all diligent zeal and caution."[12]

All this served the autocracy's preference for maximum centralization at Moscow of ultimate authority over military operations. One naturally wonders whether this was already being carried to impractical lengths, with secretaries at Moscow trying to micromanage operations on a changing front hundreds of miles away and commanders on that front left unauthorized to respond to new developments that had not been foreseen in their instructions from Moscow, Moscow in turn having failed to anticipate these developments because reports from the front had been in error or late arriving. There were indeed instances when unforeseen developments, even ones of minor import, left commanders hesitant to act and entreating the Military Chancellery to "decree to us, thy slaves, what to do." Muscovite commanders very likely operated under tighter constraint from the center than their Polish counterparts, but assuming over-centralization was a chronic problem rendering Muscovite army operations generally less effective probably goes too far given how little we really know from the archival evidence surviving from this period.

In the seventeenth century the Military Chancellery was able to shorten its response time through further division of clerical labor (establishing specialized bureaux and sections within the Military Chancellery) and by separating incoming reports into less urgent and urgent processing categories. Already in the late sixteenth century it also appears to have recognized that some kinds of decisions were better left to commander initiative. The more ramified force deployment system in the south – with two or three arrays of corps, and town governors as well as commanders of lesser corps expected to be ready to march in reinforcement (*v skhode*) to larger corps – required that working orders to these town governors and lesser corps commanders spell out the circumstances under which they were permitted to make reinforcement marches away from their original positions, but the senior commander of the Great Corps, as marshal of the corps in the field, was given greater latitude "to act according to the matter at hand, and as God so enlightens him," provided he notified the Military Chancellery of his decisions immediately thereafter.[13]

If the system aimed at maximum centralization of planning and decision-making it did not always achieve it. Orders from Moscow might not meet with compliance in the field. The best known instance of this was in 1571, when the inability of *oprichnina* and *zemshchina* commanders to coordinate operations gave Khan Devlet Girei the opportunity to cross the Oka and burn Moscow. In the last stage of the Livonian War some commanders on the northwestern front with demoralized or under-strength forces even defied Ivan IV and repeatedly disobeyed orders to move from their positions.[14]

Mobilizations and logistics

Although deployments of array corps were becoming regular biannual practice, mobilizing them still probably involved some consultation between the Military Chancellery and the tsar and Boyar Duma because of the latter's natural interest in the matter of command appointments. After the tsar and Duma had their say on choosing commanders, the command appointments were announced from the Military Chancellery. The overall plan for mobilizing troops by region and formation was worked up within the Military Chancellery from its own manpower and materiel lists and from records provided by the regional chancelleries and the chancelleries having jurisdiction over the musketeers, gunners, service Tatars, and peasant militiamen.[15]

Unless there was a full alert requiring that all available manpower be fielded at once, the troops assigned to the array corps were usually called up in two shifts, for the period 1 April to 1 July and then for 1 July to 1 October or "until the great snows." Those mobilized for the first shift usually came from districts farther away from the front. Special muster provosts (*dozorshchiki*) were used to oversee mobilizations of troops from the provinces farther from the front, whereas mobilizations from the districts near the corps stations could be entrusted to the corps commanders themselves and the governors of the nearest towns. In some instances muster provosts as well as town governors were subsequently appointed to command the troops they were sending to the corps. The actual task of riding from village to village to bring troops in to the central assembly point (preferably on staggered dates to prevent confusion and billeting problems) was entrusted to commissars (*vysyl'shchiki*) who were expected to report back frequently by courier so the muster provosts and commanders could monitor their progress and press the governors of neighboring towns into providing assistance. Troops who failed to appear for muster (*netchiki*) were to be hunted down, bastinadoed and briefly jailed, then released on surety bond and forced to reimburse the commissars for the extra costs their trackdown had incurred. In the event a shirker could not be located the commissars could select a replacement, usually a youth approaching the age of novitiate service; and if commissar interrogation of the local elected assessors (*okladchiki*) revealed no extenuating circumstances behind a subject's failure to appear for muster the Military Chancellery might choose to impose special sanctions.

The assembled troops were inspected against the town service lists and muster rolls and formed into the decuries, quinquagenies, and centuries comprising that particular corps. The centuries of middle class cavalrymen were still formed anew for each campaign, and the number of cavalry centuries in a corps varied. However, it was no longer so common for centuries to elect their own centurion, who was now more likely to be appointed by the corps commander or the Military Chancellery. Because musketeers and cossacks doubled as a peacetime constabulary, their force structure was permanent. Five centuries of musketeers comprised one command (*prikaz*) under a captain appointed by Moscow.

The middle service class cavalry centuries were expected to appear at inspection in armor with sabers and bows or firearms, mounted, and with their slave retainers. The number of such retainers each cavalryman was to bring along depended upon the number of peasant households registered for him in cadasters and censuses and on the norms established in the 1556 Decree on Service. The array corps drew especially from the middle service class of the southern frontier, of course, so array century principals were less likely to have as many retainers or to be as well equipped. Because of their smaller *pomest'e* economies, and because Moscow had not yet committed to providing firearms at treasury expense or paying special subsidies for purchasing them, southern servicemen were less likely to afford what had become the handguns of choice on the western front by the 1630s, wheellock pistols or short carbines. Muster roll data from 1639 shows that only 38 percent of Riazan's middle service class cavalry owned guns, compared to more than 80 percent in some western front districts, and most of their guns were antiquated matchlocks of sixteenth-century design, the kind of weapon western front principals preferred to relegate to their retainers guarding the baggage train; the other 62 percent of the Riazanians were armed solely with bows and sabers.[16]

Very little is known about the logistics of southern array operations in this period, primarily because provisioning and transport remained for the most part privately arranged and so went undocumented. The state played little role in corps logistics because the bulk of the corps still consisted of middle service class cavalrymen required to provide their own stores sufficient for three to four month's campaign, carried on their own packhorses and carts and sent ahead to the muster point soon after mobilization had been announced. Any additional provisions cavalrymen might subsequently need they would have to purchase or forage for themselves from the villages near where they were stationed. Musketeers and gunners did get rations money from the state, but they were still expected to purchase their own supplies with it. The government's primary contribution to logistics was therefore limited to providing transport and drivers (out of the *iam* post system, or specially requisitioned from taxpayers) to the musketeers, gunners, and artillery, which elements were usually smaller in the southern arrays than on campaigns on enemy soil on the western front.

Each corps had its own baggage train, reflecting the fact that corps traveled along separate routes and joined together for general battle on one field only under unusual circumstances. On major operations on foreign territory, at least, Muscovite army baggage trains tended to be very large even by the standards of the time and their management required the appointment of special train commanders. The 30,000-man army Ivan IV led against Polotsk in 1563 was followed by an additional 20–30,000 baggage train slaves and so many wagons the train commander had great difficulty keeping it moving along the narrow road to Polotsk; much of the column got sidetracked into forests and swamps and "lost all semblance of order. . . . Movement came to a standstill."[17] A force of 18,000 cavalrymen sent from Polotsk against Orsha the following year had a train of at least 5,000 wagons. But baggage trains for the corps of the Borderland and Riazan' arrays were probably of much smaller proportion, for these corps were not intended to make long marches across enemy territory and could draw from local supply sources along the Abatis Line.[18]

Local supply sources came in three forms. The larger or more strategically positioned garrison towns along the Bank and Abatis Line (Kolomna, Tula, Pronsk, Voronezh, etc.) held state granaries, filled by grain taxation or government purchase and designed to provision their defenders in time of siege or blockade; these could also serve as rudimentary magazines from which the corps could also draw. Merchant sutlers sometimes delivered supplies for sale, although we cannot tell whether they were operating on government contract and under instruction to provision particular units. Probably most supplemental provisioning was not state-organized but undertaken by servicemen arranging their own occasional purchases of local food and fodder from townsmen and villagers, with the government attempting some regulation by insisting these purchases be made at fair market price so as not to exploit the tsar's taxpayers (when operating on enemy territory, of course, the army was free to seize what it needed and extort "contributions").[19]

A corps could march from ten to twenty miles a day depending on the size of its baggage train and the urgency of its mission. The Military Chancellery expected commanders on the march to make frequent courier reports as to their progress and the developing intelligence, and protect the population along the marchroute from assaults and other depredations at the hands of their troops, even to the point of hearing lawsuits lodged against their troops.

Tactics

The effect of the gunpowder revolution on Muscovite tactics by the end of the sixteenth century was uneven. On the western front siege warfare had certainly been transformed by the development of heavy "wall-smasher" (*stenobitnye*) guns and the use of musketeers to support entrenching work, and cavalry tactics were beginning to abandon dense formation for extended echelon formation to counter enemy artillery fire. But tactical change on the southern front proceeded at a slower rate. There had been instances in which massed artillery fire at particular crossings on the Bank Line had helped throw back attacks upon central Muscovy (Molodi, 1572; Kolomenskoe, 1591), but there remained technical limits on the use of artillery along the defense lines: most of the tsar's ordnance still consisted of heavy large-caliber guns of limited mobility, unsuitable for deployment in the field south of the Bank, and this began to change only from the late 1620s when the Cannoncasting Yard acquired new water-powered smithies and began producing smaller caliber (two- or three-pounder) field guns.[20] Although musketeers and mercenary cossack infantry now comprised a larger part of the array corps, the inaccuracy and slow rate of fire of their unrifled matchlocks and their lack of pike support made commanders reluctant to deploy them in the open unfortified field. Southern corps commanders therefore preferred to deploy their infantry along opposing riverbanks, on river patrol boats, in ambush within dense woods, or in positions well-fortified by earthwork, palisade, *wagenburg*, or *guliai-gorod*. The *guliai-gorod*, Ivan Peresvetov's adaptation of the *wagenburg*, involved mounting loopholed wooden mantlets on small carts to provide a kind of "moving castle" within which a mass of infantry could slowly advance.[21] The battle of Dobrynichi (1605) is sometimes cited as the first successful instance of Muscovite musketeers using Mauritsian infantry tactics, but this is questionable, for it seems to have involved no more than general volley fire from musketeers massed behind a *wagenburg*, with no indication whether line or platoon firing or the countermarch had also been mastered.[22] Nor did cavalry tactics in the southern arrays change much in this period: as before, cavalry forces continued to keep to the defensive, relying on numerical superiority and waiting for the opportunity to make a sudden short flanking attack.

European observers accustomed to a different manner of warfare tended not to discern much tactical sophistication in Muscovite army operations. Giles Fletcher (*c.* 1588) maintained:

> The Russe trusteth rather to his number than to the valor of his soldiers or good ordering of his forces. Their marching or leading is without all order, save that the four *polki* or legions ... keep themselves several under their ensigns and so thrust all together in a hurry as they are directed by their general.

Isaac Massa (*c.* 1607) was even more dismissive: "They wage war without tactics, and they obtain victory only by chance, superior numbers, or against the Tatars, who have no conception of order."[23]

Whether these were fair assessments is difficult to determine, for descriptions of actual Muscovite army operations before the Troubles (when we finally have detailed accounts from Polish observers) tended to be very brief, vague, and stereotypical. One of the few exceptions was the 1572 battle at Molodi, reported in greater than usual detail in the *Razriadnaia kniga* because it was a great victory. The working order to the commander of the Great Corps at Molodi has been preserved, as were the notes of the mercenary *oprichnik* Heinrich von Staden, a participant.[24]

In response to Khan Devlet Girei's May 1571 sack of Moscow Prince M. I. Vorotynskii had been charged with the task of reforming the borderland's reconnaissance services. In April 1572, in anticipation of another major Crimean Tatar attack upon Moscow, Vorotynskii was made senior commander of an expanded 8,000-man Great Corps at Kolomna. The rest of that spring's array consisted of N. Ia. Odoevskii's Right Flank Corps (4,000 men) at Tarusa; A. V. Repnin's Left Flank Corps (2,000 men) at Lopasna; I. P. Shuiskii's Rear Guard (2,000 men) at Kashira; and A. P. Khovanskii's and D. I. Khvorostinin's Vanguard Corps at Kaluga (4,475 men, including some 900 Viatka militiamen and 1,000 hired Zaporozhian infantry based on small boats on the Oka below Kolomna). These 20,475 men were likely the maximum that could be spared for Bank deployment given that the bulk of the army was busy on the western front or with the tsar operating against Novgorod.

Vorotynskii's Great Corps included 3,000 musketeers and most of the artillery available for southern array service – about 100 guns – manned by gunners from Moscow. A company of 100 mercenary cavalry pistoleers (*reitary*) from Narva under *rotmistr* Iurii Frantsbek was ordered to keep close to Vorotynskii's hand but not so close to his Muscovite troops as to spark quarrel. All other cavalry, infantry, and artillery captains in the Great Corps were appointed by Vorotynskii. The number of slaves attending the baggage train is not recorded, but the Great Corps train must have been substantial for it included the elements of a *guliai-gorod* a few kilometers long when assembled and fully unfolded.

All five corps were to muster near Kolomna and Kashira and then march to their array positions. Towns on the Bank were to provide transport for Vorotynskii's artillery while the governors of the other borderland districts held themselves ready to march in reinforcement to the Bank and help the Bank towns prepare for siege, assisted by officers temporarily attached from

Vorotynskii's corps. Vorotynskii's working order did not attempt to manage all his actions from Moscow but gave him some discretion to use his own judgment. It listed places on the steppe to which to despatch ranger parties but allowed him to send out additional rangers "where suitable"; he was to determine where along the Oka, between Riazan' and the Zhizdra abatis, additional fortifications were to be erected, according to his own inspection, and could levy from both sides of the river whatever peasant corvée he needed to erect them; and he could choose where his and the other four corps would stand, provided these sites offered good protection for his artillery, infantry, and train and provided he kept the Military Chancellery posted as to just where the corps were deployed, how far apart they were, and how they were fortified.

But Vorotynskii's working order was specific as to his options for subsequent movement from these stations. If it appeared the enemy was taking the traditional trail towards Bolkhov to ford the Oka there, Vorotynskii's corps had to march towards Kaluga and try to turn the Tatars back before they could cross the Zhizdra. The Zaporozhians and Viatka militia would sail up the Oka to the Zhizdra to help man the fords and abatis there. If the enemy got across the Zhizdra Vorotynskii had to attempt a second stand along the Ugra, deploying in the woods or behind strong earthworks but not engaging the enemy on open unfortified field. Vorotynskii's orders also prescribed how he was to move in the event the Tatars tried to cross the Oka near Kaluga, Aleksin, Serpukhov, Kashira, Kolomna, or Riazan', or pushed up through the Meshchera Forest towards Vladimir and the Kliaz'ma River.

The general impression from Vorotynskii's working order is of the Military Chancellery's insistence on a strategy emphasizing above all else fallback and corps convergence to block enemy efforts to cross the Oka and tactics of stationary defense from fortified positions for enhanced artillery and musket firepower.

In June 1572 Khan Devlet Girei marched from Perekop, advancing up the Don towards the Oka with a large army of 60,000 Crimean Tatars, Nogais, and some Turkish janissary infantry and artillery. On 26 July the khan's army circumvented the great stone fortress at Tula and reached the bank of the Oka near Serpukhov about 70 km south of Moscow. Devlet Girei did not attempt an immediate crossing, for the Muscovites had deployed a *guliai-gorod*, some artillery, and 200 cavalrymen from Shuiskii's Rear Guard on the opposite bank. Devlet Girei brought up his own Turkish guns to silence the Muscovite artillery. On the night of 27–28 July the khan sent some Nogai cavalry under mirza Tereberdei across Senkin Ford to attack Shuiskii's cavalry from the rear. This was easily accomplished and most of the rest of Devlet Girei's army had crossed the river by morning. Tereberdei's Nogais then fanned out ahead along most of the roads leading from Senkin Ford to Moscow. Devlet Girei's main column followed up the Serpukhov road towards Moscow, passing the towns of Serpukhov and Tarusa, the latter the station of the Muscovite Right Flank under Odoevskii. Odoevskii tried to engage the Tatars on the Nara River but was defeated. The Vanguard Corps and Vorotynskii's Great Corps had been expected to throw back the enemy before it crossed the Oka and neared Serpukhov, but having arrived too late to accomplish this these two corps had to content themselves with following the khan's army at a safe distance in hope of catching some opportunity to slip ahead and block the khan's way to Moscow. When it became apparent this was not going to happen, Dmitrii Khvorostinin led part of the Vanguard Corps – about 3,000 cavalry – on an attack upon the rear of the Tatar army. This did succeed in stopping the khan's advance towards Moscow; he had to halt his column at the edge of a marsh a few kilometers north of the Pakhra River on 29 July and send 12,000 men back to reinforce his rear.

At Molodi the Muscovite Great Corps and Vanguard Corps prepared for the Tatar counterattack. Vorotynskii deployed his 3,000 musketeers behind the Rozhai River and a line of ditches, and took the rest of his corps – his cavalry, artillery, and Narva pistoleers – uphill from this line, stationing them inside a *guliai-gorod* atop the hill. The Vanguard Corps cavalry took up positions on the *guliai-gorod*'s flanks and rear.

These positions came under repeated attack over the days 29 July to 2 August – initially by the Tatar rear guard, and from 31 July, by the bulk of the khan's army. Muscovite artillery and musket fire inflicted heavy losses on the enemy and Muscovite detachments made several successful sorties from the *guliai-gorod*, managing to kill Tereberdei and capture the khan's most important field commander, mirza Divei. On 2 August Vorotynskii was forced to more desperate action – his men were now out of food and water and had begun to eat their horses – so while the Tatars were making yet another attack up the hill he took his troops out through the rear of the *guliai-gorod* and down a rear gulley, from which they rushed out by surprise against the Tatar rear. At the same moment Khvorostinin led the Narva pistoleers and part of the Vanguard Corps out of the *guliai-gorod* downhill against the Tatar front. In the ensuing melee the khan's janissaries were massacred and his own son and grandson were killed. Devlet Girei had lost too many men to continue on to Moscow, and he was under the impression that a fresh Muscovite field army was en route to reinforce Khvorostinin, so he broke camp and began withdrawing to the steppe. His rear guard came under attack several times in the days following. He was not able to assemble enough of an army for a new invasion of Muscovy.

The Battle of Molodi showed some evolution in Muscovite tactics from early sixteenth-century practice: the traditional preference for sudden flank attack continued, but when necessary units were also more able now to hold fixed positions for days running by making greater use of improvised fortifications, artillery, and musket. The *guliai-gorod*, a Muscovite innovation, did deserve partial credit for the victory at Molodi, although subsequent events would also reveal its limitations.

Combined operations

After his spectacular successes against Kazan' and Astrakhan' in the mid-1550s Ivan IV took up the idea of going on the offensive and attacking the Crimean Tatars on their own territory. A full-scale invasion across hundreds of kilometers of empty steppe with the intent of capturing Perekop and conquering the Crimean peninsula was beyond his logistic capabilities, but it did seem possible to begin making some quick raids on Crimean border territory using smaller *corps volantes* of cavalry supported by river flotillas on the Don and Dnepr – especially if such raids could be undertaken as combined operations with some allied power based nearer the Khanate. The window of opportunity for such combined operations would prove small, however, for the unsettled diplomatic circumstances of the 1550s did not permit lasting military alliances. It would be another thirty or forty years before Muscovy found its first real strategic partner on the Black Sea steppe – the Don Cossack population – and even then combined operations would long remain limited largely to intelligence-sharing, the first significant Muscovite–Don Cossack raids on the Khanate becoming feasible only in the 1640s.

In 1554–1558 the government of Ivan IV attempted to negotiate an anti-Crimean coalition with the Grand Duchy of Lithuania, Muscovite diplomats trying to assure the Lithuanians that Ottoman retaliation was unlikely as long as the sultan was preoccupied with his Persian war. Their efforts never stood much chance of success, and after Ivan IV's invasion of Livonia in 1558 they stood no chance at all.

However, another ally was found for a while in the person of Dmytro Vyshnevets'kyi and the Kanev and Cherkassk cossacks he had garrisoned on Khortytsa Island to defend Ukaine against Crimean Tatar raiding. Vyshnevets'kyi had intended to use Khortytsa as a base for cossack operations down the lower Dnepr and had sought support for this from Zygmunt II, King of Poland, along with a pledge of neutrality from the Ottoman sultan; when Zygmunt II refused Vyshnevets'kyi turned to Ivan IV. He entered the tsar's service, was granted a *votchina* at Belev, and helped plan and lead four joint operations against the Khanate. In 1556 a small force of Muscovite troops and Ukrainian cossacks took longboats down the Dnepr and made an overland march to raid for prisoners and livestock near the enemy fortresses of Islam Kerman and Ochakov. In a second raid later that year Vyshnevets'kyi's cossacks managed to seize Islam Kerman and cart off its guns. In 1558 a larger joint expedition of 5,000 men sailed down the Dnepr and raided near Perekop. The most ambitious of these joint operations occurred the following year, with Vyshnevets'kyi and the Muscovite commander Ignatii Veshniakov moving down the Donets to the Don to build a fortress and wharf from which flotillas could be sent downriver to make raids upon the Kerch Straits while Danilo Adashev took several thousand troops down the Dnepr and landed by longboat on the northern Crimean coast. Adashev's raid inflicted "considerable damage in the horde:

they killed the Tatars themselves, took many of their wives and children prisoner, freed many Christians from slavery and returned home safe and sound" even though pursued back up the Dnepr by Crimean Tatar forces.[25] After this campaign, however, Ivan IV became preoccupied with his Livonian venture; Vyshnevets'kyi left his service, returned to Ukraine, and was subsequently captured and executed by the Turks while fighting in Moldavia.

The 1550s also saw efforts to enlist as ally Ismail *Bey*, leader of the Great Nogai Horde. Ismail reportedly swore some kind of vow of alliance or vassalage in 1557. But this proved to be of little real military value for Muscovy, as the Great Horde was already in decline. Ivan IV's conquest of the Kazan' Khanate had eliminated the Horde's traditional trading partner; famine and epidemic had greatly reduced its herds; several of Ismail's kinsmen still refused to recognize the legitimacy of his rule; part of the Horde had seceded, migrating to the Emba River to form a separate Dzhemboiluk Horde; and in 1557–1559 an even larger part under mirza Kazy had moved off to the Azov steppes and accepted the Crimean khan's protection. Whatever Moscow gained from alliance with Ismail was more than offset by the danger now posed by this new Kazyev Horde (Lesser Nogai Horde). The Lesser Nogai Horde helped protect the Ottoman base at Azov and the Crimean Tatar steppes above Perekop against the cossacks and contributed warriors to the Crimean Khan's invasion armies. Zygmunt II likewise recognized the military and political value of the Lesser Nogai Horde and tried to win their loyalty for Poland, pledging that he would let them nomadize in Ukraine between the Orel and Psel rivers if mirza Kazy would swear an oath of allegiance to him.

After Ismail's death in 1563 his successors Tinakhmet *Bey* and Urus *Bey* (r. 1563–1578, 1578–1590) ignored his pledge to the tsar and gradually realigned the Great Nogai Horde with the Crimean Khanate. This realignment did not involve full submission to the Crimean Khan, for the Great Nogai *beys* considered themselves his allies, not his vassals, and they expected reciprocal Crimean Tatar military aid against the Don Cossacks and Muscovites. Therefore the Great Nogais participated in Khan Devlet Girei's invasion of Muscovy in 1571 but continued waging war upon Muscovy – particularly along the Volga – long after Devlet Girei had made his reluctant truce with the tsar.

Moscow's troubles from the Great Nogai Horde peaked in the period 1585–1600. The advance of Muscovite colonization along the Volga – marked by the construction of new garrison towns like Samara, Ufa, Tsaritsyn', and Saratov – so alarmed Urus *Bey* he sought military support from the sultan; and the new Crimean khan, Kazy Girei (r. 1588–1607), encouraged part of the Great Horde to nomadize on his side of the Don in an effort to reassemble a grand coalition uniting Lesser and Great Nogais with the Khanate. The khan boasted to Moscow that with his Nogai allies he could now field over 100,000 warriors.[26] Actually the Great Horde was again fragmenting, and Kazy Girei's invitation to cross the Don just accelerated the process. In 1616 Ishterek *Bey* (r. 1600–1619) yielded to bribes from Moscow and threats from the Muscovite garrison at

Astrakhan' and gave his oath of vassalage to Tsar Mikhail. Some of the Great Nogai tribes turned renegade briefly in 1622, but the Great Nogai Horde's vassalage was restored the following year under Kanai Tinbaev *Bey*. By this time, though, the Horde had so disintegrated its submission to Moscow no longer had much consequence for the military situation on the Black Sea steppe.

The Don Cossacks would prove to be the steppe ally of most lasting strategic significance. They lived much closer than the Muscovite steppe towns to Azov, Perekop, and the Nogai *ulusy*, so they could intercept Tatar *chambuly* returning from their raids into Muscovy and free their Muscovite captives, make punitive raids upon the Nogai encampments and even upon Crimea, and, above all, provide the tsar's border towns with better intelligence. Don Cossack detachments roaming the steppe near Azov, the Nogai grazing lands, or Perekop could serve as mercenary ranger parties gathering intelligence of enemy movement along the invasion trails days or weeks before Muscovite ranger parties were likely to detect such movement. Especially valuable was the intelligence the Don Cossacks' own land and naval raids and interrogations of traveling merchants collected of enemy war preparations within Azov or the Khanate. Urgent intelligence was usually carried by detachment to Valuiki, the nearest Muscovite garrison town, and from there to Moscow.

There were probably no more than 1–2,000 free cossacks on the lower Don in the 1590s, however, and no unified Host administration had yet emerged among them, so Moscow had to use subsidy diplomacy to gradually transform them into a military client polity: first, routinizing *stanitsa* detachments' contribution to borderland defense, extending such duty to as many other detachments as possible, and turning it into a reliably and regularly rendered obligation; then encouraging detachments to coalesce into a formally unified Don Cossack Host under one supreme commander, gradually transforming their hires into regular subsidy; and finally, formally vassalizing the chief ataman and his entire Host.

By the early 1590s Moscow had succeeded in using running subsidy to hold certain Don Cossack detachments responsible for regular defense duty.

> And if Crimean or Nogai warriors come waging war against Our Borderland or returning from it with captives, you atamans and cossacks will lie in wait for them at the Don fords and give battle to them, and We will desire to show you Our bounty for your service and will send you powder and shot.[27]

Tsar Boris Godunov unwittingly undermined efforts to "tame" the Don Cossacks through his impatience to establish full control over them, however. To restrain them from further attacks on Azov (which might provoke resumed war with the khan and the sultan), he built a new steppe town at Tsarev-Borisov to monitor cossack activity, and he tried to restrict cossacks' trading rights in Muscovite frontier towns, thinking economic pressure could force them into registering in garrison service. This provoked a backlash, pushing many of the Don Cossacks into revolt on behalf of the False Dmitriis. The efforts of Tsar Mikhail and Patriarch Filaret to reestablish control over the Don Cossacks after the Troubles proved more effective because they concentrated on coopting the cossack elite. The Sovereign's bounty towards the Don Cossacks became a semiannual Don Shipment (*Donskoi otpusk*) of munitions, cloth, grain, liquor, and cash for distribution among the Don Cossack officer elite (*starshina*). Meanwhile the routinization of hired service and the practice of distributing Don Shipment bounty as political spoils were helping to knit the detachments into a single centralized Host under a supreme commander. By 1629 the Ambassadors' Chancellery was dealing regularly with the Don Cossack Host as a recognized client polity and had begun giving it more direct military instruction – more specific intelligence assignments, for example, and orders to contribute troops to campaigns on the western front.[28]

Although the Host's ataman and *starshina* were coming to rely upon Muscovite subsidy, they were by no means already fully vassalized, for Muscovite subsidy had not yet replaced plundering and captive-ransoming as the foundation of their livelihood. The 1620s–1630s in fact saw an expansion of Don Cossack raiding activity against Azov, Crimea, and Anatolia that was not authorized by Moscow and even undermined Muscovite strategic objectives. There was too little Muscovite military force near the Don Cossack encampments to intimidate them into obeying, and Muscovy had its own form of dependence upon the Host, for the latter mediated in ransoms or exchanges of prisoners with the Tatars.

Town garrisons

In the first half of the sixteenth century the town garrisons of the southern borderland played an important role in supporting corps operations. They offered rural inhabitants fortified refuge from Tatar raiding bands; they sent out cavalry detachments to hunt down the smaller Tatar *chambuly* before they could reassemble in one host to break through the defense lines; certain of them conducted ranger reconnaissance across the steppe to provide earlier warning of Tatar movements up the invasion roads; and the larger garrisons were sometimes expected to march in reinforcement to the array corps.

In the second half of the century these four garrison functions became all the more important. In part this was because the Military Chancellery had undertaken the establishment of a new outer defense perimeter through the construction of the Abatis Line and formation of the new Borderland and Riazan' arrays, yet was already finding the demands of the Livonian War limiting the corps manpower it could assign to the new outer perimeter. In part it was due to changes in *pomest'e* economy, leaving more middle service class cavalrymen less able to support themselves in the field for months at a time in corps arrays far from their home districts.

It is possible to discern over the course of the century two waves of technological and organizational change enhancing the town garrisons' effectiveness in southern borderland defense.

Between the 1520s and the 1550s the principal improvements were in resource mobilization for siege warfare. Greater experience in the production and use of artillery and firearms made it possible to place more men in service in the provinces as gunners and musketeers, thereby increasing the garrison towns' firepower; meanwhile the conduct of siege operations and especially the mobilization of corvée to repair and expand fortifications benefited from the increasing militarization of local government, that is, from the gradual transfer of local administrative authority from the vicegerents to the new fortifications stewards (*gorodovye prikazchiki*) and annually appointed town commandants (*godovye voevody*).

By contrast, the emphasis in the second phase of military reform (mid-1550s through 1590s) was upon garrison force mobility. The cavalry manpower and command-and-control procedures needed for improved reconnaissance and interception operations were provided by the 1556 Decree on Service, which laid down norms for local defense duty by the district middle service class cavalry; by the 1571 overhaul and expansion of the southern patrol and ranger network; and by efforts in the 1580s and 1590s to resettle some of the Don Cossacks as registered service cossacks.

One can likewise discern two distinct phases in the founding of new garrison towns in the south.

The first occurred in 1551–1568, in connection with the creation of the new Borderland Array and as a consequence of the greater revenue Ivan IV's reforms of local government had made available to the central chancelleries. The fortress towns of Mikhailov, Shatsk, Dedilov, Bolkhov, Riazhsk, Psel'sk, Krapivna, Novosil', Orel, Epifan', Veneva, Chern', and Dankov were all founded in this period. Most of these were built from nothing; three had recently been the appanages of prominent princes, which Ivan IV had ordered confiscated, refortified, and garrisoned by the army. The primary aim of garrison-founding in this stage was to fill in gaps in the defense system across the forest-steppe south of the Bank and along the emerging Abatis Line so that more effective network operations (ranger reconnaissance, pursuits of Tatar raiding detachments, and especially relief marches) could be mounted in support of the array operations defending the interior. Over time such network operations could of course contribute as well to security along the new edge of the borderland, making it safer for further military colonization; but this had not yet become their main purpose. They still served primarily to support a fallback defense. Hence the array corps still deployed to protect the Oka and the interior rather than attempting to move south to protect the new garrison towns.

The second phase (1585–1599) was associated with the completion of the Abatis Line and the shift of the remaining Bank corps down to the Borderland Array. In October 1585 N. R. Iur'ev, supervisor of the patrol and ranger network, and secretaries Andrei and Vasilii Shchelkalov of the Ambassadors' Chancellery recommended improving reconnaissance and striking a more defiant stance towards the Khanate by founding eight new towns – Voronezh, Livny, Elets, Belgorod, Oskol', Kursk, Valuiki, and Tsarev-Borisov – considerably farther south, some of them on the steppe, as jump-colonies far beyond the current edge of frontier settlement.[29] These new steppe towns were situated so as to command the junctions of major invasion roads and important river fords. Their garrisons provided improved steppe reconnaissance and earlier warning of enemy movements and gave pursuit to the smaller Tatar *chambuly* returning to the steppe from their raids in the north. To help meet construction and provisioning expenses the servicemen of some of these newer garrison towns were required to perform agricultural corvée on state plowlands in addition to their defense duties. Because of the great distances between these new steppe towns, however, they were themselves vulnerable to attack by larger enemy forces.

Reconnaissance, sorties, and sieges

The practice of sending out ranger parties for long-range reconnaissance of the steppe appears to have begun at the western end of Muscovy's southern borderland, at Putivl' and Novgorod-Severskii, in the early sixteenth century. This region had a good number of *sevriuki*, servicemen and townsmen holding hunting and fishing enterprises on the steppe and therefore familiar enough with the steppe to be useful as occasional guides and hired rangers. In 1541 a ranger detachment out of Putivl' had detected Khan Sahib Girei's army advancing up a trail farther east than anticipated, thereby giving the commanders of the Bank Array enough advance warning to shift their corps to reinforce Kolomna and defeat the Crimeans outside Zaraisk. By 1551 the vicegerents of Putivl' and Ryl'sk were regularly despatching long-range reconnaissance detachments (*stanitsy*) to patrol the steppe and look for signs of enemy movement along the invasion trails. These detachments consisted of a captain and a few dozen rangers who covered great distances but traveled no fixed route. When necessary the captain might split his party into smaller units riding off in various directions. They questioned travelers and kept their eyes open for fresh tracks, tell-tale clouds of dust on the horizon, and smoke from camps or burning villages, and when these signs indicated the recent passage of Tatars some of their number rode as couriers to warn each of the nearest towns while the rest continued to track the enemy from a safe remove.

The Ottoman expedition against Astrakhan' in 1569 and a 1570 Crimean Tatar penetration of the Bank defenses finally convinced Moscow of the need for an integrated frontier-wide network of patrols and ranger parties with overlapping fixed beats, systematized reconnoitering and reporting procedures, and central supervision. In January 1571 Prince M. I. Vorotynskii produced a new ordinance requiring more of the borderland garrison towns to mount ranger parties on a routine basis. This ordinance also created a network of shorter-range *storozha* patrols. *Storozha* patrols were smaller (typically two to six riders) and operated from some central surveillance point – perhaps a bluff or high riverbank providing a commanding view of the surrounding plain – riding back and forth from this point and covering a radius of up to 70 km. *Storozha* patrols were despatched from particular borderland towns four times a year, between 1 April and 1 November, on four-to-six-week shifts; their beats were fixed and recorded by the Military Chancellery; and the southernmost routes were to be ridden by joint patrols based in two or more neighboring districts, rendezvousing at designated points so that a web of interlocking patrol beats blanketed the entire south and shared intelligence with all the towns of the borderland. These patrol beats covered the region between the steppe ranger beats, so the latter in effect became the borderland's advance tripwire against enemy attack while the *storozha* beats had the effect of marking the new border of Muscovite state territory. By 1623 the number of short-range patrol beats had been increased to 180.[30]

Some of these patrol riders and rangers were middle service class cavalrymen but most were registered cossacks who had volunteered and had been enrolled in special reconnaissance formations with higher plowland and cash entitlements. Reconnaissance duty was dangerous and in the years immediately after the Troubles Moscow could not afford to remunerate patrol riders and rangers as generously.[31] This made it necessary to supervise patrol riders and rangers more closely to discourage shirking. A special inspectorate was established and the Military Chancellery required the town governors to hold more frequent inspections and issue more detailed instructions to captains, and require captains to submit written reports certifying they had completed their beats. Shirkers were knouted, and if they abandoned their posts during alerts they were executed.

The Vorotynskii Ordinance was yet another sign of the increasing divergence of Muscovite from Polish-Lithuanian southern frontier defense strategy. Moscow had chosen to assign responsibility for steppe reconnaissance to state servicemen, whereas the Commonwealth continued to depend on unregistered Ukrainian cossacks and magnates' retainers to patrol its Ukrainian borderland.

The effectiveness of this reconnaissance system depended upon the proximity of garrison towns and therefore upon further progress in military colonization. This was true as well of the active defense mounted from the southern garrison towns. Since the array corps seldom operated south of the upper tier of forest-steppe towns, the towns of the more sparsely settled lower tier had to be up to the tasks of providing siege refuge for the local population and sending out sorties against Tatar *chambuly*. This too was thought best achieved through centralization of command authority, with the Military Chancellery closely monitoring their governors' military activity and sometimes reserving for itself final say in authorizing even minor undertakings. As with corps operations, there was the risk that centralization of initiative for town defense operations in the Military Chancellery sacrificed speed and flexibility of response. Anecdotal evidence suggests, though, that the greater problem was with governors too incompetent or too short of manpower to carry out the Military Chancellery's instructions.[32]

By the early seventeenth century the Military Chancellery was routinely processing a mass of information concerning the defense resources of its borderland garrisons: rolls and annual inventories listing the number of men under arms, the ammunition and grain stores, and the revenue each district had on hand and descriptions of the district's topography in its strategic aspect and the condition of all its fortifications. The Military Chancellery used these inventories not only to provision the towns for siege but to order sometimes very specific changes in the placement of manpower and fortifications. Its working orders and rescripts to the town governors might stipulate how they were to repair fortifications and place gun crews and guard details. Moscow determined whether governors had to tear down barns or houses too near the stockade walls (to prevent the Tatars from firing them or using them as cover for an assault) or restrict the garrison's cossacks and musketeers to build their houses only inside the town's enceinte. In some instances it even dictated the hour of evening at which the town gates were to be locked.[33]

The governors of larger towns sometimes had special siege officers and fortifications stewards responsible for guard details and gun crews; in towns where corps were stationed these tasks were given to corps officers, with the governor consulting. Across most of the southern frontier guard duty in town and at outlying pickets was performed by cossacks and musketeers, with the able-bodied kinsmen of servicemen joining them in manning the walls and gates when the town came under attack. When pickets or steppe patrols detected enemy movement the governor's first duty was to send couriers to notify neighboring towns, the nearest corps, and the Military Chancellery at Moscow, and then place the district on a siege footing. During the season for Tatar raiding the governors of frontline districts generally had standing orders giving them a free hand to "act at once and without delay, without awaiting further decree," provided they report back about the measures they had undertaken.[34] The district's rural inhabitants were given two to three days to come in to town for siege with their families, livestock, and fodder, leaving behind no unharvested or threshed grain to fall into the enemy's hands. After that troops were despatched to round up and bastinado or jail those villagers who still had not evacuated to town. In the event district inhabitants disobeyed the summons and were subsequently captured by Tatars, the government refused to pay their ransoms.

Usually only the more prosperous middle service class cavalrymen of the district had permanent siege houses inside the town walls, stocked and kept ready for them by slave caretakers. The rest of the population taking refuge in town had to erect temporary cabins spaced far enough apart to discourage fires from spreading. The civilians assembled in town for siege were armed with whatever was available – spears, axes, halberds, and a few spare firearms – and organized in units under elected decurions and centurions who took their orders from a circuit watch captain who doubled as fire chief. He assigned them their positions and distributed their ammunition (which was closely supervised; at the end of the action all unused lead and powder was collected, inventoried, and replaced in the arsenal under seal). Anyone caught possessing liquor was punished, and those venturing out to gather firewood or mow hay were allowed out only in large armed and mounted groups, working in two shifts so that half their number could stand guard.[35]

After 1550 it was much less likely that borderland towns would come under actual siege by the army of the khan, but there remained the danger of protracted blockade. Some smaller garrisons were bottled up for days or weeks while the Tatars raided and burned the *posad* just beyond their citadel walls and swept through their outlying villages with impunity. The obligation to make relief marches (*skhody*) to the corps or to neighboring towns was limited to garrison towns at particular places along the defense line where sufficient numbers of experienced cossacks and *deti boiarskie* with plowlands and cash allowances large enough to outfit them for such service were based, and the circumstances allowing or requiring relief marches were spelled out in advance in their governors' working orders. Smaller garrisons still needed to maintain enough troops to make briefer sorties (*poiski*) to defeat and chase back into the steppe the smaller Tatar *chambuly* raiding the countryside, freeing their Russian captives and taking their own Tatar prisoners as "tongues" for interrogation. If they did not have enough *deti boiarskie* or cossacks for this, pursuit parties could be filled out by issuing spare mounts to musketeers or peasant volunteers. Sortie detachments were not to be sent great distances, and if there was not certain intelligence as to the enemy's strength the governor first had to get permission from the Military Chancellery or from the array commanders and reinforce the detachment with troops from adjoining districts. Command of sortie and pursuit parties was to be entrusted to the captains of the middle service class cavalry centuries or of the cossacks unless there was an associate governor in whose keeping the senior governor could leave the town.[36]

The changing social profile of military colonization

The second wave of southern borderland military colonization (1580s–1590s) took advantage of the reduced threat from the Crimean Tatars and Great Nogais but also of the increase in southward migration driven by the economic crisis in central and northwestern Muscovy. The Livonian War had significantly increased service and fiscal demands upon the population of central and northern Muscovy, spurring tenant flight and curtailment of cultivated demesne. The economic and demographic decline of the center and the north was partially offset, though, by growth in the districts along the middle of the Bank – particularly Tula, where the total area of inhabited cultivated land recorded for tax assessment more than doubled over 1585–1589, from 7,969 to 17,745 quarters per field.[37] The expansion of population and arable underway in the northernmost tier of southern borderland districts before the Troubles was achieved mostly by the more plebeian social elements, by fugitive peasant tenants and townsmen and by servicemen's kinsmen seeking *pomest'e* allotment opportunities no longer available in central Muscovy; as yet very little of it was due to the efforts of lay and ecclesiastic magnates to establish or enlarge their *votchina* estates in the region. Prior small-scale colonization by plebeian elements – in this case small settlements of *sevriuk* servicemen exploiting local hunting and fishing appurtenances – was also preparing the ground for the establishment of garrison jump-colonies on the steppe beyond the Abatis Line.[38] Fugitive peasants and defecting servicemen relocating even farther south were enabling the Don Cossack population to expand and establish new camps on the Don, Voronezh, and Oskol' rivers, thereby extending the cossack tripwire beyond the new Muscovite steppe towns.

Thus migration responding to economic dislocations in the center and the opening of new opportunities in the south was enlarging the pool of surplus manpower ready to volunteer for enlistment in the new steppe garrisons. For example, the steppe town of Elets (founded in 1592) had its full garrison initially set at 600 *polkovye* (corps-ready) cossacks, 200 musketeers, 38 gunners and sharpshooters, 8 gatekeepers, and 5 carpenters, with service lands also prepared along the Sosna River for a nucleus contingent of 200 *deti boiarskie* (their number would rise to 846 by 1615). Most of those enrolled in these services were volunteers from Tula, Kashira, Orlov, Novosil', Aleksin, Solovsk, Epifan', Krapivna, and Bolkhov districts – men recruited not only from among the nonserving kinsmen of servicemen, but from among undeeded peasants.[39] In some cases their departure for Elets was contested by governors and *pomeshchiki* in their home districts on the grounds they were actually already on the service rolls or working under deed, so roadblock control over travel to Elets had to be established and Elets' governor ordered to subject arriving volunteers to vetting to determine their legal status. The first wave of volunteers arrived in winter 1592, before Elets had even been built, and conditions in their first months must have been very challenging, as all but the *deti boiarskie* were liable for fortifications labor and their families, livestock, and harvested grain did not join them until the following autumn.

Because those volunteering for life service in new steppe towns like Elets were usually men unable to find service in the older and more populous districts of the Bank, the middle service class cavalry contingents in these new steppe towns were enrolled with much smaller cash and land entitlement rates than prevailed along the Bank. At Elets there were just three grades of *deti boiarskie*, with service land entitlement rates of 200, 150, and 100 quarters per field (their actual allotments were likely just half or less of their entitlement rates). By 1622 the average entitlement rate for a *gorodovyi syn boiarskii* at Elets was 93 quarters. By contrast, a dozen or more rates could be found at Tula, a few ranging as high as 800 or 900 quarters and the average rate at 249 quarters.[40] This differentiation in entitlement between Bank and steppe middle service class cavalrymen would become general policy after the Troubles as military colonization for local defense took on higher priority than corps service. The steppe towns founded in the 1580s and 1590s were early experiments in the *odnodvorets* format of military colonization that Moscow would come to prefer by the 1630s.

Borderland defenses after the Troubles

During the Time of Troubles the central chancelleries lost control over much of the south. The Poles, Lithuanians, and Tatars sacked Kromy, Chern', Serpukhov, Bolkhov, Tsarev-Borisov, Livny, and other districts; various Pretenders controlled Voronezh for several years; and the forces of Hetman Sagaidachnyi ravaged Elets, Lebedian', Dankov, Riazhsk, Shatsk, and Sapozhok. Although the new government of Tsar Mikhail Fedorovich (r. 1613–1645) moved quickly to heal Muscovy's rift with the Ottoman Empire by trying to restrain the Don Cossacks from naval raids on Azov and other Ottoman domains, the Great Nogais continued raiding the southern borderland, especially Dankov, Riazhsk, and the Riazan' region, which they "depopulated ... as far as the Oka." Nogai raids for prisoners came within sight of Moscow in 1613–1614, and by 1615 so many Russians had been carried off into captivity that the price of an ordinary Russian captive at the Kaffa slavemarket dropped to ten or fifteen gold pieces.[41]

The failure of Władysław's and Chodkiewicz's autumn 1618 siege of Moscow and the signing in December 1618 of a fourteen-year armistice with the Commonwealth at Deulino finally brought the Troubles to an end and enabled the new Romanov dynasty to begin restoring order in southern as well as central Muscovy. In 1619 the tsar's father Fedor Nikitich Romanov, tonsured under Godunov as monk Filaret and subsequently held in Polish captivity for nine years, returned to Moscow, was installed as Patriarch, and took effective charge of the government. For the next fifteen years Patriarch Filaret's administration gave priority to reacquiring the power to mobilize service and revenue for war – repopulating state lands and *posad* communes with taxpayers, updating cadasters and restoring accounting for arrears and future regular taxes, issuing commercial privileges to European merchants, and restoring chancellery control over the distribution of service lands and service salaries. Resources were directed less at strengthening defenses on the southern frontier, however, than at preparing for a war of revanche against the Poles. Filaret wanted Muscovy to be ready upon the lapse of the armistice to reoccupy the west Rus' territories – Seversk, Chernigov, and particularly Smolensk – ceded to the Commonwealth by the terms of the Deulino treaty.

In this period of Reconstruction (1619–1633) the southern frontier defense system was comparatively neglected. Population movement to the south resumed somewhat in the 1620s but mostly took the form of private colonization and was limited to the districts of Kursk, Livny, and Elets. The only new fortress town was on the Don River, at Lebedian' (1613); its garrison was small (just 384 servicemen as of 1626), and it had been founded largely out of private interest, to guard the holdings of the powerful boyar I. N. Romanov, the tsar's uncle. Because too little was done to fill in the garrison network with new towns it became harder to maintain the advance posts on the steppe beyond the Abatis Line. Tsarev-Borisov had to be evacuated; Valuiki was burned by the Lithuanians; and the Military Chancellery abandoned plans to build a new town at Userdsk Gorodishche on the Tikhaia Sosna, to be manned by servicemen transferred from Voronezh and Orel'.[42]

In the early 1630s the southern frontier remained very vulnerable, especially to the southeast along the Nogai Road. Dankov, Riazhsk, Shatsk, and Lebedian' had negligible garrison forces, too few big guns, and inadequate grain reserves. The villagers of rural Riazhsk district preferred hiding in the woods to taking refuge inside Riazhsk during Tatar alerts because they did not trust its defenses: Riazhsk had no siege houses within its walls, some of its towers were unroofed, there were no anti-cavalry fences, and part of its moat had filled in.[43] The garrison towns in this region lacked the cavalry effectives to defend against even the smaller Tatar *chambuly*. In 1632 the governor of Lebedian' was cut down leading a sortie against a Tatar force twice the size of his own, and later that year a force of 700 *deti boiarskie* and cossacks from Livny – an unusually large sortie force by the standards of the time – was ambushed at Savinsk Forest by thousands of Tatar horsemen and Ottoman janissaries. The Livny servicemen made a brave stand, reportedly killing 1,000 Tatars before being overwhelmed. Three hundred of the Russians were killed and the survivors were yoked for sale in the Crimean slave markets.[44]

Declining cavalry strengths and the failure to build more garrison towns tightening network defense also undermined reconnaissance missions: the smaller the patrol and ranger parties became, the more vulnerable they were to ambush. In 1623 Moscow decided to settle for a warning tripline of greater impermeability but providing later report by shortening reconnaissance beats. Patrols were no longer sent as far south as the Dnepr, lower Donets, and lower Don; and the districts of Belgorod, Valuiki, and Putivl' no longer dared send patrols more than 15 km from town.[45]

Commanders of undermanned garrisons were also less able to spare troops for *skhoda* reinforcement to the Borderland and Riazan' arrays. This in turn discouraged corp commanders from dealing more aggressively with the enemy. Thus Tsar Mikhail rebuked his corps commanders for "stupid and simple-minded" conduct and "negligence and lack of zeal":

> You did not catch them [the Tatars] at their camps, and you did not send pursuit parties after them. You did not go along the trail yourselves, nor lie in wait for returning warriors. And you did not dare to guard against them. A few Tatars came before Dedilov – they were three versts from town – and Prince Gagarin did not dare to go out of Dedilov against them. He sent cavalry centuries, but went himself [only] when the Tatars, having made their raid, turned back.[46]

It had become harder to field corps as large as those of the late sixteenth century and harder to move the arrays farther out from their traditional locations. The number of troops in the corps of the Borderland and Riazan' arrays over the period 1616–1629 averaged 8,612 (ranging from a low of 4,119 in 1622 to 11,826 in 1629). But during the Smolensk War (1632–1634) the total strength of the southern arrays did not exceed 5,000 men. When the Borderland and Riazan' arrays had been reactivated at the end of the Troubles there had been a partial fallback from the positions of 1613, for the Vanguard Corps had moved back to Dedilov from Mtsensk, and the Watch Corps had been withdrawn from Novosil' to Krapivna. Arrangements for reinforcing regiments called for the corps to move north to join garrison troops, instead of sending garrison detachments northward to meet the regiments. This deployment pattern, reflecting renewed anxiety about the security of the central districts north of the Oka, would remain in effect until after the Smolensk campaign.[47]

Part of the reason for the reduced strength and fallback of the southern arrays was manpower transfer to the western front, for most of the men recruited into the new foreign formation infantry regiments for the Smolensk campaign came from the south. But the reduction of southern corps strengths was noticeable even before preparations for the Smolensk War and probably derived as well from the problematic state of *pomest'e* economy after the Troubles.

In general – not only in the south – the seventeenth century saw a tendency for middle class cavalrymen to petition more often for leave, promotion, or additional compensation and some historians see indications of their waning zeal for campaign duty and greater willingness to foist their service obligations off on their dependents or substitutes. Yet the harsh penalties of corporal and capital punishment, fines, imprisonment, and property confiscation the Military Chancellery held over the heads of shirkers and deserters lacked real credibility, since the government could not afford to lose men to service.[48]

In principle there were still some strong incentives for the middle service class to show up for muster and go on campaign: it was at muster inspection that new servicemen underwent initiation (*verstanie*) and were assigned their land and cash entitlement rates and at muster inspection that those with cash entitlements received their payments; and those who took their pay at muster but subsequently failed to go on campaign forfeited their bounty, risked confiscation of their service lands, and damaged the appointment and remuneration prospects of their heirs. In practice the government chose to leave most southern servicemen unpaid for long periods, stringing them along in service with the promise of eventual remuneration. This promise remained enough to guarantee that most men at least would continue to show for muster; but it may not have sufficed to guarantee they would perform their service with zeal.

The more serious problem was that the 1556 norms defining the minimal material capacity to perform corps duty were no longer realistic. The Military Chancellery considered fifteen peasant households the minimum required to maintain a single *pomeshchik* cavalryman or his retainer in regimental service. But judging from their petitions the middle service class thought at least fifty households were needed, a minimum fewer and fewer of them could meet – overtaxation, famine, foreign invasion, and civil war having put too many of their peasants to flight over the past half-century.[49]

As for land allotment norms, the 1556 Decree on Service had expected that a *pomest'e* of 100 quarters per field of inhabited land would suffice to maintain one fully equipped mounted servitor. But fewer men had allotments of this size by the seventeenth century, in part because natural increase in the number of servitors had fragmented holdings over the generations, and because novitiates often had to serve several years before they could obtain land entitlements, much less actual allotments. For some time the inadequacy of *pomest'ia* had been eroding service fitness even on the southern frontier. Of 168 Putivl' and Ryl'sk *deti boiarskie* in 1577, 99 had not yet received allotments and many of the rest had grants at only a third or quarter of their entitlement rates. At Riazhsk in 1597, only 44 men – 11 percent of those who mustered – had entitlement rates adequate (150–300 quarters) to outfit them for corps service; seven years later only 28 Riazhsk servicemen were deemed able to afford corps duty.[50]

Further work with muster rolls and other records from multiple districts is necessary to gauge to what extent the enervation of *pomest'e* economy was driving up shirking and desertion rates across the southern frontier. The records of the Military Chancellery do suggest it was at least reducing the length of combat effectiveness on the arrays. Servicemen with small *pomest'ia* and few peasants still mustered in order to take the Sovereign's bounty but subsequently found it difficult to maintain themselves in the field for several months and petitioned for early leave. Even the more prosperous worried about the neglect of their estates when stationed far from their home districts. As long as Riazan' servicemen were stationed in corps at nearby Mikhailov, Pronsk, and Pereiaslavl'-Riazan', for example, they had found their duty bearable: between inspections they could revisit their homesteads and work in their fields. But after their corps was shifted to Veneva for five years running they petitioned that such distant service was beyond their capacity and threatened their economic survival. The Military Chancellery had to grant their requests for leave.[51]

The *pomest'e* system of mobilizing cavalrymen for campaign service might have entered a decline as steep and protracted as that of the Ottoman *timar* system if Patriarch Filaret and then boyar I. B. Cherkasskii had not devoted so much effort to shoring up its foundations. Between 1619 and 1642 the chancelleries issued special short term cash subsidies and temporary tax immunities to servicemen; took some lands out of reserve funds to distribute to those in greatest need; sped up the process of assigning entitlements to novitiates; permitted some gradual juridical fusion of *pomest'e* and *votchina* tenure rights; and reassured the middle service class they would do more to help them find and win remand of their fugitive peasants by gradually extending the recovery time limit. In 1649 the government finally abolished the recovery time limit altogether, thereby completing the process of the enserfment of the peasantry for the benefit of the middle service class.[52]

Military reform for the Smolensk campaign

Ever since his return from Polish captivity in 1619 Patriarch Filaret had made the recovery of Smolensk and Seversk the primary objective of Muscovite foreign policy. Most of the political arrangements for this campaign of revanche were in place by 1630. The Zaporozhians were again in revolt against the Polish Crown; the Swedes were well entrenched in Pomerania and King Gustavus Adolphus had made it clear to Filaret he would welcome a Muscovite attack on the Commonwealth as a diversion essential to the success of his own invasion of Germany; Sultan Murat IV had promised an Ottoman invasion of the Commonwealth from Ochakov if the Russians would invade Lithuania and render additional military assistance against the Persians in the Caucasus. A successful invasion of Lithuania would of course require that Filaret order many troops shifted from the southern frontier garrisons to the western front, but he considered this affordable because the sultan had pledged to forbid Crimean Tatar raids upon Muscovy. Khan Janibek Girei was even negotiating Crimean attacks upon Poland or the Habsburg domains on behalf of the Swedes.[53]

Filaret's government had also done much to strengthen the army. Its machinery for mobilizing revenue and troops, seriously damaged during the Troubles, had been rebuilt, bringing the number of effectives in corps and garrison service on the western and southern fronts in 1632 to about 60,000.[54] It had also recognized the need to reform force structure, tactics, and equipment to keep pace with the Commonwealth's efforts at military modernization.

Poland's Crown Prince Władysław had once observed the Spanish siege of Breda and had become interested in the new siegecraft and infantry line tactics pioneered by Maurice of Nassau. In the course of the 1625–1629 Polish–Swedish War Gustavus Adolphus had shown that the Maurician military revolution could be adapted to eastern European conditions and exploited to counter the Poles' traditional tactical advantage in cavalry. Indications that the Polish army was itself moving to embrace the Maurician military revolution could be seen in the *Sejm*'s new willingness to vote expenditure for a larger military establishment. By 1629 the Commonwealth could mobilize over 34,000 troops and had expanded its artillery corps, which now had regular commands and staffs. The proportion of infantry to cavalry had been raised, to 62 percent; and the formation of foreign contingent (*autorament cudzoziemski*) infantry regiments organized, equipped, and trained in the Western European manner had begun. In Władysław's first campaign as king, the summer 1633 operation to relieve the Polish garrison at Smolensk, he would rely heavily upon foreign contingent infantry regiments under Butler, Donhoff, Rosen, and Weyher and dragoon regiments under Du Pless and Kreuz.[55]

Filaret's efforts to counter Polish military modernization began in earnest in 1630. Julius Coyet was brought to Moscow to cast light cannon while additional gun barrels and musket barrels were purchased from Sweden, England, and the United Provinces. Carbines, pistols, rapiers, and armor of the pattern used in Swedish regiments were also imported. The formation of Muscovy's own foreign contingent (*inozemskii stroi*) began in 1631 with the hiring of about 190 foreign mercenary officers, mostly Swedes and Scots out of Swedish service, at wages competitive with the rates prevailing in Wallenstein's Imperial army. Through the mediation of the Swedish crown, boyar I. B. Cherkasskii, brother-in-law of Patriarch Filaret and director of the Musketeers' and Foreign Mercenary chancelleries, contracted with a Scots colonel, Alexander Leslie, and his deputy, the Holsteiner Heinrich von Dam, to raise four regiments of mercenary *lansquenets*. Leslie managed to bring over 4,000 soldiers into the tsar's service by the end of the year. Some of them had been mercenaries serving Gustavus Adolphus, but the greater number had been recruited in Swedish-occupied Germany.

Leslie and von Dam were also directed to form and train *inozemskii stroi* regiments of native Muscovite recruits. In 1630 efforts were made to organize two Dutch-model infantry regiments of 1,000 men each by reassigning *deti boiarskie* lacking *pomest'e* lands and otherwise incapable of equipping themselves for campaign duty. Each of these recruits was to be issued arms at treasury expense and paid a generous annual subsidy of five rubles plus daily rations money (*kormovye den'gi*) of three kopeks. Only sixty men had been enrolled in these regiments by September, however, for even impoverished *deti boiarskie* considered infantry duty in the ranks under foreign officers beneath their dignity. Moscow therefore decided to focus instead on taking volunteers – in reality some coercion was used to meet the quotas – and recruiting primarily cossacks, baptized Tatars, and other more plebeian elements from the southern frontier districts, selecting from free men twenty to forty years of age. This had greater success: by the end of 1631 3,323 men had been recruited for two infantry regiments, each now set at 1,600 men in eight companies (*roty*) under 176 officers, subalterns, and staff. The proportion of musket to pike in these regiments was 3:2. These *soldaty* of lower estate had the added advantage of being cheaper; their average annual pay was 2.24 rubles, about a third of what infantrymen in European regiments received. When the war began in August 1632 four infantry regiments were ready under the command of Leslie, von Dam, Unzen, and Rosworm. Two more infantry regiments would join them at Smolensk a year later. Yet another two regiments were raised by war's end, but too late to see action at Smolensk.

Cavalry units of foreign formation were also formed for the Smolensk campaign. Colonel Charles D'Hebert was put in command of a fourteen-company regiment of 2,000 heavy cavalry pistoleers (*reitary*) and 400 dragoons (*draguny*) for fire support. The nucleus of this regiment was formed by "Germans of old and recent arrival" with some Russian volunteers enrolled to bring it to full strength; in this case enrolling Russian *deti boiarskie* was easy enough, for this was cavalry service, of greater honor than slogging on foot, and *reitary* were offered three rubles each per year plus fodder money of two rubles a month. The dragoons received annual pay of four rubles but smaller monthly fodder support. Later in the war an entire regiment of dragoons – 1,440 troopers and 136 officers – was raised to reinforce the cavalry serving at Smolensk.[56]

In all ten regiments of foreign formation infantry and cavalry with a total paper strength of about 17,000 men were organized during the Smolensk War. Further indication that the government pinned its hopes for victory on its new foreign contingent was the size of the wage bill it paid for its Smolensk expeditionary army. The traditional formation cavalry was, as in the past, responsible for outfitting itself and bringing along its own rations and fodder; but the new foreign contingent troops were equipped at treasury expense and paid monthly rations money in addition to their annual service allowances, making them considerably more expensive to maintain in the field. From the initial invasion in August 1632 until November 1633, when the expeditionary army came under full Polish blockade, about 500,000 rubles were spent on pay to its foreign formation infantry and the cossacks and peasant militiamen receiving rations money.[57]

The Smolensk campaign also required more elaborate logistics than previous operations. The traditional formation cavalry *sotnia* (century) could not be expected to cart in enough of their own food and fodder to last through the entire siege, which would likely be a protracted affair given the imposing fortifications at Smolensk; but there would have to be controls upon their efforts to supplement their stores by foraging lest they provoke resistance from the rural population of Dorogobuzh and Smolensk districts and frustrate the aim of "restoring" them to Muscovy. On arriving at Smolensk the army would in fact find most area foodstuffs already gathered up by the Poles for storage inside Smolensk, the residue to be had only at astronomical prices; purchasing would therefore be abandoned for exactions remunerated at below market price. These forced deliveries were organized by assigning particular villages to provision particular regiments.

Some supplemental stores – especially fodder for the cavalry – had been cached at two marchroute magazines on Muscovite territory – at Mozhaisk and Viaz'ma. A third magazine was founded at Dorogobuzh once it was liberated from the Poles. The Mozhaisk and Viaz'ma magazines appear to have been inadequate, for the army experienced serious provisioning problems while it was still on the march to the Lithuanian border. The Dorogobuzh magazine fell back into the hands of the Poles in October 1633.

The most significant complication, though, was the much larger proportion of this expeditionary army dependent upon rations money. This left the government more responsible for collecting and delivering provisions than on previous campaigns.

The provisions carted to Smolensk to be purchased with rations money had to come from two sources. One source was private contract. The Chancellery of Foreign Provender contracted with hundreds of merchant sutlers to purchase provisions for the Smolensk army, arranging with particular sutlers to deliver to particular regiments, which bought these stores at prices fixed by the government, usually at a little below Moscow market price. The other source was the Germans' ration (*nemetskii korm*), a tax in kind levied on Muscovite taxpayers at the rate of 19–26,000 kg rusks, 9–13,000 kg barley flour, and 1,600 kg salt pork per *sokha*. These stores were delivered to Smolensk by the same sutlers and sold at the same prices; the money given for them was then used by the Chancellery of Foreign Provender to buy up additional supplies.

In its first months on enemy territory (August–December 1632) very little reached the army, either through private sutlery or through the Germans' ration. Deliveries of the Germans' ration did improve from December 1632 to October 1633; by the end of this period about 2.45 to 3 million kg of rye flour, 1.4 to 1.9 million kg of rusks, and 9,100 kg of salt pork were delivered. But this was still inadequate, for it had become necessary to allow traditional formation servicemen as well as troops in the foreign contingent to purchase Germans' rations in order to survive.[58] The campaign revealed how much the government had yet to learn about the logistics – both provision collection and transport – needed to support large-scale operations on foreign soil with foreign formation troops.

The Smolensk War and its impact on southern Muscovy

The death of King Zygmunt III in April 1632 meant there would be an interregnum in Poland during which the *Sejm* would likely be even more preoccupied with factional intrigues. Filaret therefore launched his invasion in August 1632. The Great Corps under generals M. B. Shein and A. I. Izmailov (26,000 men, including 9,000 foreign formation troops) captured Serpeisk on 12 October and Dorogobuzh on 18 October and by 5 December reached Smolensk, the campaign's primary objective. The Vanguard and Rear Guard corps, commanded by S. V. Prozorovskii and B. M. Nagoi, took Belaia on 10 November and rendezvoused with Shein in late January for the investment of Smolensk. A small fourth corps under I. F. Eropkin pushed south into Seversk and captured Novgorod-Severskii and Starodub. In these operations some twenty western Rus' towns fell to the Muscovites and the Lithuanian towns of Velizh and Polotsk came under attack.

Smolensk was one of the largest fortresses in eastern Europe. Its 6.5 km of outer brick wall, erected in 1595–1602 when Smolensk had been in Muscovite hands, was 13–19 m high and 5–6 m thick, and the Poles had subsequently added an earthen *kronwerk* on its western side. But the fortress mounted only 32 guns and its Polish garrison comprised just 884 infantry and 932 cavalry. The only other Commonwealth forces in the area were 3,000 men under Krzysztof Radziwiłł, the Lithuanian Grand Hetman.[59]

Shein's corps camped on the southern bank of the Dnepr about 5 km east of Smolensk and fortified their position with a palisade wall and ditch. Prozorovskii's corps made its camp 5 km west of Smolensk, also on the Dnepr's south bank. The units engaged in siege and observation were deployed in fortifications running southeast and southwest from these camps; the largest concentration – the foreign formation regiments under Rozworm, Fuchs, Leslie, Unzen, and Sanderson – manned trenches to Smolensk's southeast, while the bulk of the Muscovite force west of town was placed in two redoubts (under D'Hebert and von Dam) close to the Dnepr to defend Prozorovskii's camp. This left the line running southeast from here to the main trenches comparatively undermanned by units in four small redoubts connected by abatis. But it was to the north that the besieging Muscovite army was most vulnerable: the only sizeable unit stationed on the northern bank of the Dnepr was Mattisson's regiment, in a redoubt on Pokrovska Hill. Siegeworks and artillery emplacement were in the hands of hired foreign specialists (Jan Cornelius van Rodenburg, Christoph Dalhammer, Just Mansen, and David Nichol). Eventually there would be 154 guns deployed, including 19 heavy siege guns, but most of the heavier ordnance would not arrive until winter – some of it not until March – because the roads to Smolensk were a muddy mire. Furthermore provisioning during the first two months of the siege was inadequate: deliveries from Viaz'ma and Moscow had not yet been made and most of the grain and fodder in the surrounding countryside had already been carted off to Smolensk by the Poles. Shein's cavalry was therefore largely immobilized and unable to prevent Radziwiłł's small Lithuanian force from raiding his redoubts and even bringing the Smolensk garrison a few hundred reinforcements.[60]

By early summer some conditions had improved: deliveries of state rations for the foreign formation troops became more frequent, there was a spring harvest to be requisitioned from the villagers of Smolensk and Dorogobuzh districts, and the arrival of the heavy guns made it possible to step up the bombardment of Smolensk. Bombardment and mining were succeeding in blowing breaches in Smolensk's outer walls. But Shein's infantry was unable to break through Smolensk's inner ring of earth wall; his army wanted bread, not just rusks and flour, yet there were too few bakers on hand; and there was grumbling that Shein and Izmailov were buying up area provisions for speculation rather than turning them over to the regimental quartermasters. Over the spring about 5,000 of Shein's troops deserted. Meanwhile Władysław IV, newly elected King of Poland, had been granted revenue by the *Sejm* to raise an army for the relief of Smolensk.

On 23 August 1633 a Polish army of about 12,850 infantry, 2,450 dragoons, and 8,800 cavalry under the command of Władysław IV approached Prozorovskii's and Shein's positions from the north. A force of 15,000 Zaporozhian cossacks also advanced upon the Muscovites from the south. By pinning down Prozorovskii's and Mattisson's forces in their earthworks the King was able to slip reinforcements into Smolensk. A combined attack by Polish troops and cossacks then drove Mattisson's force out of its redoubt on Pokrovska Hill and pushed it eastward all the way to Shein's camp (22 September). After striking south from Pokrovska Hill and driving off D'Hebert and von Dam the Polish army turned east to fall upon the regiments and siege guns in the trenches below Smolensk, which likewise had to fall back to Shein's camp (3 October). This left the Muscovite forces divided, bottled up in Prozorovskii's and Shein's fortified camps, about 10 km apart; and because they now had reduced access to fodder their cavalry effectives had been reduced by a third and neither corps could hope to counter the superior mobility of the Polish cavalry in order to break through to the other. Shein ordered Prozorovskii to evacuate his position and withdraw to Shein's camp under cover of night, but the carters ordered to haul back Prozorovskii's stores and munitions feared Polish ambush and refused to drive. Prozorovskii had to leave most of his supplies behind. He tried to blow them up but a sudden downpour extinguished his fuses. His stores therefore fell into Władyslaw's hands. On 16 October the King sent a *corps volant* of 3,000 Polish and Zaporozhian cavalry under Piaseczyński to raid Shein's main magazine at Dorogobuzh, about 90 km to the east; substantial stocks of food and munitions fell into their hands or were burned.

Then the King's army marched eastward along the heights along the northern bank of the Dnepr and took up positions on both sides of Kolodnia Creek and on Zavoronkova Hill (19–23 October). Shein's foreign formation infantry regiments fought fiercely to drive the Polish infantry and dragoons from Zavoronkova Hill but were driven back by Polish heavy cavalry attacking their flank. Over the four days of fighting for Zavoronkova Hill the Muscovites lost about 2,000 killed and wounded, the Poles about 600–700. By 23 October the Poles were firmly in command of the hill and had begun using it to bombard Shein's camp. Shein could not elevate his own guns enough to suppress the fire of the Polish guns. By the end of the month Shein's camp was cut off from any reinforcement from the east: Władyslaw's main force occupied the Bogdanov Dunes on the northern bank of the Dnepr, while Zaporozhian cossack regiments now held the southern bank of the river. In December Polish and cossack forces under Kazanowski and Orendarenko began raids across the border into Belyi, Viaz'ma, Rzhev, and Kaluga. Shein's troops, bottled up in their camp, began to succumb to starvation, but as of early January the three Muscovite relief armies ordered mobilized at Mozhaisk, Rzhev-Vladimira, and Kaluga in late October had still not completed their inspections and were not ready to march.

On 16 February 1634 Shein capitulated to the King, giving his parole and abandoning his position – along with his guns and banners and about 2,000 wounded – in exchange for the King's pledge to let him withdraw unmolested to Mozhaisk with the 8,000 men he had remaining.[61]

Perhaps preparations to reinforce Shein had not been given greater urgency because the futility of this war had become apparent to the Boyar Duma and the Ambassadors' Chancellery already by November 1633. The war's chief architect, Patriarch Filaret, had died in October 1633. No aid could be expected from Sweden: Gustav Adolph had fallen at Lutzen in November 1632, leaving Swedish forces in Pomerania more vulnerable to a Polish attack, and Chancellor Oxenstierna had never shared Gustav Adolph's enthusiasm for Swedish–Muscovite coalition. Although Abaza Hasan Pasha had taken an Ottoman army into southern Poland in autumn 1633, it had been largely as a demonstration; the larger Ottoman invasion promised for 1634 was no longer expected because Sultan Murat IV was preoccupied with suppressing internal revolts and prosecuting a new war against Persia. Above all the Crimean Tatars had made devastating incursions into central Muscovy in 1632 and 1633, taking advantage of the shift of most of the southern corps' manpower to the Smolensk theater.

Shein's capitulation at Smolensk made it impossible for the government to demand the Poles evacuate Smolensk and Dorogobuzh as the price of peace. Upon his return to Moscow Shein was therefore charged with treason and executed by order of the Boyar Duma. The armistice signed at Polianovka on 4 June 1634 left the Smolensk, Chernigov, and Seversk lands in Polish hands. Filaret's project of recovering the western Rus' territories had failed. For Muscovy there was some partial compensation in Władysław IV's agreement to abandon his claim to the Moscow throne, but the likelihood that Władysław would continue to press this claim through war had passed.

It appears to have been strategic blunders, especially in provisioning and the faulty circumvallation of Shein's and Prozorovskii's forces, that wrecked the Smolensk campaign. Tactically the foreign formation regiments performed as well as they could given these circumstances and given that they were but recently formed and could not have had much serious training. They had been very expensive to maintain, but it was probably not to reduce expenditure that Cherkasskii, who had helped raise them and who now took control of military policy after Filaret's death, disbanded the foreign formation regiments in 1634; the terms of the Treaty of Polianovka had required their disbanding, and we soon enough find Leslie and other foreign officers returning to Muscovite service to reorganize *soldat* and dragoon units.

The launching of the King's counteroffensive in summer 1633 had been accompanied by attempts by royal *starostas* and magnates in Ukraine (Aleksander Piaseczyński, Adam Kysil, Jeremi Wiśniowiecki) to use cossack forces to carry the war into the Seversk borderland of southern Muscovy. Some 5–6,000 Ukrainian cossacks made unsuccessful attacks on Putivl' and Sevsk in 1633 and 1634 and briefly managed to seize Valuiki and advance upon Belgorod.

The Smolensk War's greatest consequence for southern Muscovy, however, was in shifting so much Muscovite manpower from the western front that the south and even the center were left vulnerable to Crimean Tatar raids. More than 20,000 Tatars had invaded Muscovy in the spring and summer of 1632, hitting the districts of Novosil', Mtsensk, and Livny especially hard and forcing Shein to postpone his march on Smolensk. In 1633 they came in even greater strength – over 30,000 strong – and this time circumvented the fortifications of the Abatis Line and crossed the Oka into central Muscovy, taking thousands of captives in Sepukhov, Kolomna, Kashira, and Riazan' districts and probably contributing to the defeat at Smolensk by provoking mass desertion by those of Shein's troops whose home districts had come under Tatar attack.[62]

Khan Janibek Girei had been under the sultan's orders to limit his operations to attacks upon the Poles, so Muscovite diplomats assumed the Poles must have bribed him into betrayal. Actually the Khan had been unable to stop the 1632 raids, which had been led by certain Crimean *beys* and by the princes of the Bucak Horde, Lesser Nogai Horde, the Azov Tatars, and even some bands of Great Nogais, and undertaken mostly out of economic need: several years of civil war between Janibek Girei and Shahin Girei followed by plague, drought, harvest failure, and high inflation had left them desperate for booty in slaves, and having borne heavy losses in their 1629–1631 attacks upon the Commonwealth they now considered southern Muscovy the more inviting source of such booty, especially now that its southern garrisons had been stripped of men for Shein's army at Smolensk.

But the 1633 attacks were made mostly by Tatar forces out of Perekop, led by the khan's son Mubarek Girei. Unable to restrain his nobles, the khan had decided he had no choice but to follow them into war upon Muscovy. This demonstrated that much more than diplomatic engagement with the khan was needed to secure the southern frontier and central Muscovy against the Crimean Tatars. Moscow would have to postpone further operations against the Commonwealth in order to strengthen its defenses on the Crimean-Nogai front.

CHAPTER THREE

The Belgorod Line

New danger from the Khanate

The Crimean Khanate was now more dangerous than ever, for its behavior was increasingly unpredictable and more resistant to diplomatic means of containment. Khan Janibek Girei's power over the Crimean *beys* and Nogai confederates had never been very firm, but the events of 1632 and 1633 showed he could no longer stop them from assembling their own renegade military coalitions large enough to throw 20,000 warriors against the Muscovite border towns – nearly as many men as the khan himself could raise. On past occasions Muscovite diplomats had been able to appeal to the Ottoman sultan to rein in the Crimean Tatars. This was less possible now because of the growth of anti-Ottoman and separatist sentiment among the Crimean nobility. To placate his *beys* Janibek Girei had refused to provide Crimean troops for Sultan Murat IV's campaign against Safavid Persia. For this he was overthrown in 1635. But the new khan, Inaet Girei, proved an even less biddable vassal. In 1636 he invaded the Belgorod steppe in southern Moldavia to overthrow his rival Khantimur, *bey* of the Bucak Nogai Horde. Khantimur was the most loyal of the Sultan's Tatar vassals, protector of the Ottoman fortresses of Ochakov, Akkerman, and Bendery, and bearer of the title *beylerbey* of Bendery; and in seeking military support for his attack on Khantimur Khan Inaet Girei had gone so far as to propose an anti-Ottoman alliance to King Władysław and promise to relocate his capital to the Belgorod steppe to serve the Commonwealth as a bulwark against Ottoman power in Moldavia.[1]

Meanwhile Muscovy had lost considerable leverage over its own allied polities on the Kipchak steppe. The fealty of the Great Nogai *beys* was no longer of much strategic advantage, for their Horde was in disintegration; elements of it had participated in the 1632 raids upon Muscovy, and many of the remaining Great Nogais had been driven west across the Volga by the Kalmyks and forced into alliance with the Crimean Tatars and the Lesser Nogais. Nor did Moscow have much control over the Don Cossack Host. Although some Don Cossack detachments had participated in the Smolensk campaign, the Host had balked when called upon to support a punitive expedition out of Astrakhan' against the Lesser Nogais in 1633, and the Don Cossacks continued to make naval raids on

Tatar and Ottoman domains. Efforts to discourage their raiding by reducing the Don Shipments had little effect, for the Host saw itself justified in responding to Tatar and Azov Turk attacks upon its own settlements. Don Cossack intransigence caused mounting anxiety in Moscow, for Fedot Elchin had returned from Constantinople in April 1635 with word that Sultan Murat IV was just as insistent as Khan Inaet Girei that the tsar restrain the Don Cossacks if peace was to be preserved. In May Moscow put the Don atamans on notice that continued raiding on their part would expose the cossack settlements and the sovereign's frontier districts to massive retaliation by the Crimean Tatars, the Nogais, the Kazyev *ulus* Tatars, and Turkish troops out of Azov.[2]

The shift of manpower to the Smolensk front had reduced the corps defending the southern Borderland and Riazan' arrays to less than 5,000 men. Most of the towns to the south of the arrays – particularly those to the south of the Riazan' array – had garrisons of no more than 2–300 cossacks and *deti boiarskie*, too few to deal with more than one small *chambul* at a time much less offer any serious resistance to larger Tatar forces. There were so many Tatar raids up the Nogai Road towards the Riazan' Array in early 1635 that the region had to remain on full invasion alert through late autumn.

The Boyar Duma and central chancellery apparatus, now dominated by the boyar I. B. Cherkasskii, therefore decided to break with the grand strategy Patriarch Filaret's government had pursued. Military revanche on the western front had to be postponed. Priority had to be given instead to strengthening defenses in the south. Between summer 1635 and late autumn 1638 the government launched six major reforms to enhance security along the southern frontier. It more than doubled the total strength of the corps in the Borderland and Riazan' arrays. It repaired much of the Abatis Line. It demobilized most of the expensive foreign formation regiments, except for a few it now deployed along the Abatis Line. It stepped up garrison colonization of the particularly vulnerable southeast, the forest-steppe and steppe below the Riazan' Array, accelerating the colonization process by calling on volunteers and reducing its long-term costs by enrolling them as yeomen holding small *pomest'ia* in collective bloc grants. It linked up two of these new southeastern garrison towns, Kozlov and Tambov, by building an earthen wall across the Voronezh-Tsna steppe. And as soon as these new towns and their steppe wall proved effective in blocking Tatar movement up the Nogai Road, it began the enormous project of building a dozen more garrison towns, colonized in similar fashion, athwart the other major Tatar invasion trails and connecting them along a vast new fortified line, the Belgorod Line, thereby establishing a new outer defense perimeter far to the south of the old Abatis Line.

Refortifying the Abatis Line

In 1631–1634 the total strength of the corps in the Borderland and Riazan' arrays remained under 5,000 men. But the Cherkasskii government raised it to

12,759 men for 1635 and 17,055 men by 1636. The additional manpower permitted greater flexibility in operations, making it easier for the Borderland and Riazan' arrays to reinforce each other and even making it possible for the Great Corps to march south from Tula to the relief of towns south of the Abatis Line.[3]

The Crimean Tatar attacks on the Tula and Riazan' regions in 1633 had shown that several sections of the approximately 1,000-km Abatis Line were in urgent need of repair. A general survey of the Abatis Line by V. P. Shcherbatyi, N. N. Gagarin, S. F. Bolkonskii, and L. F. Volkonskii and the foreign engineers Jan Cornelius van Rodenburg, Just Monsen, and David Nichol was therefore undertaken in autumn 1635. Actual repair work began in spring 1638, partly spurred by the war scare provoked by the Don Cossacks' capture of the Ottoman fortress of Azov. Because of the urgency and magnitude of this project jurisdiction over the Abatis Line was temporarily shifted from the Gunners' Chancellery to the Military Chancellery. This centralized control in the hands of the experienced secretary Ivan Gavrenev, who reported directly to the tsar and Boyar Duma. Twenty-two of the twenty-eight sections of the Abatis Line – about two-thirds of its total length – were scheduled for reconstruction. An abatis general (*zasechnaia voevoda*) was appointed to each and instructed to report to Tula to Prince I. B. Cherkasskii, the commander-in-chief of the Abatis Line. The abatis generals were mostly men of court eminence, but some were veterans of southern frontier campaigns, and their appointments had been made *bez mest*, exempt from precedence challenge.

The Military Chancellery had projected that refortification work would require 27,400 laborers and 3,500 draft horses, with 16,900 troops defending the work sites and then manning the full length of the line upon completion. The labor force would consist of peasants and townsmen, men of draft (*tiaglye liudi*) conscripted from the eighteen districts along both sides of the Abatis Line; the troops defending the line were to be a mix of local garrison troops, free volunteers enrolled in reconstituted dragoon and *soldat* regiments, and draft militiamen – peasants and townsmen levied at the rate of one foot militiaman from every twenty households. The militia levies, enrollment of dragoons and *soldaty*, and mobilization of revenue for the Abatis Line project were entrusted to the new Chancellery of Troop Levies (*Prikaz sbora ratnykh liudei*, founded 1637), which thereby became for awhile the second most important chancellery of military function.[4]

These forces did succeed in rebuilding some 600 km of the Abatis Line between May and September 1638. This was an impressive accomplishment considering that the number of laborers actually mobilized topped out at about 20,000 men, their provisioning was inadequate, and there were numerous desertions as well as armed resistance to the labor levies. Efforts to mobilize troops to man the line were initially unsuccessful. The peasant militias were far below projected strength and poorly equipped. During construction only a small number of *soldat* infantrymen, mostly from Eremei Rosworm's regiment, were deployed along the line. Later in the autumn it did prove possible to station about 13,000 *soldaty* and dragoons along the Abatis Line by rehiring Smolensk veterans and enrolling uninitiated or land-poor *deti boiarskie*, musketeers and cossacks, and free men not previously in service. Besides receiving their firearms and dragoon mounts from the treasury they got daily rations money of .07 ruble per man (.08 ruble for Smolensk veterans). But they served only through November, when they were disbanded and their rations money stopped. However, it was of significance that a second mobilization of foreign formation infantry and dragoons for the Abatis Line was made for spring to late autumn 1639; it meant that Moscow had established a precedent for foreign formation units to play a regular role in southern frontier defense, if only to help man the defense line on a seasonal basis.

The records of the Abatis Line refortification project provide some idea of the strengths and limitations of Muscovite command-and-control practice in this period. On the one hand, the Muscovite preference for highly centralized control promoted some error and delay at the local level: the abatis generals had to report up to commander-in-chief Cherkasskii at Tula to get manpower and provisions from the town governors of the districts along their line sections, and Cherkasskii had to process so many such reports (as well as inquiries and instructions from the Military Chancellery) that most of his replies to the abatis generals took stereotyped form, harping on the need to maintain discipline and accelerate work while providing very little technical advice. Most technical guidance came from the Military Chancellery, from Secretary Gavrenev's clerks and engineers, but it was not always realistic and up to date; some of the Military Chancellery's maps and manpower estimates were incorrect and some of its instructions contradictory. On the other hand, highly centralized control appears to have kept the abatis generals under such pressure that most of the repairs were completed as early as mid-July and to the Military Chancellery's general satisfaction. The Abatis Line did not have to undergo further repair until 1659–1660, and then without much emendation to the plans for the 1638 reconstruction.[5] The greatest costs of refortifying the Abatis Line in 1638 were indirect, falling upon other chancelleries and especially upon the tsar's subjects, for boyar I. P. Sheremetev, the director of the Chancellery of Troop Levies, managed to embezzle 190,000 rubles from other chancelleries in the course of transferring funds for the project, and the unrealistic labor quotas and the coercive methods used to meet them had the effect of provoking great numbers of taxpayers to flight.

New methods of military colonization

The new buildup along the southern frontier did not stop with the strengthening of inner perimeter defenses along the Oka; it also involved resumed military colonization beyond the Abatis Line to establish a new outer perimeter farther to the south.

The garrison towns of Chernavsk and Kozlov were founded in 1635, and Verkhnii Lomov, Nizhnii Lomov, and Tambov in 1636; the next year Userdsk, Iablonov, and Efremov arose and Orel was rebuilt; Korocha arose in 1638, and Chuguev in 1639. Responsibility for organizing and supervising this new colonization drive, the most ambitious since the 1580s–1590s, was concentrated in the Military Chancellery and conformed to a plan to provide greater defense in depth by blocking the major Tatar invasion roads on the steppe and forest-steppe hundreds of kilometers below the Abatis Line. The first phase of this plan focussed on planting new garrison towns in the east, to secure the territory endangered by the Nogai Road; while these were under construction Fedor Sukhotin and Evsei Iur'ev were already surveying for townsites in the west to cut the Kal'miuss and Iziuma trails. The cost of these new towns and of the refortification of the Abatis Line was met in part by disbanding most of the expensive foreign formation regiments used in the Smolensk theater while doubling the rate for army grain taxes.[6]

The eleven garrison towns founded in 1635–1637 represented a new approach to mobilizing manpower and service land for southern frontier military colonization, one relaxing some of the social restrictions on eligibility for garrison enrollment and adapting land entitlements and tenure rights to the specific circumstances of the steppe frontier. This made military colonization more cost-effective, and in this regard the nine new garrison towns could be considered a more important development in Muscovy's southern strategy than the refortification of the Abatis Line.

The Military Chancellery wanted to settle these new garrison towns as quickly and cheaply as possible. It could not afford to transfer servicemen to them from the older districts to the north, however, as this would reduce garrison strengths across the northern tier at the very time Moscow was planning to strengthen the fortifications and manpower deployments of the Abatis Line. Past experience suggested orders for transfers would also meet with some resistance on the part of town governors, who would delay in despatching transfers or select for transfer the less fit or less prosperous of their garrison troops and taxpayers.

Fortunately the districts to the north did have some "superfluous" population available for voluntary resettlement farther south – men who, because of their declassé origins and marginal economic condition, were likely to welcome the prospect of resettlement in the new garrison towns with plowlands and annual service bounties. One such superfluous category comprised the male kinsmen of servicemen – particularly the kinsmen of cossacks and musketeers – who were unlikely to ever follow their relatives in service because of the fixed size of the local service plowland funds and cash bounty budgets.[7] Another category consisted of "free itinerants" (*vol'nye guliashchie liudi*). Not all of these itinerants were true vagrants. Many were hired laborers boarding in the households of servicemen or renting their own houses and crofts from servicemen; others lived under landlords much like peasant tenants, performing agricultural corvée as rent on their tenements but remaining legally free because they had not been registered in deeds or cadasters. Men came into free itinerancy by different routes: some were manumitted serfs or slaves; while others were clergymen's sons unable to get their own parishes; or former *deti boiarskie*, cossacks, or musketeers who had dropped out of state service due to some calamity; or men escaped from Tatar captivity.

Together these two categories constituted an unascribed manpower surplus large enough that about two-thirds of the service postings in the new garrison towns could be filled by volunteers.

Forming new garrisons from volunteers was nothing new; we have already seen it at work in the 1590s, in the settlement of Elets, Voronezh, and other frontier districts. But in settling most of the new frontier towns built in 1635–1639 the Military Chancellery went to unprecedented lengths to mobilize volunteers. In March 1636 it relaxed standards of juridical eligibility to permit the enrollment of former servicemen who had been forced by poverty or other calamity to abandon their service postings and service land after 1613 and had taken up tenancy under a *pomeshchik* or *votchinnik*. Such men could be reenrolled and restored to freedom even if they had been recorded in cadasters as someone's peasants – provided their loss of freedom had occurred after the Time of Troubles. The sons of such men were likewise reclaimable for service provided they had been born before their fathers had lost their freedom. Fugitive peasant tenants who met the test of this "1613 clause" were not to be remanded to their former owners but were permitted to register in service in the new garrison towns. This was an indication of how important the government considered the resumption of military colonization in the south: even the proprietary interests of the serfowning nobility were to be subordinated to it.

The 1613 clause was very successful in speeding up military colonization in the new districts. M. A. Vel'iaminov reported encountering a column of over 3,000 men, "with their wives and children and livestock and ten priests," on the road from Voronezh to the new garrison towns of Kozlov and Tambov. Within six months of announcement of the opportunity to enroll for life at Kozlov, Kozlov's cossack and musketeer contingents were near full strength, and by January 1639 over 1,000 *deti boiarskie* had been enrolled, giving Kozlov a total garrison strength of 2,141 men – one of the largest anywhere on the southern frontier.[8]

But the flood of volunteers also created some new problems. Many enrolled at Userdsk and Korocha deserted when the government was too slow in issuing them their cash bounties. Among the volunteers heading south were servicemen's kinsmen, free itinerants, and former servicemen ruined after the Troubles, but also men currently enrolled in service in other districts and seeking larger plowlands, and peasants on deed and cadastral registration who had never been in state service but who had seized upon this chance to flee their masters and assume false identities as free servicemen. Already by June 1636 Moscow was receiving complaints from southern landlords that the enrollment opportunities in the new frontier towns were depopulating their estates, even of families that had been in tenancy for generations. Vel'iaminov reported, "Voronezh is empty, Sovereign. Many churches are without singing, [lacking parishioners] ... and the people who are left are continually leaving without registering for permission."[9] Servicemen were deserting from Voronezh, Elets, and other towns to enlist at Kozlov and Tambov. The Military Chancellery had to remind Kozlov's governor, "It is good to settle a new town, but do not depopulate old ones."[10] Uncontrolled migration to the new garrison towns was overloading the courts in the new garrison towns with remand suits filed by landlords (at Kozlov, for example, remand suits indicted as fugitive peasants about a quarter of those enrolled in garrison service); the Military Chancellery also had to deal with complaints that the governors of Voronezh, Lebedian', Shatsk, and other older districts were jailing families trying to depart for or pass through to the new garrison towns and extorting large cash sums for their release.

The Military Chancellery responded to this disorder with three measures. In November 1637 it returned to more stringent standards of eligibility for enlistment; the terms of the 1613 clause were abandoned and governors in the new towns were instructed to turn away volunteers whom vetting revealed to be deeded peasants or men already registered in service elsewhere. On the other hand, from late 1639 it offered those who had already enrolled in the new garrison towns greater protection from remand by altering judicial procedures so that all fugitive peasant remand cases were henceforth investigated, heard, and resolved in the court of the Military Chancellery at Moscow rather than in the governors' courts. Enlistees in several of the new frontier towns had requested this, convinced that their own governors were unable or unwilling to protect their rights in court; and centralizing remand cases in the Military Chancellery had the added advantage of reducing the caseload on the governors of the new garrison towns so they could return their attention to defense matters. Meanwhile, difficulties in retaining volunteers at Userdsk and Iablonov had begun to be taken as argument for tightening central contol over manpower flows. Voluntarism had proven to be a powerful force, but a force difficult to manage; whereas colonization by transfer brought less rapid results but was more amenable to central planning, making it less likely enlistments would outstrip bounties or bleed older northern districts of their garrison veterans and taxpayers. Transfer therefore became the primary mechanism for garrison formation from 1638.

This did not mean that voluntarism ceased playing any role in Moscow's southern frontier strategy. Volunteer enlistment was later used to form special expeditionary armies sent down the Don and the new foreign formation regiments stationed along the Belgorod Line. Furthermore, the precedent set in 1635–1637 for enrolling in garrison service volunteers from nontraditional social categories would enable the Military Chancellery to take advantage of the "Cherkas immigration," the successive waves of Ukrainian refugees entering southwestern Muscovy after 1637.

The *odnodvortsy*

The new garrison towns founded in 1635–1637 were also of lasting significance for Muscovy's evolving southern frontier strategy in that they were settled almost exclusively by smallholders – cossacks and musketeers with small crofts, or middle service class *odnodvortsy* with small *pomest'ia* and no peasants.

In the older southern districts settled before the seventeenth century – Tula, Voronezh, Belgorod, etc. – there could still be found significant numbers of *gorodovye deti boiarskie* with middling entitlement rates, *pomest'ia* of 100 or 200 quarters or more, and peasant tenants. But the circumstances of southern frontier life – its heavier military service burden, the higher risk of devastation by Tatar raiders, and the greater opportunity for peasant tenant flight – made it difficult to spread or even maintain classic *pomest'e* economy in the south. Already by the 1570s–1580s in several southern districts there were too many impoverished *deti boiarskie* unable to inherit or obtain *pomest'e* allotments large enough to equip them for duty in the corps of the Borderland and Riazan' arrays, at least for duty on the terms set by the 1556 Decree on Service, forcing Moscow to reorganize these poorer *deti boiarskie* into special detachments of mounted arquebusiers with considerably lower land entitlement rates. Most of these mounted arquebusiers were *odnodvortsy*, "single-household" yeomen with no peasant tenants, for which reason they were not held to the same terms of array duty as traditional *deti boiarskie*: their primary duty was for local defense, and if called up for seasonal duty in the array corps they were not expected to bring slave or peasant retainers with them.

The Cherkasskii government essentially made the *odnodvorets* the preferred form of middle service class manpower in the new towns founded in the late 1630s. Because *odnodvortsy* had substantially lower service land and cash bounty entitlement rates, they cost the treasury far less than *deti boiarskie* of the traditional type; and for the same reason they were better suited to accelerated volunteer colonization, it being much easier to recruit into them sons of cossacks and musketeers, ruined former servicemen, and other declassé elements. Yet they still differed from lower service class cossacks and musketeers in that their service was hereditary, not contractual. This meant that their contingent in the garrison was not fixed in size and could expand as long as the district plowland reserve fund held out. The fact that they were not suited for distant campaign service in the corps of the Borderland and Riazan' arrays no longer mattered, since the primary purpose of the new garrison towns built far to the south of the arrays in the late 1630s was not to contribute troops to the Array corps but to provide greater defense in depth, to mount smaller-scale local-level operations against Tatar raiding parties moving up the invasion roads. In theory this kind of duty even yeomen with small service lands and no peasant tenants could perform.

Besides making it possible to settle a larger number of *deti boiarskie* at less cost to the Sovereign's *pomest'e* fund, *odnodvorets* colonization in the new frontier towns also favored the transformation of *pomest'e* tenure rights by spreading the *siabr* system of tenure, in which servicemen continued to have personal plowland entitlement rates (*oklady*) but held their actual land allotments (*dachy*) in the form of shares within a block grant managed by the village commune rather than as discrete personal farmsteads.

Under the *siabr* system the governor's surveyors simply set the common boundaries of the village's service land fund by marking off a tract commensurate in area with the total allotments to be awarded the village's resident servicemen and the plowland reserve estimated needed for future allotments to their heirs and other new villagers; the actual apportionment of this land among individual members was done by the village commune, which divided the block for current allotment into smaller parcels, each usually consisting of ten narrow parallel strips of standard dimensions, and then had its members form teams of ten "comrades" (*siabry*) to cast lots for strips in each parcel. Every *siabr* thereby obtained several strips interspersed with those of his neighbors, the other members of his team, so that risks and advantages in quality of strip soil or strip location were shared across the team. Trading of particular strips required the consent of the whole team, as did general redistribution of strips or redivision of parcels into new strips. Haymeadows were distributed in similar fashion. But the reserve fund for future allotments and the village pasturage, forest, fishing sites, and church lots remained undivided as village commons.

This *siabr* system mixed elements of individual and collective tenure. A *siabr* was of course not free to sell or mortgage his lands to outsiders. But field labor was not collectivized: the individual *siabr* was not under obligation to labor on his neighbor's allotments (although he did have to observe the same crop rotation as his neighbors). He had to relinquish his strips for redistribution or redivision only when new members joined the collective or neighbors complained their allotments were not in accord with their entitlements. The number of strips he held depended on his personal grant right, so his total allotment might be smaller or larger than his neighbor's. In practice, though, there was very little variation in allotment totals because *siabry* were smallholder *odnodvortsy* and the range of variation in *odnodvorets* grants was negligible.

Siabr tenure probably originated among smallholders in eastern Ukraine and spread into the Seversk lands and westward across southern Muscovy in the late sixteenth and early seventeenth centuries. It was the joint creation of the colonists and the state, serving the interests of both. Many of those migrating south to enroll in service in the new garrison towns had traveled in *arteli*, small bands or brotherhoods of a dozen or more men of common geographic origin (sons of Riazhsk cossacks, for example, or Don cossacks demobilized from the Smolensk army), and on arrival it was natural for them to request allotments at the same site and offer surety on each other's service constancy. It made sense as well for the government to grant an *artel'* plowlands in collective allotment at the same village because this preserved *artel'* solidarity and harnessed it to agricultural colonization and garrison duty by reinforcing collective surety bonds and encouraging settlers to rely upon mutual aid in establishing and defending their economies. Collective allotment to teams of *siabry* of common *artel'* origin also fit with the preference of both the state and the colonists for a nucleated pattern of settlement (it being easier to defend a dozen or so village collectives than a host of scattered isolated farmsteads). *Siabr* land tenure offered common use of haymeadow and woods and some mutual aid among neighboring households as some compensation for the reduced size of plowland allotments available to yeomen *odnodvortsy*. The *siabr* commune redistributed or redivided plowland strips when necessary, contracted to bring in outsiders as new members assuming their shares of the service burden, blocked outsiders unwilling to assume service from obtaining *siabr* strips or commons, and protected the commune's fund of reserve lands for allotments to future generation members. Furthermore *siabr* collectivism eased the burden of policing and justice administration on the local governor's office by submitting some village-level conflicts to arbitration by the village commune.

The *odnodvorets/siabr* model followed in districts colonized after 1635 thus represented a radical reconfiguration of the middle service class for duty on the southern frontier. This process was reflected in the gradual shift of jurisdiction over *pomest'e* allotments to southern *odnodvortsy* from the Service Lands Chancellery to the Military Chancellery, and in the Military Chancellery's commitment (for the time being) to particular measures to maintain the *odnodvorets/siabr* as the dominant form of service economy in the south. The Military Chancellery kept entitlement rates low and held allotment norms at low proportion to entitlement rates in order to maintain the reserve fund for future allotments and thereby promote expansion of the service smallholder rolls. A series of Forbidden Towns decrees (1637–1676) forbade men of Moscow rank to obtain virgin land or deeds to service land in particular southern frontier districts so as to keep the reserve fund intact for allotments to service smallholders. The Military Chancellery pressed the treasury to review the southern forest and river appurtenances it leased to nonservicemen and turn the less profitable over to local *odnodvortsy* to support their households. Throughout the 1640s the Military Chancellery used its power of verdict in fugitive peasant cases to limit remands out of southern garrison populations. True, the 1649 *Ulozhenie* code made it much easier in principle for serfowners to win remand of fugitive peasants, for it authorized inquisitorial method, mass dragnets, and conviction solely on the basis of cadastral registration, but in practice most southern frontier military colonists remained protected from remand: a decree of 1653 declared that those who had settled in southern frontier garrisons before 1649 were immune from remand "so as not to depopulate the defense line," and a decree of 1656 extended this immunity to those who had settled in the south before 1653.[11]

This policy of protecting *odnodvorets/siabr* settlement lasted until the outbreak of the Thirteen Years' War. After that the viability of smallholder economy came under threat from increasing population pressure on the reserve fund, conscription of many smallholders into the foreign formation regiments campaigning far off in Ukraine, and gradual subjection of the remaining smallholders to heavy taxes to support the Ukrainian campaigns.

The Azov crisis and the founding of the Belgorod Line

Kozlov, the first of these new garrison towns, stood near a strategically important fork in the Nogai Road and a vast expanse of open steppe not easily patrolled. The Military Chancellery and Kozlov's governors had therefore decided in early 1636 that the best way to block enemy infiltration up the Nogai Road was to extend Kozlov's force eastward across the steppe in the form of a short defense line. In just five months, using 950 laborers and spending just 6,500 rubles, Kozlov's governors succeeded in building an earthen wall across 25 km of steppe between the Pol'noi Voronezh and Chelnovaia rivers. This wall stood nearly 4 m high and had seventy bartizans, four earthen forts, breastworks, and ditch and anti-cavalry fences. It was an important example of further Muscovite familiarization with Western European military engineering, for it had been built to a plan devised by Jan Cornelius van Rodenburg, a Dutch engineer in Muscovite service, and under the direction of Ivan Andreev, a veteran of the engineering of the Smolensk siege.

The Kozlov Wall already proved effective by spring 1637. Kozlov troops engaged in a few successful actions against Tatar *chambuly*, but no significant Tatar raids occurred in the districts north of Kozlov. The Military Chancellery noted that Riazhsk, Riazan', Shatsk, and Lebedian' now seemed secure, while intelligence from the lower Don reported Tatar princes complaining the new steppe wall had "shut down" the Nogai Road.[12]

This persuaded the Boyar Duma to adopt surveyor Sukhotin's recommendation to cut the other Tatar invasion roads in similar manner. In January 1637 the Duma authorized 111,000 rubles to erect segments of earthen defense line in three places: across the Murava Trail, from the Vorskla River to the Northern Donets River; across the Iziuma Trail, blocking the corridors between the Korocha River and the Iablonov Forest, and between the Iablonov and Kholansk forests; and across the Kal'miuss Trail, running from the Valuiki Forest across the mouth of the Userda River as far as the left bank of the Tikhaia Sosna River. This new construction was important in three respects. The new segments of earth wall lay in such proximity as to facilitate subsequent linkage of Belgorod and the newer garrison towns of Iablonov, Userdsk, and Korocha into a single defense line network, the trunk of the future Belgorod Line. Furthermore, because they were erected just to the north of Belgorod and Valuiki they had the effect of cutting the other invasion roads much farther south – by about 250 km – than did the Kozlov Wall. And the Iablonov segment represented another new application of European earth fortification techniques, for unlike Kozlov Iablonov town had outer walls of earth with sunken profiles and bastion traces – a precedent which would later be followed in the construction of Bolkhovets, Novyi Oskol', and Nezhegol'sk and the reconstruction of Belgorod, all of which would also be built directly into the earthen steppe wall.[13]

The Azov Crisis (1637–1642) initially threatened to provoke not only

Crimean Tatar retaliation but direct military conflict with the Ottomans. Refortification of the Abatis Line was therefore given priority for awhile over the construction of new towns and defense line segments farther south. Once the crisis passed the government was emboldened to return to a policy of forward defense and the resumption of military colonization and defense line construction farther south.

Although small Ottoman detachments out of Azov did occasionally support Tatar raids upon the cossack *gorodki* of the lower Don, Azov was not actually intended as a *place d'armes* for larger-scale Ottoman operations against Muscovy's southern frontier towns. Its garrison was too small (at most 4,000 men, distributed among three forts) and it did not even have a military commandant (*muhafiz*) before 1642. Azov's importance to the Porte was mostly commercial, and its military value was defensive, serving as a reminder the Khanate was under Ottoman protection (and Ottoman suzerainty), as a naval base for policing the Black Sea against cossack piracy, and finally as a tripwire providing the Sultan with cause, if he chose to make use of it, to retaliate directly against Don Cossack or Muscovite aggression. Moscow understood Azov's purpose in the same ways and had repeatedly warned the Don Host not to attack Azov lest this shatter Muscovy's peace with the Porte, damage Muscovite trade at Azov and Kaffa, and divert the Don Host from its task of confining the Nogais to the steppe on the eastern side of the Don.[14]

A Don Cossack campaign to capture Azov was therefore not in Moscow's interest, and so the Host did not openly acknowledge to the tsar's government that it had begun preparing for such a campaign in January 1637. The Host had attacked Azov in 1574, 1593, 1620, and 1626, partly for plunder and partly to protect Razdory and other cossack settlements, and new developments seemed to favor another attack. Khan Inaet Girei's revolt against the Sultan meant that the Azov garrison could not count on assistance from the Crimean Tatars, most of whom were off in Bucak waging war against the Sultan's vassal Khantimur. The Turks could not be expected to rush reinforcements to Azov, for Murat IV was preoccupied with wars in Persia and Hungary. The risk that an attack on Azov would wreck the Host's relations with Muscovy could also be disregarded, for the Karamyshev affair (1630) had already done much to estrange Moscow and since that time Moscow had made no effort towards rapprochement by increasing the size of its Don Shipments.[15] Ataman Ivan Katorzhnyi may even have calculated that by seizing Azov he could present Moscow with greater reason to increase its Don Shipment subsidies to the Host.

In April 1637 a force of 3,000 Don Cossacks and 4,000 Zaporozhian Cossacks under Mikhail Tatarinov placed Azov under siege. On 5 June the Don Cossacks captured the sultan's envoy Foma Cantacuzene en route from Azov to the upper Don and executed him for espionage. On 18 June Tatarinov's forces breached most of Azov's outer defenses after a German mercenary instructed them in placing a mine beneath its walls; the remaining Ottoman troops made a last stand in Azov's keep but had to capitulate three days later. Tatarinov and

Katorzhnyi moved quickly to garrison Azov with several thousand cossacks and on 15 July they sent a delegation to Moscow to beg the tsar to place Azov under his protection and send them reinforcements.

Moscow sent a commission to Azov to determine whether this was worth the risk. It found Azov's fortifications and stores in deplorable state and calculated it would cost about 120,000 rubles a year to adequately reinforce Azov – about ten times as much as the cost of the average annual Don Shipment. It was therefore decided to send some grain and munitions to the Host but refuse its request for troops. Moscow recognized that any more overt association with the Don Cossacks' actions would give the sultan pretext for war upon Muscovy. A rescript was sent to the Host condemning them for the murder of Cantacuzene and a letter sent to the sultan insisting the tsar's government had not been complicit in the events at Azov, which had been the work of "brigands ... acting for reasons unknown ... without Our instruction."[16]

The crisis could not be quickly defused, for the cossacks were able to reinforce and hold Azov for the next five years: Murat IV's wars in Hungary and Persia and then his death in 1640 delayed plans for an Ottoman expedition to retake Azov, and Crimean Khan Bahadur Girei (r. 1637–1641) pleaded lack of experience in besieging stone fortresses. Meanwhile merchants out of Don and Volga towns found it profitable to provision the cossack garrison at Azov, which by spring 1641 numbered 5,300 men and 300 guns.

Because the Don Cossacks lacked the forces to extend their control across the surrounding Azov steppe and the Kerch Straits, Hussein Deli, the Pasha of Silistria, was able to land an Ottoman army of 70–80,000 men and 120 siege guns and invest Azov in June 1641. But it had to evacuate in late September after encountering heavy resistance, provisioning shortfalls, and disease (Hussein Deli and Khan Bagadur Girei both took ill and died).

The question of going to war against the Turks for mastery of Azov was put to an Assembly of the Realm in January 1642, which approved sending 10,000 troops and 200,000 rubles, but the tsar's government was far more cautious, for new inspections showed Hussein Deli's siege had spared very little of Azov's fortifications, and there was concern that finances and manpower were not up to the task of a protracted war with the Turks when so much remained to be done to complete and man the Belgorod Line.[17] Therefore the government instead resumed paying tribute to the new Crimean khan, even though the envoys it had sent to Crimea were being abused. When Sultan Ibrahim issued a new ultimatum to Moscow (March 1642) Tsar Mikhail complied and ordered the Don Cossacks to evacuate Azov. Ottoman forces reoccupied Azov in September 1642 and reinforced its garrison.

War with the Ottoman Empire had been avoided. The new Turkish garrison at Azov carried out some retaliatory raids on Don Cossack settlements but left the southern Muscovite border towns alone. There had been Crimean Tatar raids into southern Muscovy in 1637 and 1641–1643, but they had been undertaken by *beys* and princes acting on their own, driven by famine and livestock epidemics in Crimea, khans Bahadur Girei and Kamil Mehmet Girei (r. 1641–1644) being no more able than Inaet Girei to curb the Crimean nobility.

But Muscovite–Ottoman relations had suffered a permanent setback. Henceforth Moscow would have to move very cautiously to avoid provoking war. The Don Cossacks had rebuilt their forts and settlements near Azov and were again attacking Ottoman troops, and Sultan Ibrahim had responded by demanding the tsar remove the Host from the lower Don, a request beyond the tsar's power to fulfill. There were rumors the sultan was ready to take military action to clear the Don of cossacks all the way up to Voronezh.[18] The new Crimean Khan Islam Girei III (r. 1644–1654) set about taming his nobles by realigning with the Ottoman sultan and organizing major invasions of the Commonwealth and Muscovy. In the summer of 1644 20,000 Tatars invaded the Commonwealth while another 20,000 swept across southern Muscovy, carrying off about 10,000 prisoners. Another 6,000 Muscovite captives were taken the following year. Sultan Ibrahim reportedly sanctioned these attacks to obtain slaves to row his galleys in his new war with the Venetian Republic for mastery of Crete, and because prosecuting this Candian War required that he deter Muscovy and especially the Commonwealth from accepting Venetian proposals for an alliance. The khan's raids succeeded in this, pushing Władysław IV to renew peace with the Porte and resume tribute gifts to the khan in 1646.

These Tatar incursions had taken advantage of the weaknesses remaining in southern Muscovy's defense system: the absence of unified command in the corps of the southern field army, and the overcentralization of command initiative in the Military Chancellery; the inability of the field army (still stationed along the Abatis Line) to offer a forward defense for the districts to its south; large gaps in the Belgorod Line, especially between Voronezh and Kozlov and between the Tikhaia Sosna and Oskol' rivers; and Moscow's inability to stop Don Cossack raids further provoking the Tatars and Turks. The new government of Tsar Aleksei Mikhailovich therefore gave priority to addressing each of these weaknesses.

The remaining gaps in the Belgorod Line were filled in and eighteen new forts and garrison towns were founded along the Line by 1653. On its eastern end the course of the Voronezh River between Voronezh and Kozlov was strengthened with new abatis and earth wall and the garrisons of Dobryi, Sokol'sk, Belokolodsk, Usman', and Orlov. Garrisons were founded at Kostensk, Uryv', and Korotiak to reinforce the lower Voronezh River as far as the Don. Ol'shansk, Verkhososensk, and Novyi Oskol' were built across the Kal'miuss Trail, while Vol'nyi, Khotmyzhsk, Lositskii Ostrog, Karpov, Valki, Bolkhovoi, and Oboian' were built to guard the Murava Trail. An unbroken Belgorod Line now ran for over 800 km from Akhtyrka on the Vorskla River to Chelnavsk. In 1647 work began on other defense lines running eastward from Chelnavsk: a 50-km Tambov earth wall running north along the Tsna to Shatsk; from Shatsk, another new line of abatis and other fortifications extending all the way to the new garrison town of Simbirsk on the Volga; and from Simbirsk yet another new defense line, the Trans-Kama Line, running 450 km eastward to Menselinsk on the Ik River. Most of this new construction was completed by 1655. These additional eastern segments meant Muscovy's southern frontier was now protected by over 1,800 km of fortified line stretching from the Polish-Lithuanian border all the way to the Urals.[19]

In February 1646 a new deployment scheme for the corps of the southern frontier field army was introduced. The corps previously stationed in the Borderland and Riazan' arrays were henceforth posted much farther south along the new perimeter formed by the Belgorod Line. The Great Corps now stood at Belgorod every spring, with the Vanguard Corps at Karpov or Novyi Oskol' and the Rear Guard at Iablonov.[20] This marked the abandonment of a fallback strategy for one of more active forward defense — and not just for the corps, but for the detachments sent by town governors to reinforce the corps at their new stations upon alert.

Because southern garrison forces could now play a more valuable role in reinforcing corps operations it became possible to reform command-and-control practices. Some elements of this reform reflected changes in force structure, but others testified to the harnessing of military command authority to a broader range of nonmilitary administrative functions across the territory of the Belgorod Line.

The first stage of this reform (1646–1649) placed the garrison forces of the towns on the Belgorod Line, together with those of some important garrisons far behind the Line (Tula, Orel, Livny, Elets, Mtsensk, Novosil'), under the ultimate command authority of the senior commander of the Great Corps at Belgorod. Initially this command authority was only for military operations, so that it differed little from the authority permitted commanders of the old Borderland Array during general alert.

In its second stage (1650) the senior commander of the Great Corps at Belgorod was given additional authority, less directly military, over these districts: to supervise military construction, to survey and allot lands, and to hear court cases on the first or second instance (land suits, fugitive remand suits, dishonor suits, and felony cases). Under certain circumstances he could even replace town governors in his Array.

The third stage (1652–1653) focused again on military command-and-control. The old concept of a Great Corps no longer accurately described the structure and size of the force under the command of the senior commander at Belgorod, given the growing number of new Belgorod Line garrisons coming under his ultimate authority and the creation of new foreign formation infantry regiments in preparation for the war with Poland-Lithuania. A mass review of troops in 1653 therefore introduced the term Belgorod Army Group (*Belgorodskii polk*) to reflect the more elaborate force structure for field operations. In the early years of the Thirteen Years' War force expansion and force ramification on Muscovy's northern and western front was likewise accompanied by references to a Novgorod Army Group and Smolensk Army Group.

The final stage came at the height of the Thirteen Years' War, in 1658, when mass review records introduced the term *Belgorodskii razriad* to describe the venue of military and administrative authority of the Belgorod commander, which now extended to all the towns on the Belgorod Line as well as seventeen southern frontier towns beyond or behind the Line.[21] Given that the Belgorod commander now held broad civil as well as military authority over a vast territory, it would be misleading to continue translating *razriad* here as "Array": an old term was being applied to something quite new, a "military administrative region" somewhat akin to a province or governor-generalship. Thus the men appointed to head the Belgorod and later Military-Administrative Regions tended to be boyars of considerable influence in court and counsel, men of political and managerial as well as military experience – Repnins, Odoevskiis, Romodanovskii, Trubetskois, Cherkasskiis, and Khovanskiis – and in several respects the Military-Administrative Regions came to resemble the eight *guberniia* provinces Peter I would create in 1708.

The formation of Army Groups and Military-Administrative Regions continued into the 1660s and 1670s. In 1664 Sevsk, Bel'ev, Bolkhov, Orel, and Kromy – collectively a large manpower pool which, however, lay to the north of the Belgorod Line – were split off to form a separate Sevsk Army Group and Sevsk Military-Administrative Region. By 1680 field army troops in European Russia (i.e., excluding Siberia) were assigned among nine Military-Administrative Regions (Belgorod, Sevsk, Novgorod, Smolensk, Moscow, Vladimir, Riazan', Kazan', and Tambov).[22]

Although it had the potential to tighten control over district administration by town governors, the main intent behind the formation of a Belgorod Military-Administrative Region was to improve military logistics by devolving upon the Belgorod commander some of the mobilizing, provisioning, and monitoring functions that used to be centralized at Moscow in the Military Chancellery. However, it would take many years before the clerical staff at the Belgorod headquarters would be up to the task of processing all this information and town governors compliant in providing it in timely fashion.

The last time foreign formation troops had been used for the defense of the southern frontier had been in 1642 when a few thousand *soldaty* and dragoons had helped man the Abatis Line. Thereafter the practice had been discontinued because of doubts it was cost-effective. But in 1646 the government decided foreign formation troops could be useful in helping to defend the new Belgorod Line fortifications and the colonists behind the Line – provided these troops were dragoons, suited for mounted as well as foot duty, and were locally recruited, drilling in their villages and provisioning themselves from their own plowlands rather than from treasury rations money.[23] Moscow intended to use these "settled dragoons" for local defense rather than campaign duty in the field army. Settled dragoon service was also seized upon as a way of shifting some of the local defense burden from households of servicemen to households of peasants, of whom there was now a greater number because of the security offered new colonists by the Belgorod Line. A new general census in 1646, conducted to shift tax assessment from an inhabited *chetvert'* basis to a household basis, also had the effect of simplifying recruit levies and therefore may have contributed to this decision. In 1642 the Military Chancellery had raised some settled dragoons by enlisting kinsmen of servicemen, but now it turned to making peasant households provide settled dragoons. In 1646–1647 the court peasants of Komaritskaia canton, in the Sevsk region, were placed under the jurisdiction of the Military Chancellery and required to provide recruits for dragoon service at the rate of one man from each household. This yielded 5,125 dragoons, who were organized into three regiments under the command of foreign officers. In 1647 dragoon service was introduced into the villages west of Kozlov as well by removing private peasants from the manorial authority of A. N. Trubetskoi, the Chudov and Novospasskii monasteries, the Veliaminov and Pleshcheev families, and Dmitrii Pozharskii's widow; this provided another 1,800 or so settled dragoons.[24]

By 1648 it had been decided to introduce foreign formation service in the Belgorod Line field army as well, for the outbreak of cossack revolt in Ukraine and the alliance of the revolt's leader, Bohdan Khmel'nyts'kyi, with the Crimean Khanate raised the danger that the districts behind the Belgorod Line might again become vulnerable to Tatar raiding, this time out of Ukraine. Four regiments (8,000 men) of *soldat* infantry were ordered formed at Iablonov, filled largely from "volunteers" levied from the boarders and kinsmen of servicemen in sixteen southern districts. The governors of these districts were instructed to enlist about half of the available nonserving population of their districts, so the registration of volunteers actually took on the character of a conscription. The greater number of men levied in this fashion came from the eastern end of the Belgorod Line, from populous Kozlov and its satellite districts. The length of service term for these *soldat* recruits was not specified. They were issued muskets, pikes, and sabers from the treasury and were remunerated with monthly rations money rather than annual cash and grain bounties and service land allotments. By October 1653 they had been assigned to their regiments for training and deployment: to Alexander Crawford's regiment at Iablonov, John Crawford's at Belgorod, John Leslie's at Userdsk, and George Goodson's at Karpov. At this time Moscow decided to begin recruiting another 1,237 infantry on the Belgorod Line and to start forming *soldat* regiments in the northwest as well, on the Smolensk front.[25]

The years 1646 to 1653 thus saw a significant concentration of manpower on the Belgorod Line for defense against the Crimean Tatars and, soon, for reinforcement of operations in Ukraine. By 1650 there were 4,045 middle service class cavalrymen from central and southwestern Muscovy serving in Repnin's and Golovin's divisions in the Great Corps at Belgorod, and probably another 2–4,000 men in the Vanguard and Rear Guard corps at Karpov and Iablonov; another 5,000 or so Komaritskaia dragoons serving behind the Line; and about 17,000 garrison troops performing local defense duty in twenty-two districts along the Belgorod Line. This was a total of about 28–30,000 men (Muscovy's full military establishment numbered 133,210, not counting seasonally levied sappers and slaves manning army baggage trains). By 1653, on the eve of the war with Poland-Lithuania, the newly formed *soldat* regiments would increase the strength of Belgorod Line manpower by another 8,000 men.[26]

The first Don expeditions by Muscovite forces

After 1645 Moscow also reexamined its relations with the other steppe polities it had traditionally cultivated as counterweights to the Khanate. As alliance with the Great Nogais could no longer offer much of value, Moscow began pursuing alliance with the Kalmyks instead; and it also sought new ways to tighten its control over the Don Cossack Host.

Inter-*ulus* conflict and especially the increasing frequency of Kalmyk attacks across the Volga had by this time completed the disintegration of the Great Nogai Horde. Most of the Edisan, Edishkul', and Dzhemboiluk Nogai princes had joined the Kalmyks; the rest of the Great Nogais had fled towards the Terek steppe or westward towards the Dnepr. Initally the Kalmyks had been seen exclusively as a threat to Muscovite power on the Volga, not as potential allies, and it had been thought necessary to use garrison forces out of Astrakhan', Ufa, and Samara to push the Kalmyks back from the Volga in retaliation for their attacks upon caravans and upon the tsar's Great Nogai and Bashkir allies. But in 1645 the Kalmyk *taishi* Daichin entered negotiations with the Muscovites and Don Cossacks in order to win formal recognition of his *ulus*' right to nomadize on the steppe between the lower Volga and the Iaik. Over the next four years Muscovite envoys conducted further talks with Daichin and agreed to restrain the Bashkirs from attacking his people, in return for which Daichin gave assurances that the new wave of 20,000 Kalmyks arriving from Dzhungaria would confine their nomadizing to the Iaik steppe. By 1650 Muscovite–Kalmyk rapprochement had reached the point that it was now possible to discuss forming a Kalmyk–Don Cossack military alliance against the Crimean Khanate. For the time being these discussions had to be discreet and Moscow's role in mediating them plausibly deniable, for the Crimean khan had not yet broken with Bohdan Khmel'nyts'kyi and was still contributing significantly to his struggle against the Poles. Thanks to these talks, though, the Kalmyks stood ready for alliance once the khan abandoned Khmel'nyts'kyi and Khmel'nyts'kyi placed Ukraine under Muscovite protection. In 1655 the tsar pledged that the Kalmyks would be free to nomadize much farther afield – along the eastern bank of the Volga as far as Tsaritsyn and along its western bank as far as Samara. In return the Kalmyk *taishis* took oaths of eternal loyalty to the tsar and promised to join in operations against the Crimean Tatars and the Poles.[27]

Since reducing the annual Don Shipments had not worked to rein in the Don Cossacks, the opposite tack was now tried and their size expanded: 5,000 rubles, 3,000 quarters of grain, and 6,700 kg of gunpowder were sent in 1644, and 6,400 rubles, 6,300 quarters of grain, and 6,550 kg of gunpowder in 1647.[28] The Military Chancellery decided to try reinforcing the Host with new Muscovite manpower in such a way as to bind it to Moscow-directed operations. In 1646 Moscow *dvorianin* Z. V. Kondyrev was ordered to recruit a force of 3,000 volunteers at Voronezh and the other garrison towns of the Nogai Front to accompany the Don Shipment to Cherkassk. From Cherkassk these volunteers were to join the Don Cossacks in diversionary raids by longboat along the eastern Crimean coast while a second force of 1,700 Muscovite troops and 2,000 Nogais under S. R. Pozharskii marched west from Astrakhan' against the Crimean isthmus fortress at Perekop. On completion of this mission Kondyrev's volunteers were to enlist in the Don Cossack Host. Kondyrev's instructions emphasized that Don Cossack forces were expected to act only in consultation with Kondyrev and Pozharskii, that they were not to provoke the Turks by attacking Azov, and that Kondyrev was to discreetly collect intelligence on Don Cossack force disposition and intentions in the region.

This was the first major offensive operation against Crimean Tatar territory since Dmytro Vyshnevets'kyi's raid nearly a century before. But it was largely unsuccessful. The decision to recruit free volunteers from the population of the eastern Belgorod Line districts backfired on Kondyrev: over 10,000 men, many of them fugitive peasants or garrison deserters seeking the freedom of Don Host residence, enrolled in his expedition, disrupting manorial agriculture and garrison service along that part of the Belgorod Line. It proved hard to keep under discipline enlistees who had been promised release into the liberty of the Don Host, and Kondyrev's 15,000 rubles sufficed to pay enlistment bounties only for a third of the enlistees. The government was forced to throw together a special flotilla of rivercraft to ship additional emergency stores to feed the rest, but this provisioning was never adequate. Furthermore the Don Cossack *starshina* refused to place itself under Kondyrev's and Pozharskii's command and "borrowed" Kondyrev's volunteers for their own operations: in June they convinced some 500 of Kondyrev's men to join them in a landing on the Azov coast and night raid upon the outer fortifications of Azov, in contravention of Kondyrev's orders. Their raid failed, but they put back out to sea and attacked some Ottoman galleys. Subsequent attempts at raiding the Crimean coast were frustrated by storms and a shortage of seaworthy craft. Pozharskii's troops had more success in their overland attacks on Nogai and Azov Tatar encampments along the Ei River but were defeated near Kagal'nik in August by 10,000 Crimean Tatars under the command of the *nuraddin*. In September Kondyrev's force of volunteers began to melt away from hunger and demoralization; by spring he was apparently left with just 2,000 men. They were taken into the Don Host upon his recall to Moscow.[29]

The Kondyrev expedition did succeed in pushing the Nogais back to their traditional grazing lands in the east for awhile and in pressing the Khan to divert to the Azov region forces he might otherwise have sent raiding into southern Muscovy. The attacks upon Azov and Ottoman galleys had provoked new threats from the sultan, but because of the demands of the Candian War the Turks limited their response to small raids on Cherkassk by troops out of the Azov garrison.

Although the first Don campaign had been poorly executed, Moscow did not repudiate its underlying strategy – maintaining a small Muscovite force on the lower Don to harass the Crimean Tatars, deter Ottoman attack on the cossack *gorodki*, and keep a closer eye on cossack activities. Troops were therefore sent down to Cherkassk again in 1648. This time, however, it was a smaller force of 1,000 men under A. Lazar'ev, and they were foreign formation infantry (*soldaty*), not untrained volunteers. Whereas Kondyrev's volunteers had been assigned a season's mission and then turned over to the Don Host, Lazar'ev's infantry were expected to remain under their officers' discipline and to erect their own fort for several seasons' deployment on the lower Don; their mission was more carefully defined, and limited to defensive, deterrent operations; and whereas Kondyrev's volunteers had originally been expected to feed themselves out of their own enlistment bounties, the provisioning of Lazar'ev's infantry became Moscow's full responsibility. More wharves were therefore founded on the Voronezh River to expand production of rivercraft for troop transport and supply to the lower Don (they turned out over 160 barques and barges). Moscow's planning still had not anticipated the problem of cholera, however, and for this reason only about a third of the regiment remained alive on the Don after Lazar'ev's recall to Moscow in spring 1649.[30]

Fortunately the threat of Tatar and Ottoman retaliation against the Don Cossack forts and Muscovite borderland towns had diminished by this point. The measures taken since 1646 to strengthen southern defenses helped deter attack, but it was also the case that events to the east and west of Crimea gave Khan Islam Girei III reason to turn his attention from southern Muscovy. His eastern domains were now threatened by the Kalmyks, who had attacked the Nogais of the Urmamet *ulus* and pushed them across the Don towards the Dnepr and Perekop. The westward flight of the Nogais in turn strengthened the hand of the *beys* and princes of the Crimean steppe *ulusy* against their Khan; they demanded he let them undertake raids upon the Commonwealth or Muscovy in defiance of the orders of Sultan Ibrahim, who had feared this would provoke the Poles and Muscovites to accept Venetian offers of alliance. *Bey* Tugai Shirin and mirza Karachi joined with Khmel'nyts'kyi, seeing the chaos in Ukraine as presenting greater opportunities for plunder than were available in southern Muscovy. The factional conflict within the Ottoman Empire following the assassination of Sultan Ibrahim gave Khan Ismail Girei the opportunity to follow suit and slip the bonds of Ottoman control.

Cossack unrest in Commonwealth Ukraine

While Filaret and I. B. Cherkasskii were rebuilding and expanding Muscovy's southern frontier defense system the military security of Commonwealth Ukraine was approaching breakdown. Part of the reason for this was the intensification of social and cultural changes already underway in the late sixteenth century, particularly in Left Bank Ukraine: the confessionalization of the Orthodox Church in response to the perceived threat from the Crown-sponsored Uniate Church; magnate engrossment of the land and commerce, and magnate domination of palatinate and urban government; the marginalization of the Ukrainian petty nobility; and the increasing attractiveness of the cossack calling as a status alternative even in the Settled Lands.

The Polish Crown's strategic priorities in the 1610s–1630s were also partly responsible. The cossack militias in Ukraine had long borne most of the burden of defending the steppe frontier so as to spare the Crown the expense of enlarging its Quarter Army. Now cossacks were expected to serve en masse outside Ukraine – in Livonia and Ducal Prussia, in Moldavia, and in western Muscovy. Military reliance on cossack volunteers was becoming essential to Zygmunt III and Władysław IV, their way of pursuing foreign adventures without the regular army, for which the magnates and gentry in the *Sejm* and provincial dietines were reluctant to continue voting funds for long. This encouraged many Ukrainians to remake themselves as cossacks to qualify for the king's bounty. By 1611 some 30,000 cossacks were on Zygmunt III's service in Muscovy and there were several thousand more in independent freebooting bands such as the *Lisowczyki*.[31] These cossack formations were never remunerated to their satisfaction, however, for this ultimately required the consent of the *Sejm*, which saw expansion of the cossack population and royal military adventurism as equally dangerous to the stability of the Commonwealth. Unpaid and underprovisioned, the cossacks who had served in Livonia or Muscovy resorted to collecting their own "contributions" from the Lithuanian population on their way back to Ukraine and for years after each great campaign importuned Commonwealth authorities for recognition of their permanent place on the register and their rights to quartering and provisioning anywhere in Ukraine. They presented a further danger in that those not maintained on the register were more likely to join the Zaporozhian Host in plunder raids on Crimean and Ottoman territory, thereby provoking enemy retaliation on some other part of the Commonwealth's frontier. In 1616, for example, Ukrainian cossacks raided the Crimean coast and burned Kaffa. The next year 50,000 Turks and Tatars and 24,000 Moldavian and Wallachian troops marched on the Commonwealth's Dnestr borderland in retaliation. The invaders withdrew when Crown Hetman Żółkiewski promised he would "curb and punish" the cossacks; Zolkiewski then had to use Crown troops to force the Zaporozhians to accept the more moderate Petro Sahaidachnyi as their *koshevoi* ataman. In 1619, however, Żółkiewski found he needed many thousands of cossack volunteers for his project to conquer the Black Sea coast as far as the Danube and reimpose Crown vassalage on the Moldavian hospodar.

Two events in 1620–1621 worked to transform cossack dissatisfaction into cossack insurrection.

The first of these events was the collapse of Żółkiewski's campaign in Moldavia, which resulted in massive Turkish retaliation at Cecora (October 1620), where Żółkiewski was killed along with all but 1,000 Polish troops and Field Hetman Stanisław Koniecpolski taken prisoner. What remained of the Polish army – some 35,000 men, under Crown Prince Władysław and hetmans Lubomirski and Chodkiewicz – came under siege by the much larger army of Sultan Osman II at Khotyn, on the Moldavian side of the Dnestr (August–October 1621). The *Sejm* had to put aside its contempt for the cossacks and call on them to save the Polish army at Khotyn. It voted to take 20,000 cossacks into royal service, at pay of 100,000 złoties a year. Sahaidachnyi saw this as the opportunity to confirm further rights and privileges for the cossacks, so he mobilized twice this number and requisitioned whatever they needed from the Ukrainian towns. His cossacks bore the brunt of the fighting at Khotyn and performed brilliantly, forcing the Turks to withdraw with heavy losses. Polish and cossack forces at Khotyn lost about 14,000 killed, missing, dead of disease, or deserted; Osman II reportedly lost 40,000, about a third of his army. Khotyn represented "the apogee of cossack glory" in the Commonwealth, and Sagaidachnyi and other cossack leaders took advantage of it to petition King Zygmunt, pledging their obedience and promising to end unauthorized raiding if the king would grant further rights to the Orthodox Church, remove the cap on the size of the cossack register, recognize cossacks' rights to reside on lands other than those belonging to the Crown, and permit the cossacks to take occasional service with other sovereigns. But Zygmunt refused all these requests and even instructed his commissioners to further reduce the cossack register to 1–2,000 men.[32]

The second event was the visit to Kiev of Theophanes III, Patriarch of Jerusalem, in the autumn of 1620. His visit was of great importance to the Orthodox Church in Ukraine, an opportunity to remind Warsaw the Ukrainian metropolitan and archbishops were representatives of a larger Orthodox ecumene protected in part by the Muscovite tsar. Theophanes III performed a service for the Polish Crown as well by issuing a call to the Zaporozhian Host to come to the aid of the Polish army at Khotyn. But the Ukrainian cossacks reaped the greatest political benefit from his visit. They provided his escort, and thereby came to dominate his entourage, and under their pressure Theophanes III agreed to consecrate a new metropolitan (Iov Boretsky) and five bishops in defiance of royal authorities. This did much to reinvigorate Orthodox discipline, and it put the cossacks in a role with which they had not been previously associated: acknowledged leaders of the defense of the Orthodox faith.[33]

A political partnership between the Orthodox hierarchy and the cossack leaders was emerging. The newly consecrated metropolitan and bishops accepted cossack assistance in the construction of a more centralized, disciplined, and militant Orthodox Church, while the cossack leaders gained access to a new vocabulary for political resistance – the idea of a Ruthenian nation rooted in the Orthodox faith and protected by a free cossack knighthood. This made it easier for cossack leaders to enlist the support of the church, and ultimately of the Orthodox Ukrainian petty nobility, peasantry, and townspeople, for their struggle for expansion of the register, quartering privileges, and immunity from remand into serfdom.

The mounting cossack defiance of the Crown – naval raids on Ottoman towns, including Istanbul, and cossack intervention in the succession crisis in the Crimean Khanate – threatened to derail the king's plans for war with Sweden. Cossack willfulness "has become so hardnosed that indeed, forgetful of loyalty and obedience, it is founding its own sovereign state," Zygmunt wrote. "They are attacking the life and property of innocent people. All of Ukraine is under their authority. The nobleman is not free in his own home. In small and medium-sized towns, the entire administration is in the hands of the cossacks." Crown Hetman Koniecpolski had to use military force to bring the cossacks back under royal discipline. The Treaty of Kurukove (1625) forced the cossacks to accept a register capped at 6,000 – 1,000 allowed to garrison Zaporozhia, the rest to be relocated across the steppe frontier, outside the Settled Lands, and under the Crown Hetman's command, ready to campaign when and where he ordered. Unregistered cossacks living on lands other than Crown lands had twenty weeks to leave.[34]

These terms proved impossible to enforce for very long. An armistice with Sweden was signed in 1629 and thousands of demobilized cossacks returned home to Ukraine to find that they faced enserfment if denied legal haven on the cossack register. Koniecpolski, already despised in Ukraine, arranged to billet the Crown army on the inhabitants of eastern Ukraine in order to make up the army's pay arrears; and a synod at Kiev seemed to dash any hope of reconciling the Orthodox and Uniate churches.

Major cossack rebellions therefore erupted in 1630 and 1637–1638 and in the wake of the latter King Władysław IV punitively reduced the cossack register to 2,000 and ended the Zaporozhian Host's right to elect its own hetman and colonels. The Polish fortress of Kodak, attacked and burned in 1635, was rebuilt to block the Zaporozhians' war trail to the Black Sea. The Polish magnates, *starostas*, and officers commanding cossack forces imagined that the Ordinances of 1638 had brought Ukraine a Golden Peace, that cossack grievance as well as cossack revolt had been vanquished.

Impact on Muscovy

The unrest in Ukraine of course had consequences for neighboring Muscovy. For decades Ukrainian cossacks had been slipping back and forth across the border into southern Muscovy to forage and graze their livestock, but by 1640 many were also entering for banditry – some striking as far into the interior as the Don basin, forcing the government to consider building a new garrison town on the Boguchar River. More Zaporozhian detachments were also joining Don Cossack bands in raids on the Khanate, increasing the likelihood that the Tatars and Ottomans would retaliate against the Muscovite frontier towns.

After the suppression of the Rebellion of 1637–1638 great numbers of Ukrainians – especially cossacks, but also townsmen, peasants, and some petty nobles – emigrated to Muscovy and requested enrollment in the tsar's service. Moscow's response to this *Cherkas* immigration was generally welcoming but not yet actively encouraging. On the one hand, the Military Chancellery found immigrant Ukrainian cossacks useful for colonizing the garrison towns of the emerging Belgorod Line as corps cossacks or ranger atamans and therefore offered them generous resettlement subsidies (typically 5–8 rubles and 5–8 quarters rye per adult male); it also resettled along the Line, with special privileges of duty-free trade, immigrant townsmen and peasants who had skills as millers, distillers, smiths, or saltpeter-makers. On the other hand it turned away solitary and impoverished refugees less likely to establish successful homesteads, and it tried to channel most arrivals through one border station, Putivl', for vetting and policing purposes. To avoid the potential security risk of too many *Cherkas* colonists concentrated too close to the Ukrainian border it resettled many of them farther east along the Line, at Korocha, Valuiki, Voronezh, and even as far as Kozlov. By the late 1640s some 2,500 adult male Ukrainian refugees were enrolled in military service in fourteen districts of the Belgorod Line.[35]

The full scale of the Ukrainian immigration of 1638–1648 is difficult to gauge. Polish officials complained that some 20,000 tenants had abandoned the estates of Prince Jeremi Wiśniowiecki in 1637–1638 and found refuge in Muscovy. While this was probably an exaggeration, it is likely there were many more Ukrainians entering Muscovite territory than the Military Chancellery could accommodate in its garrisons.

Ukrainian immigrants may have wanted the tsar's cash and grain bounty, but many were likely to find the actual terms of resettlement in Line garrisons uncongenial. They were accustomed to founding and subsequently expanding their own homesteads by *zaimka*, free "squatting" occupation of virgin steppe land, while it was the policy of the Military Chancellery to treat virgin steppe land as the tsar's patrimony and tightly control its allocation, authorizing allotment raises only after many years' service and forbidding altogether cultivation beyond the Line. In some Line districts there were enough Ukrainians to be allowed to settle together in special suburban colonies (*cherkasskie slobody*) under their own elected atamans, but their atamans in turn had to answer to a special Muscovite *syn boiarskii* charged with keeping them under surveillance. Many of the recently enrolled Ukrainians at Kozlov in 1647 had to settle on Muscovite servicemen's homesteads as *polovinshchiki*, service and land shareholders, because their own land allotments were too small and they had still not been paid their cash and grain bounties. The governor of Kozlov considered them an unruly element (two-thirds of them had been charged with insubordination, assault, or attempted desertion) and urged they all be transferred elsewhere.[36]

Some Ukrainian immigrants therefore sought resettlement on the steppe beyond the Line rather than in the garrisons along it. In the 1620s and early 1630s Moscow had found it necessary to legalize squatter settlements of Ukrainian refugees and foragers on the steppe near Kharkov and Izium. In 1638 Zaporozhian Hetman Iatsko Ostrianyn defected to Muscovy with an entire regiment of 1,000 men and won permission to found his own fortified settlement at Chuguev on the Donets River. The Chuguev colony broke up in 1652 when Ostrianyn's regiment, angered at harassment at the hands of Muscovite officials and swayed by Polish propaganda, mutinied against him and returned to Ukraine. Nonetheless the Chuguev experiment established an important precedent: resettling Ukrainian cossacks en masse in the tsar's service but in their own self-governing regimental colonies on the steppe dozens of kilometers south of the Belgorod Line.

The Khmel'nyts'kyi Revolt and then the Thirteen Years' War brought other Ukrainian cossack regiments over into Muscovite service, and rather than break them up and try to find room for them in the garrisons along the Belgorod Line it came to make more strategic sense to use them to found forward garrisons on the steppe below the Line. A region called Sloboda Ukraine was designated for this, a forward wedge of steppe running from Valuiki and from Akhtyrka south to Izium and the former site of Tsarevborisov. Thus when Colonel I. N. Dzikovsky came over from Chernigov in 1652 with a regiment of 883 cossacks and requested to settle on the Bitiug steppe south of Voronezh he was instructed instead to settle his regiment in Sloboda Ukraine at the new garrison of Ostrogozhsk near the Tikhaia Sosna. Later that year Gerasim Kondrat'ev's regiment was settled at Sumy. Ukrainian military colonists were likewise established at Kharkov in 1654 and Saltov in 1659 and with Muscovite servicemen revived Tsarevborisov in 1656.[37]

The alternative to defection and emigration to Muscovy – convincing the tsar to intervene in Ukraine – became feasible only from the late 1640s.

In the 1620s and early 1630s certain Ukrainian Orthodox bishops and two successive metropolitans, Iov Boretsky and Isaia Kopynsky, had concluded that the outlawing of their church left them with no choice but to begin invoking the principles of ethnic and especially religious solidarity to convince the tsar to place the Orthodox population of Ukraine under his protection. Boretsky, in a 1624 letter to Tsar Mikhail, compared himself to Benjamin, supplicant younger brother to Joseph, a simile that would later take on a significance greater than Boretsky had anticipated, as justification for considering Ukraine itself "Little Rus'," junior brother to Muscovite Great Rus'.

While Orthodox Ukrainians in Boretsky's time undoubtedly felt some religious affinity with Muscovites and some respect for the tsar as the only independent Orthodox sovereign, the notion of affinity so strong as to necessitate political union was not yet widely held. It would take another three decades of propaganda work by the bishops and even deeper cossack estrangement from Polish authority before it would be seriously entertained by a large part of Ukrainian society. Getting the Muscovite tsar and patriarch to recognize their obligations to protect the Ukrainian Orthodox people was also a long struggle, for the Muscovite church after the Troubles was inclined towards "self-isolation, suspicion, and vigilance towards the surrounding world" and reluctant to recognize that Ukrainian subjects of the Polish-Lithuanian Commonwealth could be true Orthodox at all.[38] Muscovites had suffered recent humiliations at Ukrainian cossack hands – during the Troubles, in subsequent raids on the southern frontier, and most recently during the Smolensk War. In Muscovite discourse in the 1630s Ukrainians were still *litovtsy* or *liakhy* (Lithuanians, Poles), or *cherkasy* if they were cossacks, but they were not yet considered *russkie* (Russians), despite the rhetoric from Ukrainian churchmen on the shared ethnopolitical and religious heritage of Little Rus' and Great Rus'.

Appeals to religious filiality were therefore not enough; convincing the tsar to intervene required that he be made to see real strategic gain from it and minimal risk. Moscow was indeed closely following events in Ukraine, and by the 1620s there were some circles in the government (boyar I. B. Cherkasskii, secretary Ivan Gramotin) already considering the possible gains and risks of intervention. But at the time Muscovy was far from ready to go to war against the Poles. When Muscovy was finally ready – in 1632, for the recovery of Smolensk – the Ukrainian cossacks "betrayed" her by campaigning for Wladyslaw in exchange for his promise to legalize the Orthodox church. The deposition of Metropolitan Kopynsky further muffled Ukrainian Orthodox propaganda appealing for Muscovite intervention, for his successor, Petro Mohyla, favored cooperation with the King and negotiations to reunite the Orthodox and Uniate churches (on terms favoring the former) rather than rapprochement with Moscow.

Bohdan Khmel'nyts'kyi's revolt

In December 1647 a feud with the Polish vice-*starosta* of Chyhyryn drove Bohdan Khmel'nyts'kyi, a captain in the Chyhyryn cossack regiment, to take refuge with the Zaporozhian Sich. Rather than distrusting him as a privileged registered cossack of the Settled Lands, the Zaporozhians elected Khmel'nyts'kyi as their hetman. Many years before he had been demoted to captain from colonel because of his suspected sympathy for the rebels of 1638; but he also had some credibility at Warsaw, having been included among cossack representatives invited to negotiate with King Władysław IV in 1646. His leadership therefore appeared useful to the Zaporozhians' plan to threaten revolt in order to press the King to accommodation on cossack rights and the rights of the Orthodox church. As in the past, this revolt was meant to target the magnate landowners like Jeremi Wiśniowiecki and the *starosta* administration, not the Crown itself. It initially intended to teach the King he could save the Commonwealth by defending his cossacks against the *korolev'iata*, the "marchlord kinglets" who had usurped his power in Ukraine for their own selfish purposes.[39]

At first Khmel'nyts'kyi had only a few hundred followers and the king assumed they could be dealt with as in the past – encouraged to win his gratitude by taking to sea and making boat raids against the Crimean Tatar and Ottoman domains. But this newest cossack insurgency was qualitatively different, for the last two decades of religious propaganda had evidently prepared the Zaporozhians to consider more than the traditional independence of their own host and to identify themselves with the cossacks, townsmen, and peasants of the Settled Lands. They would not take to the sea for the king, for their duty was to fight in Ukraine for the defense of the Orthodox faith, which they considered in mortal danger from the Uniate Church imposed by the Poles. The psychology of religious war was in fact about to turn Khmel'nyts'kyi's cossack rebellion into a general Ukrainian revolution uniting Sich and Settled Lands, cossacks and Ukrainian petty nobles, and peasants and townsmen against Polish domination.

Bohdan Khmel'nyts'kyi's revolt also differed from past rebellions in that its strategy depended from the start on military alliance with the Crimean Tatars. Khmel'nyts'kyi realized that without an alliance with the Khanate his army might be crushed between the Commonwealth and Crimean Tatar armies; but in alliance with the Tatars it could achieve overwhelming numerical superiority over the enemy.

Khan Ismail Girei III had reason to accept such an alliance proposal. There was famine in Crimea and factional strife among his nobles, but Sultan Ibrahim was denying them plunder opportunities by forbidding them to attack the Poles and Muscovites, demanding instead they assemble in Rumelia for operations elsewhere. By accepting Khmel'nyts'kyi's alliance offer the Khan could placate his nobles with the opportunity to plunder under ideal circumstances – with the approval and protection of the cossacks, on their own territory. The Khan himself would gain the opportunity to punish the Poles for their own recent attacks upon Crimea; he could demonstrate again how important his own mediation was to the balance of power in Eastern Europe, and assert for some greater independence from his Ottoman suzerain; and he could require Khmel'nyts'kyi to restrain the Zaporozhians and deter the Don Cossacks from raiding Crimea.

In March 1648 Khmel'nyts'kyi traveled to the Crimea, quickly negotiated an alliance with the Khan, and, leaving his son behind as hostage, returned to the Sich with several thousand Tatars under the command of *Bey* Tugai Shirin. Sultan Mehmet IV would sanction this Crimean–Cossack alliance in August.[40]

Tugai Shirin's Tatars played a significant role in Khmel'nyts'kyi's first great victories over Polish forces: at Zhevty Vody (22 April 1648), Korsun (15–16 May), and Pyliavtsi (11–13 September). The Polish hetmans' armies were smashed and the death of Władysław IV left it uncertain as to when they would be rebuilt and who would command them. Jeremi Wiśniowiecki and his private army were driven across the Dnepr. The cossack rebellion ignited in Zaporozhia now spread across Ukraine as far west as the Bug. A cossack-led insurgency also broke out in southern Lithuania in emulation. In the autumn Khmel'nyts'kyi's forces levied a contribution upon L'viv and turned northward against Warsaw itself. Not only the defeats of Polish forces but the spread of the insurrection probably owed a great deal to Tugai Shirin's Tatars, for many inhabitants who might otherwise have stood aside from the revolt may have elected to support it to spare themselves Tatar raiding as a punishment.

Despite these cossack victories the Muscovite government saw no reason yet to intervene militarily in Ukraine. In early 1649 Khmel'nyts'kyi made his first serious attempt to recruit the tsar as ally by sending Patriarch Paisios of Jerusalem and Colonel Syluian Muzhylovsky to Moscow – Paisios to make the argument for honoring Orthodox religious solidarity, Muzhylovsky to propose that if the tsar invaded the Seversk region he would "recover" this territory for Muscovy while protecting the new Hetmanate's northern flank against the Lithuanians. But Moscow was not interested in breaking armistice with the Commonwealth at this time; the passing of Władysław IV (May 1648) seemed to present an opportunity to negotiate a Polish–Muscovite alliance against the Crimean Tatars (Adam Kysil was proposing such alliance in hope of pressing the khan to abandon Khmel'nyts'kyi), or perhaps even for the election of Tsar Aleksei to the Polish throne; there was the possibility the cossack revolt might yet fail; and above all Moscow remained uneasy about Khmel'nyts'kyi's alliance with the Crimean Tatars and his oath of fealty to the sultan. Khmel'nyts'kyi appeared unable to control his Tatar allies, for the khan had accepted Polish bribes and lifted his siege of Zbarazh, forcing Khmel'nyts'kyi to accept an unfavorable armistice with the Poles (signed at Zboriv in mid-August), and Tatar *chambuly* had ceased raiding Polish-controlled territory and were now taking most of their human plunder from Khmel'nyts'kyi's Hetmanate. Khmel'nyts'kyi was not in the position to protest this lest his alliance with the Tatars collapse altogether. He still needed their aid, for the Zboriv Armistice was unpopular with his colonels and unlikely to last and he needed Tatar detachments to station near Ukrainian towns of questionable loyalty to the Hetmanate.[41]

Under these circumstances it was not difficult for Moscow to imagine Khmel'nyts'kyi's dependency on the Tatars eventually pressuring him to join the khan in attacks on southern Muscovy or at least leaving him unable to stop such attacks. The khan and the sultan were already protesting Don Cossack raids on their territory and had put Khmel'nyts'kyi on notice they expected him to deter such Don Cossack raids or even undertake retaliatory attack on the Don Host as the price for their continued friendship. Moscow was alarmed by reports that Khmel'nyts'kyi's son Demka was camping on the Mius' River with 5–6,000 men, awaiting Tatar reinforcements before attacking the Don Cossack settlement at Cherkassk, as well as by intelligence suggesting Tatar forces might attack out of Ukraine and circumvent the Belgorod Line. The khan and his mirzas

> cannot in any way pass across the steppe with an army to attack the Sovereign's Borderland towns, because a strong wall has been erected and deep ditches dug, and many towns have been built behind the wall and many troops established in the towns. But when the khan's sons go with troops to Hetman Bohdan Khmel'nyts'kyi, to aid him against the

Poles ... [they] can attack the Sovereign's Borderland towns from the Lithuanian side.[42]

After the Zboriv treaty Polish diplomats made some effort at negotiating an anti-Muscovite military alliance with the Khanate – probably not with the expectation such an alliance really could be achieved, but with the intent of deterring the Muscovites from intervening in Ukrainian affairs and undermining Khmel'nyts'kyi's efforts to strengthen his own alliance with the khan. These efforts were for awhile (summer–autumn 1650) successful in convincing Khan Islam Girei III he would be supported in a war against Muscovy by a coalition comprising the Poles, Khmel'nyts'kyi's cossacks, the Nogais, and perhaps even the Swedes. The *Sejm* then voted to renounce the Zboriv armistice, raise a gentry levy, and enlarge the Quarter Army for an invasion of the Hetmanate.

In spring 1651 King Jan Kazimierz led an unusually large Polish army into Bratslav and Volhynia while Lithuanian Grand Hetman Janusz Radziwiłł prepared to march on Kiev from the north. In June the king's army crushed the cossacks at Berestechko, a victory made possible by the flight of the 50,000 Tatars entrusted with defending the cossacks' left flank. Radziwiłł's forces took Kiev on 25 July. The subsequent outbreak of partisan resistance in Bratslav palatinate blocked the king's further advance and forced Radziwiłł to withdraw from Kiev to rendezvous with the king at Pavoloch, and in September Khmel'nyts'kyi won a great victory at Bila Tserkva. But if the military situation at the end of 1651 could be called a stalemate, the political situation was more clearly one of setback for Khmel'nyts'kyi: the armistice signed at Bila Tserkva on 18 September cut back the cossack register and restored Bratslav and Chernigov to the Commonwealth, reducing the territory of the Hetmanate to Kiev palatinate.[43]

The decision to intervene

Despite its distrust of Khmel'nyts'kyi and doubts about his prospects for success, the Muscovite government could not afford to close the door altogether on negotiations for alliance with him. It was important that it indicate its readiness to continue such talks at least as a means of countering Polish efforts to push the Ukrainians and Crimean Tatars against Muscovy.

Hence Tsar Aleksei suddenly became more truculent towards the Polish crown and *Sejm* in 1650. The tsar had now chosen to cast recent Polish breaches of protocol (omission of certain of his titles, the publication in some recent books of insults to his honor) as affronts so grave as to threaten the peace signed at Polianovka in 1634. He demanded a compensation of 500,000 złoties and the execution of Wiśniowiecki and other slanderers of his honor. He even insisted upon the return of Smolensk if peace was to be preserved. He threatened the Poles with the prospect of a Muscovite–Swedish military alliance, and he reminded the king "the Ukrainian Hetman has petitioned the Grand Sovereign to take him, with all the towns, under his lofty hand, as the Zaporozhian Ukrainians' Orthodox faith is perpetually persecuted and mortally endangered by Your Highness and the Commonwealth." In February 1651 the tsar convened a Church Council and an Assembly of the Realm to discuss these affronts as well as the charge that King Jan Kazimierz was conspiring with the Crimean khan to invade Muscovy. The tsar's report to these councils noted that Bohdan Khmel'nyts'kyi and the entire Zaporozhian Host had asked to be received as his vassals, and it asked the councils to advise as to whether these circumstances warranted the breaking of the Polianovka peace. The Church Council agreed that they did; the response of the Assembly of the Realm is not known.

This did not mean the tsar had decided to ally with Khmel'nyts'kyi and go to war against the Commonwealth; rather his actions aimed at showing the Poles he would not be intimidated. In March 1652, when Khmel'nyts'kyi's envoy Iskra asked the tsar to take the Zaporozhian Host under protection, Tsar Aleksei answered he was prepared only to allow the Host to resettle on Muscovite territory along the Donets and Medveditsa and other parts of the steppe.

It was only in February 1653 that Tsar Aleksei decided to accept alliance with the Hetmanate and prepare for war against the Commonwealth.[44] Four developments appear to have led him to this decision.

After the signing of the Bila Tserkva Treaty in September 1651 Khmel'nyts'kyi had come under greater pressure to offer Muscovy not only military alliance but some form of political union (*edinoe derzhavtsvo*). He recognized his treaty with the Poles was unlikely to stand for very long; its harsh terms were already provoking unrest among the rank-and-file cossacks, peasantry, and townsmen, so that he would have to resume war with the king if he was to remain in power as hetman; yet past experience showed that going back to war with the Crimean Tatars as his only significant allies would inevitably leave him abandoned and betrayed again. Meanwhile his secretary Ivan Vyhovs'kyi was conducting his own correspondence with Moscow, presenting himself as the real architect of the Host's diplomacy and zealous spokesman for the tsar's interests in Ukraine. The tsar could not afford to pass up this opportunity to secure the Zaporozhian Host as his subjects, Vyhovs'kyi wrote, for "many people" were urging Khmel'nyts'kyi to pledge instead formal vassalage to the Ottoman sultan and permanent alignment with the khan, making it all the more likely the hetman would then be forced to join the Tatars in attacks on southern Muscovy. But if the tsar acted quickly to offer Ukraine military assistance this could be avoided and Vyhovs'kyi would even be able to restrain the khan from retaliating against Muscovy because the khan knew all too well Vyhovs'kyi was the real power in the Zaporozhian Host.[45] Vyhovs'kyi's letters appear to have made much impression on Moscow.

In late 1651 Khmel'nyts'kyi wrote again promising Tsar Aleksei he would immediately abandon his alliance with the Crimean khan if the tsar would "take the Zaporozhian Host under His lofty hand." The questioning given envoy Samuilo Bogdanovich by boyar G. G. Pushkin and the secretaries of the

Ambassadors' Chancellery suggested that the hetman had not yet specified the terms of such protectorate. Bogdanovich was asked, "How and by what means are Hetman Khmel'nyts'kyi and the whole Zaporozhian Host to be under His Sovereign's lofty hand? And where are they to reside: there, in their towns, or somewhere else? What have you been instructed about this?" He had to reply that he did not know, as the hetman had not instructed him on this matter.[46] This suggested Khmel'nyts'kyi had not yet decided upon the specific terms of protectorate and they could still be negotiated to greater advantage for Muscovy.

The second development was the autocratization of Khmel'nyts'kyi's power as hetman. His compromise at Bila Tserkva, his costly adventure in Moldavia, and his inability to protect his own people against Tatar raiding had done much to alienate the Ukrainian townsmen and gentry and the cossack rank-and-file. There was growing dissatisfaction in the Sich, in the original Zaporozhian Host, which resented its eclipse by the new Hetmanate which had borrowed its name. Because Khmel'nyts'kyi was unable to secure any lasting truce with the Poles his need to maintain a constant war footing and maximum unity of command made him loath to submit decision-making to general councils of cossacks, so he tended all the more to decide policy just with Vyhovs'kyi and his entourage – even consultations with councils of his colonels were becoming less frequent. Khmel'nyts'kyi had greater need now to legitimate his power as a divinely elected sovereign, which required recognition of his sovereignty not only by the metropolitan of Kiev (who was stinting in such propaganda, still hoping for reconciliation with Warsaw) but also by Patriarch Nikon at Moscow. This suggested, first, that Khmel'nyts'kyi had greater reason to endorse and adopt the idea of religious filial duty propagated by Ukrainian churchmen – perhaps even to the point of accepting its recasting by the Patriarch as the duty of submission of the younger Little Russian brother – and second, that Muscovite diplomats were now free to work out the concrete terms of alliance and political union with Khmel'nyts'kyi and his secretary Vyhovs'kyi alone and did not need to risk presenting them for discussion by Ukrainian cossackdom as a whole.[47]

The third development inclining Tsar Aleksei to accept Khmel'nyts'kyi's offer of political union was the breakdown of the Bila Tserkva Treaty. The deaths of Chancellor Jerzy Ossoliński (1650) and royal commissioner Adam Kysil (spring 1653) had left Poland's Ukraine policy in the hands of warhawks uninterested in pursuing any further rapprochement with Khmel'nyts'kyi or preserving the armistice. The *Sejm* had never ratified the Bila Tserkva treaty, viewing its terms as too generous and forgiving. In early spring a Polish army of 15,000 men under Stefan Czarniecki suddenly invaded the Hetmanate, burning ten towns and killing thousands; at the same time other Polish forces joined the Wallachian Hospodar Matei Basarab and Transylvanian Prince Gyorgy II Rakoczy in defeating Khmel'nyts'kyi's project of placing his son Tymysh on the throne of Moldavia. By the time boyar B. A. Repnin arrived in Warsaw (April 1653) to deliver a final ultimatum from the tsar it was obvious the Poles were not inclined to offer any significant concessions to keep Muscovy out of the war; if the tsar wanted the Poles to offer him a pretext for war, it was now possible to obtain it. The Repnin mission therefore repeated the tsar's demand for punishment of those who had insulted his honor and demanded as well that King Jan Kazimierz renegotiate peace with the Hetmanate on the more liberal original terms of the Zboriv Treaty, dissolve the Uniate Church, and guarantee the rights of the Orthodox church in Ukraine. In June the king refused these terms and issued his own ultimatum for the Zaporozhian Host to overthrow Khmel'nyts'kyi, lay down its arms, and request amnesty.

The collapse of the Bila Tserkva peace signaled to Moscow that Khmel'nyts'kyi would now be desperate for military assistance from abroad and ready to concede more politically for it; but it also suggested Muscovite diplomats had to move quickly to guarantee his alliance would be with the tsar and not with the Ottoman sultan. The danger that the Hetmanate might become an Ottoman protectorate seemed real enough. Although troubled by Khmel'nyts'kyi's meddling in Moldavian affairs, Sultan Mehmet IV was pressing Khmel'nyts'kyi to formally accept vassalage, seeing this as a way to detach from the Commonwealth the strategically valuable Podolian borderland and thereby secure Moldavia against Polish as well as cossack adventurism; and Khan Islam Girei III was insisting upon it too, as the price for full Crimean Tatar military support.

The final consideration inclining Tsar Aleksei to war was the destabilization of Lithuania, which seemed to offer him the opportunity to finally recover Smolensk and the other western territories lost in 1618. The outbreak of Khmel'nyts'kyi's rebellion in Ukraine had immediately inspired uprisings by townsmen, peasants, and newly cossackized elements in Brest, Gomel', Minsk, Mogilev, Bykhov, and other districts in Lithuanian Belarus'. Detachments of Ukrainian cossacks had entered Lithuania to try to link up these insurgencies with Khmel'nyts'kyi's operations. King Jan Kazimierz had entrusted the task of suppressing these revolts and launching a counteroffensive into northern Ukraine to Janusz Radziwiłł, Lithuanian Grand Hetman and Palatine of Vilnius. But Radziwill was expected to accomplish this with comparatively small forces – a few thousand Lithuanian gentry militia and German mercenaries. The fighting in Lithuania had been especially savage, and although Radziwiłł managed to take most of the rebel strongholds by the summer of 1651 he was never able to completely pacify the region, so that fear of renewed rebellion in his army's rear kept him from sending it into northern Ukraine for extended operations. Furthermore, Radziwiłł, a Calvinist, was a fervid opponent of Polish "military absolutism" and sought to expand his family's power in Lithuania at the crown's expense; it was at his instigation that the *liberum veto* was first used to paralyze the *Sejm*; and it was therefore of considerable interest to Moscow that Radziwill began forming a peace party in February 1653 and that Khmel'nyts'kyi had obtained letters Radziwiłł had sent to the Wallachian hospodar expressing his anxiety that the king's war with the hetman could leave the Commonwealth vulnerable to Swedish invasion.[48] This intelligence identified the most effective way of assisting Khmel'nyts'kyi, then: directing the larger part of Muscovite forces against Lithuania, the Commonwealth's most vulnerable region, defeat of which would then restore to the tsar Smolensk, Seversk, and the lands of west Rus'. Khmel'nyts'kyi's cossacks had been operating in Lithuania from 1648 with the purpose of bringing their insurgency to the Orthodox population of west Rus', so there was good precedent for requiring Khmel'nyts'kyi support Muscovite army operations in west Rus' in return for assistance in Ukraine.

On 22 June 1653 Tsar Aleksei sent *stol'nik* Lodyzhenskii to Chyhyryn to notify Hetman Khmel'nyts'kyi he had decided to place Ukraine under his protection and was readying his army for war: "We have deigned to take you under the lofty hand of Our Tsarist Majesty so that you may not be a proverb and a byword to the enemies of the cross of Christ." The hetman responded on 9 August, gratefully accepting the tsar's offer, reassuring him the Ukrainians desired to serve no other sovereign, and expressing hope that the Muscovite army would arrive soon. On 17 August, in talks with Moscow's envoy Fomin, Khmel'nyts'kyi and Vyhovs'kyi reportedly agreed to place Ukraine under the tsar's hand "in eternal servitude" (*vechnoe kholopstvo*). Khmel'nyts'kyi also announced he would send appeals to the Orthodox of Orsha, Mstislavl', and other districts to rise up against Lithuanian rule and aid the coming Muscovite campaign in Belarus'. On 1 October the Boyar Duma and the Assembly of the Realm heard the report of Warsaw's rebuff of Repnin's final appeal and quickly assented to "undertake war against the Polish king ... and receive the Zaporozhian Host with its towns and lands." They approved the tsar's choice of Vasilii Buturlin to head a mission to Ukraine to arrange the terms of protectorate.[49] On 6 January 1654 Buturlin began negotiating protectorate and union with Khmel'nyts'kyi and his officers at Pereiaslav. On 8 January their agreement was presented to a general assembly (*rada*) of cossacks for acclamation. Moscow's ratification of the agreement was announced on 21 March. The territory of the Hetmanate thereby came under the tsar's protection: Kiev, Bratslav, and Chernigov palatinates, part of Volhynia, and the Starodub region in Belarus' (at the time claimed for the hetman). The tsar recognized a cossack register of 60,000 men in ten territorial regiments on the Right Bank and seven regiments on the Left Bank. Envoys from Moscow subsequently visited 117 towns and villages in the Hetmanate and administered the oath of allegiance to 127,000 adult male cossacks, petty nobles, townsmen, and churchmen.[50]

Thus Tsar Aleksei's decision to take the Hetmanate under protection and break the Polianovka peace with the Commonwealth was based on perceptions of particular short-term advantages without sufficient consideration of their longer-term outcomes. It assumed that Lithuanian west Rus' could be quickly seized and held and that this in turn would give the Muscovite–Ukrainian alliance such preponderance of strength the Polish king would have to abandon his attempts to reconquer Ukraine. It assumed that announcement of the Muscovite–Ukrainian alliance would frustrate the sultan and the Crimean khan but that they could be induced to resign themselves to it, that Khmel'nyts'kyi and Vyhovs'kyi would have the diplomatic skill to maintain their alliance with the khan or at least secure the khan's neutrality. It also assumed that political union as Moscow understood it would be accepted by the Ukrainians and this consensus would not be significantly altered by the circumstances of the coming war.

The consequences of the Pereiaslav Agreement

Khan Islam Girei III had not been left ignorant of Khmel'nyts'kyi's negotiations with Moscow over the course of 1653 and had already warned the hetman his attempts to ally with the Muscovites could provoke retaliation by the Khanate in alliance with the Commonwealth. The possibility the khanate might switch sides and ally with the Poles seemed all the more real after December 1653, when Islam Girei suddenly suspended operations against the Poles and signed a separate peace with them at Zhvanets in return for the king's promise to resume tribute gifts. By February 1654 there were reports the khan was seeking approval from the sultan and military support from Moldavia, Wallachia, and the Lesser Nogais for an attack on the Hetmanate. After the formal announcement of the Pereiaslav Agreement in March 1654 Moscow sent envoys to Bakhchisarai to try to reassure the khan the new Muscovite–Ukrainian alliance in no way aimed at abrogating their peace with the Khanate. But the Polish envoy M. Jaskulski was already at work persuading the khan to accept King Jan Kazimierz's offer of military alliance against Muscovy and the Hetmanate. For the time being Islam Girei dealt cautiously with both sides. He inclined towards accepting Jaskulski's proposal, but his nobles were divided on the issue; his army was not ready for war, having lost many of its mounts to recent famine; he was not yet sure he could send the bulk of his army into Ukraine and simultaneously protect his domains against raids by Zaporozhian and Don cossacks; and he still needed to secure the sultan's approval. Islam Girei's death in July further postponed Crimean Tatar mobilization. The new khan, Mehmet IV, issued a final ultimatum calling on Khmel'nyts'kyi to break off with Moscow and make peace with the king. Finally on 22 November 1654 Khan Mehmet IV accepted the Polish offer of military alliance. But Kamil Mehmet Girei, perhaps deterred by the tsar's Belgorod Line, told the Muscovite envoys his army was mobilizing only to punish the Ukrainians and would not attack the tsar's border towns as long as the tsar continued paying tribute and restraining the Don Cossacks. For the time being the tsar did not have to worry about engaging Ottoman forces, either, for although the sultan approved the new Crimean–Polish alliance he was too preoccupied with his war in Dalmatia to commit any troops to the Ukrainian theater.[51]

But this respite was brief. By autumn 1655 Muscovy was embroiled in war with the Crimean Khanate, the khan – and the sultan as well – having taken alarm at the dramatic Muscovite military successes in Lithuania and the sudden Swedish invasion of Poland, which threatened to destroy the Commonwealth altogether and overturn the balance of power in Eastern Europe.

Furthermore, the political union established by the Pereiaslav Agreement was unstable from the start, for the Ukrainian and Muscovite negotiators had brought to Pereiaslav very different understandings of the character of political union, the Agreement had not clarified and settled these differences, and its vagueness encouraged both sides to try to revise union terms unilaterally according to military and political convenience.

Pereiaslav may not even have produced a treaty in the formal sense. The documentation surviving from the Pereiaslav talks is limited to envoy Buturlin's report to Moscow, Khmel'nyts'kyi's proposed terms – the twenty-three "Articles of Petition" delivered to Moscow in early March – and the responding "March Articles" issued by the tsar later in the month. A number of Ukrainain historians have argued that the original text of the tsar's March Articles was suppressed and these articles doctored in 1659 by Kiev *voevoda* A. N. Trubetskoi to revise terms of union to Muscovy's advantage. Even Khmel'nyts'kyi's Articles of Petition might have been doctored, they argue, as their only surviving variant is in a Russian translation made at Moscow.[52]

The long-term objective of the Kiev metropolitans had been the institutional confessionalization of the Ukrainian Orthodox Church, while for Hetman Khmel'nyts'kyi and his colonels, it had been the construction of an autonomous cossack state confirming cossacks' "ancient rights and privileges" as a knightly nobility. The Hetman saw himself as protector of the sovereignty of a strengthened Ukrainian Orthodox Church headed by the Metropolitan of Kiev, and expected the Church to legitimate him as a divinely elected Sovereign in return. Over the course of the Ukrainian Revolt military and diplomatic exigencies had worked to undermine the principle of cossack *krug* "democracy" and render the power of Hetman Khmel'nyts'kyi more effectively autocratic. This in turn had allowed Khmel'nyts'kyi to conduct an imaginative and wide-ranging diplomacy establishing temporary foreign alliances (Crimean, Moldavian, Muscovite, Swedish) that had been crucial on several occasions in safeguarding the new Ukrainian state.

Under these circumstances it was unlikely that the Ukrainian Orthodox Church would willingly embrace a political union leading to its full absorption into the Muscovite Patriarchate. The rhetoric from Ukrainian churchmen suggests, rather, that they saw the Pereiaslav Agreement as securing the tsar's protection over the Kiev Metropolitanate in accordance with his duty to defend the Orthodox faith. They expected this protection to preserve their church's privileges and liberties, and for this reason they spoke of the prestige of Kiev as the symbol of the original unity of Orthodoxy and of Rus'.

Nor was it likely that Hetman Khmel'nyts'kyi would volunteer to surrender his hard-won sovereignty to become a *kholop* of the tsar. More probably he expected political union to strengthen his authority – by giving him the military assistance needed to consolidate Ukraine's independence from the Commonwealth, but also by winning the Moscow Patriarch's recognition of his own patronage power over the Ukrainian Church, thereby securing the Ukrainian

Church's legitimation of his sovereignty and guaranteeing that the Hetman's headquarters at Chyhyryn rather than the Metropolitan's court at Kiev would become the true capital of the independent Ukrainian state. In exchange for sacrificing some freedom to conduct an independent foreign policy the hetman would receive Muscovite military protection against his enemies and, thereby, support for the construction of a viable Ukrainian cossack state. The Hetmanate's relationship with Muscovy would be that of a *protegé* regime.

The model of political union most familiar to Khmel'nyts'kyi and Vyhovs'kyi would have been the 1569 Union of Lublin joining the Grand Duchy of Lithuania and the Kingdom of Poland – an act of federation that Lithuanians considered preserved the separate sovereignty of their Grand Duchy. Their expectations of the consequences of vassalage to a foreign sovereign were likely shaped by the examples of the Danubian gospodars, whom the Ottoman sultans allowed fairly significant autonomy in domestic affairs. And in offering to place Ukraine under the tsar's lofty hand the closest precedent to guide them would have been the Commonwealth's elective monarchy, to which the *Sejm* had elected foreign princes (an Anjou, a Bathory, Vasas) prevented by constitutional contract from exercising absolute dominion or annexing the Commonwealth to their foreign patrimonies.[53]

However, Moscow, while endorsing the discourse of Rus' unity issuing from Ukrainian church and cossack leaders, revealed at the Pereiaslav talks its intention of reinterpreting that discourse to its own advantage. The cossack colonels, for example, expected Buturlin to give his own oath that the tsar would honor the terms of the agreement, as Adam Kysil and other representatives of the Polish king would have done; but Buturlin refused, replying that this was not Muscovite custom: he was merely the bondsman of the autocratic tsar, commissioned to communicate the tsar's will. Khmel'nyts'kyi's Articles of Petition expected the tsar to recognize the Ukrainian hetman's right to continue conducting his own foreign policy, with the sole qualification that the hetman would keep the tsar informed of major developments; but the tsar's March Articles responded that the hetman did not have the right to treat with the Polish king or Ottoman sultan without the tsar's permission. Khmel'nyts'kyi's Articles of Petition tried to restrict Muscovite *voevody* and garrisons to Kiev and Chernigov and stipulated the *voevody* were not to interfere in civil and judicial administration in those towns, except perhaps to offer hearings on appeal; the tsar's March Articles confirmed the Ukrainian towns' right to elected self-government under Magdeburg law but did not explicitly affirm any limit to the number of *voevody* the tsar could station in Ukrainian towns nor any limitation on their authority. Already by February 1654 Tsar Aleksei was essentially asserting his own dynastic patrimonial claim to Ukraine by taking the titles of Autocrat of Little and Great Rus' and Prince of Kiev and Chernigov in rescripts issued to Ukrainian towns.[54]

The next five years of war would give Moscow reason to further reduce the de facto autonomy of the Hetmanate. Muscovite garrisons and *voevody* would be established in other Ukrainian towns and Muscovite taxes and levies introduced for their maintenance. The perceived imperatives of *voevoda* military administration would increasingly conflict with the traditional liberties of these towns. Khmel'nyts'kyi's expectations that southern Belarus' would be united with his hetmanate rather than with the tsar's domains would be frustrated. Moscow would exert greater pressure to limit his right to conduct an independent foreign policy on the grounds that it hindered the tsar's own diplomatic flexibility, especially vis-à-vis Sweden. Representatives of the Hetmanate would not be included in the 1656 peace talks at Vilnius, where the Muscovites suddenly signed armistice with the Poles in order to redirect their armies against the Swedes. This in turn would so alienate the cossack *starshina* and rank-and-file that many of them would follow Vyhovs'kyi in re-allying with the Crimean Tatars and seeking reunion with the Commonwealth and the expulsion of Muscovite troops from the Ukraine. Ukrainian and Muscovite leaders would thereby come to view each other as irredeemably perfidious. "To what sovereign have the cossacks not appealed? To whom have they not submitted – and then betrayed?" wrote Prince Grigorii Kozlovskii in 1659.[55]

CHAPTER FOUR

The Ukrainian quagmire

The Thirteen Years' War: the first phase, 1654–1657

On 15–18 May 1654 three Muscovite army groups invaded Lithuania. V. P. Sheremetev's Army Group North, about 15,000 men out of Novgorod, Pskov, and Velikie Luki, marched against Nevel', Polotsk, and Vitebsk; A. N. Trubetskoi's Army Group South, another 15,000 troops out of Briansk, advanced towards Mstislavl', Orsha, and Smolensk. The largest force, the 41,000-man Army Group Center, marching from Moscow against Dorogobuzh and Smolensk, consisted of Great, Vanguard, and Rear Guard corps under Ia. K. Cherkasskii, N. I. Odoevskii, and M. M. Temkin-Rostovskii and the elite Tsar's Corps under the personal command of Tsar Aleksei. Foreign formation cavalry and infantry comprised a large proportion of these forces, particularly in the Tsar's Corps, and Tsar Aleksei even had a regiment of Polish-model hussar lancers. The artillery taken into Lithuania reportedly exceeded 4,000 guns. Jakob Kettler, Duke of Courland, observed, "No one has such an army."[1] Hetman Khmel'nyts'kyi had also pledged Ukrainian troops for the campaign in Lithuania: Colonel I. N. Zolotarenko was to take 20,000 mounted and foot cossacks north through Starodub into Lithuania to occupy territory along the line Gomel'–Propoisk–Staryi Bykhov, support Army Group South, and protect the Hetmanate from Lithuanian counterattack.

The primary objective of this invasion was the recapture of Smolensk and the west Rus' territories ceded to the Grand Duchy twenty years before. Beyond this, the three army groups aimed at seizing other Lithuanian Belarus' domains north of the Western Dvina and Dnepr. The tsar's armies were remarkably successful in both missions in 1654: in June they took Belaia, Dorogobuzh, and Roslavl'; by August they held Mstislavl', Orsha, Mogilev, and the capital of the Grand Duchy at Vilnius; Smolensk fell to them in September, and Vitebsk in November.

One reason for Muscovy's initial success on the Lithuanian front was overwhelming numerical superiority. Counting Zolotarenko's cossacks the invaders numbered about 100,000 men, whereas the field army of Lithuanian Grand Hetman Radziwiłł had only about 6,000 men, a third of whom were *szlachta* levy cavalry of limited reliability. Most of the Lithuanian towns coming under siege had tiny garrisons: Smolensk's garrison was outnumbered 20:1, Staryi Bykhov's 17:1.[2] The Muscovites faced fewer obstacles to reinforcing their armies in Lithuania: new mobilizations did not require the approval of a *Sejm*, and their largest reservoirs of reinforcement manpower were much closer to the front (in the Novgorod-Pskov region, the districts around Moscow, the Briansk-Sevsk region) than was the case for Commonwealth forces. On the whole their logistic preparations had been sound. They used the Dnepr and Western Dvina to move their heavy guns and stores into the Lithuanian interior. Velikie Luki had already been prepared as a forward base and magazine for most of the invading corps; the middle service class troops had shipped their personal stores here in advance of the invasion, and about 3.9 million kg of state grain had been stored here in new barns for the foreign formation infantry and cavalry contingents.[3]

After the Battle of Shepeleviche in late August Radziwiłł's army no longer posed much threat to the Muscovite advance. Thereafter most of the fighting took the form of siege operations. Muscovite commanders tended to resort to heavy bombardments and storm assaults in order to bring sieges to a quick end so their armies could move on and take other underdefended towns deeper in the interior before the onset of winter. Their numerical superiority generally allowed them to absorb the heavy losses these tactics incurred.[4] Meanwhile political and strategic differences divided the Lithuanian high command. Grand Hetman Radziwiłł blamed King Jan Kazimierz for the invasion because he had not settled with Khmel'nyts'kyi when there had been the chance and had then failed to fund expansion of Lithuanian forces. By early 1655 Radziwiłł was in secret contact with the Swedes, trying to arrange a coup against the king as the only chance of stopping the Muscovite advance into Lithuania. But Field Hetman Wincenty Gosiewski and Pawel Sapieha preferred seeking truce with Muscovy to inviting in the Swedes.

By contrast Tsar Aleksei sought to enhance central control over Muscovite operations and reduce delays in decision-making by spending protracted periods (June–October 1654, March–September 1655) at the front as supreme commander. This was a significant departure from custom. Athough Ivan IV had twice accompanied the army on foreign soil (against Kazan' and Polotsk), his presence with the army had served largely symbolic functions. But Tsar Aleksei genuinely strove to serve as *generalissmus* while at the front, using his new personal secretariat (headed by Tomilo Perfil'ev) to process information from his commanders, issue instructions, and monitor commanders' performance. The tsar's personal secretariat largely took over from the Military Chancellery responsibility for directing troop movements and issuing battle orders, and by 1655 it had expanded its staff and emerged as a Privy Chancellery, the *Prikaz tainykh del*, with supervisory authority over the entire chancellery system as well as the army.

The tsar intended by his presence at front headquarters to discourage squabbling and precedence suits among corps commanders and improve coordination of operations. The working orders issued from the tsar's secretariat set objectives and general directions of movement but usually allowed field commanders to make their own decisions as to engaging the enemy.

Tsar Aleksei was bent on making himself a martial monarch in the style of Władysław IV or Gustav II Adolf, and he had intelligence, diligence, and attention to detail to help him towards this goal. But he was young and had no prior military experience – he knew military affairs from books and parade but had not before lived with the army in the field. He was also determinedly autocratizing, certain that he should and could make all the decisions of strategic and political importance. He was ever ready to tutor or even savagely rebuke his generals, threatening them with disgrace or even execution. Romodanovskii, one of his best generals, he excoriated as "thrice-damned and shameful hater of the Christian race, our faithful traitor, most true son of Satan and friend of devils." His command style therefore put even his most experienced corps commanders in an anxious state. At every turn they had to decide whether to keep to his injunction against any undertakings he had not explicitly authorized or to rise to his expectations that they show initiative in exploiting sudden opportunities. Even experienced commanders like V. P. Sheremetev sometimes found this pressure paralyzing.[5]

The war in Lithuania was an especially atrocious one. Part of the reason for this was that it was a war of sieges, some protracted and costly and provoking the besiegers to bloody reprisals against finally vanquished garrisons. But it was also due in part to deliberate policy, for Tsar Aleksei had embraced the spirit of religious crusade and had authorized Trubetskoi to execute Lithuanian or Belarus'ian prisoners who had refused surrender calls and refused to convert to Orthodoxy. Trubetskoi's corps massacred thousands at Amtsislavl' and Mstislavl'. Thousands of prisoners were taken back to Muscovy as slaves. On the eve of the war the population of Lithuanian Belarus' had stood at about 2.9 million; by war's end in 1667 it had been reduced to 1.35 million.[6]

The Lithuanian campaign also presented a special problem in requiring joint operations on an unprecedentedly large scale. Friction between Zolotarenko and the Muscovite commanders quickly developed as their strategic objectives began to diverge. Zolotarenko's 20,000 cossacks were successful in capturing Chechersk and Novyi Bykhov, but from July on the tsar's generals grew frustrated at his unwillingness to coordinate operations (to immediately reinforce them at Smolensk, for example), his calls on Belarus' town authorities to swear allegiance to the hetman rather than to the tsar, and his troops' practice of stripping for their headquarters at Staryi Bykhov grain, cattle, and mounts Russian commanders had hoped would provision their own forces at Smolensk and Mogilev. "I cannot serve alongside Zolotarenko here, I fear him more than the Poles," complained M. P. Voeikov (an officer) to Moscow.[7]

Operations in Ukraine in this period involved much smaller Muscovite forces than the fighting in Lithuania, reflecting the fact that the tsar gave the reconquest of Lithuanian West Rus' paramount importance and did not initially think

Khmel'nyts'kyi needed much Muscovite reinforcement to defend Ukraine. But the fighting in Ukraine would quickly make heavier demands upon Muscovite manpower and significantly affect the situation in Lithuania and Greater Poland.

In late spring 1654 Khmel'nyts'kyi's position in Ukraine appeared reasonably strong; he claimed to have 100,000 men under arms, and Polish operations against him were not yet supported by significant numbers of Tatars. Radziwiłł's army, trying to force its way south from Gomel' through Starodub to strike at Kiev, had been thrown back at Borodenets, about 30 km from Kiev, in March, and the Muscovite invasion of Lithuania in May substantially reduced Radziwiłł's ability to threaten the Hetmanate again from the north. Polish Crown Hetman Stanisław Potocki had failed in his drive eastward against Uman' and Bila Tserkva, had lost many of his 20,000 troops due to desertion, and had been forced to withdraw to Kamianets.[8] This freed Khmel'nyts'kyi to rest his forces in the Bila Tserkva/Fastov region just south of Kiev. Khmel'nyts'kyi's and Vyhovs'kyi's letters to Moscow at this point even expressed confidence the new Muscovite–Ukrainian alliance would inspire the hospodars of Moldavia and Wallachia to join them against the Commonwealth.

Moscow therefore saw no need to send great numbers of troops into Ukraine. It expected Khmel'nyts'kyi's army could afford to spare Zolotarenko's 20,000 cossacks for the Lithuanian campaign while still securing the Tatar invasion roads, protecting the western flank of the Belgorod Line, and throwing back any new Polish offensive from the west. The subsequent frustration of these unrealistic expectations would begin to feed distrust towards the hetman. For his part, Khmel'nyts'kyi already had cause for dissatisfaction with Moscow: the cash salaries the tsar had promised his cossacks sufficed to pay only a fifth of his army.

When the invasion of Lithuania began in May 1654 three Muscovite corps remained along the Belgorod Line to protect the southern borderland against Tatar attack. At Belgorod V. B. Sheremetev commanded a corps of a few thousand *deti boiarskie* and cossacks and 6,763 foreign formation infantry (the regiments of colonels Alexander Crawford, John Crawford, John Leslie, and George Goodson). At Karpov, F. V. Buturlin headed a second corps comprising several centuries of traditional formation cavalry, 568 Tula dragoons under Colonel Rafael Korsak, and 335 Don Cossacks. I. I. Romodanovskii's corps at Iablonov had orders to reinforce Sheremetev at Belgorod or Buturlin at Karpov upon alert.

A fourth southern corps – A. V. Buturlin's, based at Ryl'sk – was sent into Ukraine for joint operations with Khmel'nyts'kyi's army. This corps comprised just 3,950 Komaritskaia dragoons, 246 *deti boiarskie*, a few dozen cossacks, and some artillery. It arrived at Kiev on 19 June and rendezvoused with the hetman's army at Fastov on 11 July. Meanwhile Kiev was being garrisoned by roughly 2,000 *soldaty* and middle service cavalrymen under the command of F. S. Kurakin and F. F. Volkonskii. The total strength of Muscovite forces in Ukraine therefore did not much exceed 6,000 men. Moscow's expectation that A. V. Buturlin detach part of his command to reinforce A. N. Trubetskoi's corps near Lutsk in Lithuania was further indication of the secondary importance Moscow accorded the Ukrainian theater at this time. In fact Buturlin could not fulfill this order: his corps was already low on provisions and many of his dragoons had deserted. Kurakin's force garrisoning Kiev was also inadequate, for it had only twenty guns and had dilapidated fortifications to repair.[9]

Khmel'nyts'kyi likewise decided he could not afford to spare Ukrainian troops to reinforce Trubetskoi at Lutsk. Khan Mehmet Girei was still participating in peace talks with Muscovite and Ukrainian envoys, but only to play for time and prepare against expected Don Cossack and Kalmyk raids; power in the Khanate was once again in the hands of Vizier Sefer Gazy Aga, a long-term proponent of alliance with Poland, and there was intelligence out of Moldavia that the vizier and khan had already promised King Jan Kazimierz a spring 1655 invasion of Ukraine and southern Muscovy by 100,000 Tatar warriors. Small *chambuly* were already raiding between the Dnepr and Dnestr by mid-August. Furthermore, by late October Crown Hetman Potocki and Field Hetman Stanisław Lanckoroński had assembled a new army of 15,000 cavalry and 5,000 infantry near Bar for a new Polish offensive, and Crimean Tatar and Nogai warbands had begun crossing the Bug to rendezvous with them.[10] Khmel'nyts'kyi had to distribute some of his regiments across the Tatar invasion trails while leading the rest of his army (the Uman', Bratslav, Kal'nitsk, Bila Tserkva, and Kiev regiments) towards Korsun' to secure the Dnepr basin. A. V. Buturlin's understrength corps was to remain at Bila Tserkva and guard the approaches to Kiev.

Moscow finally recognized it needed additional troops in Ukraine and would have to take most of them from Sheremetev's corps at Belgorod. Initially it was thought this could be postponed until spring when the Don Cossack Host would be ready to make diversionary descants on the Crimean coast. But by late November Potocki and Lanckoronski had already pushed deep into Bratslav palatinate, forcing the Military Chancellery to send F. V. Buturlin's Karpov corps into Ukraine at once. John Leslie's and Alexander Crawford's infantry regiments were attached to it, giving Buturlin command over some 4–5,000 men in all; and about a week later V. B. Sheremetev was ordered to enter Ukraine with his Belgorod corps, now numbering about 9,000 men. These two corps joined A. V. Buturlin's corps at Bila Tserkva on 13 January.

By this time Potocki and Lanckoroński had rendezvoused with 30,000 Crimean Tatars under Kammambet Mirza and placed Uman' and Okhmativ under siege. A. V. Buturlin sent six squadrons of Christopher Graff's dragoons ahead to reinforce the 1,500 cossacks garrisoning Uman'. On 15 or 16 January Khmel'nyts'kyi's army and a large part of the Muscovite expeditionary army began moving south from Bila Tserkva to engage the enemy near Uman'. Potocki and Lanckoroński responded by leading the larger part of their army north to intercept them. Most of the Crimean Tatars remained in their rear, plundering the villages around Uman' and Okhmativ.

On 19 January 1655 the Ukrainian–Muscovite army (totaling about 25–32,000 men) set its wagon camp at Drizhipol'e, a few kilometers outside Stavishche. This was a vulnerable position on open, unwooded ground, without adequate water, and the troops were exposed to a harsh frost. Polish cavalry soon managed to break through Khmel'nyts'kyi's line of wagons and seize several guns but were beaten back when cossack cavalry under Colonel Bohun, just arriving from the recapture of Okhmativ, fell upon their rear; subsequent Polish assaults on the wagon camp, continuing through the twenty-first, were repulsed by Muscovite artillery fire. By the morning of 22 January it was clear the camp could no longer hold its ground, so it began evacuating as a *wagenburg*, moving slowly towards Okhmativ castle to join up with a cossack regiment under Pushkarenko. Polish cavalry attacks were unable to break up the *wagenburg*. One of the Polish commanders, Zamojski, opined that it could have been destroyed if Kammembet Mirza's Tatars had been sent against it; but they were off raiding in the rear. Potocki and Lanckoronski therefore decided to withdraw. The battle at Drizhipol'e had produced no clear victor.[11]

Khmel'nyts'kyi's army retired to Tetev, the Muscovite corps to Bila Tserkva. V. V. Buturlin did send some troops north into Belarus'; otherwise Muscovite forces in Ukraine remained in recuperation through the spring. But Drizhipol'e had also exhausted the Polish army. It had to abandon its drive upon Kiev and the Dnepr and return to the Bug, and Potocki and Lanckoronski laid down their commands, to be replaced by Krzysztof Tyszkiewicz, *wojewoda* of Chernigov, and Stefan Czarniecki, *wojewoda* of Kiev. Most of the Polish *szlachta* militia went home. Most of Kammambet Mirza's Tatars withdrew across the Bug, having taken enough plunder. In February the *kalga* Fetih Girei did bring into Ukraine a new Tatar army, reportedly exceeding 100,000 men, promising Tyszkiewicz his warriors would launch a new offensive against Khmel'nyts'kyi in June, but in the interval Tyszkiewicz permitted them to "feed" off some two dozen small towns and villages in Bratslav palatinate. Tatar requisitions of grain and livestock quickly degenerated into slaveraiding. By Tyszkiewicz's count, in just four months the *kalga*'s army took more than 200,000 captives, strangled some 10,000 children and dumped their bodies along the roadsides, and left 1,000 churches in ruins. Fetih Girei's plundering did much to undermine the Polish army's combat-readiness in Podolia and Bratslav by driving townsmen and peasants to flight – making it harder for Polish forces to obtain provisions – and by provoking other civilians to join the cossacks or form their own partisan detachments; and by March it had even become apparent the *kalga* was not going to honor his pledge of a June offensive, as two-thirds of his army were already en route back to Perekop with their prisoners and plunder. Meanwhile desertion had reduced Tyszkiewicz's own army to just 5,000 men; his cavalry was immobilized, the Tatars having rustled many of their mounts; and his artillery had no more than 100 rounds. In April cossack forces under colonels Bohun and Zelenetsky were able to regain control of much of Bratslav palatinate. The only significant Polish troop concentrations now were far off at Kamianets and L'viv.[12]

V. B. Sheremetev and F. V. Buturlin were recalled to Moscow. Vasilii Buturlin, one of the tsar's closest advisors, and Grigorii Romodanovskii replaced them at Bila Tserkva headquarters and the losses incurred at Drizhipol'e were partly offset by the arrival of 3,000 more troops transferred from Trubetskoi's corps campaigning in southern Belarus'. This gave them about 13–15,000 men: traditional formation cavalry, *strel'tsy*, foreign formation cavalry and infantry, and Chuvash and Cheremis irregulars. A. V. Buturlin's garrison at Kiev had another 3–4,000 men. The plan of campaign for summer 1655, devised in consultation with Khmel'nyts'kyi, called for Vasilii Buturlin and Grigorii Romodanovskii to join forces with Khmel'nyts'kyi and push southwest across Bratslav palatinate towards Lanckoroński's army in Podolia. To prevent the khan from counterattacking out of Perekop a force of Don Cossacks, Kalmyks, and cavalry and musketeers out of the lower Volga garrisons was to make a simultaneous attack upon the Azov steppe.

Khmel'nyts'kyi, Buturlin, and Romodanovskii began their march south from Bila Tserkva on 1/2 July. An outbreak of plague along the lower Volga prevented the Volga garrison troops and Kalmyks from marching against the Khanate, but a force of 2,000 Don Cossacks managed an effective naval blockade of the Kerch Straits and raids upon Taman, Sudak, Kafa, and other towns along the Black Sea and Azov coasts, keeping the bulk of the Crimean Tatar army confined in Crimea and on the defensive until mid-September.

The summer of 1655 held another development of immense consequence: Sweden's entry into the war. King Karl X Gustav had become alarmed that Muscovite successes in Lithuania were endangering his project of bringing Polish Livonia, Courland, and Prussia under his hegemony. He no longer saw any chance of reaching an alliance accord with the Commonwealth to block Muscovite expansion, as it was apparent to him that Commonwealth forces were *in extremis*: Radziwiłł had no more than 4,000 regulars now, and Polish forces in Ukraine about 10,000.

So in mid-July the great Deluge (*Potop*) began. Magnus de la Gardie invaded northwestern Poland from Pomerania while a second Swedish army under Arvid Wittenberg entered from Brandenburg and swept across Poznan and Kalisz palatinates. By the end of the month Poznan and Kalisz had accepted Swedish sovereignty. On 17 August Radziwiłł capitulated at Niejdany and accepted a Swedish protectorate over Lithuania. On 8 September Swedish forces entered Warsaw, forcing Jan Kazimierz to flee into exile in Silesia.

For Khmel'nyts'kyi, Sweden's entry into war initially appeared a godsend. He could negotiate with Karl Gustav to coordinate operations against the Poles and even perhaps secure Karl Gustav's guarantee to the sovereignty of the Hetmanate as a counterweight to Tsar Aleksei's perceived attempts to further limit his real sovereignty. When Swedish forces advanced on Warsaw the Transylvanian prince Gyorgy II Rakoczi threw his support to Khmel'nyts'kyi and arranged to join 12,000 Ukrainian cossacks on a march to Warsaw to link up with Swedish forces. The Swedish invasion had also hastened the collapse of

Lithuanian resistance to the Muscovite advance – Vilnius had surrendered to the tsar's forces in August – and could therefore be exploited to destroy Polish resistance in west Ukraine as well.

Khmel'nyts'kyi therefore thought it urgent that Ukrainian–Muscovite forces beat the Swedes to L'viv, the last major city remaining loyal to King Jan Kazimierz. Possession of L'viv would extend the Hetmanate westward to the Carpathians, and it seemed to be a fruit within reach, for the Tatars were still preoccupied with Don Cossack raids along the Crimean coast, and the only Polish army standing before L'viv was Grand Hetman Stanisław Potocki's, comprising just 6,000 Crown troops and 300 horse of *szlachta* militia.

Khmel'nyts'kyi, Buturlin, and Romodanovskii advanced on L'viv in early September, capturing most of the small towns in reach along their marchroute. They reached the outskirts of L'viv on 16 September. Potocki had taken most of his small army a few kilometers off to Solonoi Gorodok, choosing to harass the Ukrainian–Muscovite besiegers from their rear rather than sacrifice his men in a desperate stand at the gates of L'viv. But Khmel'nyts'kyi and Buturlin decided Potocki's army needed to be driven off before they began their siege of the city. On the night of 18 September Romodanovskii and the Ukrainian Colonel Lisnytskyi therefore led a large force (Goodson's infantry regiment, Fonvizin's *reitar* regiment, Korsak's dragoons, a command of elite Moscow musketeers under Artemon Matveev, and cossacks of the Mirgorod *polk*) into the dense forest and tangle of small creeks on the flanks and front of Potocki's camp. Using lumber commandeered from nearby huts, Lisnytskyi's cossacks threw up some rudimentary bridges across the creeks and ambushed Potocki's outer line of pickets. Romodanovskii's troops followed them across. They drove back a counterattack by Polish cavalry and reached the edge of Potocki's camp. For the next three hours Potocki fought to drive them back, first throwing his infantry against them, and then, more effectively, his *husarz* cavalry; but then his front lines mistook Polish cavalry militia arriving in reinforcement from Peremyshl' as fresh Muscovite troops and panicked and broke. Potocki's army fled into the darkness. Romodanovskii and Lisnytskyi did not give pursuit. Potocki's army had escaped largely intact, but his nephew *rotmistrz* Jan Potocki had been taken prisoner, and Khmel'nyts'kyi's and Buturlin's forces were now securely positioned before L'viv and could afford to detach smaller *corps volantes* on raids as far beyond the city as the Sana and Vistula rivers. The objective of these raids was to break through to Brest and rendezvous with A. N. Trubetskoi's corps, marching west from Lithuania, and thereby link up the Lithuanian and Ukrainian fronts. Detachments of traditional formation cavalry and cossacks under Petr Potemkin and Dmytro Vyhovs'kyi got as far as Lublin (20 October), on whose citizens they levied a contribution before turning back towards L'viv. Trubetskoi never reached Brest either. On 28 October 1655 Khmel'nyts'kyi and Buturlin extorted a contribution of 50,000 gold złoties from the citizens of L'viv and lifted their siege. This was a regrettable decision in that it left King Jan Kazimierz a refuge from which to assemble the Tyszowce Confederation, which would go on to defeat the Swedes and save the Commonwealth,[13] but it could be argued it was necessary to withdraw from L'viv now that the Crimean Tatars endangered the Dnepr above Kazyev Ford and Bila Tserkva and the road to Kiev. Khan Kamil Mehmet Girei, alarmed at the seemingly imminent prospect of the total collapse of the Commonwealth, had taken a large army across the Dnepr near Kodak and joined forces with *nuraddin* Aadil Girei near Zbarazh.

To make greater haste towards Bila Tserkva Khmel'nyts'kyi's regiments separated from their baggage train and the Buturlins and Romodanovskii, who were moving in their own columns. This presented the khan with the chance to cut off and destroy each column in turn. On 8 November he attacked Romodanovskii's *wagenburg*, marching on Khmel'nyts'kyi's right flank near Zalozhitsy. On 10 November the khan made a more concerted attack on Vasilii Buturlin's corps just as it was following Khmel'nyts'kyi's train over a difficult river crossing at Ozernaia. An assault on A. V. Buturlin's *wagenburg* on the left flank was also attempted.

Vasilii Buturlin's only hope was to continue moving forward. After a day-long battle he managed to get his force across the river and throw up a fortified camp with Khmel'nyts'kyi's train (he was severely wounded, however, and would die a month after). On 11 November the khan sent an envoy to Hetman Khmel'nyts'kyi, offering his Ukrainian regiments safe passage on parole if he would hand over the Muscovite commanders and their troops. Khmel'nyts'kyi refused. The khan then made another attack on Vasilii Buturlin's section of the Ozernaia camp. It failed, however, reportedly costing the khan more than 10,000 casulaties. On 13 November Memet Girei agreed to an armistice with Khmel'nyts'kyi in return for the hetman's pledge to stop Zaporozhian raids on Crimea. Crimean Tatar forces withdrew from central Ukraine towards the Bucak steppe and the Moldavian frontier. Fear of a Kalmyk attack upon the Khanate kept the khan on the defensive for the next few months.[14]

But in winter 1655–1656 the Sapiehas and other magnates rejected Radziwiłł's peace with Karl X Gustav and formed a confederation to expel the Swedes, and King Jan Kazimierz's own Tyszowce confederates brought him back to Poland and called for all Poles to rise up against the Swedes and restore him to his throne. By March they had managed to assemble an army of 30,000 men. Khmel'nyts'kyi's efforts to bring Sweden into alliance with the Hetmanate and Muscovy in order to complete the destruction of the Commonwealth had encountered a new obstacle: Karl X Gustav's concern that the Muscovite conquests in Lithuania were encroaching upon his conquests in the Commonwealth's Baltic provinces. Conversations with the Swedish envoy Udda Edda convinced Tsar Aleksei, "They are really afraid of us, the Swedes. ... It is not Smolensk that vexes them so much as Vitebsk and Polotsk because it gives us the route up the Dvina to Riga."[15] The Swedes had already tried to block the Muscovite push down the Dvina, by preemptively seizing Dünaburg just as it had come under Muscovite siege, and Muscovite troops under A. L. Ordyn-Nashchokin had skirmished with Swedish pickets along the right bank of the Dvina. A dramatic shift in the tsar's war plans was about to occur.

The death of Vasilii Buturlin after Ozernaia had reduced the influence of those advisors who called for strengthening military support for the Hetmanate and fighting on to total victory against Poland. The tsar was instead increasingly attentive to Ordyn-Nashchokin, who argued for reaching a truce with Jan Kazimierz in order to turn against the Swedes and drive them from Livonia. Swedish control over Livonia was a threat to Pskov and Novgorod, he contended, and perhaps to the tsar's territorial gains in southern Lithuania; but in driving out the Swedes the tsar could occupy the rest of the course of the Dvina and the strategic port of Riga, thereby gaining what had eluded Ivan IV: direct access to the Baltic. The Empire, Denmark, the Netherlands, and Brandenburg would likely join a coalition against Sweden – and perhaps even the Crimean Khanate. Furthermore, war with Sweden could advance Tsar Aleksei's dynastic ambitions, for Jan Kazimierz's still-desperate position seemed to offer the chance to revive the tsar's own candidacy for the Polish succession.

At peace talks at Niemiez, outside Vilnius, the tsar's representatives demanded that Tsar Aleksei be proclaimed successor to the Polish crown *vivente rege*, in Jan Kazimierz's lifetime. Polish diplomats agreed to this in order to secure an armistice, but the election of the tsar was unlikely to ever be ratified for it was in contravention of Polish law and would likely enrage the Emperor at Vienna as well as the Dutch and Danes. The armistice agreement reached in October did not establish a Polish–Muscovite coalition against Sweden; both states would merely continue their own separate campaigns against Karl Gustav. Nor did the armistice agreement address the issue of Polish operations against the Hetmanate.[16]

Tsar Aleksei did not even wait for the armistice or a coalition agreement with other Baltic powers to launch his war upon the Swedes. He declared war on Sweden on 17 May 1656. The tsar returned to the front in early July and began moving his army down the Dvina against Riga.

The Muscovite volte-face had three important consequences. It forced Karl Gustav to draw down his forces in Wielkopolska and Małopolska to meet the new Muscovite threat in the east – thereby allowing Jan Kazimierz to regain control of much of the Vistula basin and reenter Warsaw. The Riga campaign proved beyond Muscovite tactical capability, for Riga's fortifications were stronger than those of the towns in the Lithuanian interior and the tsar, lacking the fleet to blockade Riga from the sea, had to lift his siege in October. Muscovite and Swedish forces in Livonia remained at stalemate through 1657. And the Niemiez Armistice severely damaged Muscovite–Ukrainian relations. Khmel'nyts'kyi felt betrayed. His diplomacy to form a coalition with Sweden to finish off the Commonwealth had been repudiated by Moscow. He had been anticipating completing the destruction of the Polish monarchy, or sparing it on the condition it cede to him the rest of Ukraine, but the tsar had suddenly offered the Poles an armistice at peace talks to which Khmel'nyts'kyi's representatives had not been invited. The tsar's attempt to secure the Polish succession alarmed him for it raised the prospect that Tsar Aleksei might reduce the borders of the Hetmanate or even restore Ukraine to the Commonwealth in order to win the support of the Polish magnates.

In the final year of his life the ailing Khmel'nyts'kyi witnessed the disintegration of his coalition with Transylvania, the Danubian hospodarates, and Sweden. The Khanate was also an increasing concern to him; the Tatar–Ukrainian armistice negotiated at Ozernaia still held but might soon collapse. There had been a harvest failure and massive loss of livestock in Crimea after an especially harsh frost, and the Khan had been forced to forbid the export of grain under penalty of death – the sort of circumstances likely to drive many mirzas back to war. The Ottoman sultan was still ostensibly forbidding Crimean raids on Ukraine, but this might soon change, for the Sultan had reason to resent recent Ukrainian interference in Wallachian affairs and his new Grand Vizier Mehmet Köprülü was requesting more galley slaves for the war against Venice. Khmel'nyts'kyi was also concerned about the continuing loyalty of the Kalmyks, who were receiving envoys from the Crimean khan.[17]

Khmel'nyts'kyi's Hetmanate had been held together by the force of his personality, by his imaginative diplomacy and talent as a commander. But there remained significant differences in political culture in western and eastern Ukraine and therefore the possibility of the Hetmanate's split in the absence of his leadership. The ideology of his cossack state was most developed on the Left Bank, where his revolution had begun. In the more polonized west, however – in Volhynia, Rus' Czerwona, and Belz palatinates – allegiances to the Commonwealth were more likely to have been concealed than repudiated. Catholics and Jews were more numerous in the towns here, with Catholic patricians dominant in town administration; magnate manorial authority was more deeply rooted; leaseholding semivassalized or client petty nobles more likely than cossacks to play the mediating role between landed elites and the peasantry.

Khmel'nyts'kyi died on 27 June 1657. It had been his wish that his son Iurii be proclaimed his successor as hetman. But Iurii was only sixteen and widely judged to be incapable (Sheremetev considered him "better suited for herding geese than ruling as hetman").[18] The Hetmanate's general secretary Ivan Vyhovs'kyi soon sent Iurii Khmel'nyts'kyi off to the Kiev Academy and assumed the hetmancy himself at an officers' council at Chyhyryn (26 August 1657). Unlike Bohdan Khmel'nyts'kyi, Vyhovs'kyi did not seek preliminary approval from the Zaporozhian Sich and even waited three weeks before writing to inform the Sich of his election.

The revolt of Hetman Vyhovs'kyi, 1657–1659

It is often asserted that Vyhovs'kyi took power already committed to breaking with the tsar's protectorate and reuniting Ukraine with the Commonwealth. Stalin-era Soviet historiography in particular sought to explain his pro-Polish orientation in class terms, as the natural consequence of his gentry background and his solidarity with the cossack and urban elites. There is no question he favored the propertied cossack *starshina* rather than the rank-and-file *chern'* and was suspicious especially of the Zaporozhian Sich, but this by itself does not explain his decision to "betray" the Muscovites, for Bohdan Khmel'nyts'kyi could be accused of the same autocratic and elitist tendencies after 1650. Vyhovs'kyi had played a crucial role in negotiating political union with Muscovy in 1652–1654, sometimes to the point of offering more concessions and reassurances than Khmel'nyts'kyi himself had been prepared to give. If by autumn 1657 Vyhovs'kyi was close to giving up on the Muscovite protectorate we should at least ask what had transpired since 1654 to change his views.

The exclusion of the Hetmanate from the Niemiez armistice talks and Tsar Aleksei's efforts to obtain the Polish throne had already raised real concerns among cossack leaders as to Moscow's intentions towards Ukraine. Urban elites in Ukraine were not entirely assured the tsar would continue to respect their rights of self-government under Magdeburg law. Moscow, citing its preoccupation with the war, was still deferring decision as to whether the Kievan metropolitanate was to remain under the jurisdiction of the Constantinople patriarch or come under the authority of the Moscow patriarch. Tsar Aleksei's insistence that Novgorod-Severskii, Pochep, Starodub, and Chernigov now belonged to his patrimony rather than to the Hetmanate had angered many cossack leaders, and the tsar's demand that the cossacks turn over Staryi Bykhov was about to drive that town's commandant, Colonel Ivashko Nechai, to revolt. Bohdan Khmel'nyts'kyi's negotiations with Karl X Gustav showed that Khmel'nyts'kyi too had already concluded the tsar's protectorate was not by itself enough to guarantee the hetman's sovereignty. But the opportunity to obtain meaningful Swedish guarantees had now passed.

Furthermore Vyhovs'kyi worried that the Poles might now induce the Crimean Tatars to rejoin them in alliance against the Hetmanate. Tatar detachments were reportedly crossing the Dnepr near Ochakov and rendezvousing with Polish units near Vinnitsa, Bratslav, and Uman'. It seemed necessary either to prepare for resumed war with the Tatars or find some new basis for deeper rapprochement with them. Report that Moscow was sending Grigorii Romodanovskii to Pereiaslav with a new Muscovite army for the purpose of coordinating frontier defense against the Tatars suggested Moscow was moving to deny Vyhovs'kyi the latter option. Moscow expected Vyhovs'kyi's colonels to draw down their own resources in order to prepare stores, transport, and militia support for Romodanovskii. Subsequent news that a second Muscovite army under the ruthless A. N. Trubetskoi would be arriving caused further anxiety. Colonel Lisnytskyi circulated letters declaring the arrival of these Muscovite armies a plot against cossack liberties.

> They want to set up *voevody* in the towns in Ukraine: at Kiev, Pereiaslav, Uman', and all the others, so that we would have to give them

maintenance everywhere, and they will be collecting for the Sovereign all those taxes we used to pay to the Polish nobles. And all that will remain of the cossack host in Zaporozhia will be 10,000 men ... and the rest will all have to become townsmen or peasants or ... they will be in the dragoons and *soldat* infantry. The Crimean Khan is treating with us and asking that we be friends with him as we were before, and he is not demanding such imposts from us.

In September Vyhovs'kyi began negotiating an alliance with the khan for joint operations against rebel colonels. About this time he may also have begun giving a more attentive hearing to the envoy Stanisław Bieniewski's proposals for alliance with the Commonwealth.[19]

Like Khmel'nyts'kyi, Vyhovs'kyi sought to autocratize the hetmancy, keep the Zaporozhian Sich fully in hand, and govern through the colonels of the regiments on both banks of settled Ukraine. But from the start the Zaporozhian Sich opposed him, and they intercepted Vyhovs'kyi's correspondence with the khan and informed the Muscovites of its contents. Martyn Pushkar, the Colonel of the Poltava cossack regiment, soon joined with the Zaporozhian ataman Iakov Barabash in efforts to overthrow Vyhovs'kyi. Hoping to secure Moscow's backing, they denounced Vyhovs'kyi to Moscow for conspiring to ally with the Crimean Tatars and the Poles.

Muscovite diplomacy was not adroit in responding to this crisis. On the one hand, Tsar Aleksei was still awaiting his election as the Polish royal successor and did not want to get drawn into civil war in Ukraine, so he held back from decertifying Vyhovs'kyi's election and recognizing Pushkar or Iurii Khmel'nyts'kyi. Several missions were sent to Vyhovs'kyi to try to resolve differences and win reassurance of his loyalty while envoys went to Pushkar and Barabash to ask them to end their revolt. On the other hand Tsar Aleksei, his suspicions regarding Vyhovs'kyi's loyalty deepening with every new denunciation received from Barabash and Pushkar, also withheld official recognition of Vyhovs'kyi's election, and his decision to send Romodanovskii's and Trubetskoi's armies back into Ukraine probably aimed as much at intimidating Vyhovs'kyi as defending against the Tatars.

Vyhovs'kyi's subsequent experiences with Muscovite forces in Ukraine inclined him to suspect the tsar was already surreptitiously supporting Pushkar and Barabash and preparing his overthrow. Vyhovs'kyi warned Romodanovskii of the "treachery" of Barabash and the Zaporozhians, "who want to destroy the *starshina* and submit to the Crimean khan,"[20] and asked Romodanovskii to take his army across the Dnepr to guard against Tatar or Polish attack while Vyhovs'kyi marched against the Zaporozhian Sich. But Romodanovskii replied he could not move his troops without the tsar's authorization (even though he had already apparently violated his orders from the tsar by taking his army into Ukraine, to Pereiaslav, instead of halting on the border). In spring 1658 the tsar appointed A. P. Chirikov to serve at Poltava with 300 *soldaty*, to strengthen its defenses against possible attack by the Crimean Tatars. But Poltava was also the headquarters of Pushkar, so this looked to Vyhovs'kyi like open Muscovite support for Pushkar's rebellion. Colonel Lisnytskyi's warning that Muscovite *voevody* were about to be imposed on all the major Ukrainian towns seemed to be coming true: the tsar had just ordered Buturlin at Kiev to send *voevody* not only to Poltava, but to Bila Tserkva, Korsun', Nezhin, Chernigov, and Mirgorod. Each *voevoda* was to be given a garrison force of 200–300 foreign formation infantry. This could be taken as a violation of the terms of the Pereiaslav agreement.[21]

Ultimately Moscow's refusal to assist Vyhovs'kyi against the rebels Pushkar and Barabash drove him to seek assistance from the Crimean Khanate. In February 1658 Vyhovs'kyi negotiated an alliance through one of the *karachi beys*. To reassure the Poles this new Ukrainian–Tatar alliance was not directed against them Vyhovs'kyi invited them into coalition later that month. On 19 April 40,000 Tatars arrived at Chyhyryn – crucial reinforcements for Vyhovs'kyi, who could field only about a quarter of the cossack forces Bohdan Khmel'nyts'kyi had commanded. The Polish military commitment to Vyhovs'kyi was comparatively minor, and unofficial; just before the great battle at Konotop Andrzej Potocki was seen in Vyhovs'kyi's camp at Zenkov, but with just 5,000 Poles, mostly mercenaries.[22]

On 30 May 1658 Vyhovs'kyi's regiments, supported by the Tatars, attacked Pushkar's and Barabash's forces near Poltava. Pushkar was killed and his head presented to Vyhovs'kyi on a pike. Poltava was sacked and burned. The Tatars raided the neighboring countryside for four days. Barabash and a few of his officers fled to Romodanovskii, who took them into his army without the tsar's authorization. Vyhovs'kyi therefore chose not to believe Moscow's assurances that Romodanovskii's army was present to maintain order, not to threaten him. Vyhovs'kyi now considered his break with Moscow to be final and informed the Poles and Tatars of this fact. The coalition formed to help Vyhovs'kyi crush the rebellion in the Hetmanate was thereby transformed into a coalition against the Muscovite military presence in Ukraine.

The sack of Poltava and liquidation of Pushkar forced the tsar to abandon plans to appoint *voevody* and garrisons to the other Ukrainian towns; this additional manpower was all recalled to Belgorod. The Muscovite military presence in Ukraine was for the time being limited to the small garrison at Kiev. Towards the end of June a new *voevoda*, V. B. Sheremetev, arrived in Kiev to replace Buturlin. He brought 1,159 Komaritskaia dragoons and 413 Moscow musketeers. Romodanovskii sent from Belgorod another 1,000 *reitary* (under majors Shepelev and Skorniakov-Pisarev) and 1,325 dragoons (the regiment of Rafael Korsak). This brought the strength of the Kiev garrison up to 6,075 officers and men. Part of the Kiev cossack *polk* was also ready to assist in defending the city. But the Kiev arsenal was short of powder, lead, and match; the *reitary* had carbines but no pistols; the new *reitary* and dragoons were untrained; grain stores were low; and these troops' rations money was 12,000 rubles in arrears.[23]

Vyhovs'kyi moved to drive the Muscovites from Kiev, entrusting the task to his bother Danilo and a force of 20,000 cossacks and a few thousand Tatars under the command of *nuraddin* Selim Girei. On 16 August the vanguard of this army attacked some of Sheremetev's troops while they were cutting lumber outside the city. On the twenty-third the rest of the cossack army arrived, made its camp near the Pecherskii Monastery, and set to work on entrenchments. But Sheremetev gave them no time to strengthen their position. He sent his infantry on a night sortie which drove them from their trenches and took 150 prisoners. Danilo Vyhovs'kyi was wounded and withdrew his force. Sheremetev's force lost just twenty-one killed and wounded.[24]

His failure to force the Muscovites from Kiev led Ivan Vyhovs'kyi to convene an officers' council at Hadiach on 8 September. With the encouragement of his advisor Nemyrych and the Polish commissioner Bieniewski, Vyhovs'kyi crafted an ambitious proposal for restoring Ukraine to the Commonwealth as an independent co-equal "Grand Duchy of Rus'" with its own administration, coinage, taxes, and army and ruled by an elected Hetman confirmed by the Polish King. The Uniate Church was to be abolished on the territory of the Grand Duchy of Rus' and the Rus' Orthodox Church given equal legal status with the Catholic Church across the rest of the Commonwealth. The Hetman would periodically present the King with lists of cossacks for ennoblement so as to gradually equalize cossack with *szlachta* status within the Commonwealth.

Vyhovs'kyi's willingness to surrender some of the Hetmanate's sovereignty for the ennoblement of the cossack *starshina* was not lost on the King, the Senate, and the *Sejm*; when they finally ratified the Hadiach agreement in May 1659 it was with several important "emendations" that went farther than Vyhovs'kyi had intended in limiting Ukraine's sovereignty. The *Sejm*'s version of the agreement included in the Grand Duchy of Rus' only the palatinates of Kiev, Bratslav, and Chernigov, that is, the territory recognized by the Treaty of Zboriv (Podolia, Volhynia, and Galicia were to remain under the authority of the Polish Crown, would be policed by the Crown Quarter Army, and would presumably be recolonized by Polish magnates); the Hetman would be chosen by the King from four candidates elected by the Ukrainians; the cossack register would be limited at 30,000, although the Hetman could maintain a hired army of 10,000 more troops; the Uniate Church would not be allowed to establish new churches, but it would not be removed from Ukraine either; and most important, the Hetman would not be able to receive any foreign missions without the King's consent. The Hadiach Articles passed by the *Sejm* were in some respects more restrictive of Ukrainian sovereignty than the Pereiaslav Agreement Vyhovs'kyi had repudiated. When Colonel Peretiatkovich, Vyhovs'kyi's envoy to Warsaw, returned with the articles ratified by the *Sejm* Vyhovs'kyi is reported to have cried that he had brought him his death.[25]

Grigorii Romodanovskii and a Muscovite army of about 20,000 men reentered Ukraine in November 1658 and set up winter quarters at Lokhvitsa. This encouraged or intimidated some of the Left Bank cossack regiments into electing Ivan Bespalyi as a temporary alternative hetman and reinforcing Romodanovskii at Lokhvitsa. Romodanovskii's work to establish a counter-hetman may not have been authorized by Moscow, for it had the effect of giving Vyhovs'kyi reason to rebuff Moscow's latest attempt to negotiate a peaceful solution. In December Vyhovs'kyi accepted a force of 3,800 Polish infantry under the command of Andrzej Potocki; soon after Selim Girei brought him another 15,000 Tatars. He rejected Moscow's proposal for a new *rada* and reconciliation talks set for Pereiaslav in February 1659 and instead held his own *rada* at Chyhyryn which declared war upon the Zaporozhians and Muscovites (January 1659). In February and March he moved to suppress the mutiny on the Left Bank by occupying Mirgorod, Poltava, and other towns and placing the Zaporozhian cossacks holding Zenkov under siege. He also sent a force of cossacks under Colonel Skorobogatenko on an unsuccessful attack on Romodanovskii's and Bespalyi's forces at Lokhvitsa.

In March 1659 a new corps under Prince A. N. Trubetskoi entered Ukraine from Sevsk to join Romodanovskii's army and Bespalyi's cossacks. On the one hand, Trubetskoi's working order instructed him to make a final appeal to Vyhovs'kyi: send the Crimean Tatars home and submit to a new *rada* to be held at Pereiaslav and in return Moscow would withdraw Sheremetev's garrison from Kiev, remove Trubetskoi's army, pledge to send no more armies into Ukraine, and install Vyhovs'kyi as *voevoda* of Kiev. Meanwhile Trubetskoi was authorized to take military action against Konotop, which Vyhovs'kyi's cossacks and some Crimean Tatars were using as a base for raids against Putivl', Ryl'sk, and Sevsk. On 16 April Trubetskoi's corps, reinforced by Bespalyi's cossacks, reached Konotop; Romodanovskii's army arrived four days later. Some historians follow Tadeusz Korzon in claiming this gave Trubetskoi a force of almost 150,000 men. It was more likely just a third this size.[26]

Konotop, defended by Colonel Gulianytsky and 4,000 cossacks, was stormed by Trubetskoi's forces on 29 April. Nine musketeer *prikazy*, four infantry regiments, and eight dragoon regiments – perhaps 21,500 men in all – assaulted Konotop's walls for five hours. They were forced to withdraw after losing 514 killed and 2,980 wounded. Subsequent attempts to weaken Konotop's defenses by bombardment also failed: heavy return fire from Konotop's walls kept Trubetskoi's men from making progress with their entrenchments, and sorties by Gulianytsky's cossacks seized some of the Muscovite guns. On 24 June Vyhovs'kyi's 16,000-man army, now reinforced by 30,000 Tatars under the khan and *nuraddin* Gazy Girei, began advancing upon Trubetskoi's position. Trubetskoi was unaware of this, for the reconnaissance detachment he had sent out to Shapovalovka had been destroyed. Vyhovs'kyi and the khan were therefore able to prepare a trap for the Muscovites at a marshy crossing over the Sosnovka River a few kilometers below Konotop. They deployed the bulk of their forces behind a screen of forest opposite the marsh and sent the remainder in two smaller columns across the river to attack the rear of the besieging army from left and right and lure it across the Sosnovka into ambush. On 27 June one of these columns suddenly struck the rear of Trubetskoi's camp, driving off many cavalry mounts and then falling back across the Sosnovka. It took Pozharskii and L'vov a few hours to overcome their confusion, saddle up, and begin pursuit with a force of 3–4,000 *deti boiarskie*, *reitary*, and dragoons.[27] The next morning (28 June 1659) found Pozharskii and L'vov camped just across the Sosnovka, their backs to the marsh and the bridge, and apparently unaware of the size of the Ukrainian–Tatar force just behind the treeline and on their flanks. Trubetskoi and Romodanovskii had left a small reserve below the walls of Konotop and were bringing their infantry slowly up behind Pozharskii and L'vov but were still separated from them by the river.

Cossack cavalry under Colonel Bohun suddenly emerged from the woods on Pozharskii's right flank, destroyed the bridge over the Sosnovka, and dammed the river. This flooded Pozharskii's ground, making it harder for him to move his armored *reitary* and field guns, and he began losing many of his men to cossack musket fire. Bohun's cossacks then made a wide sweep and fell upon the right flank of Trubetskoi's and Romodanovskii's troops while Tatars hit them on the left flank and half of Gulianytsky's command sortied out of Konotop to hit them in the rear. A charge by Vyhovs'kyi's center out of the woods finished off Pozharskii and L'vov and then struck at Trubetskoi's and Romodanovskii's column across the river, now withdrawing towards Konotop. The Muscovite siege was lifted and after a difficult crossing over the Sosnovka the remnants of Trubetskoi's army withdrew by *wagenburg* towards Putivl' under harassment by Vyhovs'kyi's cossacks and the Tatars. Pozharskii and L'vov were turned over to the khan and soon died of wounds or were executed; the few survivors of their command were reportedly put to death by the Tatars.

Although some writers repeat the claim that 30,000 Muscovites were killed or captured at Konotop, lists Trubetskoi submitted to the Ambassadors' Chancellery report total losses of 4,769 men: 2,830 of L'vov's and Pozharskii's column sent across the Sosnovka, and 1,896 during the attacks upon Trubetskoi's withdrawing *wagenburg*. Soloviev's judgment that "the flower of the Russian cavalry had perished in one day" is true only in the sense that at least 259 of those killed or captured were officers or men of Moscow rank (*zhilets* and above). But Konotop was undoubtedly a brilliant victory for Vyhovs'kyi and Khan Kamil Mehmet Girei. Trubetskoi's army had suffered such heavy losses it was unable to continue operations in Ukraine; Sheremetev was left isolated in Kiev and had to resort to terror raids against neighboring towns and villages to deter another attack upon him. There was no longer any obstacle to the Crimean Tatars swinging around the western end of the Belgorod Line and ravaging Muscovy's southern borderland as far east as Voronezh and Usman'. That August the Tatars raided eighteen Muscovite districts, most of them behind the Line, burning 4,674 farmsteads and carrying off 25,448 prisoners. Trubetskoi's army was ordered to redeploy between Putivl' and Sevsk to block further Tatar incursions. There were rumors Tsar Aleksei intended to abandon Moscow for Iaroslavl'.[28]

The victory at Konotop did not preserve Vyhovs'kyi's power, however, for the towns and cossack regiments began turning against him, driven by suspicion the Hadiach Treaty would not actually restore cossack liberties and by anger at Vyhovs'kyi's attempts to billet his Polish, Serb, and German mercenaries on them. The Zaporozhian Sich continued to defy him, and its *koshevoi* ataman Ivan Sirko carried out raids near Uman' and Chigirin as well as attacks upon the Belgorod Horde and Crimea that prevented Vyhovs'kyi from concentrating his forces to complete his pacification of northern Ukraine. Sirko's victories also emboldened young Iurii Khmel'nyts'kyi to contribute men for the raids on Crimea. Sirko and Ivan Briukhovets'kyi, one of Bohdan Khmel'nyts'kyi's trusted lieutenants, began working to convince cossack commanders that it was time to restore to young Iurii the hetmancy that Vyhovs'kyi had usurped from him.

Vyhovs'kyi also faced insurgencies at Pereiaslavl' and Nezhin, where colonels Vasilii Zolotarenko and Timofei Tsytsura had taken power by coup. Trubetskoi's army reentered Ukraine to support them; Sheremetev sent troops from Kiev to garrison Pereiaslav, while A. V. Buturlin's corps occupied Nezhin. By early September 1659 cossack commanders from Priluki, Baturin, Glukhov, Chernigov, and Novgorod-Severskii had abandoned Vyhovs'kyi and renewed their loyalty to the tsar's protectorate. Vyhovs'kyi held a *rada* at Germanovka on 11 September to make a final appeal for support of his hetmancy and his Hadiach Treaty. But he was shouted down and nearly lynched, escaping only with the help of his 1,000-man Polish guard. The Germanovka *rada* proclaimed Iurii Kheml'nyts'kyi his successor. Vyhovs'kyi accepted this verdict because Iurii, unlike Tsytsura and Zolotarenko, had not joined in open revolt against him.

Expanding the foreign formations

By April 1658 the stalemate in Livonia had forced the tsar to begin peace talks with the Swedes at Vallisaari, near Narva. In December these talks produced a three-year armistice allowing the Muscovites to retain for the while the Livonian territory they had captured since 1656 but with the prospect of further border readjustments at future talks. But the death of Karl X Gustav in February 1660 left Muscovy unable to secure its gains in Livonia, for the regency guiding the five-year-old Karl XI decided to sign a peace treaty with the Polish-Lithuanian Commonwealth (the Treaty of Oliva, May 1660) that essentially reestablished the status quo ante 1655, with the important exception that the Commonwealth recognized Swedish control of Livonia. Upon the lapse of the Vallisaari Armistice Tsar Aleksei therefore was unable to bring enough pressure to bear upon the Swedes to enforce his own claim over Livonia. He had to settle for a permanent peace with Sweden in exchange for abandoning the districts taken since 1656 (the Treaty of Kardis, 1661). Muscovite access to the Baltic had been lost again. Nothing had been gained from the war with Sweden.

The Vallisaari Armistice had immediately raised the prospect that the Commonwealth would resume its war with Muscovy. Talks to extend the Polish-Muscovite truce in May–October 1658 made no progress and even before they recessed two Lithuanian armies under Grand Hetman Pawel Sapieha and Field Hetman Wincenty Gosiewski put Vilnius under blockade. On 11 October 1658 Muscovite forces launched a surprise attack on Gosiewski's army at Warki. Muscovy and the Commonwealth were again at war.

Although Vyhovs'kyi had not obtained much direct military support from the Poles, his overthrow in September 1659 had by no means left the Muscovite forces in Ukraine any more secure, for King Jan Kazimierz was again in alliance with the Khanate and he was fielding larger forces than had been available to him before. The Commonwealth's desperate struggle to expel the Swedes had finally given the king enough leverage over the *Sejm* and provincial dietines to win their consent to emergency excise taxes and loans to expand the army. By the second quarter of 1659 the Commonwealth had 54,000 regulars under arms – 36,000 men in the Polish army, and 18,000 in the army of Lithuania. This did not include the gentry cavalry militia of the *pospolite ruszenie*. Polish crown regular forces had increased 85 percent over their 1655 strength, and even more significantly, the relative weight of the *cudzoziemski autorament* had tripled, from 6,628 men to 20,320. The traditional formation *narodowy autorament*, comprising the *husarz* lancers, *pancerni* armored cossack cavalry, Tatar-Wallachian cavalry, and *łanowa* hearth-levied infantry, had grown by 30.8 percent, from 14,870 to 19,450 horse and foot.[29]

The last five years of war in Lithuania and Ukraine had attritted Muscovy's own foreign formation infantry regiments. In 1653 2,275 recruits from the Kozlov region had been taken into the infantry regiments at Belgorod; by 1658 only 1,778 of them remained under arms.[30] As regional levies into the infantry regiments no longer sufficed to make up losses and outpace Polish military reconstruction a nationwide levy, taking one recruit (*datochnyi chelovek*) from every ten to twenty-five households of taxpayers, was instituted in late 1658. This first nationwide levy yielded 18,000 *soldaty* by early 1659. Another 15,000 men were recruited by July of that year; the levy of 1660 yielded another 17,000 men; and 58,000 more were raised in the three levies of 1661–1663. In 1661–1663 there were 42 infantry regiments containing 24,377 officers and *soldaty*. By war's end in 1667 an estimated 100,000 men had been levied into the infantry regiments.[31]

The term of service for infantry recruits was for life. But the infantry regiments did not yet represent a standing army in the true sense, for only the officers and a core cadre of infantrymen remained under arms year-round; the rest of the regiment was sent back to their villages at campaign's end (usually at winter's outset) and their rations money payments resumed only when they were called up again for the next campaign. The only exceptions to this were the troops assigned to garrison duty in the towns of Left Bank Ukraine, and the two elite Moscow infantry regiments, which were supposed to remain under discipline all year. None the less the levies of 1658–1663 were a major step towards the foundation of a large standing Western-formation infantry and dwarfed what the Poles could raise through mercenary hire and *łanowa* levies.

In committing to expanding the foreign formation infantry the Military Chancellery had concluded that their tactical value outweighed their greater equipping and maintenance costs. The infantry *soldat* was in principle equipped with a matchlock musket, pike, or *berdysh* halberd; cuirass with cuisses, morion helmet, and bandolier with twelve charges; rapier; a winter fur coat; and occasionally, grenades; this was usually all issued at state expense. His rations money allowance averaged 7.5 to 11 rubles a year. Colonel Alexander Crawford calculated that four regiments of infantry (8,700 men) required 3.5 tons of powder, 1.5 tons of match, and 35.5 tons of ball annually for drill and guard duty; another 3.5 tons of powder might be expended in a full day's intensive battle.[32]

The period 1658–1663 also saw significant expansion of Muscovy's foreign formation cavalry. In 1659 the government began transferring southern frontier middle service class cavalrymen out of the traditional formation cavalry centuries into the *reitar* heavy cavalry now considered more resilient against either European or Tatar forces. Men of lower social order – cossacks, monastery peasants, bondsmen, and taxpayer *datochnye* recruits – were also taken into the *reitar* regiments, so that by 1663 there were 22 *reitar* regiments with 18,795 officers and men – a nine-fold increase over the *reitar* formation of 1653. The *reitary* received service land and annual cash allowances like the traditional formation cavalry, and at comparable rates, so they were expected to provide their own mounts and sometimes to purchase their own equipment (typically cuirass and helmet, rapier or saber, a pair of pistols, and a wheellock carbine). Their equipment was therefore much less standardized than that of the infantry. Those pleading poverty could receive treasury arms as the Sovereign's bounty or purchase them at reduced prices.

The dragoon (*dragun*) formation was expanded through *datochnyi* levy and transfers out of the cavalry centuries and *reitar* squadrons. In 1658 the Belgorod Army Group formed four dragoon regiments totaling 5,000 men. By 1663 the number of dragoons in service had been brought up to 9,334 in eight regiments. Ideally, the dragoon was supposed to be armed with a pair of pistols and rapier (by the time of the first Turkish War, a saber), and for dismounted combat, a carbine or musket and *berdysh* halberd. The formation of lancer units also began in 1658. By 1663 there was one regiment (757 men) of Polish-model *husarz* lancers (*gusary*) and two regiments (1,185 men) of *kopeishchik* lancers carrying shorter, stouter lances.[33]

By 1663 the foreign formations comprised 54,448 officers and men in 75 regiments and accounted for about 79 percent of the total field army strength. Foot (counting dragoons with *soldat* infantry) now counted for 55.3 percent of foreign formation troop strength, and the relative weight of foot in the traditional formation units had also increased, for there were 18,800 elite Moscow *strel'tsy* and another 30,000 provincial *strel'tsy* – a three-fold increase from the mid-1630s – many of whom could be called into field army duty. Meanwhile the number of *dvoriane* and *deti boiarskie* serving in the traditional formation cavalry centuries had declined from 39,400 at war's start to 33,600.[34]

At mid-century the field army had perhaps 1,000 guns, including trophy guns and small-caliber swivel-guns (another 4,000 guns were distributed across Muscovy's garrison towns for defense; about 5,000 men were registered as gunners). Assessing the state of regimental artillery in the late 1650s and 1660s is difficult because the foreign formation regiments were still operationally subsumed within the traditional force structure of corps and most inventories listed guns by corps. The largest number of guns (200 or more) were usually concentrated in the Tsar's Corps or the Great Corps and 50–80 guns allotted to the other corps. Tactical as well as cost considerations limited the number of guns assigned to the infantry and dragoon regiments as their own in the late 1650s and 1660s, but by the late 1670s foreign formation troops were more often called on to fight on open ground outside *wagenburgs*, supported by their own regimental artillery, with dragoon regiments typically given six field guns (two-, three-, and six-pounders) and *soldat* regiments having six to twelve. General Kravkov's elite Moscow Select Infantry Regiment had twenty bronze two-pounders. These were higher ratios than in western Europe, where a ratio of one gun to every 1,000 men was still considered ideal. Sevsk became the principal artillery park for field army guns used on the southern frontier and in Ukraine. Under the supervision of the Armory and the Gunners' Chancellery the foundries at Moscow, Tula, and Kashira increasingly concentrated on turning out smaller caliber guns more suited for use in the field. They also produced grenade-firing mortars for siege operations and experimented with rifled barrels. But because the army still had to rely partly on imports and could not afford to dispense with older or trophy guns it had to deal with a wide variety of calibers, making it difficult to find cannonballs of appropriate size.[35]

Until the 1680s Muscovy remained dependent on the expertise of foreign mercenary officers, especially in the infantry and dragoons. Of 277 identifiable staff officers (colonels, lieutenants-colonel, majors) in the 1660s, only 18 were Russians; 648 of the 1,922 captains, lieutenants, and ensigns were Russians; for the time being Russians prevailed only among the sergeants and corporals. Moscow aimed at maintaining a high proportion of officers to men (1:20 on average in the infantry and dragoon regiments) in order to instill drill sense and maintain order on the battlefield. To recruit and retrain experienced foreign officers the treasury offered salaries generous even by international standards. Colonels, for example, received 250–400 rubles a month, with bonuses if they converted to Orthodoxy. The pay of the 2,524 officers of the active field army therefore accounted for nearly a third of the army's total cash wage bill in 1663 (between 227,000 and 282,000 rubles, out of a total of .95 million to 1 million rubles).[36]

An obvious question is whether these investments in recruitment, equipment, and training had produced by war's end a field army tactically competitive by western European standards.

The ordinance for Muscovite infantry evolutions, firing systems, and tactics was still the *Uchenie i khitrost stroeniia pekhotnykh liudei*, a 1647 translation of a 1615 manual by Johann von Wallhausen – representative perhaps of Mauritsian military thought, but anachronistic by the 1660s. It sold just 135 copies in its first decade of use. An ordinance for heavy cavalry training may have been translated from the Dutch in 1650 but apparently circulated only in manuscript.[37]

Lacking contemporary descriptions of any detail, we can only speculate as to what was recognized as standard order of battle. If commanders did still follow Wallhausen's prescriptions, the army would have approached the enemy's position with its forces highly concentrated, cavalry in the front and along both flanks, followed by the strongest infantry regiments, the main body, and finally the baggage train. The infantry regiments marched with their companies of pike in mid-column, preceded and followed by their companies of musket. Upon sighting the enemy the infantry and artillery were to be ready to fall back to the baggage train and take shelter in *wagenburg* formation; the cavalry then struck the advancing enemy – sometimes in caracole, more often "cossack style" in no discernible order – and pulled back to fall behind the *wagenburg*. In the event regiments had to fight on open ground they would deploy into line by company square – ten ranks deep by ten files across, one to two paces between rows – usually with the pike companies sleeved on right and left by musket companies (Wallhausen's *kriegsbuch* offered rectangles sixteen ranks deep as an alternative deployment). The shallower six-rank line favored by the Swedish army would still be a long time in finding favor. Firing by rank in sequence was the norm. Firing by file or division does not seem to have been practiced; there is no evidence of platoon firing before 1698; and even the Swedish Salvee, the three-rank volley fire used with such success by Gustavus Adolfus, appears to have been considered a novelty when Patrick Gordon and the Second Moscow Select Infantry Regiment demonstrated it to young Tsar Peter in the early 1690s. Holding rank and line was emphasized over advancing fire. Charge by pike, or even pushing by pike, was probably not much attempted; the pike companies' primary function was to defend the musket companies, and the proportion of pike to musket was lower than in most other armies. When confronted with a cavalry charge the two front ranks of musket dropped to their knees and held their fire while the third and fourth ranks fired over their heads; the third and fourth ranks then dropped to knee while the fifth and sixth ranks fired over them; then the first and second ranks would fire from knee at close range.[38]

Compared to the Gustavan system these were deeply conservative tactics delivering less in both shock and firepower. That they were apparently still retained into the 1660s should probably not be attributed to ignorance or failure of imagination – Moscow was paying good money to hire the most experienced officers it could find, many of them out of the Swedish army. More likely the

Muscovite preference for static defensive tactics owed to limitations on training time and to the particularities of warfare in a steppe environment.

The best trained Muscovite infantry regiments were the two elite Moscow-based Select Infantry Regiments founded in 1642 and commanded by Matvei Kravkov and William Drummond. These regiments were recruited mostly from the middle service class and stationed in special colonies outside the capital. When deployed at the front they were used as shock troops – hence they were larger than other regiments and had more regimental guns. When not at the front they served as training camps for officers for other regiments. The Moscow Select Infantry regiments were expected to drill daily. In reality they drilled intensively only on the eve of campaign, for they also engaged in agriculture and trade during the rest of their time in quarters. The other infantry regiments based in the provinces probably received no more than a month of drill in a typical year. Furthermore, the high attrition rate at the Lithuanian and Ukrainian fronts and the huge scale of the annual *datochnyi* levies meant that the proportion of raw recruits among the rank-and-file remained high. It is therefore not surprising that officers complained their troops did not know how to advance in order and could not attain good rates of fire. Colonel Crawford reported that it was common for an infantryman in his regiment to get off no more than twelve rounds in a day-long battle. Infantrymen often wasted their rounds by firing before the enemy came within effective range (the recommended range was ten *sazheny*, about 21 m).[39]

When facing Polish or Swedish forces fronted by infantry unprotected by earthworks or *wagenburg*, the first line of attacking Muscovite cavalry consisted of companies or squadrons of *gusar* or *kopeishchik* lancers, if these were available, followed by the *reitary* using pistol and rapier, with the dragoon companies providing fire support. Lancer charges were considered much less effective against Tatar light cavalry. The foreign formation cavalry regiments were likewise only seasonally mobilized and spent little time in drill. Many of the *reitary* had been recruited from southern *odnodvortsy* and lacked the service land and labor resources to provision themselves for protracted campaign, so such men tended to shirk service or arranged to appear on active duty only once every two or three years by dividing up their duty with kinsmen or boarder shareholders. Kozlov, one of the largest manpower pools on the Belgorod Line, sent Romodanovskii 1,200 *reitary* in 1668, but another 980 *reitary* and lancers were left behind because they were impoverished and had no mounts or had deserted and hidden themselves in the forest near Chelnavsk. This was especially disturbing to headquarters at Belgorod, which considered the Kozlov *reitary* and lancers "the best troops, and the best mounted, in the regiments."[40] The multipurpose dragoons could have been of great tactical value – Peter I would recognize this, and build a cavalry almost exclusively of dragoons – but because Tsar Aleksei's government recruited most of them from state peasants with even smaller economies they were even more likely to shirk service, and their combat effectiveness was limited by a shortage of carbines which forced them to make do with older heavy matchlocks completely unsuited for mounted service.

However, it should be kept in mind that the training and discipline necessary for the mastery of the latest European line tactics may not have been as necessary in Ukraine, where *wagenburg* massing of troops made more sense than line deployment for battle.

Muscovite strategy for war in Ukraine called for seizing, garrisoning, and reinforcing a limited number of towns scattered across a vast but sparsely populated plain – much of it uncultivated steppe – providing fewer opportunities for foraging and contributions extortion than central Europe. To achieve this Muscovite commanders needed to convey large forces several hundred kilometers – from Belgorod to Bila Tserkva, for example – moving not only cavalry to defend against Tatar or cossack attack but enough infantry and artillery for siege operations. This in turn required that provisioning for much of the campaign come out of the army's baggage train. Relying on a vast train of great numbers of small wagons slowed the army's rate of march and rendered it especially vulnerable when fording rivers or ascending hills, but it had two advantages: a larger train could be formed into a defensive *wagenburg* on the steppe or used to augment earth fortifications when the army camped below enemy walls for siege, and a larger train could carry enough provisions to support more infantry and artillery to defend a *wagenburg* position.

The war thus far in Ukraine showed that Muscovite forces were most likely to come under attack when their trains were crossing or camped on difficult terrain (Drizhipol'e, Zalozhnitsy) or encamped to besiege an enemy town (L'viv, Konotop). It was therefore understandable that Muscovite commanders would give greater attention to training their troops in the tactics of stationary defense behind fortifications (a *wagenburg*, a *guliai-gorod*, or a fort of ditch, earthen berm, and *chevaux-de-fris*), and this choice had the further advantage of providing some compensation for what by western European standards would be considered their troops' greatest tactical deficiencies: mastering the more complex firing systems, providing advancing fire, making offensive use of the pike, maintaining line and rank. What their infantry and artillery could provide was the heavy if not very accurate firepower delivered by a numerically superior host from a fortified position.

Polish and Lithuanian forces were more successful than the Crimean Tatars in developing an effective response to Muscovite *wagenburg* tactics. If large Tatar auxiliary forces were available to them they used them to blockade the Muscovites' fortified position, cut them off from reinforcement, and gradually starve them out. Otherwise they would set their infantry and artillery to improvising their own earthworks while their cavalry worked to provoke the Muscovite horse into making a sortie, which was then countercharged by the tactically more proficient *husarz* lancers. Jan Chryzostom Pasek witnessed how Czarniecki accomplished this against a Muscovite *guliai-gorod* in Lithuania (1660).

There's no way to charge these things, no way to break in upon the enemy, for the horses would be speared. Being behind those things, it's as if an army were behind a fortress, whence the name: moving forts. No sooner had Czarniecki heard about this stratagem, but he ordered earthworks thrown up forthwith in front of the ranks, small in size but close together. Both infantry and retainers threw themselves into the task at once, carrying earth away in whatever they had, cap or coat tails, as the army did not have many spades in its weaponry. Within an hour or so, the bulwarks were up, the infantry and small cannon brought, all very speedily. Our battle ranks did not have to advance beyond the fortifications, they were to fight from there *defensive*, moving forward by regiments and taking *refugium* behind the earthworks if the fighting was burdensome.

Polish cavalry sorties eventually provoked the Muscovite commander, Iurii Dolgorukii, into ordering his

> regiments to be led out to the field from those moving forts, leaving inside a part of the infantry with the cannon, and mixing some field pieces and foot soldiers among the horse. He was expecting to overwhelm us at one blow, relying on the great size of his army. ... Our cavalry also came forward, leaving those fieldworks at their rear. ... As Muscovy was suiting its own design and not ours, it charged our right wing first ... We engage then in bloody combat. Their ranks are fearsomely dense, several of them to one of ours; but even so we do not let ourselves be smashed, we stand firm. ... Plainly, the hand of God was protecting us. ... I consider it a great wonder: when 3,000 Muscovites let fly all together at those four squadrons of ours, which had galloped too far in pursuit of the enemy and had been driven aside and nearly led into the lines of fire, as usual only one cavalier and four retainers perished, and my horse was shot down. ... At least half of us ought to have dropped from our horses under such fire. ...
>
> The hussars then charged with lances as into a wall: some splintered, others held. ... They encountered a weak spot in the wall – some who were anxious about their bellies. The wall stepped aside and our men bored like a drill through the enemy's lines, nearly without a single broken lance: they came straight to that place which served as the gateway between those moving forts. ... Upon taking up their position at that gateway, they turned and with their standard faced the enemy's rear lines. ... Fearful lest they be overwhelmed there ... the Governor [Czarniecki] ordered the rest of his troops to give charge. ... Now was Muscovy thrown into confusion; now did they take to their heels. ... Whenever a Muscovite squadron races towards that gateway hoping to escape behind the moving fortresses, those hussars, who had pierced

through the enemy ranks, present their lances: the Muscovites were turned aside. A huge number of them pressed about those movable bastions then, wanting their men to give fire and repulse our hussars, but their men could not shoot without doing greater harm to their own. Nor were they firing from the cannon anymore, it being to no avail amid the tangled armies.... Vast numbers of the enemy were laid low there, corpse falling upon corpse in a heap.[41]

Sustaining operations in both Ukraine and Lithuania over these five costliest years of the war created special problems for command-and-control. Military and diplomatic intelligence had to be routed between the Military Chancellery and Ambassadors' Chancellery and coordinated by the Privy Chancellery, so clerks of the Privy Chancellery had to be attached to envoys as well as to the commanders sent to the front. Beginning in 1657 commanders were required to send their reports directly to the Privy Chancellery, which then sent copies to the Military Chancellery. The Privy Chancellery attempted to review commanders' communications with the Military Chancellery closely enough to enable the tsar to discipline commanders for operational blunders and even for underreporting combat losses. By the end of this period Tsar Aleksei began relaxing supervision by the Privy Chancellery, having concluded that it had been taken to extremes undermining the effectiveness of decision-making within the Military Chancellery. But he still relied on his secretary Dementii Bashmakov to oversee matters, for he transferred Bashmakov out of the Privy Chancellery into the directorship of the Military Chancellery.

The expansion of arms production and the foreign formations had been accompanied by the creation of several new chancelleries with specialized military functions. But the Military Chancellery remained the principal central organ for managing the war and the armed forces. Peter Brown considers its range of functions during the Thirteen Years' War to have been about as broad as that of the Prussian *Generalkriegskomissariat*: it appointed to commands and planned operations, at least in the broad sense; supervised recruiting and cavalry militia call-ups; inducted recruits and determined rank and compensation entitlements; managed the quartermastery; and maintained the provincial garrisons and defense lines. It also administered occupied territory. A Lithuanian Chancellery was created in 1656 but did not actually administer occupied Belarus' and Lithuania because they were not fully pacified. Left Bank Ukraine's occupation likewise remained under the Military Chancellery until 1663, when a Little Russian Chancellery – *Malorossiiskii prikaz* – was created to administer the Left Bank garrisons and manage relations with the cossack regiments and the Zaporozhian Sich.

Brown finds the Military Chancellery generally effective in foreseeing time horizons, forecasting, gathering information, and computing manpower and supply needs. Ivan Gavrenev, who served as its director from 1630 to 1661, had by this time considerable experience, and as its range of tasks expanded the division of labor within the Military Chancellery had become more ramified: by 1668 it had been subdivided into five bureaus with regional or functional specializations (Moscow, Novgorod, Chancellery, Cash, and Grain). Belgorod and Sevsk bureaus would be added by 1680.[42] Furthermore, by 1663 the Belgorod and Sevsk territorial military administrations (*razriady*) had obtained the authority to conscript recruits and tax and on their territories, allowing the Military Chancellery to devolve much of the responsibility for military resource mobilization on the Belgorod and Sevsk commanders stationed just off the Ukrainian front.

Despite the considerable expansion of the foreign formation logistic practice had not changed much since the days of Filaret's Smolensk War. The traditional centuries of middle service class cavalrymen but also the regiments of *reitary* and lancers were still expected to provision themselves from their *pomest'e* lands. State provisioning was limited to the *strel'tsy*, to whom the government paid musketeers' grain (*streletskii khleb*), and the *soldaty* and the foreign officers, who depended mostly on rations money (*kormovye den'gi*) up to 1663.

The *streletskii khleb* tax, collected from taxpayers in kind or cash according to inhabited acreage norm (*sokha* assessment) or from a certain number of households (*dvor* assessment), had become a semiregular levy from 1613. Its yield was not sufficient to provision the *strel'tsy* – whose number had tripled over the 1630s–1650s – because neither *sokha* assessment nor *dvor* assessment were flexible and specific enough to let the chancelleries adjust levies to the current number of working taxpayers. Using *streletskii khleb* to provision musketeers on the Belgorod Line or serving in Ukraine in Belgorod and Sevsk corps was especially problematic because the southern frontier had far fewer taxpayers than central or northern Muscovy; most southern *strel'tsy* therefore had to be given small land allotments (*nadely*) to help maintain them in service. Grain provisioning of garrison and field army troops, including foreign formation troops, would only become effective after 1663, when a Grain Chancellery (*Khlebnyi prikaz*) and an "eighth-grain tax" (*chetverikovyi khleb*) were introduced.[43]

This meant the army had to find ways to mobilize more cash for its maintenance. Of the roughly one million rubles the state spent on military cash salaries in 1663, 736,672 rubles went to the foreign officers, *soldaty*, and dragoons receiving rations money for the purchase of food stores (annual cash *zhalovanie* allowances accounted for the rest: 92,903 rubles to musketeers, 5,786 rubles to cossacks, and 81,015 rubles to the middle service class cavalry).[44] But Muscovy's economy remained undermonetarized, and the assessment problems that rendered grain taxation inefficient affected direct taxation in cash as well. Since the late 1640s, partly in anticipation of resumed war with the Commonwealth, there had been efforts to improve the yield from indirect taxation, by establishing of state salt and potash monopolies, reorganizing the state tavern system (1652), and introducing a simplified and standardized customs rate (1653). The scale of Muscovy's grain exports to the United Provinces had also been expanded, taking advantage of the record high prices in the Baltic grain trade in the wake of the Thirty Years' War; grain exports out of Arkhangel'sk yielded 250,000 rubles in 1653.⁴⁵ But none of these measures could keep pace with the expansion of the foreign formation.

In 1656 the government therefore resorted to currency debasement. It reminted 223,405 rubles' worth of silver joachimthalers as silver *efimki* and issued 3.95 million rubles in copper coins at the same face value – meanwhile requiring that all debts to the state be repaid in silver. By 1663 about 20 million rubles in copper had been issued. This unleashed horrific price inflation. The price of a silver ruble at Moscow rose from 1.08 ruble in spring 1659 to 15 rubles in June 1663. Inflation of grain prices further complicated *streletskii khleb* provisioning and the rations money system. The market value of the *streletskii khleb* tax at Charonda quadrupled over 1654–1663; grain prices at Vologda, which had remained stable at about .30–40 rubles per quarter in 1646–1656, reached 24 rubles per quarter in January 1663. The Copper Crisis also contributed to the growing unpopularity of the tsar's protectorate over Ukraine. Vyhovs'kyi had cited it in arguing for rejection of the protectorate: "The Moscow tsar wants to pay us in copper money. But what good is this money, what can you get for it?"⁴⁶ The growing refusal of Ukrainian merchants to accept copper undermined the provisioning of the Muscovite garrisons in Ukraine. Of the 3,206 Muscovite troops in Kiev in 1662, 458 were sick of malnutrition; 250 of the 737 *reitary* and all 92 dragoons had lost their mounts.⁴⁷ In July 1662 report there was about to be yet another extraordinary levy of "fifths money" sparked riots in Moscow. This finally pushed the government to begin restoring silver coinage and withdrawing the copper coins (June 1663).

From Chudnovo to Glukhov, 1659–1664

Moscow greeted Iurii Khmel'nyts'kyi's election as hetman in autumn 1659 but insisted he had to swear allegiance to the tsar at A. N. Trubetskoi's headquarters at Pereiaslav and pledge that he would receive no foreign envoys, campaign only when and where the tsar commanded, and execute all those inciting treason against the tsar. These new Pereiaslav Articles also required the Ukrainian cossacks to evacuate Belarus'. Novgorod-Severskii, Chernigov, Starodub, and Pochep were declared annexed to Muscovy; the Hetmanate could no longer lay claim to them. *Voevody* and Muscovite garrisons in Ukraine were no longer officially limited to Kiev and Chernigov but extended to Nezhin, Pereiaslav, Bratslav, and Uman'. Registered cossacks were still exempt from having to billet Muscovite troops or provide them transport, but non-cossacks were no longer. Fugitive Muscovite peasants resettling in Ukraine had to be deported.

Not surprisingly these terms, presented to the cossack colonels in the camp of Trubetskoi's army, were a great disappointment and revived much of the anti-Muscovite feeling that Vyhovs'kyi had exploited. Stanisław Bieniewski began working to win their support for the Commonwealth.

The Military Chancellery made plans at this time for a major offensive against the Poles. Over the winter and spring of 1660 a new campaign army of 27,000 men was assembled at Kiev under V. B. Sheremetev. Sheremetev met with Khmel'nyts'kyi and the Moldavian *gospodar* Konstantin Shcherban in a council of war at Vasil'kov, where the cossack Commissioned Hetman (*nakaznyi hetman*) Tymofei Tsytsura argued that Polish forces had been so weakened by four years of war with Sweden the Muscovite and Ukrainian armies should be able to push deep into Polish territory, driving even as far as Cracow. Grigorii Kozlovskii, commander of Muscovite forces at Uman', strongly disagreed, observing that they had no good intelligence as to the deployment and condition of Polish forces and suggesting that it might be unwise to rely too much on the enthusiasm of the cossack regiments. He recommended instead a defensive strategy, which would force the Poles to stretch out their supply lines trying to reach and invest the Muscovite garrisons on the Left Bank. But Sheremetev endorsed Tsytsura's proposal for a drive on Cracow.[48]

In fact Sheremetev did not know the full size of the Polish forces now assembling against him. The signing of the Oliwa Treaty with Sweden had freed Field Hetman Jerzy Lubomirski to lead his army (6,000 *reitary* and other cavalry; 900 dragoons; 7,000 infantry) out of Prussia towards Volhynia, to join forces with Crown Hetman Stanisław Potocki. Potocki, assumed to be camped at Ternopol with just 6,000 men, was already marching towards Ozhekhovtsy with 13,600 *reitary* and cavalry, 2,000 dragoons, 3,000 infantry, 15,000 Crimean Tatars, and twelve guns. The Polish regiments certainly had logistic problems – Lubomirski was having to pay his troops out of his own pocket – but Volhynian landowners were at least generous in quartering and feeding them, considering them their final hope to end the cossack problem. By late August Potocki and Lubomirski had joined forces near Mezhibozh'e on the Upper Bug, where the *nuraddin* Gazy Girei brought them more Tatars.

Sheremetev's, Kozlovskii's, and O. I. Shcherbachev's corps marched west from Kiev on 8 August with a total of 19,200 troops (6,100 *reitary*, 5,100 other cavalry, 4,000 dragoons, and 4,000 *soldaty* and *strel'tsy*). This was most of the Muscovite military presence in Ukraine. Only 5,000 men had been left to garrison the Ukrainian towns. Tsytsura accompanied Sheremetev with six regiments of cossack infantry (20,000 men). There were twenty field guns and a baggage train of 3,000 wagons carrying 9.1 million kg of stores and enough ammunition for two months, driven and escorted by about 10,000 slave and peasant retainers. Tsytsura's cossacks were apparently reluctant to provide reconnaissance, so Sheremetev had to use part of his cavalry for this, and they were far less familiar with the region.

Iurii Khmel'nyts'kyi marched with 30–40,000 cossacks and thirty small guns in a separate column along the Goncharikha Trail with the task of rendezvousing with Sheremetev near Slobodishche.[49]

At the end of August Sheremetev, still unreinforced by Khmel'nyts'kyi, advanced from Kotel'na towards Lubar. Kept abreast of this by Polish scouts, Potocki asked *nuraddin* Gazy Girei to throw his vanguard against the Muscovites while Potocki followed up their attack with two of his regiments of dragoons and two infantry regiments. On 4 September they attacked the three Muscovite corps while they were camped on open ground outside Lubar, defended only by their baggage train and a low earth wall. Some 600 Muscovites and cossacks were killed. Sheremetev finally managed to beat off the attackers but they had succeeded in cutting his lines of communication with Khmel'nyts'kyi. For the next twelve days Sheremetev sat encamped, his supplies dwindling, awaiting reinforcement from Khmel'nyts'kyi.

On 16 September Potocki, Lubomirski, and the *nuraddin* brought their main forces up near Sheremetev's position in preparation for a general attack. Only now did Sheremetev learn how large an enemy army he faced. This finally convinced him he had to find a safer position. That night the three Muscovite corps abandoned their earthworks and formed a great square *wagenburg* defended by their field guns. A party of peasant sappers cut a passage through nearby woods for their escape. As the Muscovite corps followed they were attacked from the woods in front by Tatar cavalry and hit on the flanks by Polish hussars. They also came under bombardment by Potocki's artillery. Part of the *wagenburg* – about 1,000 wagons and seven guns – was separated and presumably overwhelmed when it came under fire while trying to cross a log road hastily laid across the marsh, but sorties by Muscovite cavalry and some of Tsytsura's cossacks enabled the rest of the column to keep moving through the darkness towards Chudnovo. Over the next few days the army slowly skirmished its way towards Chudnovo. On the morning of 26 September Potocki and Lubomirski awoke to find that the Muscovites were in movement again, passing through woods towards the hills. At mid-day they bombarded the Muscovite column and attacked it from rear and flanks as it was ascending a steep hill. Yet the Muscovite *wagenburg* held, losing just eighty wagons and seven or eight guns. Even Lubomirski was impressed by their good order: "The Muscovites flee from us like a wolf baring its teeth, not like a rabbit."[50]

Sheremetev reached Chudnovo on 27 September and built a new camp on the banks of the Teterev River while part of his army seized whatever stores they could find in town. But the Poles soon arrived and occupied the surrounding Chudnovo heights, from where they could train their guns down on Sheremetev's new camp. Sheremetev's cavalry had no pasture for their mounts here, and any of his men venturing out for wood or water were likely to be captured by the Tatars encamped in the surrounding ravines. The next several days saw no major movement on either side – rather an artillery duel during which Muscovite supplies again ran low.

Lubomirski learned from a cossack prisoner on 6 October that Iurii Khmel'nyts'kyi had reached Slobodishche, several kilometers to the east, and was resting his army there for a march to reinforce Sheremetev. With some misgivings Potocki permitted Lubomirski to take 9,000 troops (mostly cavalry), a few thousand Tatars, some of Ivan Vyhovs'kyi's cossacks, and ten field guns against Khmel'nyts'kyi. On the seventh Lubomirski attacked the cossack army at Slobodishche. Lieutenant Patrick Gordon was wounded while leading an advance by dismounted dragoons across the marsh but managed to break through Khmel'nyts'kyi's barricades.[51] Khmel'nyts'kyi suffered heavy losses but found his withdrawal blocked by the Tatars. Fearing that larger Polish and Tatar forces were approaching and that Sheremetev could no longer reinforce him, Khmel'nyts'kyi capitulated sometime between 8 and 17 October. He pledged his allegiance to the Commonwealth, having been given to understand it would honor the terms of the Hadiach Treaty.

Sheremetev finally tried to break out his own trap on 13 October, forming eight or more columns within another vast *wagenburg* and setting out for Slobodishche to reach Iurii Khmel'nyts'kyi's army. Lubomirski's division followed behind, while Potocki's division tried to get ahead to block its advance. Three times the Poles and Tatars fell upon the *wagenburg*. At one point Tatar cavalry broke through but then fell to plundering, allowing Sheremetev to make a counterattack with cold steel and push them out. Muddy roads, flooded meadows, and the absence of bridges made it impossible to advance any further, however; he had to halt his column on 14 October and form a new camp on the edge of the forest, the only available expanse of dry ground. He had managed to get just a few kilometers east from his previous position and had lost another 1,000 men in the process.

News of Khmel'nyts'kyi's surrender spread among the cossack infantry. Tsytsura went over to the Poles with about 2,000 cossacks on 21 October. Potocki and Sikorski had begun a heavy bombardment from guns atop an earth berm erected around Sheremetev's position. Sheremetev's stores were nearly depleted and it was raining almost incessantly. On 26 October Sheremetev sent I. P. Akinfiev to the Polish camp to propose a truce. He hoped this would buy enough time for reinforcements from Kiev to arrive, unaware a Polish detachment had already driven them back to Kiev.

Potocki and Lubomirski offered a truce if Sheremetev's army would lay down its arms and leave Ukraine, withdrawing all the way to Putivl'. They also demanded Sheremetev order the removal of all other Muscovite forces from Ukraine (which he did not have the authority to do) and remain hostage in the Polish camp with 200 of his officers until the evacuation was completed. Sheremetev complied and his troops disarmed on 4 November. But *nuraddin* Gazy Girei raised objections to this agreement, viewing it as an unnecessary compromise with the Muscovites and perhaps a sign the Commonwealth was about to abandon its alliance with the Tatars in order to regain control of the Left Bank. To placate the *nuraddin* Sheremetev offered twenty-four Muscovite hostages and 60,000 thalers and even turned over 8–9,000 surviving cossacks of Ceciura's command. But this was not enough for the *nuraddin*; he demanded more Muscovite prisoners. Potocki and Lubomirski finally decided they could not afford to lose their alliance with the Tatars – another 30,000 Tatars were deployed on the Polish frontier at this moment – and it had become clear to them that the Muscovite *voevody* were not going to obey Sheremetev's call to abandon the Ukrainian towns. They removed the German infantrymen guarding the Muscovite camp and the Tatars poured in, massacring some 7,000 unarmed Muscovites and enslaving 1,000 more. Sheremetev himself was turned over to the *nuraddin*. He would spend the next twenty-two years in Crimean captivity.[52]

A Muscovite-Ukrainian army of almost 40,000 men had been completely destroyed. Sheremetev bore much of the responsibility for this debacle through his overconfidence, his impatience to proceed without good intelligence, and his contempt for his cossack allies, which undermined their faith in his plans. His army had made the best it could of *wagenburg* tactics, however, and showed good order in moving from Lubar to Chudnovo and beyond while under repeated attack. But the longer his army stayed behind its wagons, the weaker his cavalry became, so that effective sorties were probably no longer possible after the final camp was set on 14 October.

The Polish hetmans' victory at Chudnovo did not immediately make Iurii Khmel'nyts'kyi master of both Left and Right Banks. There was some Left Bank support for him in Poltava, Priluki, and Mirgorod, but the Zaporozhian hetman Sirko opposed him, as did Iakiv Somko and Nezhin's Colonel Zolotarenko. Muscovite garrisons remained in several Left Bank towns, and Grigorii Romodanovskii, a more capable commander than Sheremetev, arrived at Nezhin in mid-April 1661 with another army from the Belgorod Line. The arrival at Poltava of Grigorii Kosagov's corps of 7,000 troops (mostly foreign formation, with some Don Cossacks) helped Somko and Zolotarenko suppress Iurii's supporters there. Nor was the Right Bank solidly behind Khmel'nyts'kyi: many cossacks were troubled by his dependency upon the Poles, others still hoped to restore Vyhovs'kyi, and the peasantry and townspeople were preoccupied with fears of famine and Tatar raiding.

From spring 1661 to summer 1662 Khmel'nyts'kyi's regiments and Polish forces under Field Hetman Stefan Czarniecki struck across the Dnepr a number of times, causing devastation but failing to break the resistance on the Left Bank. The Crimean Tatars provided support to the Polish offensives but also continued to raid the Right Bank, forcing Iurii Khmel'nyts'kyi to make his own alliance with the khan in October 1661. The khan made his first joint campaign with Iurii against Pereiaslav later that month but did not remain long on the Left Bank.

Khmel'nyts'kyi's final attempt to subjugate the Left Bank – a June–July 1662 attack on Pereiaslav supported by Polish cavalry squadrons and the Crimean Tatars – failed when Romodanovskii brought 10,000 Muscovite horse to the aid of Somko and Zolotarenko and drove Khmel'nyts'kyi back across the Dnepr. The Tatars did not assist Khmel'nyts'kyi and his camp was destroyed on 17 July. He fled to Chyhyryn pursued by Muscovite cavalry. Having lost the confidence of his colonels he abdicated the hetmancy in January 1663 and took the tonsure at Chyhyryn monastery. Pavlo Teteria, a supporter of the Hadiach Articles and alliance with the Poles, was elected his successor.

Meanwhile Zolotarenko was working to unify the cossack resistance on the Left Bank. He organized a *rada* at Kozeletsk to elect a Hetman of Left Bank Ukraine. The colonels and *starshina* were not one mind, however; the *rada* proclaimed Somko the new hetman, but supporters of Ivan Briukhovets'kyi would not accept the results and convinced Moscow, which had not sent a representative to Kozeletsk, to insist upon a new election *rada* held in the presence of the Muscovite army. This second *rada* occurred at Nezhin in June 1663 and elected Briukhovets'kyi, who subsequently did everything he could to ingratiate himself with Moscow. In September he had Somko arrested and executed on charges of treasonable conspiracy with Tsytsura and the Poles.[53]

This war owed its length and human cost not just to Muscovite and Commonwealth territorial ambitions but to the ambitions of the Ukrainian hetmans, none of whom could accept the permanent division of Ukraine. Sheremetev had led his army to destruction in Volhynia upon the urging of Tsytsura, who had believed it was still possible to reunite both banks of Ukraine by military force. Now Right Bank Hetman Pavlo Teteria urged the Poles to invade the Left Bank in pursuit of the same goal.

In September 1663 the Poles still had 40,000 field army troops in Ukraine: a division under Crown Hetman Potocki, a division under Field Hetman Czarniecki, a division under Jan Sobieski, and now a division under King Jan Kazimierz himself. Dedysh Aga had also brought 40,000 Crimean Tatars up to Bar to rendezvous with Sobieski's regiments.

At a council of war at Bila Tserkva there were voices urging the army be used to consolidate control over the Right Bank, but Teteria and Dedysh Aga insisted it should be taken across the Dnepr to destroy Briukhovets'kyi and expel the Muscovites. Their view prevailed, perhaps because it also seemed to offer the king the opportunity to use a subjugated north Ukraine as staging-area for a push north into southern Lithuania to join with Sapieha and Pac and throw the Muscovites out of Lithuania as well.

A central magazine for all four divisions was established at Stavishche. It was decided not to march on Kiev itself, where a successful siege would undoubtedly take too long and consume too many supplies; rather the four divisions were to circumvent Kiev and concentrate on seizing the smaller cossack and Muscovite garrisons in the northern interior of the Left Bank. The king's division was the first to cross the Dnepr, at Rzhishchev on 13 November, followed by the Crimean Tatars at Tripol'e. Jan Kazimierz counted on speed to carry him deep into the Left Bank, so his division traveled without many wagons and relied on foraging. He was fortunate in not encountering much Muscovite resistance – to his surprise Romodanovskii's army was still in its winter quarters on the Belgorod Line – but Briukhovets'kyi's cossacks did harass his foragers. Food shortages therefore left his troops impatient to complete sieges of Left Bank towns. Towns that put up protracted resistance were burned. In January 1664 the king captured Oster and made it his winter quarters. His Tatars went home with their captives, so Jan Kazimierz had to call Teteria's division from

Kremenchug to reinforce him at Oster. Czarniecki's division was already about 100 km to the east, having just captured Romny; this put them within reach of Sumy and Sloboda Ukraine.

Towards the end of January the king's division left Oster and advanced upon Baturin, bypassing Nezhin, which was well fortified and had one of the larger Muscovite garrisons. The small cossack garrison at Saltykova-Devitsa, however, was massacred after beating back several storm assaults. Intelligence that Briukhovets'kyi had reinforced Baturin convinced the king to turn north to rendezvous with Sapieha's and Pac's Lithuanians. This move was blocked by Muscovite forces under Boriatinskii, Kurakin, and Cherkasskii, however, and the king had to turn back to Novgorod-Severskii and then to Glukhov. His intelligence of the enemy's movements had been inadequate and his marchroute had repeatedly changed to avoid garrisons too large for his division to capture.

Czarniecki's division reached the king at Glukhov and placed it under siege. Teteria's division was also called to Glukhov, for taking this town was desperately necessary: Polish stores were now very low, the winter frost was becoming unbearable, and Briukhovets'kyi and Romodanovskii were reportedly coming en masse to Glukhov's relief. But Glukhov stood firm, its frozen soil hampering Polish mining efforts and its small garrison (100 or so cossacks and some Muscovite troops under Avraamii Lopukhin) throwing back every storming party. In late February Romodanovskii and Briukhovets'kyi arrived and there was a great battle on open ground outside Glukhov. The account of it given in the *Chronicle of Samuil Velychko*, written decades later, describes it in detail but probably without much accuracy. Apparently the Polish forces were defeated, though, for Romodanovskii pursued the king's division all the way back to the Desna.[54]

Stalemate

The battle at Glukhov marked the end of the Polish offensive in Ukraine. The Crimean Tatars were no longer reinforcing Polish forces, most having returned to Crimea after harvesting captives to their satisfaction, and a raid on Perekop by Kosagov's troops and Sirko's Zaporozhians made it unlikely the Tatars would return to Ukraine soon. Furthermore, Czarniecki's brutality along his marchroute to Romny had provoked resistance on the Right Bank. Rebels had seized Stavishche and the Polish army's stores, and Colonel Bohun was executed for allegedly secretly working for Briukhovets'kyi. Teteria had to return to the Right Bank to put down revolt. Czarniecki therefore withdrew from the Glukhov region and returned to Liubech while the king took his army from Starodub back into Lithuania.

By this point Jan Kazimierz had in fact lost the ability to finance further operations in Ukraine. Many of his troops had not been paid for two years.

The breakdown of Polish military finance was not so much a technical as a political problem. In 1659 the king had succeeded in significantly expanding the army, particularly its foreign contingent, by introducing a centrally administered excise tax. But the *Sejm* and provincial dietines considered this to be an extraordinary tax, to be run only through the next *Sejm*. To regularize war taxes the king needed to strengthen his authority vis-à-vis the magnates in the *Sejm*. He had sought to accomplish this through particular political reforms: transferring some power from the *Sejm* to the Senate Council; running the *Sejm* on an agendum set by royal proposal rather than deputies' own proposals; reducing the fiscal authority of the provincial dietines; and insisting upon the election of a successor *vivente rege* in the hope this would break down factionalism. But these proposals had alarmed those magnates who noted the king's popularity with the officers of the foreign contingent and feared reform might be a cover for royal military absolutism. By 1662 they had defeated reform. The *Sejm* and dietines retained control of war taxes and began withholding them to protest royal actions they considered dangerous to Commonwealth liberties. When Jan Kazimierz impeached the popular Grand Hetman Jerzy Lubomirski for refusing to continue campaigning against the Muscovites, Lubomirski's supporters in the army's national contingent rose up in *confederatio* against the Crown. Confederate forces marched back into Poland from Ukraine collecting their pay arrears along the way by plundering. A civil war had begun. In July 1666 the *confederatio* decisively defeated the royal army at Matwy. Jan Kazimierz abdicated two years later.[55]

Muscovite forces in Ukraine were also losing their combat effectiveness. Desertion had become pandemic. Only 200 Muscovite troops remained at Uman' by 2 September 1664; by the end of the month Kosagov had just 68 *reitary* and 160 infantrymen under arms. The garrisons at Kiev, Nezhin, and Pereiaslav were dangerously undermanned and low on stores. The shortage of troops made it impossible for Kosagov and Briukhovets'kyi to reinforce the rebels at Stavishche, who surrendered to the Poles on 8 October. Simple war-weariness was undoubtedly part of the problem, but so was the inflation unleashed by the new copper coinage, which had not been brought under full control even though the government had finally begun withdrawing the copper coins. An English observer thought it would take forty years to repair the damage done by the debasement scheme. Muscovite forces on the Left Bank did finally get 7,000 men in reinforcement in spring 1665, but they were mostly Kalmyks, and Briukhovets'kyi was supposed to pay them out of his own revenues.[56]

Fortunately for the Muscovites the Lubomirski Revolt and the collapse of the Polish war effort provided a breathing-spell they could exploit to tighten their political control over the Left Bank. In September 1665 Hetman Briukhovets'kyi accepted a new treaty, the Moscow Articles, which conferred further privileges on the *starshina* while simultaneously expanding the authority of the Muscovite *voevody* and establishing garrisons at more towns. The garrison at Kiev was to comprise 5,000 men; there would be garrisons of 1,200 men each at Chernigov, Pereiaslav, Nezhin, and Poltava, and 300-man garrisons at

Novgorod-Severskii, Kremenchug, Kodak, and Oster. These garrisons were now to be maintained from Ukrainian revenue sources – mill and tavern revenues and other cash and kind taxes – collected by Muscovite officials into the tsar's treasury. Briukhovets'kyi reportedly allowed *voevody* to be stationed in Glukhov, Gadiach, Mirgorod, Lubny, Priluki, and Baturin as well, to help him maintain order.[57]

Ukraine remained divided along the Dnepr, however. Most of the Right Bank remained under Hetman Teteria, and when conflict among his colonels forced him to flee to Wallachia, his aide-de-camp Petro Doroshenko was elected the new hetman.

Petro Doroshenko, grandson of the revered Zaporozhian *koshevoi hetman* Mikhaylo Doroshenko, had been colonel of the Chyhyryn regiment under Vyhovs'kyi and Iurii Khmel'nyts'kyi's aide-de-camp from 1662. He was strongly committed to reunification of Ukraine under one hetman, with Ukrainian autarchy guaranteed by a loose protectorate. He did not believe a Muscovite protectorate would respect the Hetmanate's independence, however; a Polish protectorate might, if the king and *Sejm* could be brought to honor the terms of the Hadiach Treaty, but a Turco-Tatar protectorate seemed to him more achievable. He had good relations with the khan and the sultan. In August 1665 he negotiated an alliance with mirza Kammambet to defeat Drozd and Detsik, the colonels who had overthrown Teteria and were challenging Doroshenko's election.

Doroshenko initially swore fealty to King Jan Kazimierz. But he continued to cultivate secret ties with the Crimean Tatars and the Ottomans in anticipation of an opportunity to expel the Poles and Muscovites. The Polish military presence was the more negligible – just small garrisons of German mercenaries, Polish volunteer irregulars, and royal cossacks at Chyhyryn, Korsun', and Bila Tserkva – and would therefore be the first to be challenged. The Muscovite forces on the Left Bank were much larger but were increasingly despised by the townsmen on whom they were billeted; there were already anti-Muscovite disturbances at Kiev, Kotel'va, Nezhin, Pereiaslav, and other towns. Doroshenko believed that he might be able to drive out the Muscovites through further agitation work and alliance with the Zaporozhian Sich.

In February 1666 Doroshenko convened a *rada* at Lisianka and announced he had entered an alliance with the Crimean Khanate and was demanding the Poles leave Ukraine.[58]

The Andrusovo Armistice and the new Ottoman threat

In 1666 Andrusovo, near Smolensk, became the site of peace talks between Muscovy and the Commonwealth. The Poles were under strong inducement to end the war: Lubomirski was seeking alliance with the tsar, and Doroshenko's army of 25,000 cossacks, now reinforced by 30,000 Tatars and a detachment of Ottoman janissaries, was trying to drive the Poles from Bratslav palatinate. Open

Ottoman military support for Doroshenko's revolt was a deeply alarming development threatening to pull the Commonwealth into war with the Turks. It was just as alarming to the Muscovites, for part of Doroshenko's forces were making raids across the Dnepr against Muscovite-garrisoned Pereiaslav and Priluki districts and calling on the people to throw off Muscovite occupation before the tsar's diplomats handed their realm back to the Poles. If Doroshenko managed to bring Sirko and the Zaporozhians over to his side there was the real possibility they could drive out the Muscovite armies and garrisons and turn all of Ukraine into a vassal protectorate of the Ottomans.

On 13 January 1667 Muscovy and the Commonwealth signed a thirteen-year armistice agreement at Andrusovo. Muscovy retained Smolensk and the Seversk districts, Chernigov, and part of Vitebsk palatinate (Dorogobuzh, Belaia, Nevl', Sebezh, Krasnoe, Velizh), but the rest of Belarus' and Lithuania was reconfirmed for the Commonwealth. The problem of Ukraine was addressed in Solomonic fashion, by dividing it along the Dnepr, the Left Bank to remain under the tsar's lofty hand, the Right Bank (assuming Doroshenko's revolt could be ended) to be restored to the Commonwealth. Polish diplomats allowed Kiev, standing on the right bank of the Dnepr, to remain under Muscovite control for the next two years only (by which point they hoped to have suppressed Doroshenko). Muscovy and the Commonwealth were somehow supposed to exercise joint sovereignty over the Zaporozhian Sich.

Besides formalizing the division of Ukraine the Andrusovo Armistice had the great consequence of committing Muscovy and the Commonwealth to cooperative diplomacy to obtain Ottoman and Crimean Tatar neutrality and keep both banks of Ukraine from falling under Ottoman-Tatar domination. Ordyn-Nashchokin even went so far as to consider the armistice the possible foundation for an eventual military alliance uniting not only Muscovy and the Commonwealth but other European powers in a great Holy League against the Porte and Khanate. He developed a plan for a Muscovite attack upon Perekop with a simultaneous Polish strike across the Danube at Belgrad. In May and June the tsar sent missions to the Empire, France, England, Spain, the Netherlands, Denmark, Sweden, Brandenburg, Venice, and Persia to solicit their recognition of the Andrusovo settlement, to determine which of these powers might be willing to mediate in negotiating a permanent peace with the Commonwealth, and to sound out interest in an anti-Ottoman alliance.[59] One could argue that it was at this point Muscovy emerged from comparative geopolitical isolation and sought to become a regular player in European diplomacy.

But Ordyn-Nashchokin's project of a great anti-Ottoman alliance was not yet realistic. Some major obstacles to it remained. Uncertainty about Polish intentions remained because the Commonwealth's policy towards the Ottomans continued to be pulled between competing pro-Austrian and pro-French factions. King Jan Kazimierz longed to abdicate and the succession might fall either to Emperor Leopold I's candidate, the Prince of Lorraine, or Louis XIV's candidate, the Prince de Conde. Second, the Muscovite mission to Vienna experienced protocol difficulties and had only limited success; the Emperor was willing to mediate in future Polish–Muscovite peace talks but was not ready to commit to a coalition against the Turks. Third and most important, neither Muscovite nor Polish envoys were able to get Doroshenko to give a firm commitment to peace. That autumn the Polish Crown Hetman Jan Sobieski did manage to extort from Doroshenko a pledge to accept the King's sovereignty over the Ukraine, and from Doroshenko's Tatar commanders, a pledge to end raids upon the Commonwealth in return for the resumption of Polish subsidies to the khan. But Doroshenko had no intention of honoring his promise for he had been pressed to it merely to rescue his army at Podgaitsy, his Tatar allies having decided to return to Crimea upon news that Sirko and the Zaporozhians had burned Perekop and raided the *ulus* of the Shirin *bey*. In December the tsar sent Vasilii Tiapkin to Chyhyryn to convince Doroshenko to abandon his alliance with the Turks and Tatars and accept again the tsar's protectorate over Ukraine. Doroshenko refused and charged Moscow with betraying the Hetmanate's freedom by negotiating the Andrusovo Armistice without consulting the cossacks. Report of his rebuff even had the effect of increasing Doroshenko's popularity among the cossack regiments on the Left Bank, as a defender of Ukrainian liberties more resolute than the servile Briukhovets'kyi. Abuses of authority by Muscovite *voevody* and garrison troops, along with the unresolved issue of the future status of Kiev, were feeding discontent with the Muscovite occupation. The *voevoda* of Kiev noted that the townspeople and rural inhabitants were no longer paying their taxes.[60]

The alternative to forming an immediate military coalition against the Tatars and Turks – achieving real diplomatic rapprochement with them, and getting them to accept the terms of the Andrusovo settlement – was no more possible at this time. The sultan and the khan were prepared to make vague offers of peace but held back from any clear and firm commitment to the terms of Andrusovo. Sultan Mehmet IV saw in continued alliance with Doroshenko the opportunity to exploit Poland's weakened state and annex Kamianets and much of Podolia. He therefore ignored Warsaw's argument that his formal endorsement of the Andrusovo peace would enable Muscovy and the Commonwealth to finally put an end to Zaporozhian cossack raids on Ottoman territory. Khan Aadil Girei was prepared to assure the Muscovites he would leave the Left Bank towns in peace, but he exempted Kiev from this on the grounds the Andrusovo agreement had identified it as a Commonwealth town, and he expected the tsar to make good his tribute arrears. Subsequent Muscovite efforts to negotiate with Aadil Girei were undermined not only by Doroshenko's agents, but by the Zaporozhians, who executed a Crimean envoy en route to Moscow and the envoy the tsar had sent to the Sich to protest this act. Moscow attributed these deeds to Doroshenko's influence but it is possible they were committed by Doroshenko's enemies in the Sich to prevent the Muscovites from coming to terms with Doroshenko. Negotiations with the Crimean Tatars therefore continued over the next three years with no sign of reaching any meaningful agreement.

The magnitude of the danger now posed by Doroshenko and his Ottoman and Tatar allies prevented Muscovy from reducing its army strength after the Andrusovo Armistice. Troop strength along the Belgorod Line in fact had to be increased. In 1668–1669 the Belgorod and Sevsk military administrative regions had 112,062 in three army groups under Grigorii Romodanovskii, G. S. Kurakin, and S. A. Khovanskii. Of these, about 25,000 infantry and 42,500 cavalry were available for campaign duty; the rest were assigned to defense duty along the Belgorod Line. The buildup on the Belgorod Line was enough to beat back attacks on Sevsk and Komaritskaia by Doroshenko's cossacks and Tatars and to keep the khan in peace talks with Muscovite envoys.[61]

Up to early 1668 Doroshenko's military struggle had been primarily with Commonwealth forces. Moscow had still thought it possible to induce him to repudiate his alliance with the Ottomans and Tatars by indicating it was prepared to jettison Briukhovets'kyi – increasingly unpopular even with the *starshina* of the Left Bank – and confirm Doroshenko's authority over both sides of the Dnepr. Ironically, it was Briukhovets'kyi who now presented Doroshenko with another way of eliminating his rival and taking control of the Left Bank.

In January 1668 Briukhovets'kyi and Doroshenko made a secret rapprochement. It was agreed that Briukhovets'kyi would raise the Left Bank against the Muscovite garrisons and receive assistance from Doroshenko's cossacks and the Tatars; once the Muscovites had been driven out Doroshenko would step aside for him, for he claimed he wanted nothing more than to see all Ukraine and Zaporozhia reunited under a single hetman. The security of the reunified Hetmanate would then be guaranteed by the Ottoman sultan and Crimean khan.

Briukhovets'kyi trusted to this pact and made attacks on the undermanned Muscovite garrisons at Gadiach, Starodub, and Glukhov. His agents even agitated for revolt among the cossacks of Sloboda Ukraine. The Military Chancellery ordered Romodanovskii into Ukraine to suppress the revolt, but a harsh late winter and shortage of fodder delayed his army's arrival until May. Briukhovets'kyi considered his revolt on the verge of succeeding, for Doroshenko's forces and the Crimean Tatars were crossing the Dnepr to reinforce him. He had no suspicion that Doroshenko had remained in negotiation with Moscow and was coming to attack him, nor that some of his own colonels were preparing to betray him. At Oposhna his Tatars and many of his officers turned against him and he was given into Doroshenko's custody, chained to a gun carriage, and beaten to death.[62]

Doroshenko now reportedly had about 50,000 men – half of them Crimean Tatars – and faced no significant opposition force on either side of the Dnepr. He counted on his alliance with the Khanate and Porte to reconcile the Poles and Muscovites to his reunification of the Hetmanate. Both were indeed continuing to negotiate with him through the rest of the year. But Warsaw and Moscow were unable to reach terms with him because they doubted his willingness to repudiate his Tatar and Ottoman allies. Furthermore, if either unilaterally recognized the unification of the Hetmanate it would break the Andrusovo agreement, which had divided Ukraine along the Dnepr in order to reach armistice.

By the end of 1668 the Muscovites had discovered an alternative course of action. Doroshenko had overestimated the depth of his own popularity on the Left Bank. The Zaporozhians still resisted him and had elected their secretary Sukhoveenko as "Hetman of all Ukraine." Doroshenko had returned to Chyhyryn leaving Dem'ian Mnogogreshnyi, former colonel of the Chernigov regiment, in charge of the Left Bank as Commissioned Seversk Hetman. The Muscovites decided to split Mnogogreshnyi from Doroshenko. Romodanovskii reentered Ukraine and besieged Mnogogreshnyi's forces at Nezhin, and then, assisted by Chernigov archbishop Lazar Baranovich, turned negotiations for Mnogogreshnyi's withdrawal into talks towards an alliance.

On 27 February 1669 Romodanovskii and Artemon Matveev called the colonels and *starshina* of several Left Bank regiments to a *rada* at their headquarters near Glukhov to elect a Hetman of Seversk – essentially a new Hetman of Left Bank Ukraine. The *rada* proclaimed Dem'ian Mnogogreshnyi their new hetman without discussion. They did, however, stipulate that the tsar return to the principles of the 1654 Pereiaslav agreement and withdraw the Muscovite *voevody* and garrison troops from all towns save Kiev. But Moscow's Glukhov Articles did not concede them this. They offered in compromise loosening of the restraints borne in the days of Briukhovets'kyi – pledges that Muscovite *voevody* would not interfere in administration in the towns or the cossack regiments and would pay for all requisitions, that all taxes for the support of Muscovite garrisons would be collected into the hetman's treasury, and that the *starshina* could petition the tsar directly. But *voevody* were to remain in Kiev, Pereiaslav, Nezhin, Chernigov, and Oster. Romodanovskii explained that this was necessary for defense. He reminded them that their new hetman's authority did not extend over the Right Bank, and told them they had no right to demand the removal of the Muscovite garrisons.

> Bohdan Khmel'nyts'kyi became the subject of the Great Sovereign and served him faithfully to his death. But what happened after him? You had hetmans – Ivashka Vygovs'kyi, Iuraska Khmel'nyts'kyi, Ivashka Briukhovets'kyi – and they all compiled treaty articles, signed them in their own hands, and pledged their souls upon them ... and then betrayed them.[63]

CHAPTER FIVE

The Chyhyryn campaigns and the wars of the Holy League

Ottoman military intervention in Ukraine, 1669–1676

Mnogogreshnyi's election as Hetman of the Left Bank shocked and enraged Doroshenko. He held his own *rada* at Korsun' in spring 1669 and formally pledged his vassalage to the Sultan.

For the time being this seemed the best response available to him. While his Tatar allies were driving Polish garrisons out of the Right Bank and raiding Małopolska Doroshenko could threaten the Poles and Muscovites with Ottoman military intervention to keep them negotiating with him; and by spreading rumors of his imminent reconciliation with one or the other he could sow suspicion between them and press for further concessions. For the sultan Doroshenko's fealty offered a means of blocking the extension of the Andrusovo Armistice into an Eternal Peace between Muscovy and the Commonwealth. Envoys from the Porte informed Warsaw that the Commonwealth would have to abandon all claims to Right Bank Ukraine and repudiate the Andrusovo Armistice to secure peace with the Crimean Khanate and Ottoman Empire. The Muscovites were likewise put on notice: if they chose the course proposed by Ordyn-Nashchokin and joined the Poles in attempting arbitration of the issue of the status of the Right Bank, they would have to be prepared to join the Commonwealth in military coalition not only against Doroshenko and the Tatars but against the Turks; if they were to negotiate peace with the Khan and Sultan they would have to be ready to break with the Commonwealth. To further complicate Moscow's position, peace talks with the Khan had provoked the Zaporozhians to assassinate envoy Lodyzhenskii on his way to Bakhchisarai, while talks with Polish representatives about coalition and permanent peace alarmed Left Bank cossacks that the handover of Kiev and perhaps most of the Left Bank to the Poles was imminent. Such fears were beginning to incline cossack officers from Baturin, Poltava, and Mirgorod to Doroshenko's cause.[1]

But Doroshenko's influence would begin to erode once Ottoman forces actually invaded Ukraine.

After Polish Crown Hetman Jan Sobieski defeated Doroshenko's forces at Bar, Bratslav, and Kalnik Mehmet IV sent an ultimatum to King Michał Korybut

Wiśniowiecki demanding he withdraw all Polish troops from Ukraine. In the spring of 1672 Mehmet IV declared war upon the Commonwealth and sent a army of 50–80,000 troops across the Dnestr to besiege Kamianets-Podol'sk.

The Ottoman invasion is often characterized as an opportunistic imperialist adventure, an example of the Köprülü viziers' strategy of waging wars of territorial expansion as a panacea for the Empire's internal problems. There is some truth to this. The invasion took advantage of the political and military weakness of the Commonwealth under King Michał – the deadlock between pro-Habsburg and pro-French factions, the reduced strengths of the Crown and Lithuanian armies – and it did result in Ottoman annexation of Podolia, the Empire's last significant territorial acquisition. But it could also be seen as a defensive action, an effort to safeguard Ottoman hegemony over Moldavia and Transylvania by deterring Polish intervention in Petriceicu's rebellion against Moldavian Hospodar Gheorghe Duca and by discouraging the wavering Michael I Apafi of Transylvania from joining King Michał and his brother-in-law Leopold I in coalition.[2]

The course of the Polish–Ottoman War of 1672–1676 established Jan Sobieski's reputation as one of the more talented commanders of the seventeenth century at the same time as it dramatized again the political constraints upon Polish military power. Because of the reduced size of the Commonwealth's military establishment on the eve of the war – 12,000 Crown troops and 5,400 Lithuanian troops – the invading Turkish and Crimean armies initially encountered little effective resistance. The fortress of Kamianets, though well-fortified, was defended by only 1,500 troops and capitulated after just a week's siege (August 1672). Mezhibozh'e, Zhvanets, Bar, and other towns fell soon after. The Turks and Tatars placed L'viv under blockade and extorted from its inhabitants a "contribution" of 80,000 thalers. Tatar raiding parties swept across Małopolska and took thousands of captives. In September Jan Sobieski finally managed to assemble militia levies and private troops into an army of 16,000, which he divided into several *corps volant* of 1–2,000 men to attack the camps of the Tatar raiding parties. These small corps would likely have been annihilated if isolated and cornered by the main Turkish army, but because they moved so quickly and usually struck Tatar encampments in teams they were able to smash most of the Tatar *chambuly* and free several thousand prisoners. King Michał, however, had no confidence that this would drive the Turks from Podolia and on 17 October he signed a peace treaty at Buchach ceding all of Podolia to the Sultan, recognizing the independence of the Right Bank under Hetman Doroshenko, and pledging payment of an indemnity of 22,000 ducats.

Jan Sobieski joined other commanders in a *confederatio* that succeeded in forcing the *Sejm* to reject the Buchach treaty and to resume the war. The *Sejm* voted to increase the size of the Crown and Lithuanian armies to 31,000 and 12,000 men; with militiamen and private troops the forces available for campaign numbered nearly 60,000. This, and the additional fact that the Crimean Tatars had not mobilized to reinforce the Turks in Podolia, enabled Sobieski to launch a three-pronged offensive against Halil Pasha's 8,000 troops at Kamianets, Kaplan Pasha's corps of 3–4,000 men at Cecora, and the largest Ottoman force concentration (30,000 Turks and Wallachians) under Hussein Pasha at Khotyn.

On 10 November 1673 King Michał died. That same day Sobieski, commanding about 30,000 men, attacked Hussein Pasha's fortified camp at Khotyn. On the following morning the northeastern ramparts of Hussein Pasha's camp, undermanned after a night of heavy rain and the defection of some 5,000 Wallachians, fell to a storm by dismounted Polish dragoons. Polish heavy cavalry then poured into the Turkish camp while Polish reserve regiments deployed to block the Turks' escape across the Dnestr. The bridge over the Dnestr soon collapsed under heavy artillery fire, leaving Hussein Pasha's army completely encircled. Twenty thousand Turks were killed or captured; Polish losses ranged from 1,500 to 2,000 men.[3] Upon news of this defeat Kaplan Pasha withdrew across the Danube.

The onset of winter soon forced the Poles to lift their blockade of Kamianets, however, and the political factionalism of the interregnum prevented Sobieski from executing his plan to carry the war deeper into Moldavia. Although Sobieski's great victory at Khotyn led to his election as King Jan III on 21 May 1674, he could no longer command resources on the scale the *confederatio* had mobilized during the emergency of 1672–1673. He managed to assemble just 6,000 men to throw back a Turco-Tatar attack upon L'viv in the summer of 1675, and 18,000 men to fight the army of Ibraim Shaitan Pasha to a stalemate at Zurawno in September 1676. Only the smaller Turkish garrisons on the Right Bank and in Podolia fell to him, and Kamianets remained in Ottoman hands. On the other hand Khan Selim Girei, disinclined to suffer further losses on behalf of an Ottoman *eyalet* in Podolia, had offered to mediate in peace talks with the Sultan; and at Jaworow in June 1675 representatives of Louis XIV had pledged a French subsidy if Sobieski ended his war with the Sultan and returned to his old project of seizing East Prussia from Elector Friedrich Wilhelm. Sobieski therefore signed an armistice at Zórawno on 17 October 1676. By its terms the Commonwealth ceded Podolia to the Porte for all time and pledged to evacuate most of its garrisons beyond the Bug. To extend this armistice the *Sejm* would finally ratify the Buchach treaty in 1678. Podolia would remain under Ottoman control until the treaty of Karlowitz in 1699.

Attacks upon Crimean Tatar territory by Muscovite troops, Zaporozhians, and Don Cossacks had helped reduce Tatar support for Ottoman operations against the Poles but had not drawn Muscovy into direct conflict with the Turks. But this situation changed in 1674, when Muscovy took advantage of the waning power of Doroshenko and invaded the Right Bank.

For several years Moscow had clung to the hope that with appropriate concessions it could regain Doroshenko's loyalty; and it had been constrained from taking concerted military action against him by fear that such a violation of the Andrusovo Armistice might reignite war with the Commonwealth. But by 1674 these constraints had lifted. Moscow's patience had been exhausted by

Doroshenko's repeated demands that he be ceded Zaporozhia and all of the Left Bank as the price of his loyalty. Vasilii Daudov had returned from Istanbul to report that Doroshenko was urging the sultan to march upon Kiev. The tsar's sovereignty over the Left Bank had been reinforced, the Left Bank's Hetman Ivan Samoilovich (elected at Konotop in 1672) having reaffirmed the terms of the treaty of Glukhov. Samoilovich was just as intent as Doroshenko upon ruling a united Ukraine and was therefore his implacable enemy, eager to support a Muscovite campaign against him. Meanwhile support for Doroshenko among the colonels of the Right Bank had ebbed considerably as they came to understand the costs of his vassalage to the sultan. Nor was the sultan able to render Doroshenko much real military support; Ottoman commanders were preoccupied with holding Podolia and were unable to establish garrisons on the Right Bank large enough to hold out against the Poles or against Ukrainian insurgents. Furthermore a Muscovite invasion of the Right Bank no longer risked violation of the Andrusovo Armistice, the Commonwealth having abandoned its sovereignty over the Right Bank when King Michal signed the Treaty of Buchach.

The armies of Romodanovskii and Samoilovich therefore launched a major offensive against Doroshenko in January 1674. They captured Cherkassy, Moshnia, and Kanev and bottled him up in Chyhyryn. Most of the Right Bank *starshina* now deserted him and convened a *rada* at Pereiaslav (15–17 March 1674) which recognized Samoilovich as Hetman over a unified Ukraine. It was not until the summer of that year that an Ottoman army under Kaplan Pasha was able to come to Doroshenko's aid. Its arrival did deter Romodanovskii and Samoilovich, who lifted their siege of Chyhyryn and withdrew across the Dnepr. But Kaplan Pasha relied too heavily upon terror to restore Doroshenko's authority over the population of the Right Bank; his massacres of civilians at Lodyzhin and Uman' drove thousands of refugees eastward into Sloboda Ukraine and further discredited Doroshenko. As soon as Kaplan Pasha's army withdrew across the Dnestr King Jan III reentered Ukraine and seized Nemirov, Bar, Kalnik, Mezhibozh'e, and Korsun'. Sobieski's subsequent victories over Ottoman armies at Zamość, Zloczew, and L'viv showed that the Turks were unlikely to resume operations east of the Bug on Doroshenko's behalf anytime soon.

Doroshenko therefore surrendered to Zaporozhian *koshevoi* ataman Ivan Sirko at Chigirin on 10 October 1675. Although he declared his readiness to swear allegiance to the Tsar at this time, Moscow delayed accepting his surrender until September 1676 so as to satisfy Samoilovich (who insisted that Doroshenko capitulate to him personally, lest Sirko represent himself as the new hetman over unified Ukraine) and give the Muscovite army the opportunity to enter Cherkasy, Zhabotyn, and the other towns on the road to Chyhyryn.[4]

The surrender of Doroshenko did not put an end to the Ottoman project of establishing a vassal Principality of Lesser Sarmatia on the Right Bank, but it made it more difficult, for the role of vassal prince now fell upon the unfortunate

Iurii Khmel'nyts'kyi, a prisoner of the Turks since 1672; as there was no natural base of popular support for him on the Right Bank, one would have to be created, through intimidation; and that meant that Ottoman armies would have to play the dominant role in Iurii's campaign. But the new Grand Vizier, Kara Mustafa, accepted the risks this entailed. Perhaps he had concluded that the hospodars of Moldavia and Wallachia might switch their allegiance to Moscow if Samoilovich filled the political vacuum on the Right Bank; or that a major demonstration of Ottoman military power in Ukraine was necessary to discourage King Jan III from thinking he could repudiate the Żórawno Treaty and reestablish Polish garrisons on the Right Bank. There was no longer much likelihood that the king would respond to a new Ottoman campaign on the Right Bank by joining the Muscovites in coalition, for Sobieski was preoccupied with his Brandenburg project and had been promised that his neutrality in Ukraine would be rewarded with the cession of Kiev and Smolensk once Samoilovich and the Muscovites were defeated. Muscovite diplomacy was less likely now to present Sobieski with a compelling counter-offer, for Tsar Aleksei was dead and A. S. Matveev in political eclipse. Furthermore the Zaporozhian attacks upon Evpatoriia, Karasubazar, and Bakhchisarai and Muscovite attempts to beseiege the Ottoman fortresses on the Kalancha River were provocations the Porte could not afford to ignore.

Rolling the Muscovites back from the Left Bank may not have been among Kara Mustafa's war aims, but the seizure of Chyhyryn and possibly also Kiev for Iurii Khmel'nyts'kyi were, under the justification that King Michał had ceded them to the sultan's vassal Doroshenko with the rest of the Right Bank under the Treaty of Buchach. While Moscow's support for Samoilovich's bid to subjugate the Right Bank had its limits, Moscow had cause to fear that the loss of Kiev could bring about the collapse of its control over the Left Bank.

The First Russo-Turkish War, 1676–1681

In June 1677 Vizier Ibraim "Shaitan" Pasha, *muhafiz* of Ochakov, led an army of 45,000 men (some 30,000 Ottoman and Moldavian horse, 15,000 janissaries, and Iurii Khmel'nyts'kyi's guard of 300 cossacks) across the Danube on campaign against Chyhyryn. His objective was to join with Khan Selim Girei's army of 20,000 Tatars and reach Chyhyryn before it could be relieved by Romodanovskii and Samoilovich, capture the town by early October at the least, and install Iurii Khmel'nyts'kyi there. This would then allow him to erect bridges across the Dnepr for a spring attack upon Kiev.[5]

Samoilovich and Romodanovskii had argued forcefully for defending Chyhyryn at all costs. Since the time of Bohdan Khmel'nyts'kyi Chyhyryn had been recognized as the de facto capital of the united Zaporozhian Host, so its loss to Iurii Khmel'nyts'kyi and the Turks would be a major blow to Samoilovich's project to extend his sovereignty over the towns and villages of the Right Bank. The loss of Chyhyryn would also make it harder to rein in the Zaporozhian

Sich, for Samoilovich was convinced the Sich's *koshevoi ataman* Sirko had turned renegade by signing an armistice with the Crimean Tatars. Above all the fall of Chyhyryn would give Ottoman and Crimean armies a convenient staging area for attacks upon Kiev and the towns of the Left Bank. This last consideration was the argument most weighty in Moscow's eyes. Therefore the Tsar and Duma had agreed to commit vast resources to the defense of Chyhyryn.

By 29 March Chyhyryn had been refortified by Nicholas von Zahlen and its Muscovite-Ukrainian garrison, now under the command of Major-General Afanasii Trauernicht, had been doubled to about 12,500 men (7,000 *soldaty*, 2,400 *strel'tsy*, and 3,100 of Samoilovich's cossacks). There had not been time to accumulate sufficient stores and most of Chyhyryn's forty-five guns were of poor quality, but its reinforced garrison gave it a much greater chance of withstanding a Turkish siege, especially given that Ibraim Pasha's advancing army may have had as few as twenty-eight guns. In July Romodanovskii and Samoilovich held a council of war at Baturin. They agreed that Romodanovskii, commanding 32,258 men from the Belgorod and Sevsk army groups, would march from Kursk and rendezvous with Samoilovich and his 20,000 cossacks on the Artopolot' River, cross the Dnepr, and proceed to the relief of Chyhyryn. V. V. Golitsyn's corps of 5,705 men at Putivl' would stand in reserve and guard their rear; additional corps would stand at Belgorod (under I. Rzhevskii), Ryl'sk (A. Khovanskii), and Novyi Oskol' (P. Khovanskii).[6]

Ibraim Pasha's army did not reach Chyhyryn until 4 August. Romodanovskii's progress was also slow because of the great size of his train. Romodanovskii and Samoilovich rendezvoused on the Artopolot' River on 10 August, and on the night of 20 August a detachment of 1,400 of their dragoons and *serdiuk* mercenaries crossed the Dnepr and slipped through the marsh and woods to reach the gates of Chyhyryn and embolden its defenders with news of the relief army's advance. By 24 August the Muscovite-Ukrainian army had only to cross the Sula River at Buzhin Ford to reach Chyhyryn. But Ibraim Pasha had shifted much of his own army to try to block its crossing.

On the night of 26–27 August, under cover of Romodanovskii's batteries, a force of 2,000 *soldaty* and 2,000 cossacks managed to cross the river by longboat and barge and take control of a sandbar along the opposite bank. These troops threw back an attack by Ottoman janissaries, seized their trenches, and drove the enemy observation corps back to its camp in the hills. This made it possible to ferry the rest of the Muscovite-Ukrainian army across the river.

On the twenty-eighth Muscovite and Ukrainian cavalry attacked and overwhelmed Ibraim Pasha's camp, inflicting heavy casualties and pursuing the enemy all the way to Krylov. This was the decisive engagement of the first Chyhyryn campaign. The next day Ibraim Pasha lifted his siege and began withdrawing to the Ingul' River. Romodanovskii and Samoilovich chose not to pursue him, as this would have required following in force, slowed by a large baggage train and harassed by Tatar cavalry, and their more immediate concern was relieving and refortifying Chyhyryn (5–10 September).

If prisoner testimonies are to be believed Romodanovskii and Samoilovich had won a victory to rival Sobieski's at Khotyn. The Turks and Crimean Tatars had suffered 20,000 casualties, most of them in the 28 August attack upon their camp. Upon his return to Istanbul Ibraim Pasha was imprisoned; Selim Khan was ordered deposed and exiled to Rhodes. Casualties in the army of Romodanovskii and Samoilovich were 2,460 dead and about 5,000 wounded; Trauernicht lost 500 men in holding Chyhyryn's walls.[7]

On 22 June 1678 a second Ottoman army of 70,000 men under the command of Grand Vizier Kara Mustafa Pasha crossed the Dnestr and rendezvoused with Khan Murat Girei on another attempt to take Chyhyryn. Kara Mustafa had taken precautions to avoid the mistakes of Ibraim Pasha; he had a considerably larger artillery train and larger auxiliary of Tatar cavalry, and his army made an impressive forced march in double time across the Ukrainian steppe, reaching the Ingul' River (six hours' ride from Chyhyryn) on 18 July.[8] Moscow again entrusted the relief of Chyhyryn to Romodanovskii and Hetman Samoilovich. They followed essentially the same strategy that had led them to victory over Ibraim Pasha the previous year. But this time, for reasons unclear, they halted their armies on the far side of the Tias'min River, just two miles from Chyhyryn, making no serious effort to attack the Ottoman camp. On 11 August Romodanovskii ordered the Chyhyryn garrison evacuated across the river and its citadel burned to prevent it from falling into enemy hands. For decades thereafter Ukrainian political and cultural figures were outraged by "the incompetence and perfidy" of Romodanovskii and blamed him for the loss of the entire Right Bank to the Turks. Van Keller, the Dutch resident in Moscow, noted that feeling against Romodanovskii was so high in the capital that Romodanovskii did not dare show his face there.

But it should be noted that in their consultations with emissaries from Moscow over the winter and spring of 1677–1678 Romodanovskii and Samoilovich had remained firm about the necessity of defending Chyhyryn against a second Ottoman invasion and had argued that a second campaign to defend Chyhyryn had good prospects for success. The defeat of Ibraim Pasha had shown that Russo-Ukrainian forces could stand up against a full-size Ottoman army; the new Crimean Khan, Murat Girei, was unlikely to have any more stomach than his predecessor for a pitched battle to capture Chyhyryn for the Sultan, given that this would have the effect of further limiting the Khan's sovereignty over his own Ukrainian *yurt*; and Samoilovich even went so far as to endorse Lithuanian Hetman Michał Pac's proposal that King Jan III be convinced to repudiate the shameful Żórawno Treaty and negotiate an alliance with Muscovy against the Ottomans.[9]

Rather it was Moscow that now had reservations about the risks and benefits of a second Chyhyryn campaign. The new thinking as of spring 1678 was that Samoilovich's efforts to extend his authority over the Right Bank should no longer be allowed to place Kiev and the Muscovite garrisons on the Left Bank at risk of Ottoman attack. Moscow took Samoilovich's representations with greater skepticism now: his feuding with Sirko and the Zaporozhians, his requests for a regiment of Muscovite *reitary* as a personal guard, and his remarks betraying anxiety that the cossacks garrisoning Chyhyryn might surrender the fortress without a fight all suggested that Samoilovich exaggerated the support he enjoyed among Ukrainians. While the Crimean Khan probably had no strong desire to help establish an Ottoman garrison at Chyhyryn, surely the retention there of a Muscovite military presence would provoke the khan more than the demolition of Chyhyryn.

Second, Moscow saw no indication that a Polish–Muscovite coalition against the Turks was in the offing. Sobieski had just rebuffed the offer to negotiate a coalition on the grounds that it would place upon the Commonwealth the task of fighting the Turks while Muscovy merely skirmished with the Crimean Tatars. Might not Sobieski welcome resumption of war between the sultan and the tsar for diverting Muscovite attention from the Baltic, giving him a freer hand against Brandenburg and perhaps even leading to the restoration of the Commonwealth's sovereignty over Kiev palatinate and Smolensk? (In fact the *Sejm* was still insisting upon the return of Kiev and Chyhyryn as the price of any alliance with Muscovy.) Worse, if Samoilovich should now realize his ambition of consolidating his authority as Hetman over the reunified Right and Left banks it might sabotage negotiations to renew the Andrusovo Armistice or even plunge Muscovy into a new war with the Commonwealth over the status of the Right Bank. There was already dismay at intelligence from Istanbul that Sobieski had proposed to the Sultan an alliance against Muscovy upon the lapse of the Andrusovo Armistice and was urging the Sultan to march upon Kiev in the summer.[10]

The tsar's government was no longer as convinced of the strategic value of Chyhyryn, either. It was certainly of political importance to Samoilovich as the capital of hetman authority over the Right Bank, but it did not command the approaches to the Left Bank, the nearest crossing of the Dnepr lying some distance off at Buzhin. If Chyhyryn fell to the Turks, Kiev would of course be placed in greater danger; but if Chyhyryn was *destroyed* in the course of siege the Turks could not proceed on towards Kiev until they had rebuilt it and installed Khmel'nyts'kyi.[11]

On 12 April the Tsar and Duma ordered Romodanovskii and Samoilovich to mobilize for a second campaign on behalf of Chyhyryn. But their campaign was to pursue the larger aim of defending Kiev and the Left Bank, and in supplemental instructions delivered by *stol'nik* Semen Almazov Romodanovskii was told to initiate negotiations with the Turks in a final attempt to forestall war, and if unable to prevent the fall of Chyhyryn to the enemy, to evacuate and burn Chyhyryn and fall back to Kiev to assist in its defense.[12]

The 50,000-man expeditionary army Romodanovskii assembled at Kursk in March consisted of essentially the same units he had commanded in 1677: 22,131 troops from the Belgorod Army Group and 8,971 troops from Sevsk (foreign formation cavalry and infantry, gunners, Moscow musketeers, and a few Don Cossacks); a corps of a few thousand cavalry from Belgorod, under I. P. Likharev, from Belgorod; and about 10,000 mounted and foot reserves from Izium, under V. A. Zmeev. Samoilovich had anywhere from 30–50,000 foot and mounted cossacks at Baturin. In mid-June Romodanovskii and Samoilovich rendezvoused at the Artopolot' River and marched to Lubny, from where they could hasten to the relief of either Chyhyryn or Kiev. They left Lubny around 21 June and reached the Dnepr above Chyhyryn on 26 June.

Chyhyryn was being garrisoned by a slightly smaller force than the year before – 11,713 men, of whom 4,050 were Muscovite *soldaty*, musketeers, and gunners stationed in the fortress citadel and the rest Samoilovich's cossacks manning the lower town and its outer defenses.

Other divisions were stationed at strategic points on the Left Bank: V. V. Golitsyn commanded the Great Corps and Dolgorukii's Kazan' Corps at Putivl'; M. A. Golitsyn's musketeers and Kozlovskii's *soldaty* guarded Kiev; and Khovanskii's Novgorod Corps stood at Ryl'sk.[13]

For this campaign Romodanovskii's foreign formation infantry and cavalry did not receive their annual rations money allowances at full rate, at six rubles per infantryman and twelve per cavalryman; just one to two rubles each upon mobilization at Kursk. But the bill for this still exceeded 79,000 rubles, and Samoilovich was subsidized another 10,000 gold *chervontsy* to pay a Ukrainian infantry militia (levied from Right Bank settlements at the rate of one man from every three or five households). Romodanovskii's middle service class cavalry of course provided their own rations; his foreign formation units were provisioned with grain from government granaries at Kiev, Chernigov, and Briansk. The Ukrainian cossack regiments had cached additional stores at magazines established along part of the marchroute. Romodanovskii's army therefore experienced no serious provisioning problems until it camped on Buzhin Field awaiting reinforcements, and then only until 26 June, when 400 longboats came down the Dnepr with grain and hay from the Right Bank settlements. The provisioning of the Chyhyryn garrison was badly handled from the start, however. Moscow had pledged to send it 2.6 million kg of grain, but Samoilovich was unable to come up with the 5,000 wagons needed to transport the grain from Kiev because so many wagons were already in use hauling lumber for Chyhyryn's refortification. Moscow reminded Samoilovich continued delay in provisioning Chyhyryn for siege might finally force it to order the city evacuated and destroyed. Eventually it was decided to ship the grain by boat to Buzhin and use Romodanovskii's corps transport to take it overland to Chyhyryn.[14]

N. A. Smirnov has argued that the prosecution of the second Chyhyryn campaign may have been undermined by overcentralizing decision-making in Moscow, with the secretaries of the Military Chancellery not only dictating Romodanovskii's war plan in his *nakaz* (working order) but also every subsequent step in his campaign – perhaps even ignoring or overriding his advice – by sending him too many further orders by courier – couriers who took ten or eleven days to arrive at Buzhin. The intelligence gathered by other commanders in Ukraine had to be submitted to Golitsyn at Putivl' and transmitted from there to Moscow, which decided when and how to share it with Samoilovich and Romodanovskii. If such stovepiping of command authority helped prevent deadlocks between feuding commanders, Smirnov thinks it had the greater disadvantage of slowing the army's response time.[15]

This overstates the extent to which Moscow circumscribed Romodanovskii's initiative. Romodanovskii and Samoilovich played the leading role in developing the plan of campaign for 1678. Planning had begun during 2–6 October 1677, when Vasilii Tiapkin consulted with Romodanovskii at Sudzhi and Samoilovich at Baturin, after which Samoilovich sent Moscow his own eighteen-point memorandum on strategy and provisioning. Romodanovskii and Samoilovich held their own council of war at Ryl'sk in November and in early December Samoilovich submitted additional recommendations. Only after this did the Tsar appoint the commanders and set the place and date of mobilization. Moscow's 22 March 1678 orders instructing Romodanovskii to begin his march from Kursk to the Dnepr were general and stereotypical, and on the more specific matter of rendezvousing with Samoilovich they were open-ended. The couriers subsequently sent to Romodanovskii's and Samoilovich's headquarters were usually envoys of high rank, sent to consult with them and carry their responses back to Moscow; even the secret instruction read to Romodanovskii and Samoilovich at Kryza on 8 April by Semen Almazov presented the idea of evacuating and burning Chyhyryn as an option of last resort, not a command, and Romodanovskii and Samoilovich responded at the time with objections as to why this was undesirable. The most explicit and detailed instruction from Moscow – the fourteen-point instruction delivered in April from the Ambassadors' Chancellery – dealt not with military operations but with how to initiate and carry on peace talks with the sultan. It was entirely appropriate that the Ambassadors' Chancellery exercise the closest supervision over the negotiating process.[16]

If Romodanovskii was operating under greater restraint from Moscow than in the preceding year's campaign, it was a restraint on general strategy rather than operations or tactics and derived from the changed political situation. The tsar's government restrained Romodanovskii lest he throw away on an objective of diminishing value to Moscow an army that might soon be desperately needed for the defense of Kiev. Moscow had already expressed its reservations about making a full-out effort to hold Chyhyryn long before Romodanovskii's army had reached the Dnepr, as early as October 1677, in its instructions to attempt peace talks with the Turks and to consider the destruction of Chyhyryn if it proved impossible to keep it from the enemy's hands.

An additional political reason for keeping Romodanovskii on a tighter leash was to better manage relations with Samoilovich. The defense of Chyhyryn was above all Samoilovich's project, and to maintain the tsar's credibility as his patron and protector it was important to acknowledge the hetman's claims over the Right Bank, claims symbolically embodied in the hetman's continued occupation of Chyhyryn. A gesture, even an effort of low risk, towards saving Chyhyryn was therefore necessary, as was a provision in Romodanovskii's instruction that he not proceed with evacuating and burning Chyhyryn if this seemed likely to provoke revolt on the Left Bank; and for similar reason much attention had to be given to communications protocol, to sharing intelligence, to reassurances that reinforcements were on the way, and to subsidizing Samoilovich's militia.

Nor were these restraints exercised entirely from the chancelleries at far-off Moscow. The territorial *razriad* principle was adapted to devolve some command-and-control functions to a regional authority in the Left Bank rear. During the 1676 and 1677 campaign seasons, Romodanovskii's political rival V. V. Golitsyn had been stationed at Putivl' as *voevoda* of the Great Corps with the tasks of collating and interpreting intelligence and liaising between the Military Chancellery and the Left Bank garrisons and field army. This had the advantage of minimizing the semiliterate Romodanovskii's responsibility for diplomatic correspondence with the Poles and Zaporozhians, and it had no apparent negative repercussions for Romodanovskii's military operations until spring 1678, when Romodanovskii and the other corps commanders were officially subordinated to Golitsyn and Golitsyn's corps was greatly expanded and tasked with serving as the principal concentration of reserves for operations on both sides of the Dnepr, Putivl' being better positioned for this than Belgorod.

This change in the chain of command did have some connection with factional rivalries at court (Golitsyn was the rising star of the Miloslavskii bloc, while Romodanovskii and Samoilovich were leagued with the Naryshkins), but it also reflected Moscow's growing skepticism as to the political advantage of a second costly campaign to defend Chyhyryn. By placing Golitsyn above Romodanovskii (and between Romodanovskii and the Military Chancellery) Moscow could more easily rein in Romodanovskii, authorizing Golitsyn to deny him reinforcements once it appeared further struggle on behalf of Chyhyryn was in vain or was diverting manpower needed for the more important task of defending Kiev. This is how Golitsyn "sabotaged" the final stage of the 1678 Chyhyryn operation – not by withholding or distorting intelligence about the enemy's intentions but by halting his and Shcherbatov's reinforcement marches.[17]

Samoilovich and his deputy Ivan Mazepa observed squabbling among Romodanovskii's generals and colonels that may also have contributed to the campaign's failure. There were so many officers Romodanovskii found it difficult to coordinate their actions and bring them to recognize the supremacy of his command authority. According to Samoilovich whenever Romodanovskii ordered some new troop disposition "there would start up such protests and insubordination among the colonels that reprimand was ineffective. We don't have such men in our regiments – we are at liberty – but when I order my army to march, it marches without making excuses for itself."[18] These conflicts may have issued from the composite organization of Romodanovskii's army – many smaller foreign formation regiments under foreign as well as Russian colonels alongside larger traditional formation divisions – exacerbated by distrust or jealousy between Romodanovskii's Russian officers and Samoilovich's cossack colonels. Failure to coordinate movements complicated the final attempt to relieve Chyhyryn, on the night of 10 August, when General Franz Wolf arrived with 15,000 reinforcements but neglected to inform Gordon where in the town his force was located; the following morning Wolf made his own halfhearted and unsuccessful attack on the Turks, ignoring Gordon's pleas to coordinate it with a sortie by his garrison.

Foreign formation infantry and cavalry comprised two-thirds of Romodanovskii's army in 1677 and 1678 and about 60 percent of the 110,000 Muscovite troops deployed across the Ukrainian front in 1679.[19] On both campaigns Gordon noted signs of inadequate training and discipline in the foreign formation units as well as in the traditional formations, in Romodanovskii's army but especially among the Muscovite garrison troops under his command inside Chyhyryn. The majority of his troops were traditional formation – gunners "so inexperienced in firing and concealing their guns that in a short while the Turks rendered seventeen of the best guns useless" and Moscow musketeers "not especially well trained" – but his foreign formation troops, if better trained, were not much better disciplined, for which he blamed the unreliability of their officers, especially the subaltern officers of Russian birth, some of whom showed such cowardice Gordon had to cast lots to assign command of sortie parties. Some of Samoilovich's cossacks also accused the Muscovite garrison troops of "showing not the slightest bravery – they could hardly hold their positions along the wall much less undertake sorties or any other measures to hurt the enemy." As for Romodanovskii's troops, Samoilovich noted there were many desertions from their ranks over the fifteen days the army spent motionless at Buzhin, and Mazepa complained that not only the traditional formation cavalry but the *reitary* were essentially useless, "good only for raising a shout" (he had a higher opinion of the infantry but thought it a shame that too many of them were kept in reserve at the baggage train and saw no combat).[20]

Gordon and the Ukrainian commanders may have been exaggerating the incompetence of Russian officers to imply that Chyhyryn could have been saved but for them. Gordon's own accounts of the Chyhyryn garrison under siege in 1677 (from details presumably provided by commandant Trauernicht) and 1678 (from his eyewitness perspective) generally portray an outnumbered garrison bearing up under long and very heavy bombardment and showing some proficiency in sortie tactics – using grenades as well as halberds and muskets to clear the front Ottoman trenches and occupying the trenches for several hours before falling back slowly in good order under protection of their pikes, halting when necessary to fire volleys at the enemy.[21] Their refusal to emerge from their trenches to sortie came only during the final days of the second siege, when Romodanovskii's relief army arrived just across the river, convincing them further risk and sacrifice was no longer necessary.

There is even reason to consider the Chyhyryn campaigns as a turning point in the foreign formation infantry's ability to maneuver, holding formation, on open ground unprotected by earthworks or *wagenburg* and supported only by pike and field gun. This was at least true of the elite Moscow Select regiments of Shepelev and Kravkov in Romodanovskii's army.[22]

The most striking demonstration of their improved effectiveness on the 1677 campaign was the successful 26 August night landing by longboat and barge Shepelev's First Moscow Select Infantry Regiment and 2,000 of Samoilovich's cossacks undertook across the Sula River. Despite heavy fire from ten Turkish field guns and several thousand janissaries and Crimean Tatars, the landing force managed to get across without casualties, entrench themselves on the opposite bank, set up their own four field guns, and push the enemy back far enough to secure a landing zone for the rest of the Muscovite-Ukrainian army. This operation helped decide the outcome of the first Chyhyryn campaign by enabling Kosagov's and Samoilovich's cavalry to cross the river and crush the Ottoman-Crimean observation corps on the twenty-eighth.[23]

The most successful operation of the 1678 campaign was the 3 August assault on Strel'nikov Hill about a mile south of Chyhyryn. Romodanovskii's road to Chyhyryn was blocked by an enemy observation corps of 10,000 Ottoman troops under Kaplan Mustafa Pasha, with several thousand Crimean Tatars under Khan Murat Girei and a good number of field guns. To dislodge them Romodanovskii and Samoilovich sent a third of their army up the hill in formation with pike in front, under heavy enemy bombardment. In the first wave were 6,000 musketeers, the 6,000 *soldaty* of Shepelev's and Kravkov's First and Second Moscow Select Infantry regiments to their right, and Samoilovich's cossacks on the left flank. First over the top were Shepelev's and Kravkov's infantry. Instead of immediately digging in and awaiting the ascent of the center and left flanks, Shepelev and Kravkov pushed on, driving the enemy out of their trenches, but the enemy then counterattacked and surrounded them, leaving Shepelev badly wounded and about half his regiment killed. Five hundred of his men managed to form a square "and closed order around their pikes and started up a strong fire from their muskets and two field guns," throwing back several fierce Ottoman and Tatar attacks over the course of two hours until they were finally rescued by the arrival of their reserves, Zmeev's 10,000 infantry and cavalry. Two charges by Zmeev's *reitary* drove the enemy from the hill, capturing their camp and twenty-eight guns; according to an Ottoman account, the *Ahval-i Icmal-i Sefer-i Cehrin*, the Turks

> fell into utter disorder and disarray. The sekbans and other undisciplined irregulars [*levendat*] in particular turned their backs on the enemy and wished only to put ground behind them. ... Soon the entire army fell into headlong flight until they reached the head of the bridges

across the Tias'min, which they burned to cover their retreat to Chyhyryn. By some reports this battle cost the Turks and Tatars 5,000 dead, the Muscovite-Ukrainian forces 1,500 dead and 1,000 wounded. Upon reaching Kara Mustafa's camp the khan urged him to lift his siege and withdraw from Chyhyryn "because of the arrival of so innumerable a foe."[24]

On the other hand, the plan for the 1678 campaign – which followed in most respects the strategy that had produced victory the previous summer – was botched in execution due to a few decisions holding up the army's arrival at Chyhyryn until it was too late to save the city. For example, by recalling Kosagov's vanguard from its mission to secure a crossing over the Tias'min at Krylov (10 July) Romodanovskii allowed the Turks to seize Krylov the following day and move their troops across the Tias'min to dig in atop Strel'nikov Hill, blocking his road to Chyhyryn; by order of the tsar Romodanovskii and Samoilovich waited three weeks at Buzhin in vain, awaiting promised reinforcements under Prince Kaspulat Cherkasskii (only 5,000 of whom, many unfit for combat, finally arrived on 29 July, the day Kara Mustafa's forward trenches reached Chyhyryn's outer ditch); and after his victory at Strel'nikov Hill Romodanovskii halted his army for eight days (4–12 August) on the far side of the Tias'min, just two miles below Chyhyryn. Immediately crossing the Tias'min in force might not have been practical, as the terrain was marshy and the Turks had burned the bridges; but Romodanovskii also failed to send sufficient reinforcements ahead to Chyhyryn to enable it to hold out a few more days. Probably the most consequential of these blunders was the decision to halt the army at Buzhin for three weeks. This had been Moscow's decision, not Romodanovskii's, and it may have been motivated not so much by concern that Romodanovskii needed Cherkasskii's reinforcements as by concern for Kiev, for M. A. Golitsyn had just reported intelligence (subsequently discredited) that the Turks were about to lift their siege of Chyhyryn and march upon Kiev. The fatal delay, then, may have resulted from the Military Chancellery's wavering as to saving Chyhyryn or withdrawing to protect Kiev.[25] By early August Moscow was ready to recommit to saving Chyhyryn, for courier Afanasii Khrushchev brought Romodanovskii instructions on 8 August urging him to defend Chyhyryn and announcing that K. O. Shcherbatov and Kasimov Prince Vasilii Arslanovich were ready to march in reinforcement with 30,000 men. Romodanovskii probably decided to exercise the latitude given him in his 8 April secret instruction and order Chyhyryn evacuated and destroyed only on the morning of 11 August, when it had become clear the Turks were overrunning Chyhyryn's lower town and Shcherbatov's corps was still 100 km away at Lokhvitsa.[26]

If by this point Chyhyryn's fate had already been sealed by decisions made in Moscow, it still fell to Romodanovskii to make the final order to abandon Chyhyryn. A. P. Bogdanov sees Romodanovskii as thereby selflessly "taking the fall" for Moscow, not just on the morning of 11 August but perhaps over the course of the campaign to that date, the preceding blunders all amounting to a *demarche* by Romodanovskii calculated to guarantee Chyhyryn could no longer be saved by the time of his army's arrival, Romodanovskii having recognized from the start that his government never intended to allow him to risk heavy losses in a second campaign to hold Chyhyryn. This is an intriguing idea but Bogdanov offers no explanation why Romodanovskii would knowingly accept the role of scapegoat for a foredoomed campaign, destroying his reputation and career to the benefit of Golitsyn and the Miloslavskii faction. Perhaps he was blackmailed into it, through his dependence upon Moscow for the money to ransom his son Andrei Grigor'evich from Crimean captivity.[27]

Bogdanov thinks the seemingly foolish manner in which Romodanovskii communicated the evacuation order – transmitting it first to the regiments guarding Chyhyryn's gates, so that the cossacks were already in flight from the lower town before Gordon in the citadel had any idea an evacuation was underway – was Romodanovskii's final political service to Moscow, a ploy guaranteeing that the Muscovite withdrawal would occur only after Chyhyryn had already been abandoned by Samoilovich's cossack garrison. It thereby retrieved for the tsar some political advantage from what was in purely military terms a defeat.

The official casualty toll for Romodanovskii's army in the 1678 campaign was 3,290 killed or missing and 5,430 wounded. Losses in Samoilovich's regiments are thought to have been comparable. Losses of 332 killed and 1,047 wounded were given for the Muscovite garrison in Chyhyryn, although Gordon considered this underreported by about 1,000. Estimates as to the number of Ottoman and Tatar dead range from 12,000 to 20,000.[28]

News of the burning of Chyhyryn caused dismay with Romodanovskii in both Ukraine and Moscow and the subsequent fall of Kanev, Cherkasy, Moshnia, Korsun', and Zhabotyn to Iurii Khmel'nyts'kyi (now supported by twenty *ordas* of janissaries detached from the withdrawing army of Kara Mustafa) led Sirko to blame Samoilovich as well for the devastation of their homeland. Some historians consider Chyhyryn's destruction as marking at least a stalemate if not a Muscovite defeat in that it led to the Right Bank falling to Khmel'nyts'kyi and the sultan.[29] But this interpretation treats the Chyhyryn campaigns as the centerpiece of Muscovy's first Turkish War and assumes that Moscow's war aims had coincided entirely with Samoilovich's and that the Right Bank remained within the Ottoman sphere of influence after 1681.

Subsequent events instead confirmed Colonel Iakim Golovchenko's prediction (August 1678) that the Ottomans would fail to maintain a lasting occupation of the Chyhyryn region if Chyhyryn was destroyed. This region was not like Podolia; the Turks would not bother to rebuild and garrison Chyhyryn, "as few grain stores would be reaching this place – cossack detachments would threaten them all – and Chyhyryn is far from their frontier and it is all steppe."[30] Most of Iurii Khmel'nyts'kyi's Ottoman and Tatar auxiliaries left him after the capture of Kanev, and his fortunes rapidly declined after his attack across the Dnepr against Pereiaslav failed in January 1679.

Furthermore, already from late 1677 Moscow's primary objective in the war had become the protection of Kiev and the Left Bank, and by this test the first Muscovite–Ottoman War could be said to have ended on terms advantageous to Moscow, terms won through the action of the Muscovite and Left Bank Ukrainian armies following the destruction of Chyhyryn. Victory was achieved in two ways.

First, the military buildup across the Left Bank, Sloboda Ukraine, and southwestern Muscovy in 1679 and 1680 was of such enormous scale as to deter any Ottoman strike against Kiev or across the Dnepr. In the spring of 1679 twelve Muscovite corps were deployed: 69,321 Muscovite troops on the Kiev front, along both sides of the Dnepr, reinforced by 30,000 of Samoilovich's cossacks; and another 50,000 Muscovite troops in corps holding the Belgorod Line against any Crimean Tatar attack. The following spring's deployments reflected reduced alarm as to an Ottoman invasion but continued vigilance against a possible major Crimean strike up the Murava Trail against Belgorod and Putivl': 30,000 men at Sevsk (under V. V. Golitsyn) and Sumy (under P. I. Khovanskii) stood ready to march to the defense of Kodak or Kiev in the event of an Ottoman attack, while another 100,000 guarded Sloboda Ukraine and the Belgorod Line against the Tatars. In June and July a small Crimean army under *nuraddin* Saadet Girei did manage to circumvent the defense line near Vol'nyi and raid across eighteen Muscovite and Ukrainian districts, but it had to move quickly and withdrew after capturing just 3,014 men and women and burning 889 farmsteads. Later in the summer of 1680 there was some raiding to the east around Usman', Kozlov, and Tambov by war-bands of a few hundred to a thousand Tatars and Kalmyks coming up from the Khoper steppe, but here too measures against future raiding were already underway, the government having established a new 7,000-man Tambov Corps under K. O. Shcherbatov and initiated a general inspection of Line defenses between Tambov and Userdsk. By autumn 1680 the threat to the Left Bank had so receded that Samoilovich demobilized most of his regiments and the Military Chancellery reassigned thousands of troops from the Belgorod and Sevsk army groups to erect a new defense line protecting Sloboda Ukraine. In early January 1681 Moscow learned from Don Cossack spies that the pasha of Azov was signaling the sultan's readiness to sue for peace, but news of the treaty signed with the khan at Bakhchisarai on 3 January had not yet reached Moscow and there were still reports from the Zaporozhian Sich that Iurii Khmel'nyts'kyi was assembling some Ottoman janissaries and Tatar cavalry for a strike across the Dnepr; so a reduced Great Corps of 6,000 men stood ready at Sevsk to march to the Dnepr, drawing if needed upon some of the 23,000 field army troops in reserve along the Belgorod Line.[31]

Second, the counteroffensive Samoilovich and the Muscovite army undertook between 8 February and 4 March 1679 avoided direct confrontation with the Ottoman and Crimean armies and focussed instead on making lightning terror raids upon the civilian population of the Right Bank – a revival of the tactics of "ethnic herding" used so successfully in the past by both Doroshenko and Samoilovich. This operation came to be called the Great Expulsion, and it proved considerably more decisive than the Chyhyryn campaigns in shaping the destiny of the Right Bank. Rzhishchev, Kanev, Korsun', Moshnia, Zhabotyn, Cherkasy, Drabovka, and several other Right Bank towns and villages were attacked and burned by cossacks under Samoilovich's son Semen, supported by Muscovite troops out of the Kiev garrison of *voevoda* L. Nepliuev and by the foreign formation infantry regiment of Grigorii Kosagov. In all about 20,000 refugees from these settlements were driven across the Dnepr into the Left Bank Hetmanate, leaving most of the Right Bank between the Dnepr and the Bug depopulated and Iurii Khmel'nyts'kyi in control only of the western part of Bratslav palatinate, on the other side of the Bug. The chronicler Samuilo Velichko considered the raided region still unpopulated wilderness at the turn of the century – an exaggeration, but the Great Expulsion had indeed reduced for some crucial time the human resources available to Iurii Khmel'nyts'kyi and the Ottomans and turned much of Bratslav and Kiev palatinates into a no-man's land, a buffer zone closed for the time being to both Ottoman and Muscovite territorial aggrandizement.[32] This buffer zone was officially recognized by the Crimean Tatars in the articles of armistice the khan signed at Bakhchisarai in January 1681. In the revised articles signed at Istanbul in April 1682 the sultan still laid claim to the Right Bank but pledged not to erect new towns or garrisons along the Dnepr between Kiev and Zaporozhia. The buffer zone remained in effect de facto for the Ottomans as well as the Tatars because of the Ottomans' subsequent inability to consolidate their power over the Right Bank beyond the Bug. In 1681 Iurii Khmel'nyts'kyi was replaced as puppet Prince of Lesser Sarmatia by the Moldavian hospodar Gheorghe Duca, but the latter was no more successful in rebuilding a cossack following and was overthrown in 1685. A former lieutenant of Duca, Stepan Kunyt'skyi, then went over to the Poles and placed himself at the head of a cossack campaign to drive most of the Ottoman garrison troops back over the Bug.[33]

As for the 20,000 refugees driven across the Dnepr, it proved politically unfeasible to resettle them all in the hetman's territorial regiments on the Left Bank, where competition for plowland rights was already intense, so Samoilovich and the Moscow government finally agreed to resettle two-thirds of them in cossack *polk* service in Sloboda Ukraine, particularly on the virgin steppe land along the Northern Donets and Oskol' rivers. This significantly increased cossack *polk* strengths in Sloboda Ukraine and allowed for a fifth, Iziumskii, *polk* to be spun off from the Kharkovskii *polk* in 1685. Muscovite military colonization of Sloboda Ukraine also now accelerated to counter the threat of Crimean or Ottoman invasion. There had been 146 Ukrainian and Muscovite settlements in Sloboda Ukraine in 1667; by 1686 there were 232. Some 50,000 infantrymen from the Belgorod and Sevsk army groups and troops from Belgorod Line garrisons were put to work in 1679–1680 building a new defense line extending southward along the Valui and Oskol' rivers to Tsarev-Borisov and from there turning northwestward to Kolomak, just west of Poltava. This new Iziuma Line ran for a total of 530 km, linking up some twenty existent or newly built fortified garrison towns, enclosing an area of 30,000 square km, and extending the frontier another 160 km southward. Tsarev-Borisov was no longer an isolated island deep in the Tatar steppe; in fact two new garrisons, Maiatsk and Tor, now arose to its south on the Northern Donets, thereby advancing Muscovite military colonization to within 150 km of the Black Sea coast.[34]

Driving much of the Right Bank's population into Sloboda Ukraine and strengthening defenses on the Left Bank, in Sloboda Ukraine, and southern Muscovy had the effects of depriving the Ottomans of a human resource base in Ukraine east of the Bug and deterring the Crimean Tatars from raiding around the western end of the Belgorod Line. Despite the loss of Chyhyryn the war aims of greatest importance to Moscow were therefore achieved. Khan Murat Girei was compelled to negotiate at Bakhchisarai a twenty-year armistice with Muscovy formally acknowledging Kiev and the Left Bank as Muscovite possessions. Murat Girei played a crucial role in subsequently inducing Sultan Mehmet IV to ratify these same terms. For Mehmet IV and Grand Vizier Kara Mustafa the destruction of Chyhyryn was thereby rendered a Pyrrhic victory.

Improving logistics and command-and-control

Although the conduct of the second Chyhyryn campaign showed the Muscovites were still reluctant to engage large Ottoman armies in general battle, by the end of the war Tsar Fedor's chancelleries had undertaken measures to improve manpower and revenue mobilization and command-and-control in the event such conflict became unavoidable.

A decree of December 1678 redefining minimum standards of wealth, lineage, and status eligibility for assignment to the traditional and foreign formation cavalry units in the Belgorod Army Group indicated that the Military Chancellery saw the Chyhyryn campaigns as having finally demonstrated the superior tactical effectiveness and campaign endurance of the foreign formation troops, especially the infantry.[35] The new standards stipulated that service in the traditional formation cavalry centuries was now permitted only to prosperous and "familied" men possessing at least twenty-four peasant households each and thus able to maintain themselves in cavalry service from their *pomest'ia* alone, without cash allowances. There were very few such men in the largely *odnodvorets* south, so this had the effect of dramatically reducing the proportion of traditional formation cavalry in the Belgorod Army Group. The complement of foreign formation *reitar* and lancer cavalry was correspondingly increased and the musters held in December 1679 to January 1680 in expectation of an Ottoman attack on Kiev established six foreign formation cavalry regiments, with 1,000 *reitary* and 250 lancers in each. Service in the foreign formation cavalry was open to some men with fewer than ten peasant households, but preference here too was for more propertied men who would not need cash allowances, and enrollment was in theory denied to those not born into the middle service class. Cavalrymen unable to meet these qualifications were shifted from the traditional *sotni* and foreign formation cavalry units into the *soldat* infantry regiments. This had the effect of redirecting the *odnodvorets* majority into the infantry. The infantry regiments were further expanded in the course of the muster reviews of winter 1679–1680, which saw the enrollment as *soldaty* of thousands of itinerants, pardoned shirkers, impoverished town service *deti boiarskie*, cossacks and musketeers, and even some elite Moscow musketeers. Ten 1,600-man infantry regiments were thereby formed. The subsequent extension of these new standards to the other army groups greatly expanded the relative weight of foreign formation troops in the field army and established a 2:1 ratio of infantry to cavalry. By 1681 the armed forces would have 81,000 *soldaty* in 48 infantry regiments and 45,000 *reitary* and lancers in 26 cavalry regiments.[36]

A further indication of greater confidence in the force structure, drill, and tactics of the foreign formation infantry was the decision in 1681 to restructure the *strel'tsy* musketeers, ending their old decimal *prikaz* structure under *golovy* and placing them in companies and regiments under colonels. The *strel'tsy* were now ordered to "study company formation frequently so that they will not forget it and will become entirely used to it."[37]

The general muster of winter 1679–1680 also had the consequence of extending the *razriad* principle of territorial army group administration across the rest of European Russia. All troops in field army service, either in foreign formation or traditional formation units, were now assigned to nine territorial army groups (Belgorod, Sevsk, Moscow, Vladimir, Smolensk, Novgorod Riazan', Kazan', and Tambov). Five of these *razriady* – the Moscow, Vladimir, Tambov, Smolensk, and Riazan' territorial army groups – were new or newly reestablished; the old Borderlands army group at Tula was abolished. At least two mustering points were designated within each *razriad*; thus troops in the Tambov territorial army group assembled at Elets, Efremov, Lebedian', Livny, and Chern'. Not counting troops assigned to local garrison duty, the total manpower strength of the nine territorial army groups available for service in the field army in 1680 was 164,600 men, of whom 55 percent were foreign formation cavalry and infantry. The largest territorial army group was of course the Belgorod, with a total strength in 1681 of 34,000, most of them deployed in Ukraine; the smallest was that of Tambov, with three regiments totaling 4,718 men.[38]

With field army troops and local garrison troops in every region of European Russia now permanently under a territorial army group commander the Military Chancellery obtained better information on fluctuations in regiment strengths and a wider range of options for mobilizations and reinforcement operations. It was also easier to detach regimental troops to temporary corvée on the defense lines and to use muster reviews to reassign servicemen from local town service into the infantry regiments of the field army infantry regiments. There remained some difficulties in deploying regiments outside their home territories, however;

some infantry companies and dragoon squadrons in the new Tambov *razriad* balked at being despatched to distant Kiev until Moscow agreed to pay them on monthly rations money.

The costs of rations money for the expanded foreign formation troops – even though their allowances were seldom paid in full – continued to strain state finances. A reform of state finances had begun in March 1677 with the launching of a general cadastral survey to provide updated information on taxpayer solvency (the last such national survey had been in 1646). In autumn 1679 A. S. Kirillov and I. M. Miloslavskii recognized the need to review tax rates and assessment methods to deal with the problem of mounting arrears. A decree of 5 September 1679 therefore amalgamated a number of minor direct taxes – captive ransom money, *obrok* rent paid on state leaseholds, and so on – into a single "musketeers' money" tax (*streletskii den'gi*) for the maintenance of the army. Furthermore, musketeers' money along with musketeers' grain (*streletskii khleb*) were henceforth to be assessed by household rather than by *sokha* (i.e., by area and productive capacity of cultivated land) in order to streamline collection costs; and to facilitate budgeting responsibility for direct taxation was further centralized in the Grand Treasury, which issued the first rudimentary unified state budget in 1680. The fiscal reform was also expected to ease the burden on taxpayers by setting the assessment rate of the new amalgamated musketeers' money somewhat lower than the combined rates of the older taxes it replaced (1681) and cancelling arrears of some of the older taxes. While these measures did simplify and rationalize the state's fiscal machinery, they were less successful in increasing revenue yields, however. Harvest failures, recruit levies, and various other surviving petty taxes continued to erode taxpayer solvency. Therefore the musketeers' money and musketeers' grain taxes together covered only about half of budgeted military expenditure and both taxes themselves soon fell into arrears. The government was forced to further reduce their rates and to debase the silver *kopeika* by another 15 percent, which spurred inflation that may have contributed to the uprising in Moscow in 1682.[39]

Command-and-control problems experienced in the Turkish War provided additional reason for the abolition of *mestnichestvo*, an action recommended on 24 November 1681 by a commission headed by V. V. Golitsyn and including leading officers of foreign formation regiments. Some historians have wondered why the commission felt it necessary to abolish a practice that was already largely moribund.[40] But there were important military considerations behind the government's decision to abolish the precedence system and burn the old genealogy books. In the course of the recent war the chain of command had undergone considerable restructuring, the traditional century and *prikaz* organization of the middle service class cavalry and *strel'tsy* having largely given way to the foreign formation force structure of companies and regiments with their corresponding officer staffs, and in appointing these staffs the Military Chancellery preferred veterans of lower Moscow rank above less experienced sons of men of Duma rank. The de facto subordination of Romodanovskii to Golitsyn, commander of a new Putivl' array in reserve, was also a break with the past, and new territorial army groups had been created so troops for the Ukrainian theater could be drawn from as far away as Kazan' and Novgorod and regiments deployed along the entire Tatar front from the Dnepr to the Volga. Some historians had assumed that precedence litigation had declined because commanders were less often placed in array (*v razriade*) with each other (the traditional order of battle of Vanguard, Great Corps, and Left and Right Wings having become less common); actually command appointments in array multiplied and linked up across a much larger front so more complex operations could be mounted. True, command appointments were less likely to be suspended outright in response to formal precedence suits, but there remained the problem of quarrels rooted in the anachronistic mentality of precedence honor disrupting operations; the rivalry between Romodanovskii and Golitsyn had highlighted this problem by bringing under dispute two conflicting war plans and provoking factional conflict within the Boiar Duma itself.

Thus the preamble to the 12 January 1682 decree finally abolishing *mestnichestvo* mentioned first among its justifications the need to improve the administration and discipline of the army. Beyond this it cited the need to modernize force structure (by reorganizing the traditional cavalry and *strel'tsy* forces into companies and regiments) and to master new tactics, the war having shown the need for greater caution and unit cohesion in defending against enemy attacks of a tactically innovative or unfamiliar nature.[41] Golitsyn and his circle may also have come to view the precedence system as no longer reconcilable with the new understandings of the responsibilities and rewards of military command emerging from their dealings with the Ukrainian and Polish hetmans. In publicistic literature like Lyzlov's *Skifskaia istoriia* and in the propaganda attending Golitsyn's 1687 and 1689 Crimean expeditions the new ideal of the pursuit of personal glory through martial valor was upheld as a more rewarding alternative to the service honor earned under the terms of the old precedence system.[42]

Muscovy in the Holy League

After the armistice of Żórawno King Jan III Sobieski had sought to put the Commonwealth's peace with the Ottoman Empire on a sounder footing. It was his perception that relations with Moscow were again deteriorating, and a closer modus vivendi with the sultan – perhaps even a military alliance – could provide an urgently needed counterweight to Muscovite power in Ukraine besides giving him a freer hand to campaign against Brandenburg. Initially the efforts of his envoy to Istanbul, Jan Gniński, gave grounds for optimism; it even seemed briefly possible that the sultan would offer to restore to the Commonwealth the Ukrainian territories the Turks had seized after the Treaty of Buchach if the *Sejm* recognized the permanent cession of Kamianets-Podol'sk to the Porte. But by 1678 the Gniński mission had collapsed, rebuffed by the sultan on every point. The sultan had little confidence in the durability and utility of an

Ottoman–Polish alliance against Muscovy, given the political divisions within the *Sejm* and the strength of the opposition to the king; the destruction of Chyhyryn had convinced him mastery of the Right Bank was within his reach; and he had found unconvincing Gniński's efforts to alarm him with the prospect of a Polish–Muscovite alliance against the Porte.

The failure of the Gniński mission – Zbigniew Wójcik goes so far as to call it a fiasco – forced a revolution in the Commonwealth's foreign policy. The project of rapprochement with the Porte was abandoned, as was Sobieski's Brandenburg campaign. At Grodno in the winter of 1678–1679 the *Sejm* ratified a fifteen-year extension of the Andrusovo Armistice with Muscovy, on terms less advantageous to the Commonwealth than previously demanded. Gniński was now sent to Moscow to attempt to negotiate a Muscovite–Polish alliance against the Ottoman Empire, while Prince Michał Radziwiłł attempted to enlist Emperor Leopold I as an ally.[43]

Moscow initially gave Gniński little encouragement and agreed to negotiations largely to extort from the Poles formal recognition of permanent Muscovite sovereignty over Kiev. At the time Gniński seemed unable to offer anything concrete as a credible alternative to the negotiations at Bakhchisarai the Khan was proposing. Hetman Samoilovich cautioned the tsar that Jan Sobieski would likely betray them and sign a separate peace with the sultan at the first opportunity; therefore Muscovite as well as Ukrainian interests would be better served by reaching an agreement with the Ottomans and Tatars on the basis of demilitarization of the Right Bank.

But by 1684 the Muscovite government had experienced its own diplomatic revolution. It was now prepared to break the Bakhchisarai Armistice and join the Commonwealth, the Holy Roman Empire, and the Venetian Republic in a Holy League to drive the Turks from Europe. Jan Sobieski's surprising victory over the army of Grand Vizier Kara Mustafa at the gates of Vienna (12 September 1683) undoubtedly played some role in this volte-face by redeeming the reputation of the Polish army and deflating the Ottoman army's image of invincibility. The threat from Sweden, which had repeatedly frustrated the efforts of Ordyn-Nashchokin and Matveev to forge a Muscovite–Polish alliance against the Turks, had suddenly vanished, Karl XI having realigned with the Netherlands against France and the Ottoman Empire after the treaties of Nijmegen and Lund (1678, 1679). The current political situation in Moscow favored a major redirection of foreign policy: the regent, Sophiia Alekseevna, and her favorite, V. V. Golitsyn – both inclined to further rapprochement with the Commonwealth – had succeeded in marginalizing the Miloslavskii faction and the household of co-tsar Ivan and were for now in firm control of the government. The diplomatic establishment was more confident in its knowledge of internal political affairs in Poland and perhaps more likely to appreciate the opportunity rapprochement with the Commonwealth offered for Muscovy's integration into the European great power system, for after 1674 it finally possessed a permanent mission abroad, at Warsaw, which served as a clearing house for

THE CHYHYRYN CAMPAIGNS AND THE HOLY LEAGUE

reports from the temporary envoys sent to the other European capitals. Warsaw thereby became Muscovy's "window on Europe."[44]

Even the cultural climate was now more conducive to rapprochement with Poland. The role played since mid-century by Ukrainian bookmen in introducing Renaissance learning into Muscovite literary culture had partly eroded the traditional Polonophobia at court and even in some ecclesiastic circles. A bolder and more comprehensive ideology of anti-Muslim crusade was becoming apparent in Muscovite and Ukrainian publicistics. The *Sinopsis, ili kratkoe sobranie*, first published by the Kievan Collegium in 1674, was reprinted in 1678 and 1680 with new supplements describing the two Chyhyryn campaigns and lauding those who had laid down their lives "for the freedom of the Slavs." The revised *Sinopsis* endorsed Polish Sarmatist notions of the historical brotherhood of the Slavs; held the Moscow tsars to be the heirs of the Kievan grand princes and thus legitimate sovereigns of Ukraine; implicitly compared the Chyhyryn campaigns to Dmitrii Donskoi's 1380 victory over Mamai at Kulikovo; and called for a Polish–Muscovite coalition against the Turks and Crimean Tatars. By 1678 *stol'nik* Andrei Lyzlov, an officer in V. V. Golitsyn's suite on both Chyhyryn campaigns, was circulating among B. M. Khitrovo, Patriarch Ioakim, and other important political figures a compendium of excerpts he had translated from Polish sources and Polish renditions from the Italian (Matwej Stryjkowski, Andrzej Taranowski, Szymon Starowolski, Marcin Bielski, Allesandro Guagnini, and Giovanni Botero) to marshal similar arguments for a pan-Slavic crusade against the Ottomans and Tatars. Lyzlov's *Skifskaia istoriia* (1692) would subsequently place this crusade in an even grander historical context as part of the age-old struggle between sedentarized civilized peoples and the savage nomadic "Scythian" peoples of the steppe.[45]

But two considerations above all made membership in the Holy League politically advantageous for Muscovy. In May 1684 Golitsyn had received the assurance of the Emperor's envoys, von Blumberg and Zierowsky, that Muscovy's expected contribution to the mission of the Holy League would be limited to campaigning against the Crimean Tatars in order to deprive the sultan of Tatar reinforcements on the Moldavian and Transylvanian fronts. This assured that Muscovite operations would directly support the security of Left Bank and Sloboda Ukraine and southern Muscovy while reducing the risk of a Muscovite army having to confront a large Ottoman army on the battlefield (Patrick Gordon had advised Golitsyn that the prospects for a successful invasion of Crimea were considerable, but that revenue shortfalls and continuing problems with discipline in the field army cautioned against taking on Ottoman armies in the west). Second, Golitsyn could set as price for Muscovy's acceptance of this mission a guarantee that the Commonwealth would never again challenge the tsar's sovereignty over Kiev, the Left Bank, the Zaporozhian Sich, and the regions of Smolensk, Chernigov, and Novgorod-Severskii. Golitsyn therefore demanded the Commonwealth sign a treaty of permanent peace with Muscovy on these terms as a precondition for Muscovy's entry into the Holy League.

To the dismay of the *Sejm* Sobieski's envoys to Moscow accepted these terms and signed a Treaty of Eternal Peace on 26 April 1686. In permanently ceding Kiev, the Left Bank, and Zaporozhia to Muscovy this treaty marked the point at which Muscovy achieved indisputable geopolitical preponderance over the Commonwealth.[46]

Subsequent events revealed how deeply Jan Sobieski had miscalculated. He had wagered that a coalition with Muscovy, by depriving the sultan of Tatar auxiliaries, would ensure the success of his own campaigns to drive the Turks from Podolia and Moldavia; but neither of these objectives was achieved in his lifetime and the lives and revenue he squandered on them ultimately provoked a political backlash by the magnates and provincial dietines that further reduced the military power available to the Crown. Encouraged by Hetman Kunit'skyi's success against the Ottoman garrisons in Right Bank Ukraine in 1685, Sobieski had thought it possible to restore the Commonwealth's full control over the Right Bank. While he did succeed in promoting some *szlachta* recolonization of the Right Bank, the resulting land grabs had the effect of alienating rank-and-file cossackdom and preventing the revival of a politically and militarily reliable Right Bank Hetmanate. By the end of his reign the greater number of Right Bank cossacks were in revolt under the leadership of Colonel Semen Palyi, who was in league with the Tsar and the Left Bank Hetman Mazepa.

Ratification of the Eternal Peace now obligated Muscovy to campaign against the Khanate. Over the course of 1686 a plan was developed for Golitsyn to lead a Muscovite–Ukrainian army down the Vorskla and Dnepr to seize the Perekop isthmus, thereby pinning down the Tatars in Crimea while Austrian troops engaged the Turks in Transylvania, the Poles invaded Moldavia, and the Venetians campaigned in Dalmatia. Golitsyn undertook two such expeditions against the Crimean Khanate, in 1687 and 1689. They have been widely if somewhat unfairly viewed as ignominious failures. As efforts to take the fortress at Perekop, the gateway to Crimea, they certainly failed, wasting many lives in the process and eventually destroying Golitsyn's political credibility. But some doubt remains as to whether the seizure of Perekop – an objective probably unattainable by any European army of the age – was really their purpose; and the two campaigns did have some value as demonstrations of the tremendous powers of resource mobilization Muscovy now possessed and of the potential strategic value of Muscovy's contribution to the Holy League.

Troops drawn from the Belgorod, Sevsk, Kazan', Novgorod, and Riazan' territorial army groups assembled in February–April 1687 in Sloboda Ukraine for the first Crimean expedition. Five corps were formed: the Great Corps, under the command of Golitsyn, at Akhtyrka, and four subordinate corps under A. S. Shein, V. D. Dolgorukii, M. G. Romodanovskii, and L. R. Nepliuev, at Sumy, Khotmyzhsk, and Krasnyi Kut. If Sobieski's envoy Foy de la Neuville is to be believed, it was Golitsyn's political rivals who had pressed to have him named commander-in-chief, to remove him from court and to hold him personally accountable in the event the campaign failed.[47]

These five corps together numbered 112,902 men (not counting the roughly 20,000 slave retainers, carters, and sappers marching in the army's train). Not only was this one of the largest Muscovite armies ever to take the field, but its composition reflected command's greater confidence in the foreign formations and particularly in the *soldat* regiments after Chyhyryn, for foreign formation infantry and cavalry accounted for 66.9 percent of its total strength and infantry outnumbered cavalry by 5.3:4.6. Another 50,000 Left Bank cossacks under Hetman Samoilovich were to join the expedition at the Samara River for the final march down the Dnepr past the ruins of Kodak and the Zaporozhian Sich to Perekop. Yet another force under Grigorii Kosagov was given the mission of supporting the Zaporozhians in an attack upon the Dnepr fortress of Kazy-Kermen while the Don Cossacks launched a diversionary raid upon Azov.[48]

To lead a column of 132,000 Muscovite troops and support personnel and 100,000 horses from the banks of the Samara across 300 km of empty steppe was an enormous logistical challenge. On a campaign projected to last four months these 132,000 men could be expected to consume 23,000 tons of grain. Their horses would need 9,000 tons of dry fodder to supplement their green forage. The traditional cavalry *sotni* could be expected to provide their own rations for the duration of the campaign, but they comprised only 7.7 percent of Golitsyn's army; the remainder would have to be provisioned by the Military Chancellery. It is a mark of the improved effectiveness of Muscovite logistics that the Military Chancellery did succeed in mobilizing 22,283 tons of grain for the first Crimean expedition. This was accomplished through a combination of extraordinary levies ("on-demand grain"), regular levies (musketeers' grain and "eighth-grain"), special purchases, and requisitions from the granaries along the Belgorod Line. Over the course of 1686 and spring 1687 grain was collected from across European Russia and shipped to the muster points in Sloboda Ukraine by wagon and on 125 barges launched from Briansk; some of it was delivered to Kiev as well, for resupplying the expedition by boat down the Dnepr. There is no mention of forward magazines being established along the marchroute south of the Samara, however. In any event, it was a shortage of fodder, not rations, that would plague the first expedition. Sixty-seven thousand wagonloads of hay were delivered to Belgorod and Sevsk, but merely to fatten the expedition's horses on the eve of campaign; to take supplemental feed along on the march would have required several thousand more wagons be added to the train. Golitsyn made a fatal error in wagering the expedition's success upon finding sufficient green forage in the steppe.[49]

Delays in troop mobilizations held up Golitsyn's march from Akhtyrka until 2 May. This meant that he did not rendezvous with Samoilovich's force (nine cossack regiments and three mercenary regiments) on the Samara River until 30 May, at the onset of the summer heat. The expedition, now comprising some 180,000 combatants and support personnel and 20,000 wagons of supplies, moved south along the eastern side of the Dnepr towards Konskie Vody in two formations: a vanguard of seven infantry regiments, and a monstrous rectangular *wagenburg* measuring 1.5 km across and perhaps 5 km in length. The Muscovite and Ukrainian cavalry was deployed outside the *wagenburg*, close in along each side, out of fear of Tatar attack. To maintain close formation this immense column had to move slowly and make frequent halts, so its progress averaged only about 10 km a day. In the already parching heat of early June it raised such a cloud of dust that Samoilovich came down with a serious eye infection. On 13 June the army halted on the Konskie Vody to replenish its hay and water and beheld a great reddish glow along the southern horizon: the Crimean Tatars had set fire to the steppe ahead to deprive the invaders of forage. By the time the army approached the Karachakra River on the sixteenth it had become clear no unburnt grass was to be had for many kilometers around and that the water taken on at Konskie Vody had been tainted. The army's transport horses and cavalry mounts were too sick and exhausted to continue on, even though Perekop lay another 200 km away — about six weeks' journey, at this pace — and no contact had yet been made with the enemy. On the following day a council of war made the decision to turn back. Twenty thousand Muscovite troops under Nepliuev and 20,000 cossacks under Grigorii Samoilovich were detached and sent westwards to the Zaporozhian Sich, with instructions to join Kosagov's troops and the cossacks of Zaporozhian *koshevoi ataman* Filon Likhopoi in an attack on Kazy-Kermen. The rest of the army trudged back to the Konskie Vody.[50]

In his despatches Golitsyn claimed that the steppe fires had been set to cover the retreat of the Khan's demoralized army and that the expedition had managed to get within 90 km of Perekop. For the time being Patrick Gordon said nothing to contradict these misrepresentations and even characterized the operation as a success for having diverted Crimean forces from the Moldavian and Hungarian fronts. But within the army itself there was general embarrassment, and rivals of Samoilovich among the cossack colonels soon provided Golitsyn with a convenient scapegoat: Hetman Samoilovich, who had favored preserving the Bakhchisarai Armistice and opposed the Eternal Peace with the Commonwealth. It was alleged that Samoilovich had colluded with the khan in setting the steppe fires. Although never formally charged with treason, Samoilovich was forced to resign the hetman's baton and on 23 July a cossack *rada* held under Golitsyn's supervision elected Ivan Mazepa as his successor.[51]

Measures were now taken to reinforce the Muscovite army's surveillance and control over the Left Bank cossack regiments and particularly over the Zaporozhian Sich. Save for a small engagement with Ottoman troops at Karatebenia on the Dnepr, the Sich had not exerted itself in besieging Kazy-Kermen. In the past it could excuse such inaction by pleading a shortage of manpower and materiel or fear of a retaliatory strike by Kalmyks in collusion with the Khanate. But the Sich had now been significantly reinforced by Kosagov's and Nepliuev's troops. In April 1688 the Military Chancellery therefore ordered Hetman Mazepa to contribute 20,000 cossack laborers to the project of constructing two new fortresses on the Samara River. The first of these, Novobogoroditskoe, was completed in August under chief engineer

THE CHYHYRYN CAMPAIGNS AND THE HOLY LEAGUE

Wilhelm von Zahlen and garrisoned with 4,014 Muscovite foreign formation troops; the second fortress, Novosergeevsk, was finished by July 1689 and manned by about 500 *soldaty*. Although the official rationale for their construction was to provide forward bases for the next campaign against the Khanate, their location just across the Dnepr opposite the ruins of Kodak on the edge of Zaporozhia was understandably taken by the Zaporozhian cossacks as a sign that Moscow intended to tighten its control over their supply lines from Ukraine and thereby impose the tsar's full sovereignty over the Sich.[52]

In committing to a second expedition against Perekop for spring 1689 Golitsyn may have been seeking to further intimidate and pacify the Zaporozhian Sich as well as restore his honor, vindicate the mission of the Holy League to his political opponents, give Khan Selim Girei reason to restrain his nobles from raiding Sloboda Ukraine and the Belgorod Line, and possibly press the khan and sultan to negotiate a separate peace with Muscovy. To achieve these ends another massive demonstration of Muscovite military power was needed. There is some doubt as to whether Golitsyn was truly prepared to capture and hold Perekop, however.[53]

To avoid the provisioning problems that wrecked the 1687 campaign Gordon proposed that the army follow a different marchroute, keeping closer to the course of the Dnepr and building forts for resupply at regular intervals in the army's wake. Golitsyn rejected this advice on the grounds that it would waste precious time; in his view the principal mistake made in 1687 had been the army's late departure from Sloboda Ukraine and slow rate of march, which had left it on the steppe in the heat of summer, deprived of forage by Tatar arson. Therefore the second expeditionary army (117,446 Muscovite troops and 350 guns) began mobilizing considerably earlier and was able to set out from Sumy by February. By 20 April it had rendezvoused with Mazepa's force (30–40,000 cossacks) at Novobogoroditskoe. From there it followed the same route as the previous expedition but made somewhat better time by marching in six separate columns, screened by a vanguard under the command of A. S. Shein. Greater care was also taken to send patrols ahead to reconnoitre and stop the Tatars from firing the steppe, and to send out detachments to establish a series of a small forward stations with wells and caches of hay. A reserve corps under I. F. Volynskii was left behind on the Samara to help in resupply efforts, for which 6,300 tons of grain had been deposited at Novobogoroditskoe.[54]

As a result the Muscovite–Ukrainian army reached the Karachakra River – where the 1687 expedition had turned back – by 3 May, and by 11 May it was already at the Kairka, just four days' march from Perekop. From their camp on the Kairka Golitsyn and Mazepa sent a detachment west against the Dnepr fortress of Aslan-Kermen. Then they resumed their march to the south. But as the army was now deep in the Nogai steppe Golitsyn redeployed the six columns to march in battle formation. On the fifteenth, somewhere between Zelenaia Dolina and Chernaia Dolina, a large Tatar force attacked on their right flank. After three hours' fighting it was driven back by fire from the right flank division's unlimbered artillery. When Muscovite cavalry followed in pursuit a second Tatar force fell upon the rear wagons of the main division; it too was repulsed by artillery fire. Around noon of the following day, at Chernaia Dolina, the main Tatar army attacked head on, pushing the vanguard division back to the main division's *wagenburg* before retreating under Muscovite cannonade. The Tatars then wheeled about and hit the left flank division, briefly penetrating its outer wagon line and causing heavy casualties among two regiments of Sloboda cossacks. But this attack too was finally thrown back by the Muscovite artillery. After this the Tatars no longer attempted attacks en masse and Golitsyn's army was able to resume its progress – although with its cavalry now pulled inside its six *wagenburgs* for safety, and with mounting concern about diminishing food and water supplies.

On 20 May 1689 the army reached the isthmus of Perekop. Golitsyn was dismayed to find that the grazing land here "was trampled down and stamped out, and what was more, there was nowhere to get water, neither streams nor springs, on this side of Perekop." A protracted siege of Perekop fortress by blockade was therefore out of the question. Nor could Golitsyn bring up his guns close enough for a bombardment: the Crimeans had dug a long 7-km trench across the entire width of the isthmus. The next day Golitsyn ordered the army to turn back. During its long retreat march it encountered some harassment by bands of Belgorod Tatars and by Ottoman troops out of the sultan's Dnepr fortresses, but the heavier losses it incurred were from hunger and thirst, the Tatars having burned the steppe again.

The casualty rate among the Muscovite divisions on this campaign was unlikely to have been as low as the figures of 61 killed and 441 wounded reported in Golitsyn's dispatches, but nowhere as high as the estimate of 20,000 killed and 15,000 captured offered by Tsar Peter's advisor Franz Lefort.[55] But the rumors spread by Lefort and taken up by the Polish, Swedish, and Dutch ambassadors illustrate the growing skepticism and anger that greeted the Regent's efforts to portray the campaign as a success and lionize Golitsyn as a returning hero. Gordon and a good number of the German colonels went over to the faction of Tsar Peter, joining boyars M. A. Cherkasskii and Ia. F. Dolgorukii, the Naryshkins, and Lopukhins in the coup (5–7 September 1689) that overthrew Sophia's regency and sent Golitsyn into exile in the far north.[56]

Peter's party – particularly the Naryshkins – had long doubted the wisdom of coalition with the Commonwealth against the sultan and the khan and had long expected the breakdown of the Holy League. They were convinced the Poles and Austrians were hopelessly bogged down in Hungary and Moldavia and ready to reach a separate peace with the Turks, leaving Muscovy alone to face Ottoman revanchism in Ukraine and Tatar retaliation against the Iziuma Line. Now that they were in power they considerably softened their demands upon the Porte and the Khanate in hope of negotiating a new armistice. They limited the southern army's mission to guarding the Iziuma and Belgorod lines, so that the only offensive operations undertaken against the Khanate were by the

Zaporozhians and Don Cossacks. They kept close watch over Jan Sobieski for any sign his commitment to the League was weakening.

But by 1694 it had become apparent that the Muscovite army would have to resume operations on behalf of the Holy League. Leopold I, Jan Sobieski, and the Patriarch of Jerusalem had rebuked Tsar Peter for inaction and Sobieski had even demanded the Tsar either launch a new campaign against Perekop or send Muscovite troops to reinforce the Polish army on the Dnestr. Given the government's longstanding skepticism about the durability of the Holy League, pressure from League allies was not enough to force it to change its foreign policy. But its efforts at rapprochement with the khan and sultan were getting nowhere; the khan had repeatedly rejected Moscow's negotiating points and had even allowed his mirzas to raid Chuguev, Zmiev, and Nemirov (1691, 1692) and carry off several thousand prisoners. Peter and his circle may also have concluded it was time to undertake one last great operation to salvage for Muscovy some concrete gain in the south before the League disintegrated altogether. Such an operation would provide the opportunity to test in battle the elite units (the Preobrazhenskii and Semenovskii "toy" regiments, the Moscow Select Infantry regiments, the reformed Moscow musketeer regiments) the tsar had been honing on maneuvers at Preobrazhenskoe and Kozhukhovo over the last eleven years, and it would have the additional benefit of reinforcing Mazepa's authority over the Left Bank cossacks and further coopting the Don Cossacks and Zaporozhians.

The Azov campaigns of Peter I

By late 1694 a plan had therefore emerged for a campaign against two groups of targets: the Ottoman fortresses blocking the lower Don (Azov, Liutik) and the Ottoman fortresses blocking the lower Dnepr and threatening Left Bank Ukraine (Kazy-Kermen and the smaller forts of Shagin-Kermen, Mustrit-Kermen, Mubarek-Kermen, and Aslan-Kermen). These fortresses were thought to be within the army's logistical reach, unlike Perekop, and their capture would cut off the Khanate from the Nogai *ulusy* in the Kuban and on the lower Don and the Dzhemboiluk, Edisan, and Bucak hordes in the Bug and Dnestr basins.[57] B. P. Sheremetev, the rising young star in the southern army, was assigned the task of attacking the forts on the Dnepr using traditional and foreign formation troops from the Belgorod and Sevsk army groups reinforced by cossacks of the Hetman's regiments and the Zaporozhian Host (reportedly 120,000 men in all). For the attack upon Azov Gordon, Lefort, and A. M. Golovin were placed in collegial command of a smaller army (31,000 men and 201 guns) consisting of the elite regiments trained at Preobrazhenskoe and Kozhukhovo and several infantry regiments from the Tambov army group.

Sheremetev's operation against the Dnepr fortresses had the advantages of overwhelming numerical superiority and a little good luck. The forces of Sheremetev and Mazepa placed Kazy-Kermen under siege (25–30 July 1695) while a river flotilla manned by cossacks of the Chernigov and Kiev regiments and the Zaporozhian Host cut off Kazy-Kermen from any reinforcement by the Crimean khan. Artillery bombardment did little damage to Kazy-Kermen's strong stone walls, so Sheremetev had a mine placed under one point along the wall. When it blew it also happened to set off the enemy's powder magazine. Kazy-Kermen's janissary garrison quickly surrendered. Its Tatar contingent tried to take refuge in an undamaged section of the fortress but was overcome by the spreading flames. Upon learning of the fall of Kazy-Kermen the smaller Ottoman fortresses of Mustrit-Kermen, Mubarek-Kermen, and Aslan-Kermen capitulated without a fight. Unfortunately it proved impossible for Sheremetev and Mazepa to establish a sizeable garrison at any of these sites. Kazy-Kermen, the largest and strongest of the forts, had been irreparably damaged and had to be leveled. The Ukrainian garrison left at Mustrit-Kermen, on nearby Tavan' Island, numbered only about 1,000 men, too few to hold the region, and they soon came under harassment by the Zaporozhians, who resented their presence as an infringement upon the liberties of the Sich. Sheremetev therefore had to abandon plans for a summer 1696 campaign against Ochakov, the last important Ottoman fortress in the Dnepr region, and keep his army of 46,000 encamped the entire summer with Mazepa's regiments along Berestovaia Creek to deter the khan from invading the Left Bank.[58]

The manner in which Tsar Peter, Gordon, Golovin, and Lefort conducted their first Azov campaign (1 May–1 October 1695) shows some effort to learn from the logistical errors that had undermined both of Golitsyn's Perekop expeditions. To ensure that the main corps would have sufficient stores in wait at its destination a vanguard of 10,000 men under Gordon was sent ahead to establish a forward base on the Koisuga River, a day's march from Azov. On 26 June Gordon built a dock on the Koisuga to receive the munitions and provisions being shipped down the Don from Voronezh on 1,000 longboats. A second, smaller munitions flotilla sailed down the Volga to Tsaritsyn parallel to the marchroute of the main corps, its cargo to be unloaded at Tsaritsyn for transport across the steppe to Panshin for the final leg of the main corps' journey down the Don. Additional food stores (beef, salt pork, fish, and salt) were supposed to be awaiting the army at Panshin. Unfortunately two details had not been anticipated. There were not enough horses available at Tsaritsyn to transport stores to Panshin, and because of cheating by contractors the provisions awaiting at Panshin fell far short of what had been ordered. As a result the army could not set out from Panshin until 18–19 June. A crucial week had been lost. This enabled twenty Ottoman galleys to reinforce Azov on 6 July, two days before the Muscovite trenches were close enough to Azov's walls for mortar bombardment to commence. Gordon also shared some responsibility for this; time he could have spent beginning entrenchments around Azov he had instead devoted to finishing the dock on the Koisuga.[59]

There were additional reasons for the failure of the 1695 Azov expedition. Although it outnumbered Azov's garrison by five to one, the besieging

Muscovite army was too small to establish a full circumvallation of the town; the side along the river was left unsecured, leaving the Ottomans free to resupply Azov by galleys coming upriver from the sea. The subsequent stationing of a few hundred men with a battery on the river's far bank was not enough to remedy this. Thanks to discord among the three commanders and the defection of a Dutch sailor who revealed to the Turks where the army's pickets were deployed, the Azov garrison was able to make a number of effective sorties against the Muscovites, spiking their siege guns and on one occasion even penetrating to the camp of Lefort's division. Entrenching work was conducted competently on the whole, but attempts to mine Azov's walls failed due to a shortage of experienced engineers. This placed the army in the unpleasant position of attempting to storm intact bulwarks defended by an enemy still well fed, well equipped, and unbroken in spirit. Apparently not even Peter's elite regiments were ready for this; only the Don Cossacks showed any eagerness to volunteer for the three storming parties (1,500 men each) sent against Azov's walls on 5 August, even though ten rubles was offered for every volunteer. The 5 August assault failed, as did a second assault on 25 September. Even capturing the small fort at Liutik commanding the river above Azov proved beyond the army's capability. The greatest single reason for the failed assaults and the continued vulnerability of the Muscovite positions to Turkish sorties appears to have been discord among the three co-equal commanders, especially between Gordon and Lefort. Tsar Peter did not begin to intervene in their councils of war until the final phase of the campaign (6 August–1 October), by which time the army was nearing exhaustion. On 1 October the siege was finally abandoned. The army made its way back to Valuiki in a great *wagenburg*, losing significant numbers of men and horses en route to Tatar skirmishers, frost, hunger, and thirst.[60]

But the spring of 1696 saw a second campaign against Azov, this time on a much grander scale, combining land and naval operations, and under a single commander-in-chief. The Azov expeditionary army of 1696 was over twice the size of the army of the previous year – 70,000 men, counting the 15,000 Ukrainian cossacks under Colonel Lizogub and the 5,000 Don Cossacks. The proportion of foreign formation infantry to *strel'tsy* had been increased, Peter having been greatly disappointed in the latter's lack of zeal on the previous campaign. The cavalry contingent was expanded to more than 27,000 horse, to better protect the siege troops against Ottoman sorties and Tatar attacks and to improve reconnaissance and foraging. Several German engineers had been hired to take charge of mining. The principal supply depot, holding 94,000 tons of grain, was established at Korotoiak, on the middle course of the Don – farther north than Panshin and Tsaritsyn, but situated so stores could be sent directly down the Don by longboat and barge, thereby avoiding the slow and dangerous portage across the Volga–Don steppe that had wasted a crucial week the year before. The bulk of the army followed the river flotilla down the Don; the longer marchroute along the Volga to Tsaritsyn was abandoned to save time.

Lefort, Golovin, and Gordon again commanded divisions, but now there was a commander-in-chief above them – officially A. S. Shein, a politically reliable but militarily inexperienced courtier, but in fact supreme command authority was exercised by the young Tsar.

Without doubt the most significant innovations were the vastly enlarged size of the river flotilla for provisioning and troop transport and the construction of a small seagoing fleet for seizing control of the mouth of the Don and placing Azov under full blockade. More than 20,000 laborers – town service *odnodvortsy*, lower service class troops, and urban taxpayers – were levied from districts across southern Muscovy to labor in shipyards established at Voronezh, Kozlov, Dobryi, and Sokol'sk. Despite 4–5,000 desertions from these wharves 1,066 longboats and 100 barges were built for river transport, exceeding the original quota, and a fleet of 23 galleys, 4 fireships, 2 large galleasses, and another 60 smaller seagoing vessels were produced at Voronezh. Lefort, who had no naval experience, was named admiral over the marine fleet constructed at Voronezh, but the tsar had actual command of it, assisted by the vice-admirals Lima and de l'Orsiere. Four thousand volunteers and soldiers from the Preobrazhenskii and Semenovskii regiments were assigned as crews and marines.

By following the Don marchroute and carrying troops by boat and barge Peter was able to deliver the bulk of his army to Azov a month earlier (28 May–3 June) than had been possible the year before. This along with improved engineering expertise and the availability of 15,000 men for fortifications labor enabled Gordon to complete the circumvallation of trenches and batteries by 7 June and even begin work on a rolling rampart allowing his artillery to fire upon Azov's walls from above. On 20 May an Ottoman fleet of twenty galleys and a number of smaller supply boats standing off the mouth of Azov was attacked by Don Cossack longboats and burned or driven out to sea. After this the enemy was unable to reinforce and resupply the Azov garrison. A week later the first of the Muscovite naval squadrons took up position off the Don's mouth, with the rest of the Muscovite fleet joining it by 12 June. The blockade was completed by 14 June when Gordon and Ia. F. Dolgorukii stationed regiments at two earth forts on opposite banks of the Don below Azov. Two subsequent attempts by Ottoman galleys to reinforce Azov (28 June, 13 July) were easily turned back, deterred by the deployment of 10,000 Muscovite troops near the river's mouth and by fire from the Muscovite fleet. It proved unnecessary to storm Azov's walls; the fortress surrendered on 19 July 1696 after a month's blockade and bombardment.[61]

After the fall of Azov Peter established a naval base at Taganrog and organized the southern service and taxbearing estates into fifty-two "companies" to apportion subsidy of the construction at Voronezh of a Black Sea fleet of eighty ships of the line, sixty brigantines, and six galleys. This did not assure Muscovy rights of free passage on the Black Sea, however. The Ottomans still controlled the straits of Kerch, thereby confining Peter's ships to the Sea of Azov, and Peter's new ships, having been built hastily of green wood and lacking experienced crews and masters, were unlikely to be able to seize the straits anytime soon. The Muscovite occupation of Azov had significantly weakened the Khanate's military power east of the Kal'miuss River but it could not enhance the security of the Muscovite and Ukrainian garrisons at Tavan' Island and the other captured Turkish fortresses on the Dnepr. Although 37,000 Muscovite troops were enough to secure the region of Azov and Taganrog, it took 83,000 Muscovite and Ukrainian troops to hold the Dnepr fortresses against Turkish and Tatar attacks in 1698. The mounting human and material costs of defending the lower Dnepr were provoking unrest in Ukraine and eroding Mazepa's authority.

In April 1698 Peter learned that Leopold I and Poland's new king, August II, were negotiating treaties of separate peace with the sultan through Dutch and English mediators. It was now unlikely that continued Muscovite campaigning for the Kerch straits and the lower Dnepr would receive any support from the League allies. Peter therefore decided to join in the peace negotiations underway at Karlowitz and on 26 January 1699 his envoys signed a two-year armistice with the Ottomans. The Treaty of Constantinople (3 July 1700) extended this armistice to thirty years, formally recognized the Tsar's sovereignty over Azov, and finally freed Muscovy from tribute obligations towards the Khan. But to achieve this Peter's diplomats had to drop all demands for the cession of the Kerch straits and pledge that the captured Ottoman fortresses on the Dnepr would be evacuated and demolished. The Dnepr south of the Zaporozhian Sich and the steppe east of Perekop as far as Miusskii Gorodok were to become demilitarized zones, and while the Sultan promised to restrain the Tatars from raiding, the Tsar was equally bound to restrain the Don and Zaporozhian hosts. But by this time the abandonment of Muscovite claims to the Kerch straits and the Dnepr fortresses was no longer such a painful concession on Peter's part. The peace talks at Karlowitz had revealed to him a grand new opportunity in the north in the form of a coalition with the Commonwealth and Brandenburg against Sweden.[62] Peter I had begun to think upon the project of a new Great Northern War.

CHAPTER SIX

The balance of power at century's end

Fifty years of warfare in Ukraine and on the lower Don had dramatically altered the balance of power in the Pontic steppe region. By 1699 the circle of serious contenders for hegemony had been narrowed to the Ottoman Empire and Muscovy. Although the Polish-Lithuanian Commonwealth regained control over Podolia with the Treaty of Karlowitz, it lacked the troops, funds, and reliable political clients to restore its full sovereignty over the Right Bank. Sobieski's compensatory efforts to draw Moldavia into the Polish sphere of influence had further drained the Commonwealth's resources and eroded the crown's support among the nobility. Cossack power in general was in decline: Karlowitz essentially abolished the raiding economies of the Don and Zaporozhian Hosts; the Right Bank Hetmanate was now largely a fiction, and Moscow had deprived the Left Bank Hetmanate of most of its independence in foreign and military affairs. The Crimean Khanate had been thrown on the defensive and had partly disengaged from its military partnership with the Ottomans.

The Polish-Lithuanian Commonwealth

Wladyslaw IV, Jan Kazimierz, and Jan Sobieski had pursued military modernization as avidly as the Muscovite government. They had founded and expanded foreign formations, instituted their own *lanowa* system for recruiting peasant infantry, and created territorial army groups (*komputowe* armies) at the palatinate level by fusing Quarter Army units and *szlachta* levy militias. The Poles continued to lead the Muscovites in the development of artillery science and new cavalry tactics. In the 1690s Jan Sobieski was still pursuing military reform by equipping his infantry regiments with flintlocks and reducing the proportion of pike.

But Sobieski's failed campaigns in Podolia and Moldavia (1684, 1686, 1687, 1690, 1691, 1692) show why Commonwealth military power was in sharp decline in the last two decades of the seventeenth century. Because of revenue shortfalls the maximum size of the army had been reduced to about 30,000 men, and more seriously, the reductions had most affected the infantry (both national and foreign contingents), artillery, and even the heavy *husarz* cavalry, the army's most effective formation. So Sobieski invaded Podolia and Moldavia primarily with light cavalry forces not of much use for taking Ottoman fortresses. Thus the Turks were able to continue holding Kamianets with a garrison of just 5,000. Sobieski's troops typically encountered early supply problems and had to withdraw into winter quarters without having accomplished their objectives. Asking that they repeat this pattern of operations every few years without tangible result tended to erode their morale and made the *Sejm* increasingly reluctant to continue funding such campaigns. Mounting pay arrears then further reduced the army's combat readiness. By 1697 army pay was in arrears by 26 million Polish crowns – about ten times the Kingdom's annual revenue.[1]

The great weakness of the Commonwealth's military system was the crown's inability to maintain army funding. In Sobieski's reign the Polish royal treasury was receiving about the same total annual revenue it had collected 100 years before under Stefan Bathory.

The poverty of Commonwealth military finance is usually blamed on the selfishness of Polish and Lithuanian magnates dominating the *Sejm* and exercising the *liberum veto* to prevent the transformation of royal forces into a standing royal army, which they saw as the instrument of royal military absolutism threatening their liberties. Thus Jan Kazimierz's war on Muscovy was ended by the nobles waging civil war in Lubomirski's name; Sobieski faced increasingly serious opposition from the Lithuanian Grand Hetmans Michal Pac and Sapieha. Five of the six *Sejms* held between 1688 and 1695 dissolved without voting funds for the army.

In fact the lesser nobility was nearly as reluctant to fund a standing royal army because this would encourage further expansion of its foreign contingent infantry and further reduce the need to call upon the gentry levy, the *pospolite ruszenie*. They saw the gentry levy as embodying the principle of *towarzystwo*, which gave the cavalry squadrons their cohesion and dash and bound the gentry as citizen-soldiers with their commander and King; the *towarzystwo* principle therefore had to be preserved – by strike in *confederatio*, if necessary – to maintain republican liberty. For this reason the gentry generally did not seek officer rank in the foreign contingent. This "ensured that there was no equivalent of the loyal officer corps which had such a stake in the successful military revolutions in Sweden, Denmark, and Russia. Forced to choose in the 1660s, most of the army asserted its identity as citizens, rather than as soldiers."[2] Perhaps this could have been avoided if at an earlier stage – the buildup of 1658–1659 – the king had not contented himself with the hire of foreign mercenary officers and soldiers for the infantry regiments of the foreign contingent but had also used the *łanowa* system to fill them with peasant recruits and had not limited hetmancies and other higher command positions to officers out of the national contingent cavalry.

One must hold Jan Sobieski responsible, too, for failing to acknowledge the limits of royal military power in the late 1680s and 1690s and throwing away the troops and funds the *Sejm* had granted him on overly ambitious foreign campaigns that could not have the broad support of the nobility and gentry. Rather like Bohdan Khmel'nyts'kyi, Sobieski tried to pursue a flexible foreign policy to seize advantage wherever it might arise and so had made Poland an instrument of French, Austrian, and other competing foreign interests. This had the effect of deepening political factionalism among Polish and Lithuanian ruling circles and stiffening resistance to his course changes. Meanwhile his Moldavian and Prussian projects diverted manpower and funds needed for southern borderland security. In 1688 and again in 1695 the Crimean Tatars raided as far north as L'viv, causing great panic. The continued vulnerability of southern Poland to Tatar attack in turn limited Sobieski's freedom to pursue other projects because it rendered the Commonwealth's southern borderland security all the more dependent upon alliance with Muscovy.[3]

Another factor limiting army funding was the loss of populated territory to Muscovy, Sweden, the Turks, and the Hetmanate. In 1648 the population of the Polish-Lithuanian Commonwealth stood at about 11 million. By the 1660s the Khmel'nyts'kyi Rebellion, the war with Muscovy, and the Swedish Deluge had reduced this by about a quarter. By 1716 the population had fallen to just 6–7 million, continued warfare, rising rents, and declining prices abroad for Polish grain exports having further suppressed population growth.[4] It was therefore important that the Poles reestablish real hegemony over the Right Bank and repopulate it. Sobieski did attempt this; he encouraged Polish magnates to begin resettling the Bug and Dnestr with refugees out of Podolia, and he tried to reestablish cossack *polk* administration there. But resettlement was soon slowed by conflicts over the reintroduction of the Uniate Church and respective magnate and commoner rights to the land, and by doubts in the government as to the loyalty of the new cossack colonels.

The Crimean Khanate

Muscovite, Ukrainian, and Polish towns and villages continued to lose inhabitants and livestock to raiding parties led by Crimean Tatar mirzas, but the likelihood that the entire military weight of the Khanate would be thrown against them had diminished considerably. The successors of Khan Mehmet Girei occasionally asserted their independence from the Porte in foreign policy, generally avoided adventures that might provoke massive Muscovite retaliation, and accepted Muscovite offers of reconciliation. The Turks found it necessary to depose Khan Aadil Girei (r. 1666–1671) for his lukewarm support for Doroshenko and his willingness to negotiate with the Muscovites. Murat Girei (r. 1678–1683) also sought to limit conflict with Muscovy. He tried to convince Kara Mustafa to end the second siege of Chyhyryn and played a crucial role in ending the First Russo-Turkish War by agreeing upon the demilitarization of the lands between the Dnepr and the Bug and by persuading the Sultan to ratify most of the terms of the Bakhchisarai Treaty. Although Murat Girei did not explicitly recognize Muscovite sovereignty over the Zaporozhian Sich in the treaty's text, he did so in his personal *shert'* of friendship in November 1681. He too was deposed by the Turks, as punishment for Kara Mustafa's defeat at Vienna. The general thrust of Crimean policy in the last third of the century is best illustrated in the career of Khan Selim Girei I (r. 1671–1678, 1684–1691, 1692–1699, 1702–1704). Selim Girei I was removed in 1678 for not reinforcing the Ottoman army at Khotyn and for advising Ibraim Pasha to lift the first siege of Chyhyryn, but his subjects brought him out of retirement three times because he consistently placed the security of the Khanate over his obligations to the sultan. He offered the "evildoer *giaour* Kalisin" (V. V. Golitsyn) face-saving negotiations at Perekop in 1689, and after the fall of Azov to the Muscovites he journeyed uninvited to Edirne to personally press the sultan to enter peace talks at Karlowitz. He accepted the termination of Muscovite tribute payments to the Khanate as a precondition for peace. By contrast the three khans in this period most assiduous in serving the Ottomans were unable to hold power for more than a year: Haji Girei II (r. 1683–1684) was overthrown by Crimean nobles who believed he was plotting to liquidate them upon orders of the Sultan; Saadet Girei II (r. 1691) lost his throne when he failed to arrive at Szalankemen in time to save Grand Vizier Mustafa Köprülü; and a cabal of Tatar nobles overthrew the notoriously corrupt Safa Girei I (r. 1691–1692) after the Crimean army he had ordered into Wallachia mutinied against him.[5]

It is possible the khans turned to a more independent, defensive, and cautious foreign policy in response to changes in European military technology, organization, and tactics. The many instances from mid-century on in which Tatar forces hung back from open battle – deciding conflicts not by attack but by sudden defection, as at Zbarazh in 1649 – might indicate that their commanders saw greater casualty risk than in decades before, perhaps due to Muscovite improvements in firepower and *wagenburg* movement (the Nogais in particular appear to have found it more difficult to maintain their cohesion and momentum in the face of the heavier artillery and musket fire they now encountered) or to innovations in Polish cavalry tactics. Jan Sobieski had considerable success by sweeping the steppe with small but fast-moving and closely coordinated *corps volantes*, to prevent the main Tatar force from releasing its *chambuly* and to push it to give battle on ground of his own choosing. Sobieski also experimented with deploying his infantry and artillery in small redoubts as bait for Tatar cavalry attacks, which were then countercharged by Polish cavalry attacking from behind the redoubts. But of even greater consequence was the Muscovite program of building and colonizing the Belgorod and Iziuma lines, which clearly heightened the risks and lowered the *iasyr* yields for Tatar raiding bands venturing into southern Muscovy. Slaving raids into southern Muscovy were much less frequent after 1654, generally occurring only under circumstances allowing Tatar forces to circumvent the western end of the Belgorod Line, and *chambuly* did not dare to range as far from their camps and therefore did not take as many prisoners.[6]

Crimean military adventurism was also discouraged by the growing factional divisions within the Crimean and Nogai nobilities and by the shrinking circle of foreign powers the khans could count as reliable allies. The Khanate was most successful in extorting tribute and harvesting the steppe for slaves in the years of its alliance with Hetman Bohdan Khmel'nyts'kyi. The establishment of the tsar's protectorate over Ukraine suddenly ended this. If the testimony of Tatar prisoners is to be taken at face value (they may have been telling their Muscovite captors what they thought they would want to hear), by 1659–1660 there was declining Tatar confidence in the advantages to be gained from joint operations with the Poles, who offered less support and fewer rewards than alliance with Bohdan Khmel'nyts'kyi had provided.[7] The rise of the Kalmyks as a steppe power also helped throw the Crimean Khanate on the defensive. In the time of *taishis* Daichin and Puntzuk (late 1650s–1660s) Kalmyk attacks fell mainly upon the Lesser Nogai *ulusy* on the steppe above Azov, and *taishi* Aiuki (before 1676, when he turned against the Muscovites) never contributed more than a few thousand Kalmyk warriors to Muscovite and cossack attacks upon the Crimean peninsula or campaigns against Crimean field armies. Despite this the Kalmyks were a major obstacle to the Crimean khans' efforts to reassert their real authority over the eastern Nogai *ulusy*. This was especially the case after 1683, when Aiuki resumed his fealty to the Tsar. Thereafter the Crimean khans' only option was to recognize Aiuki's hegemony over the Volga–Don steppe and to seek rapprochment with him through trade and gift exchange. In 1695 Selim Girei I addressed Aiuki as Khan of the Kalmyks, thereby acknowledging his coequal status. Meanwhile Crimea and Azov had also become more vulnerable to the larger-scale joint raids undertaken by Zaporozhian ataman Ivan Sirko, Don ataman Frol Minaev, and Muscovite commanders. Sirko's 1667 attack on Crimea caused such panic that Khan Aadil Girei put out to sea to take refuge in Anatolia.[8]

Cossack and Kalmyk raids apparently did enough lasting damage to produce a general contraction of the Crimean peninsula's population and economy. The *çizje*-bearing Greek, Armenian, Jewish, and Circassian millet communities – the Khanate's most important source of tax revenue – appear to have been the most affected; Evliya Çelebi, who visited Crimea in the late 1660s and early 1670s, likewise noted signs of significant depopulation at several towns and villages and attributed it to cossack depredations. Alan Fisher believes this population decline forced the Ottomans to reassess the costs of maintaining their administrative and garrison presence in Crimea; after 1676 they gradually ceded their jurisdiction in Crimea to the khans so that they could devote greater resources to maintaining their presence in Podolia and reinforcing their garrisons on the lower Dnepr.[9] The need to reduce expenditures and rebuild the Crimean urban economy may therefore help explain the shift to a more defensive and pacific foreign policy under Murat Girei and Selim Girei. If the Ottoman sultans recognized this need, it could help explain why they allowed the restorations of Selim Girei and grudgingly accepted the reduced frequency and scale of Crimean participation in their Hungarian campaigns.

But there was also reason for the khans to feel some genuine estrangement from their Ottoman suzerains. To compensate for the declining military support they were receiving from the khan, the Ottomans had attempted to establish a vassal cossack Principality of Lesser Sarmatia and tighten their control over the Bucak Horde and the Nogais on the western steppe. This in effect ignored the khan's claims of sovereignty over much of the steppe above Perekop, limited the territory on which his nobles could raid for *iasyr*, and reduced the number of warriors the khan could command on campaign. The most far-reaching Ottoman attempt to limit the khan's sovereignty was the Sultan's pledge in the Karlowitz and Constantinople treaties to forbid Crimean raiding activity in order to preserve the inviolability of Porte's new border with Muscovy. This restriction threatened the existence of the Nogai and Crimean raiding economies, and Khan Devlet Girei II and his brother Gazi Girei led Crimean and Bucak Tatar forces in an unsuccessful revolt against it in 1701–1702.[10]

Ottoman power on the northern Black Sea coast

Most Russian, Polish, and Ukrainian historiography has characterized Ottoman Pontic steppe policy in the seventeenth century as ruthlessly aggressive and intractable, and therefore a mortal threat to the security of Muscovy, the Commonwealth, and the Hetmanate. From the Ottomans' own perspective, however, their interests in the Pontic steppe east of the Dnestr were defensive in nature and negotiable. Developments here were of importance to the Ottomans in so far as they endangered existing assets: the reliability of the Crimean Tatars as allies; the security of Black Sea shipping and of their coastal towns; and the stability of Moldavia as a buffer shielding the Danube, Wallachia, and Dobruja. The Ottomans therefore committed significant forces to the Pontic steppe theater only when threats to these assets reached intolerable proportions. Osman II's Cecora and Khotyn campaigns (1620–1621) had been provoked by Zaporozhian naval raids and Polish attempts to conquer Moldavia; Mehmet IV's invasion and occupation of Podolia in 1672 was in response to Polish efforts to suborn the loyalty of the Moldavia and Transylvanian vassal states. Don Cossack naval raids had occasionally made it necessary for sultans to threaten the Muscovites, but the Don Cossack seizure of Azov and skirmishes with Muscovite troops supporting the Don Cossacks on the lower Don had not led to full-scale war against Muscovy. When the Ottoman Empire and Muscovy finally went to war in Ukraine in 1677–1678 it was to maintain the loyalty of allies useful for defending respective standing territorial claims (Iurii Khmel'nyts'kyi, for helping to secure the Ottoman presence in Podolia, and Samoilovich, for securing for the tsar the Left Bank, Sloboda Ukraine, and the western end of the Belgorod Line), and neither side was willing to bend all efforts for territorial gain on the other side of the Dnepr. The Ottomans accepted the terms of the Bakhchisarai Treaty because it reaffirmed the status quo ante, leaving them in control of their fortresses protecting Bucak and Moldavia, and they could afford to have Right Bank Ukraine treated as no-man's land because they recognized it was no more possible for the Muscovites than for them to establish any lasting hegemony there at the time. After Bakhchisarai the Ottomans devoted great attention to tightening their control over the vassal hospodars and trying to install more pliable Crimean khans, but they did not turn Podolia into a *place d'armes* for further aggression in Ukraine – their military presence in Podolia was pretty much limited to Kamianets, to guard the roads into Moldavia – and they did not give much aid to their vassal hetmans in Right Bank Ukraine (Duca, Iurii Khmel'nyts'kyi, Draginich).[11]

The Ottomans did, of course, recognize that the tsar's vassalization of Left Bank Ukraine and the advance of Muscovite military colonization threatened the Crimean Khanate, and, because of the Khanate's traditional role in providing cavalry for operations in Moldavia and Hungary, thereby indirectly but still significantly endangered the Ottoman Empire's Danubian frontier. At mid-century Evliya Çelebi had warned,

> These infidels [the Muscovites] are so damned that if for five or ten years they become freed from Tatar raids and if the [Moscow king's] state is given easy circumstances and allowed to be put into full order no other state will be able to face up to those accursed ones. They will invade the Cossack and the Pole and draw up to the shores of the Danube and give the State of the Ottoman Dynasty no peace.[12]

By century's end only part of Çelebi's scenario had come true. Muscovy had prevailed over the Cossack and the Pole but was still decades away from making any overt military challenge to the Ottomans' Danubian frontier. True, Muscovy was already beginning to indirectly undermine Ottoman power along the Danube through its contributions to the coalition warfare waged by the Holy League, which kept Ottoman forces engaged in four different theaters of war, straining Ottoman military resources beyond the point any other great power could have sustained.[13] In this sense Muscovite forces helped the rollback of Ottoman power from Hungary, Transylvania, Croatia, Slavonia, and the Peloponnese, as well as from Azov and Podolia.

But Muscovite operations against the Turks were a comparative sideshow and their direct outcomes of less strategic consequence than the operations undertaken by the other members of the Holy League. The terms of the Constantinople Treaty were less damaging for the Ottomans than those of the Karlowitz Treaty. Although Peter I had taken Azov and established a naval base at Taganrog, his fleet remained confined within the Sea of Azov – the sultan still controlled the Kerch straits – and the logistical problems of maintaining Azov and Taganrog would soon prove beyond Russian capabilities. The Constantinople Treaty also required Peter to abandon and demolish the Ottoman fortresses he had captured on the Dnepr; it reaffirmed the steppe south of the Sich as no-man's land; and it let the Ottomans keep their most important fortresses, the Ochakov, Bender, Akkerman, and Kilia strongholds guarding Bucak, Moldavia, and the western Black Sea coast. So it was hardly the case that all of Evliya Çelebi's nightmare had come true: the Muscovites were not yet drawing up to the shores of the Danube. Peter I would eventually begin efforts to drive the Turks from these fortresses and from Moldavia, but it would take eighty years and four great wars for the Russians to accomplish this. The Russo-Ottoman struggle had only just begun.

The late sixteenth and seventeenth centuries are often described as a period of systemic crisis in the Ottoman Empire. The decline in *timar* revenue yields; the reduction of the timariot *sipahi* cavalry formation; the compensating enlargement of the janissary and militia infantry formations, and the great increase in direct taxes and requisitions to pay for them; the resulting empowerment of the *multezim* taxfarmers, who evolved into a new landlord class in political partnership with other provincial notables; and the tendency of notables to tap state revenue to hire their own peasant *sekban* and *sarica* militias – these developments have been taken as evidence of not just the decentralization, but the degeneration of Ottoman state power. However, this characterization may rely too much upon the pessimistic "advice literature" authored by Koci Bey and other conservatives, warning the sultans that abandonment of traditional practices was bound to end in disaster. More recent scholarship takes a less dire view of Ottoman political and military power in the late seventeenth century, pointing out that the Ottoman state was grappling with some of the same problems besetting other early modern European powers and characterizing the results of its struggle as the reconfiguration of the political system rather than its collapse. The fiscal crisis was eventually managed: the government "altered fixed taxation to a more variable basis, changing the emphasis on certain taxes, exploiting cash revenue, and changing tax collectors," and in some respects these new practices – especially those promoting greater task specialization and routinization in fiscal administration – left the state "controlling and consolidating even more than before."[14] The taxbearing population, particularly the peasantry, did indeed suffer as once extraordinary taxes (*avariz*, *nuzul*) were turned into regular annual levies and added to the *ozur* grain tax, special army and granary levies, fortifications labor, and transport labor – but a similar process was underway in Muscovy, too. The crisis of the *timar* system had indeed hit the timariot *sipahi* cavalry especially hard, but the reduction of their numbers did save on expenditure and could be further justified by the fact they were increasingly obsolete tactically.[15] Nor was the *timar* system abandoned altogether; some *sipahis* with inadequate *timar* yields were eventually brought back into service with new grants, and other *timars* were issued to veteran musketeers in keeping with the higher priority now given to rewarding infantry service. The rise of the *ayanlik* system – the shift of fiscal authority, and thereby, of patronage power and political influence, into the hands of local notables – became pronounced only at the very end of the century, and anyway the notables still shared the center's commitment to reinforcing army and police power. Local *ayan* dynasties would even take much of the initiative in mobilizing troops and materiel for the empire's eighteenth-century wars with Russia.

Such reconfiguration of taxation and provincial administration made it possible for the empire to continue mobilizing and provisioning large armies on multiple fronts. The army supply system remained effective at century's end. Rhoads Murphey finds

> apart from the general effect of inflation ... no convincing evidence to suggest that mounting military costs in the late seventeenth century were serious enough to engender a resource-related crisis affecting the Ottomans' ability to wage war. At the close of the seventeenth century, the empire's position as a universally-acknowledged European "superpower" was still largely intact.[16]

There were signs, however, that the tactical effectiveness of Ottoman armies vis-à-vis Muscovite, Polish, and especially Austrian armies was beginning to decline. Hussein Pasha's defeat by Sobieski at Khotyn (1673) was followed by Ottoman defeats at Chyhyryn (1677) and even more disastrous losses on the Danubian front at Vienna (1683), Harkany (1687), Szalankemen (1691), and Zenta (1697). These defeats had some interesting commonalities: the Ottoman *sipahi* and *deli* cavalry charges were broken by European cuirassier countercharges and heavy fire from European muskets and artillery; Ottoman infantry order collapsed more quickly than in past decades, apparently because there were now fewer regulars in proportion to short-term *levendat* mercenaries and *il-eri* militiamen; this led to the Ottoman *tabor* camps being penetrated and overrun despite the depth and complexity of their earthworks; and Ottoman troops caught between their *tabor* camp and a river were then massacred. Earlier in the century the Ottomans had been very successful at the classic mode of steppe warfare, the cavalry duel between opposing *wagenburg/tabor* camps, but European innovations in the last quarter of the century may have begun to make this mode anachronistic. This is illustrated by some of the tendencies observable in Romodanovskii's army in the 1670s – an increase in the number of regimental guns; more use of grenadiers in attacks on enemy earthworks; an infantry now experienced enough to hold formation and advance across open ground; and greater continuity of fire through the use of rank salvoes, which wore down janissary infantry unaccustomed to using salvo fire themselves.

Gabor Agoston finds no evidence of Ottoman inferiority in military technology underlying these defeats. The Ottomans remained self-sufficient in musket production in the seventeenth century, and their artillery ordnance was more varied than was once thought – they produced many light, mobile *sahi* guns, not just heavy *balyemez* "wall-smashers." But Agoston does think it possible that Ottoman gunners had by the 1670s concentrated too much of their attention on siege gunnery skills and tactics and too little on adapting to recent European improvements in field artillery tactics.[17]

The Ottoman disadvantage may have extended beyond field artillery tactics and was most apparent on their Danubian front, where their Habsburg opponents could take advantage of denser population and more developed transport opportunities than were available to the Muscovites and Poles on the Black Sea steppe front.[18]

Austrian military power in the Danubian theater had been significantly enhanced by certain organizational and tactical innovations inspired by Raimondo Montecuccoli in the 1660s and subsequently refined by Charles of Lorraine, Louis of Baden, and Eugene of Savoy. Montecuccoli increased the proportion of heavy cavalry and gave closer attention to heavy cavalry training, making their charges against lighter *sipahi* cavalry and janissary infantry more effective. Matchlocks began giving way to flintlocks among the Imperial infantry after 1666, and wider use of the bayonet after 1686 (although still of the plug variety) made it possible to reduce the proportion of pike to musket. Montecuccoli favored a densely compacted four-rank infantry line protected by pike and field artillery crossfire in order to withstand *sipahi* cavalry attack and provide the continuity of fire needed to wear down janissary infantry. Combat aimed above all at destroying the most disciplined part of the enemy's army, his janissary infantry, without which he was considered incapable of continuing the campaign.

Of likely greater consequence, however, were Montecuccoli's thoughts on strategy. He placed great importance on developing the ability to continue operations through the winter: rather than waste the cold months at idleness in winter quarters the army should take advantage of the frozen rivers and roads to seize and refortify smaller but strategic enemy positions. In spring the army should advance along the rivers in separate corps, across a broad front and in carefully planned stages, rather than in one great *wagenburg* mass plodding along a single corridor. Reliance on river transport and permanent advance magazines would reduce the need to travel with an immense baggage train. Enemy strongholds not strong enough to threaten the army's lines of communication could be bypassed, for the important thing was to catch the main body of the enemy and decisively defeat it in open battle.[19]

Such a strategy was well suited to Hungary, essentially a fixed front since the 1590s. It was not yet suited for warfare on the Pontic steppe in the late seventeenth century. The forward magazines and river transport needed to permit slow advance in separate corps across a broad front were still underdeveloped here because the Muscovite steppe below the Belgorod and Iziuma lines had not yet been colonized and the Ukrainian steppe below Kodak and the southern Bug in Ukraine had been depopulated. Peter's army therefore marched towards the Pruth in 1711 in *wagenburg* tradition, in one great mass – and found itself trapped on unsupportable ground, like Sheremetev at Chudnovo. Munnich's army likewise moved in clumsy "monstrous oblongs" in the Russo-Turkish War of 1735–1739.

A Russian "Military Revolution" achieving lasting supremacy over the

Ottomans had to wait until the reign of Catherine II, when it would be demonstrated in the crushing Ottoman defeats dealt at Larga and Kagul. This mid-eighteenth-century Russian Military Revolution owed something to the spread of the rifled flintlock and bayonet and the development of artillery science, and something to the tactical ingenuity of Rumiantsev, Potemkin, and Suvorov. But it was also the result of progress in the state-organized colonization of the steppe and improvements in military resource mobilization at the regional level, the same kinds of changes that had begun pushing the Crimean Tatars out of southern Muscovy a century before.

The cossack polities

At the end of the century there were about 28,000 inhabitants in the 127 Don Cossack settlements on the middle and lower Don.[20] The Don Cossack Host retained its formal independence but its freedom of action had been significantly curtailed. As part of the pacification of the Host after the defeat of Stepan Razin, Grigorii Kosagov had used Muscovite troops to impose on Ataman Iakovlev an oath of exclusive allegiance to the tsar (1671). This by itself did not vassalize the entire Host, for oaths could be ignored or repudiated. But it was followed by measures restricting Don Cossack activity: roadblocks erected in Voronezh and other frontier districts, to check the flow of refugees to the Don and control Don Cossack movement to the borderland towns; more Muscovite troops stationed on the lower Don, ostensibly to monitor the Turkish fortresses but also to surveille the cossacks; and levies on Don Cossacks for corvée on Muscovite fortifications along the Miuss River.

Meanwhile larger processes were at work rendering the Host more vulnerable to Muscovite control. The northern reaches of the Host's domain – the middle and upper Don, Bitiug, Khoper, Medveditsa, and the Northern Donets – now faced encroachment by Muscovite military colonization and, from the 1690s, private colonization by magnates like the Naryshkins and Dolgorukiis. Plowland and profitable fisheries and saltworks in the north were also being granted to colonels of the regiments of Sloboda Ukraine.[21] The continued weakness of agriculture and trade on the lower Don left the Host as a whole more dependent upon Muscovite subsidy. Given such economic stagnation, it was unlikely there was as much socioeconomic differentiation among the Don Cossacks as some historians have claimed, so the notion there was a hegemonic pro-Moscow propertied elite (the *domovitye*) holding much of the rank-and-file as dependent laborers is probably an exaggeration, at least for the late seventeenth century. But there was underway a stratification based on political orientation: the Don Cossack leadership was becoming more dependent on the tsar's Don Shipment subsidy, to which the rank-and-file had little access, and this had the effect of heightening tensions between a *starshina* more willing to take Muscovite direction and a *chern'* more desperate than ever to find their own opportunities to obtain plunder.

The war in Ukraine had also helped stengthen Moscow's hand over the Don Host. Zaporozhian assistance to the Don Cossacks in the capture and garrisoning of Azov (1637–1642); the development in Ukraine of an ideology calling on the duty of all Orthodox to help establish and defend an Orthodox cossack state; and Bohdan Khmel'nyts'kyi's refusal to campaign against the Don Cossacks to placate his Tatar allies – these developments established an understanding that the Don Cossack Host had an obligation to coordinate its interests with those of the new cossack state in Ukraine. Moscow was then able to invoke this understanding to gain further control over Don Host military activity, for once Moscow established its protectorate over Khmel'nyts'kyi's cossack state the Don Host became obliged to coordinate its interests with the Muscovite war effort in Ukraine as well. That meant the Host could be expected to make diversionary strikes on the Khanate in support of Muscovite offensives in Ukraine when Moscow asked, to contribute cossacks to Muscovite operations in Ukraine, and to cease raiding Crimean and Ottoman territory if this was likely to provoke Tatar retaliation at inopportune times. By 1699 the Don Host – or at least its leadership – had so internalized this obligation it allowed Muscovite diplomats to abolish their raiding economy in the name of resolving the frontier with the Khanate and the Ottoman Empire. The treaties of Karlowitz and Constantinople criminalized Don Cossack raiding as banditry and required the cossacks burn their boats. The Don Host was compelled to recognize a fixed frontier – not only with the Khanate, but with Muscovy, for in 1700 Peter I would burn the cossack *gorodki* recently erected along the Khoper and Medveditsa and force their inhabitants to resettle around Azov.

For the time being the Don Cossacks accepted the fixing of the frontier and suppression of their raiding rights, for their leaders had already become more dependent on Muscovite subsidies than on raid plunder, and the rank-and-file had been led to expect compensation in the form of opportunities to trade with the new Muscovite garrisons at Azov, Taganrog, and Miussk. And abandoning the raiding economy for the role of border patrollers did not deprive them of all opportunities for military enterprise, for they were still allowed to collect ransoms on captured Tatar raiders breaking the peace.[22]

The subsequent decline of the Azov and Taganrog colonies, restrictions on cossack fishing rights, and land engrossment by outsiders would frustrate these expectations, however, and Peter I's attempts to mobilize Don Cossack troops by simple command rather than negotiation provided further justification for part of the Host to erupt in open revolt in 1708 (the Bulavin Rebellion).

Moscow had used similar techniques to increase its control over the Zaporozhian Sich: encouraging its dependency on subsidies in cash and grain and shipments of artillery, firearms, and powder; using Kosagov's expeditions to establish a tradition of joint operations and, thereby, of natural alliance; building fortresses (Novobogoroditskoe, Novosergeevsk) to monitor Zaporozhian activity and define the Sich's borders; and eventually imposing a ban on raiding activity in order to secure peace with the Khanate and the Ottomans. An additional source of Muscovite pressure upon the Sich was the colonization and absorption into the Muscovite frontier defense system of Sloboda Ukraine, which hemmed in traditional Sich steppeland on the north.

An important difference from the experience of the Don Cossack Host, however, was the fact that the Zaporozhians saw themselves as co-creators with Bohdan Khmel'nyts'kyi of the Ukrainian cossack state established in their name as the Zaporozhian Host and therefore entitled to judge whether the hetman was honoring or betraying its fundamental principles. Already by the end of Bohdan Khmel'nyts'kyi's hetmancy the Zaporozhians were experiencing serious misgivings about the direction of his foreign policy and his autocratization of the hetmancy, and from that time they began holding themselves apart from it in order to intervene to correct or recreate it. They rose in revolt to challenge the legitimacy of Vyhovs'kyi because he had been elected solely by some of the colonels of the Settled Lands, and they rose in revolt again when Iurii Khmel'nyts'kyi accepted the protection of the Tatars and the Poles. The Zaporozhians thereby contributed to the division of Ukraine into competing Left and Right Bank Hetmanates. Although the Left Bank hetmans owed their survival in part to the Sich they were frustrated that it no longer considered itself an integral part of their Hetmanate and anxious that it could still betray them. Samoilovich tried to rein in the Sich by blocking its provisioning from the Left Bank and then by repeatedly denouncing Sirko to Moscow as a collaborator with the Tatars. Mazepa likewise tried to blockade them into submission and further antagonized them by resettling too many refugees from the Right Bank on the northern edge of the Sich. This pushed the Zaporozhians to briefly consider alliance with Khan Selim Girei I (1690). In 1691–1694 the Sich placed itself under the leadership of a certain Petrik (Petro Ivanenko?), who sought to recreate the unified cossack state by allying with the Crimean Tatars to drive out the Muscovites and overthrow Mazepa. Petrik's revolt did not gather real momentum, however, for the greater number of Zaporozhians rejected alliance with the Tatars and held fewer grievances against Muscovy than against Mazepa, especially now that Peter I was offering them the opportunity to campaign against Azov.[23]

The Ukrainian Hetmanate established by Bohdan Khmel'nyts'kyi had been divided in fact if not de jure just two years after his death, by the civil war between Vyhovs'kyi and Pushkar, and this division had been formalized in the 1667 Andrusovo Armistice. Five years later Podolia had come under Turkish occupation, and the Right Bank had subsequently suffered such devastation it had become impossible to establish a militarily viable hetmancy there. What remained of Khmel'nyts'kyi's cossack state by 1699 was therefore limited to the Left Bank, under the authority of Hetman Mazepa: a population of about 800,000 to 1.2 million, on territory no more than a third the size of the original cossack state.[24] Mazepa governed under roughly the same terms as those imposed on Mnogogreshnyi at Glukhov in 1669: without the right to conduct his own foreign policy; with a cossack register army not to exceed 30,000; and under the eye of Muscovite garrisons stationed in the larger towns. The many years of war in Ukraine and the Moscow tsar's use of Ukrainian auxiliaries on the Perekop and Azov expeditions had overstrained the cossack register and Mazepa found himself increasingly dependent on mercenary cavalry and infantry units hired out of his personal funds. Like Samoilovich he also needed a special guard of Muscovite troops for his personal security.[25]

Mazepa's power was further limited by the growing gulf between the *starshina* elite and the *chern'* rank-and-file. To some extent this was unavoidable, for socioeconomic differentiation on the agriculturally developed and partly urbanized Left Bank was much farther advanced than on the lower Don. But social polarizations were further sharpened by Mazepa's collaboration with Moscow, for this had led to many old magnate *folwark* lands being redistributed to the *starshina* and the monasteries as political rewards and to Muscovite magnates like A. S. Menshikov acquiring their own vast new estates in Ukraine. Mazepa was therefore confronted by a series of revolts against *starshina* oppression (1687, 1688, 1690–1691, 1693–1696).

To keep alive Khmel'nyts'kyi's dream of a unified cossack state on both sides of the Dnepr Mazepa had to depend on Muscovite military power, which was not inclined at this time to risk exerting itself for that goal. Meanwhile Mazepa's dependence on Moscow deepened his isolation from the mass of the Ukrainian population. He therefore had to wait for some great crisis shaking the tsar's hegemony over the Left Bank and introducing a new great power on the Pontic steppe offering an alternative to the tsar's protectorate. In 1708 Mazepa would embrace Sweden as his deliverer.

Muscovy

From the reign of Vasilii III the primary objective of Muscovite policy on the Pontic steppe had been eliminating the threat from the Crimean Khanate. By 1700 this had been largely accomplished. The threat of Tatar invasion of central Muscovy had been ended and Tatar raiding of the southern frontier significantly reduced. The Khanate's frontiers had been pushed back to the Konskaia River in the north and the Miuss' and Dnepr in the east and west. Its strategic alliance with the Ottoman Empire had been weakened and it could no longer check Muscovite expansion by setting against it the Nogais, the Don and Zaporozhian hosts, or the Commonwealth, all of which had been neutralized or coopted by the Muscovites. Only a slender neutral zone and the Ottoman fortresses along the northwestern coast of the Black Sea now buffered the Khanate from Muscovy, which had directly absorbed or indirectly hegemonized the lands beyond: the Left Bank of Ukraine, Sloboda Ukraine, and the Donets, Don, and Volga steppe.

Muscovite success in rolling back Crimean Tatar power owed partly to diplomacy, but not so much to daring of diplomatic imagination as to caution, tenacity, the accumulation of diplomatic experience, and exploitation of blunders by rival powers. One of the legacies of the Mongol conquest of Rus' had been the necessity of maintaining an especially close diplomatic engagement with the Great Horde and its successor polities. This gave Muscovite diplomats a good understanding of Crimean Tatar and Nogai protocol, interests, intelligence sources, and internal political divisions and thereby the ability to sense and seize whatever opportunities presented themselves. Already by the 1480s Muscovite diplomacy was adroit enough to enable Ivan III to negotiate military alliance with the newly emerged Crimean Khanate and the Nogais against the Great Horde and Lithuania, for example; and after the circumstances permitting cooperation had passed, in the reign of Vasilii III, it gave great attention to learning how to deal with the Crimean threat to Muscovite security. Moscow was generally well informed about current and potential conflict points with the Khanate (how the Tatars were likely to respond to Muscovite settlement of particular march lands, to Don Cossack activity, to new Polish overtures towards covert alliance, etc.); alert to opportunities to press the Ottomans to restrain Crimean aggression; and aggressive in enlisting the support of elements within the Tatar steppe confederation (the Nogais) and even within the Crimean ruling circle (the Suleshev *karachis*).

Muscovy of course also faced challenges from Sweden and Poland-Lithuania on its northwestern front, and the need to engage these periodically diverted crucial resources from the southern Tatar front, stalling efforts there and sometimes carrying even graver consequences – as in 1571 and 1632–1633, when the concentration of Muscovite forces on the northwestern front exposed central Muscovy to Tatar invasion. But Muscovite security policy was complicated not just by the geopolitical fact of having to deal simultaneously with multiple fronts, but by a deficiency in its strategic culture lasting at least up to the final quarter of the seventeenth century. Muscovite understanding of the internal politics and foreign policy agenda of other European powers – even in the cases of Lithuania and the Hetmanate – was less developed than its understanding of the Khanate and other successor polities of the Great Horde, and its policy towards these European powers was therefore less adroit.

On several occasions overly hasty responses to perceived crises or opportunities resulted in unrealistic adventures on the northwestern front, for example: Ivan IV's decision to expand punitive raids into Livonia into a full-scale conquest invasion, and Aleksei Mikhailovich's decisions to risk his gains in Ukraine and Belarus' to wage war on Sweden and press for his election to the Polish throne. In retrospect the greatest Muscovite strategic gain of the era was the establishment of Tsar Aleksei's protectorate over the Ukrainian Hetmanate. But the protectorate had been undertaken suddenly, as an improvisation, primarily to exploit a window of opportunity in Lithuania; its implementation was distorted by mutual Ukrainian and Muscovite misunderstanding as to the kind of political union being negotiated; its risks were not sufficiently considered at the time; and for several ensuing decades the only apparent justification for maintaining it was the sunk-cost argument. The diplomat Ordyn-Nashchokin has been celebrated as a visionary because his prioritization of the struggle with Sweden and his endorsement of Holy League alliance against the Ottomans foreshadowed the foreign policy of Peter I, but his most significant real accomplishments, the 1656–1658 Swedish War and the 1667 Andrusovo Armistice, created as many new problems as they resolved because they underestimated force costs and settled for bilateral rather than multilateral agreements.[26]

It was only after the death of Aleksei Mikhailovich that Muscovite diplomacy towards Christian European powers can be said to have found its footing, and this was reflected not only in the regularization of diplomatic contacts with a wider range of powers but with greater caution and patience in strategic thinking: maximalist projects like securing the Polish succession for the tsar were put aside for pursuit of collective security agreements reinforced by a stronger Muscovite military deterrent. This greater diplomatic realism brought more lasting gain, too, for costly protracted war with the Ottoman Empire was avoided yet the Bakhchisarai Treaty and the 1686 Eternal Peace secured both Ottoman and Polish recognition of Muscovy's permanent hegemony over the Left Bank.

The expansion of Muscovite power on the Black Sea steppe also owed much to a series of innovations and improvements in military organization, technology, tactics, and strategy. In most instances these were responses to deficiencies exposed in previous campaigns rather than proactive reforms anticipating conditions in future conflicts. Four broad phases or waves of military change enhancing the effectiveness of the field army can be discerned.

The first phase, in the 1520s and 1530s, emphasized expansion of army size. By this period the grand princes of Moscow had achieved effective monopoly over armed force across the realm and were able to field larger armies under unified command. These were largely armies of horse archers, organized in small or large arrays of three to five corps, relying on numerical superiority and mobility to defeat the enemy. Military change in this period was predominantly political and social in character, not technological or tactical. The enlargement of the field army was achieved through the grand princes' "gathering of lands" across Rus', including territories wrested from Lithuania; through the expansion of the court and the reordering of lesser princes and boyars into a service nobility (using for this purpose treaties, surety bonds, elite hostage-holding, the spread of vicegerent administration, and the *mestnichestvo* precedence system); and the extension of the state service principle to the provincial petty nobility brought about by the growing nexus between *pomest'e* tenure right and campaign service obligations.[27]

The second phase, in the 1550s–1560s, saw the emergence of new service arms – *strel'tsy* infantry, artillery, and cossack light cavalry. All three of these elements had been present in the old army, but technical improvements in weapons production, accumulating experience in siegecraft, and further sociopolitical change (the registration of formerly independent cossacks, the ability to impose heavier and new forms of *tiaglo*) had now made it possible to greatly expand their respective weights within the field army as discrete formations. The greater size and structural complexity of the army brought into being more formal and routinized procedures for mobilization and command-and-control, as evident in the 1556 Decree on Service regulating cavalry service requirements, the practice of issuing written working orders, and the emergence of a central war office (*razriadnaia izba*, quickly evolving into a Military Chancellery) and other offices for aspects of military administration. This phase also brought new developments in strategic thinking and tactics: more concerted application of *tabor* tactics to better coordinate infantry and artillery firepower with cavalry mobility, and better integration of mobile and static defense strategies through the repositioning of the field army corps in Borderland and Riazan' arrays along the Abatis Line. Certain of these changes – the regulation of *pomest'e*-based cavalry service, the creation of standing *strel'tsy* forces, the expansion of the artillery (with emphasis on increasing the number of heavy "wall-smasher" siege guns) – appear to have been inspired by the Ottoman army, which was still paradigmatic in eastern Europe at this time.

The third phase (1658–1663) came in response to the buildup of Polish *cudzoziemski* forces and the unexpected stalemate in Ukraine and Lithuania. It involved the dramatic expansion of the foreign formation infantry and *reitar* regiments (first introduced during the Smolensk War) and their replacement of the traditional middle service class cavalry as the core of the field army. This was accomplished by instituting annual nationwide recruit levies and by debasing the currency to meet the rising military wage bill – the latter practice soon creating its own new problems for army provisioning, which began to be resolved only at the end of this period, in 1663, when the shift from rations money to grain provisioning began. The transition to a predominantly European-style army, striking as it was, did not represent a Military Revolution in the tactical sphere because of inadequate training and because the special circumstances of warfare on the Ukrainian steppe reinforced preference for *tabor* tactics. The foreign formation infantry regiments did contribute to the turning of the tide against the Commonwealth, however, for the Muscovite political system could raise them at lower political cost than the Commonwealth and could therefore continue to build army strength beyond what the Polish Crown could afford. This period also brought some important efforts to strengthen command-and-control: Tsar Aleksei's attempt to centralize control in the Privy Chancellery, and more successfully, the increasing division of labor within the Military Chancellery and the devolution of some authority for troop levies and taxation to the Belgorod and Sevsk territorial military administrations.

The fourth phase (1676–1683) of military change came about in response to the new direct threat from the Ottomans in Ukraine. The remodeling of the army upon foreign formation principles continued with the reorganization of the old *strel'tsy* units into regiments drilled in the European manner and with the reform of 1678 pushing more southern *odnodvortsy* into the foreign formation cavalry and shifting poorer *odnodvortsy* into the infantry. This, along with very aggressive troop levy efforts, assisted the great military buildup along the Belgorod Line that deterred Ottoman attack upon Left Bank Ukraine. The best-trained of the foreign formation infantry regiments began showing greater tactical proficiency in the Chyhyryn campaign, even on open ground without *tabor* protection. The most important changes in this phase affected provisioning and command-and-control, however: hikes in grain tax rates and expansion of the granary system, the reform of state finances and the shift from *sokha* to household assessment; the gradual Russification of the higher officer ranks; the Military Chancellery's willingness to permit more operational planning nearer the front, in councils of war; and the emerging practice of marshalcy, as seen in the subordination of field commanders to a supreme front commander in the near rear (in this case, to Golitsyn' at Putivl'). Romodanovskii's career, and after him the careers of Golitsyn and B. P. Sheremetev, foreshadowed a subtler change, none the less very important for the future development of Russian military science – the gradual emergence of a new, more "professionalized" conception of generalship, probably in imitation of the greater independence of authority and opportunity to pursue personal martial glory permitted the Ukrainian and Polish hetmans.

However, the single most important contribution to Muscovy's imperial project in the southern steppe in the seventeenth century was less directly linked to the field army than to the spread of the *voevoda* system of local government, which greatly enhanced the central chancelleries' control over resource mobilization at the local level and thereby allowed Moscow to pursue an ambitious program of planned military colonization along the Belgorod Line and in Sloboda Ukraine.[28] By 1654 progress in the military colonization of the Belgorod Line had greatly reduced the Tatar threat to central Muscovy and the tsar's decision that year to take the Hetmanate under his protection and introduce Muscovite forces into Left Bank Ukraine had been influenced in large part by the urge to consolidate settlement along the Belgorod Line by securing its western, Ukrainian flank.

The Belgorod Army Group lost about 10,000 killed or captured between 1658 and the end of the Thirteen Years' War, not counting losses to hunger and disease; and its desertion rate over this period averaged about 10 percent a year, in some especially hard years reaching 50 percent.[29] But the continued colonization of the Belgorod and Sevsk *razriady* and Sloboda Ukraine expanded manpower reservoirs enough to replace losses in the Muscovite regiments and garrisons in Left Bank Ukraine, wear down the Commonwealth, and finally secure Left Bank Ukraine for the tsar. By the time of the Muscovite–Ottoman War the population of Sloboda Ukraine was approaching 100,000, and that of the Central Black Soil region – comprising the southern reaches of the old Abatis Line and farther south – about 900,000. This allowed the Military Chancellery to pursue a force buildup in the south large enough to deter Tatar or Ottoman invasion. Thereafter the colonization rate picked up again, encouraged by the improved security situation: over the years 1678–1719 population in the Central Black Soil region increased by 84 percent, compared to a 20 percent increase in the population of central Muscovy.[30]

The burden of providing troops, grain, and cash for the securing of the Belgorod and Iziuma lines, the lower Don, and Left Bank Ukraine fell disproportionately upon the *odnodvorets* population of the southern frontier, however, and their smaller plowland grants, their inability to keep peasant tenant labor, and government policies restricting their ability to expand their land fund made this burden increasingly difficult for them to bear. For example, in 1673 and 1674 another 1,873 men were taken from Kozlov into the regiments at Belgorod and Sevsk even though this required breaking the pledge not to levy recruits at rates higher than one man per every three adult males per household. In many instances recruits taken into the infantry regiments were left with just one adult male kinsman or dependent to work their *pomest'e* land, while Kozlov men performing local defense duty were left with none. By 1679 command at Belgorod was receiving frequent reports from across the territory that many *odnodvortsy* had been reduced to poverty and "have run off to places unknown." In 1700 Peter I's government began levying recruits younger than fifteen years, "leaving no one on the plowland, they enroll everyone who meets the measuring stick."[31]

Servicemen not taken into the regiments were held responsible for corvée and taxes to support field army operations on the lower Don and in Ukraine. They repaired and extended the fortified lines, provided mounts for the regimental artillery, and milled and transported grain to Belgorod Line granaries; and all men in local defense service east of Belgorod were required to participate as well in "ship labor" (building, rowing, and escorting river craft for troop and supply shipments down the Don). These corvée obligations left them with too little time and labor to cultivate their own lands: "Our hay is unmowed or not stored away and is rotting, and our winter and spring rye in the fields is uncovered and rye mould comes at that time and causes bad harvest, leaving us without grain, and we are starving to death."[32] Especially burdensome was the eighth-grain tax (*chetverikovyi khleb*) introduced in the 1660s to provision the field army and granaries, for its rate increased nine-fold by 1673–1674.[33]

It can therefore be said that the ultimate advantage favoring expansion of Muscovite military power on the Don and Black Sea steppe was the comparative absence – vis-à-vis the Commonwealth, and now vis-à-vis even the Ottoman Empire – of significant restraints upon the Muscovite state's authority to command resource mobilization for war. This was illustrated yet again at the close of the century. A decree of 1696 redistributed military service and *tiaglo* obligations of the southern *odnodvortsy*, exempting the majority of them from campaign duty but making them liable for heavier cash and grain taxes to support those in the regiments; this was followed in 1699 by their subjection to a new cash tax, a prototype of the soul tax assessed by head, regardless of their land resources. This had the effect of collapsing legal distinctions between their condition and the status of state peasants paying rent on treasury lands; it placed them in a new legal category, that of *tiaglye odnodvortsy*, stripped of the juridical freedom they had once enjoyed as men of service.[34] The ensuing Great Northern War would see the burden of recruit levies and taxation grow still heavier on the population of the southern frontier.

Notes

Chapter One

1 Jackson, *The Mongols and the West*, 305–308.
2 Magocsi, *A History of Ukraine*, 131–134, 144–145, 148–149; Slabeev *et al.*, eds., *Istoriia Ukrainskoi SSR*, 272–284; Gordon, *Cossack Rebellions*, 40.
3 Magocsi, 136–137; Subtelny, *Ukraine: A History*, 106.
4 Cherepnin, *Obrazovanie Russkogo*, 715–718.
5 Ibid., 876–882; Kargalov, *Konets ordynskogo iga*, 80–114. Akhmet's defeat is often interpreted as finally freeing Rus' from the Mongol Yoke. Actually it merely accelerated the decline of the Great Horde *ulusy* (domains) nomadizing on the lower Volga. Crimean Mengli Girei would crush these *ulusy* in 1502 and assume the title of Great Khan of the Great Horde. Soon after he would turn against Moscow and reimpose tribute obligations.
6 Fennell, *Ivan the Great of Moscow*, 152, 155, 270–272.
7 Kleimola, "Holding on in the Stamped-Over District," 131–132. Observing cossacks working small plowlands on the Don at the end of the seventeenth century, Cornelius Kreutz concluded, "The land is so rich they need work only half as hard as those in other regions and without manuring they can obtain larger harvests." Dulov, *Geograficheskaia sreda*, 58; Zagorovskii, *Istoriia vkhozhedeniia*, 71.
8 Fisher, *The Crimean Tatars*, 3–7; Kolankowski, "Problem Krymu w dziejach Jagiełłonskich," 282.
9 The *beys* were the heads of the four great non-royal clans that had helped establish the Khanate. They were the chiefs of the four *ulus* tribes nomadizing the Perekop steppe; as *seraskirs* they commanded the tribes in war, and as *karachi* they sat on the khan's divan as his principal advisors and mediated between the khan and the sultan. The sultan considered that they spoke for the *kurultai*, the assembly of the Crimean nobility, on matters of war and peace, the deposition of failed khans, and the selection of new khans, so this gave them very considerable power vis-à-vis the khan. The most senior and generally most powerful of the *beys*, the Shirin *bey*, was authorized to speak for the other *beys*. The mirzas (from *emir-zade*) were lesser ennobled clan elders. Vozgrin, *Istoricheskie sud'by krymskikh tatar*, 171, 184–186.
10 But these Bucak Tatars owed fealty directly to the Ottoman sultan and sometimes waged war upon the Crimean Tatars. Fisher, *The Crimean Tatars*, 1–14, 18, 24–25; McNeill, *Europe's Steppe Frontier*, 24–25; Collins, "The Military Organization and Tactics of the Crimean Tatars," 258–259, 264; Novosel'skii, *Bor'ba*, 13–15; Kochekaev, *Nogaisko-russkie otnosheniia*, 101–108; Kargalov, *Na stepnoi granitse*, 10.
11 Ochmański, "Organizacja obrony," 362.

NOTES

12 Sultan Bayezit II also developed a plan to blow up some of the larger rocks in the lower Dnepr rapids so his galleys could ascend the Dnepr and seize Kiev. Fennell, *Ivan the Great*, 207–209; Abramovich, "Staraia turetskaia karta Ukrainy s planom vzryva dneprovskikh porog i ataki turetskogo flota na Kiev," 76–97.
13 Inalcik, "The Origin of the Ottoman–Russian Rivalry and the Don–Volga Canal (1569)," 54–55, 57.
14 Kortepeter, *Ottoman Imperialism During the Reformation*, 26–29; Burdei, *Russko-turetskaia voina 1569 goda*, 37–40; Kurat, "The Turkish Expedition to Astrakhan'," 10–12.
15 By the end of the Persian War of 1578–1590 the Ottomans were in control of most of the Caucasus. Another Muscovite fort was built on the Terek in 1587, but farther from Ottoman communication lines. Kortepeter, *Ottoman Imperialism*, 30–31, 92.
16 RGADA, F. 21, Razriadnyi prikaz, Belgorodskii stol stolbets no. 201, ll. 187–188.
17 Zagorovskii, *Istoriia vkhozhdeniia*, 46, 59–62, 66; Grekov, ed., *Osmanskaia imperiia*, 153–155.
18 Pokhlebkin, *Tatary i Rus'*, 95–103; Khodarkovsky, "Taming the Wild Steppe," 268–269.
19 Smirnov, *Krymskoe khanstvo*, 397–406; Grekov, "K voprosu o kharaktere politicheskogo sotrudnichestva Osmanskoi imperii i Krymskogo khanstva v vostochnoi Evrope v XVI-XVII vv.," 309–311.
20 Sahib Girei I's physician Remmal Khoja, quoted by Inalcik, "The Khan and the Tribal Aristocracy," 464.
21 Kortepeter, *Ottoman Imperialism*, 111.
22 Tushin, *Russkoe moreplavanie*, 22; Ochmanski, "Organizacja obrony," 362–364.
23 A maximum-scale operation led by the khan was called *seferi*; if successful it might return with several thousand prisoners. The somewhat smaller incursion led by the *nuraddin* or *kalga-sultan* and yielding a few thousand prisoners was known as *chapkul*; the small incursion of 10,000 or fewer warriors led by one or more mirzas and taking no more than a thousand prisoners was called *beshbash*. Vozgrin, *Istoricheskie sud'by krymskikh tatar*, 162; Ochmanski, "Organizacja obrony," 359–360; Alekberli, *Bor'ba*, 107–108; Kargalov, *Na stepnoi granitse*, 10–12; Collins, "The Military Organization," 258–260; Inalcik, "The Khan and the Tribal Aristocracy," 446.
24 Zagorovskii, *Belgorodskaia cherta*, 25, 49; Skrynnikov, *Rossiia nakanune "smutnogo vremeni"*, 95.
25 Bel'iaev, "O storozhevoi, stanichnoi, i polevoi sluzhbe na pol'skoi ukraine Moskovskogo gosudarstve do tsariia Alekseiia Mikhailovicha," 38–39; Zagorovskii, *Belgorodskaia cherta*, 19–21; Kargalov, *Na stepnoi granitse*, 35–38.
26 Nowak, "Walki obronne," 179.
27 *Tarih-i Sahib Giray Han*, quoted by Victor Ostapchuk, "The Chronicle of Remmel Khoja," 9–13.
28 Collins, "The Military Organization," 258–266, 268–271; Inalcik, "The Khan and the Tribal Aristocracy," 459; de Beauplan, *Description*, 50–51, 54, 57.
29 de Beauplan, *Description*, 51.
30 Including the costs of hosting Crimean ambassadors at Moscow and maintaining Russian missions at Bakhchisarai, the total expenditure over 1618–1650 was almost a million rubles. Poland paid about 20,000 złoties a year in tribute to the Crimeans in the seventeenth century. Novosel'skii, *Bor'ba*, p. 93; Fisher, "Muscovy and the Black Sea Slave Trade," 589.
31 RGADA, F. 210, Razriadnyi prikaz, Belgorodskii stol stolbets no. 176, ll. 44–54; Novosel'skii, *Bor'ba*, 317–318.
32 McNeill, *Europe's Steppe Frontier*, 22–23, 26, 28; Fisher, *The Crimean Tatars*, 8, 21.
33 Fisher, "Muscovy and the Black Sea Slave Trade," 580–582; Inalcik, "Servile Labor," 38; Ochmański, "Organizacja obrony," 366.

NOTES

34 Braudel, *The Mediterranean*, 192; Alekberli, *Bor'ba*, 104; Berezhkov, "Russkie plenniki," 357; Inalcik, "Servile Labor," 39.
35 The total population of European Russia in 1678 was about 10.5 million; in 1600 it had been about 7 million (or 11–12 million, by A. I. Kopanev's estimate). Rybakov, ed., *Istoriia SSSR s drevneishikh vremen do kontsa XVIII veka*, 200, 269; Vodarskii, *Naselenie Rossii za 400 let (XVI-nachalo XX vv.)*, 27; Keep, *Soldiers of the Tsar*, 88.
36 Novosel'skii, *Bor'ba*, 435–436; Vazhinskii, "Razvitie rynochnykh sviazei v iuzhnykh russkikh gorodakh vo vtoroi polovine XVII veka," 102.
37 Fisher, "Azov," 168.
38 Berezhkov, "Russkie plenniki," 345, 357, 358; Iashchurzhinskii, "Iuzhno-russkie plenniki v Krymu," 162; Novosel'skii, *Bor'ba*, 436; Fisher, *The Crimean Tatars*, 26; Alekberli, *Bor'ba*, 104; Fisher, "Muscovy and the Black Sea Slave Trade," 583.
39 Shmidt, "Russkie polonianiki," 31; *OMAMIu* 16, Prikaznyi stol stolbets no. 1445, ll. 1–6; Alekberli, *Bor'ba*, 103, 114, 127–128; Berezhkov, "Russkie plenniki," 359.
40 Shmidt, "Russkie polonianiki," 30, 32–33; *Ulozhenie*, Chap. VIII, arts. 1–7; Berezhkov, "Russkie plenniki," 365–366; Novosel'skii, *Bor'ba*, 436.
41 Fisher, "Azov," 164–166; Novosel'skii, "Iz istorii donskoi torgovli," 214; Bushkovitch, *The Merchants of Moscow*, 92–93.
42 Khodarkovsky, "Taming the Wild Steppe," 290.
43 Novosel'skii, *Bor'ba*, 14–15, 27–28, 78–79, 95, 139–140; Kochekaev, *Nogaisko-russkie otnosheniia*, 110–111, 125; *RIB* 2, no. 163; Inalcik, "The Khan and the Tribal Aristocracy," 459, 464; Kortepeter, *Ottoman Imperialism*, 18, 30.
44 Kortepeter, *Ottoman Imperialism*, 17; Kochekaev, *Nogaisko-russkie otnosheniia*, 86.
45 Stanislavskii, *Grazhdanskaia voina*, 7–8; Novosel'skii, "Iz istorii donskoi torgovli," 208; N. I. Nikitin, "K voprosu o sotsial'noi prirode," 99; Pronshtein, "K istorii voznikoveniia," 167–168; McNeill, *Europe's Steppe Frontier*, 49, 115.
46 Zagorovskii, "Donskoe kazachestvo," 131–133; Kortepeter, *Ottoman Imperialism*, 16; Ianchevskii, *Kolonial'naia politika*, 111, 118–122, 135, 170–171; Zagorovskii, *Belgorodskaia cherta*, 22; Stanislavskii, *Grazhdanskaia voina*, 18.
47 Nikitin, "K voprosu o sotsial'noi prirode," 99–101; Stanislavskii, *Grazhdanskaia voina*, 9–10; Pronshtein, "K istorii voznikoveniia," 168, 172; Mikhailova, "Sluzhba donskikh kazakov," 144.
48 Nikitin, "K voprosu o sotsial'noi prirode," 100; Mikhailov, "Sluzhba donskikh kazakov," 153.
49 Mikhailova, "Sluzhba donskikh kazakov," 143–144, 149, 152; Smirnov, *Rossiia i Turtsiia*, 57; Ianchevskii, *Kolonial'naia politika*, 114; Stanislavskii, *Grazhdanskaia voina*, 11; Rostovskii Gosudarstvennyi Universitet, *Istoriia Dona s drevneishikh vremen do velikoi oktiabr'skoi sotsialisticheskoi revoliutsii*, 130; Tushin, *Russkoe moreplavanie*, 86–134; Novosel'skii, *Bor'ba*, 129–131.
50 Hrushevsky, *History of Ukraine-Rus'*, VII, 41–48, 64.
51 Frost, *The Northern Wars*, 55–56; Nowak, "Walki obronne," 169.
52 Hrushevsky, *History of Ukraine-Rus'*, VII, 26.
53 Kotarski, "Wojskowość Polsko-Litewska doby Batorianskiej (1576–1586)," 145–146.
54 Frost, *The Northern Wars*, 17; Plewczyński, *Ludzie Wschodu w wojsku ostatnich Jagiełłonów*, 71–72, 142–147; de Beauplan, *Description*, 112–113; Stolz, trans., *Konstantin Mihailovic*, 171, 173; Stelletskii, "Pol'sko-kazatskaia voina," 33.
55 Wimmer, *Historia piechoty Polskiej do roku 1864*, 75–76, 139–146; Stelletskii, "Pol'sko-kazatskaia voina," 33.
56 Hrushevsky, *History of Ukraine-Rus'*, VII, 27–32, 43–44.
57 Frost, *The Northern Wars*, 57–58.
58 This reconstruction of *husarz* tactics is partly speculative and based upon an exchange posted by Radoslaw Sikora at www.jest.art.pl/taktyka.html.

59 On the notion of *wagenburg* tactics as one of the three fundamental modes of warfare in the early modern eastern hemisphere, see Chase, *Firearms*, 197, 205–207; Inalcik, "The Khan and the Tribal Aristocracy," 460–461.
60 Hrushevsky, *History of Ukraine-Rus'*, VII, 68, 80, 83–84, 110, 121.
61 Artamonov, "Ochagi voennoi," 59; de Beauplan, *Description*, 11.
62 de Beauplan, *Description*, 13; Iavornitskii, *Istoriia zaporoz'kikh kozakiv. Tom I*, 376, 378–379.
63 They looted and scuttled Ottoman galleys rather than taking them as prizes, since they did not have experience sailing larger craft. For more on the cossack naval threat to Ottoman coast districts, see Ostapchuk, "The Landscape of the Ottoman Black Sea," 23–95, and Tolmacheva, "The Cossacks at Sea," 483–512.
64 Serczyk, "Rech' Pospolitaia," 174–193.
65 Hrushevsky, *History of Ukraine-Rus'*, VIII, 299.

Chapter Two

1 Smith, "Muscovite Logistics," 38–39; Keep, *Soldiers of the Tsar*, 87–88; Alef, "Muscovite Military Reforms," 77–78, 122.
2 Chernov, "Tsentral'nyi gosudarstvennyi arkhiv drevnikh aktov," 150.
3 Chernov, *Vooruzhennye sily*, 78; Kalinychev, *Pravovye voprosy voennoi organizatsii Russkogo gosudarstva vtoroi poloviny XVII veka*, 40; Hellie, *Enserfment*, 37–38.
4 Zimin, "K istorii voennykh reform 50-kh godov," 344–345, 348; Zimin, *I. S. Peresvetov i ego sovremenniki*, 356–359, 361; Chernov, "Tsentral'nyi gosudarstvennyi arkhiv drevnikh aktov," 138–139; Hellie, *Enserfment*, 161, 164.
5 Iakovlev, *Zasechnaia cherta*, 20–21, 37–38; Margolin, "Oborona," 13–15. For a reconstruction of the Abatis Line see Nikitin, "Oboronitel'nye sooruzheniia zasechnoi cherty XVI-XVII vv.," 116–213.
6 There is some dispute as to whether the Abatis Line system included two shorter segments farther south on the steppe, one uniting the towns of Kromy, Livny, and Elets, the other connecting the towns of Kursk, Oskol', and Voronezh. Hellie, *Enserfment*, 174–176; Shaw, "Southern Frontiers of Muscovy," 123–124; Keep, *Soldiers of the Tsar*, 17; Kargalov, *Na stepnoi granitse*, 157–160.
7 Chernov, "Tsentral'nyi gosudarstvennyi arkhiv drevnikh aktov," 151; "Nakaz voevode kniaziu Ivanu Kugushevu," 1–9; *PSZ* 2, no. 728; Iakovlev, *Zasechnaia cherta*, 39–40.
8 *AMG* 2, no. 1081; Iakovlev, *Zasechnaia cherta*, 78–81, 87–88.
9 Zagorovskii, *Istoriia vkhozhdeniia*, 165; Novosel'skii, *Bor'ba*, 22–23, 43–44, 428–431; Kargalov, *Na stepnoi granitse*, 165–166; Kochekaev, *Nogaisko-russkie otnosheniia*, 109.
10 Markevich, *Istoriia mestnichestva v Moskovskom gosudarstve v XV-XVII v*, 359–368; *AI* 5, no. 251; *SGGD* 3, no. 54; Bel'iaev, "O storozhevoi," 78; *AAE* 3, no. 187.
11 Grala *et al.*, eds., *Pamiatniki*, 189–236; Chernov, "Tsentral'nyi gosudarstvennyi arkhiv," 120; Kalinychev, *Pravovye voprosy*, 111; *AMG* 3, no. 647; Demidova, *Sluzhilaia biurokratiia v Rossii XVII veka i ee rol' v formirovanii absoliutizma*, 179.
12 Kalinychev, *Pravovye voprosy*, 110.
13 *AAE* 3, no. 187, 271–274; Novosel'skii, *Bor'ba*, 158–160; Kargalov, *Na stepnoi granitse*, 154; *RIB* 2, 467–471.
14 Grala *et al.*, eds., *Pamiatniki*, 213–220, 223–226.
15 The middle service class cavalry centuries received their mobilization instructions from the Military Chancellery, but the Musketeers', Gunners', and other chancelleries announced mobilizations for the formations over which they had jurisdiction. Chernov, "Tsentral'nyi gosudarstvennyi arkhiv," 121; Veselovskii, "Smety voennykh sil Moskovskago gosudarstva, 1661–1663 gg.," 1–60; Stashevskii, *Smeta voennykh sil Moskovskago gosudarstva v 1663 godu*.

16 Bogoiavlenskii, "Vooruzhenie russkikh voisk v XVI–XVII vv.," 260–262; Vorob'ev, "Konnost', liudnost', oruzhnost' i sbruinost' sluzhilykh gorodov pri pervykh Romanovykh," 103–104; *RIB* 15, no. 216; Chernov, *Vooruzhennye sily*, 126.
17 Skrynnikov, *Ivan the Terrible*, 56.
18 Except for the Great Corps, which included some men of Moscow rank traveling with retainers, tents, and more extensive supplies. Smith, "Muscovite Logistics," 48. On the size of trains of early modern western European armies, see Perjes, "Army Provisioning," 1–51.
19 Smith, "Muscovite Logistics," 48–50; *AAE* 3, no. 187, 274.
20 Kolosov, "Razvitie artilleriiskogo vooruzheniia v Rossii vo vtoroi polovine XVII v.," 259–260.
21 Fletcher, "Of the Russe Commonwealth," 185; Margeret, *The Russian Empire and the Grand Duchy of Muscovy*, 45.
22 Kostomarov, *Smutnoe vremia Moskovskogo gosudarstva v nachale XVII stoletiia. 1604–1613*, 114–115.
23 Fletcher, "Of the Russe Commonwealth," 185; Massa, *Massa's Short History of the Muscovite Wars*, 85.
24 Andreev, *Neizvestnoe Borodino*, 119–125, 205–212, 220–223, 245–250; Zagorovskii, *Istoriia vkhozdeniia*, 171–175; Kargalov, *Polkovodtsy X–XVI vv.*, 248–255.
25 Fennell, ed., *Kurbskii's History*, 125; Hrushevsky, *History of Ukraine-Rus'*, VII, 89–97; Floria, "Proekt antituretskoi koalitsii serediny XVI v.," 72, 74, 79.
26 Novosel'skii, *Bor'ba*, 13–17, 28–36; Kochekaev, *Nogaisko-russkie otnosheniia*, 90–98, 101–105; Fennell, *Kurbskii's History*, 123.
27 Mikhailova, "Sluzhba donskikh kazakov," 144, 146–148; Ianchevskii, *Kolonial'naia politika na Donu*, 118–122; Pronshtein, "K istorii voznikoveniia," 168–172.
28 Stanislavskii, *Grazhdanskaia voina v Rossii v XVII v.*, 17–19; Svatikov, *Rossiia i Don*, 39.
29 Zagorovskii, *Istoriia vkhozdeniia*, 95–105, 189, 197–199; Miklashevskii, *K istorii khoziaistvennago byta*, 22; Zagorovskii, "Nekotorye osobennosti kolonizatsionnogo protsessa," 88.
30 Margolin, "Oborona," 5–13, 23; Miklashevskii, *K istorii khoziaistvennago byta*, 72–75; Buganov, "Gramota livenskomu voevode Ivanu Osipovichu Polevu 1595 g.," 180–185; Chermenskii, *Ocherki po sitorii kolonizatsii tambovskago kraia*, 11–14; Zagorovskii, *Istoriia vkhozdeniia*, 79–83, 89, 109, 152–160; *AMG* 3, no. 181; Bel'iaev, "O storozhevoi," 5–21, 64–65.
31 In 1625 rangers were entitled to 50–100 quarters per field of service land and cash allowances of 5–10 rubles. By 1660 the rangers of Valuiki were complaining:

> We, thy slaves, have become beggared ... and our horses have fallen. Many of us serve thee ... on foot and without firearms, which cannot be obtained anywhere. And we have not been granted thy cash allowance for eight years or more. We have a grain shortage at Valuiki and are dying of hunger.

Miklashevskii, *K istorii khoziaistvennago byta*, 72–75; Vtorov and Aleksandrov-Dol'nik, eds., *Drevniia gramoty* 1: no. 37; *AMG* 3, no. 181.
32 Novosel'skii, *Bor'ba*, 66, 68, 69; *PSZ* 3, no. 1540; *DAI* 4, no. 19.
33 *AI* 3, no. 116; Chicherin, *Oblastnyia*, 115; *AMG* 3, no. 62; *PSZ* 1, no. 320.
34 *PSZ* 3, no. 1540; Iakovlev, *Zasechnaia cherta*, 64.
35 *AI* 4, no. 161; *AAE* 4, no. 206; Piskarev, *Sobranie materialov dlia istorii zapadnago kraia Tambovskoi gubernii i eparkhii*, 67–69.
36 *AIuB* 3, no. 165; *AMG* 1, no. 135; *AAE* 4, no. 206; *AI* 4, no. 161; "Nakaz voevode kniaziu Ivanu Kugushevu," 1–9; *AI* 5, no. 161; *Chuvash*, no. 4; *DAI* 2, no. 100; *PSZ* 3, no. 1585; *AI* 5, no. 161; Chicherin, *Oblastnyia*, 115.

37 Belotserkovskii, *Tula i Tul'skii uezd v XVI i XVII vv.*, 165; Tikhomirov, *Rossiia v XVI stoletii*, 384.
38 Zagorovskii, "Nekotorye osobennosti kolonizatsionnogo protsessa," 88; Pallot and Shaw, *Landscape and Settlement*, 21–22.
39 Priakhin, Glaz'ev et al., eds., *Rossiiskaia krepost' na iuzhnykh rubezhakh*, 5–100.
40 Belotserkovskii, *Tula i Tul'skii uezd*, 207–209, 219, 227.
41 Kochekaev, *Nogaisko-russkie otnosheniia*, 112; Novosel'skii, *Bor'ba*, 55–56, 67–69; Smirnov, *Rossiia i Turtsiia v XVI i XVII vv. Tom vtoroi*, 56.
42 Zagorovskii, *Belgorodskaia cherta*, 25, 27, 65; Novosel'skii, *Bor'ba*, 163, 165; Stashevskii, "K istorii kolonizatsii iuga," 242, 244, 290–293.
43 Stashevskii, *Smolenskaia voina 1632–1634 gg*, 238–239, 294–301, 304–305, 314; *AMG* 1, no. 372, 374–375.
44 Novosel'skii, *Bor'ba*, 154, 210–213.
45 Chermenskii, *Ocherki po istorii kolonizatsii*, 10–11; Bel'iaev, "O storozhevoi," 11; Novosel'skii, *Bor'ba*, 160–161.
46 Novosel'skii, *Bor'ba*, 150–154; Solov'ev, *Istoriia Rossii s drevneishikh vremen*, 161.
47 Bel'iaev, "O storozhevoi," 40–46; Novosel'skii, *Bor'ba*, 158; Kargalov, *Na stepnoi granitse*, 107.
48 Keep, *Soldiers of the Tsar*, 34.
49 Ibid., 49; *Solov'ev* 5: 278–279; Vorob'ev and Degtiarev, *Russkoe feodal'noe zemlevladenie ot "smutnogo vremeni" do kanune petrovskikh reform*, 140, 144; Abramovich, "Novgorodskoe pomest'e v gody ekonomicheskogo krizisa poslednei treti XVI v.," 5–26. At the national level the typical *gorodovyi syn boiarskii* in 1638 held only five or six peasant households. Iakovlev, *Prikaz sbora ratnykh liudei*, 259.
50 Skrynnikov, *Sotsial'no-politicheskaia bor'ba v Russkom gosudarstve v nachale XVII veka*, 117–118.
51 Novosel'skii, *Issledovaniia po istorii epokhi feodalizma*, 183–184.
52 Vazhinskii, *Zemlevladenie i skladyvanie obshchiny odnodvortsev v XVII v.*, 77–78; Stashevskii, *Ocherki po istorii tsarstvovaniia Mikhaila Fedorovicha do epokhi Smolenskoi voiny*, 212–234; Hellie, *Enserfment*, 52–69, 111–147.
53 Porshnev, *Muscovy and Sweden in the Thirty Years' War*, 12, 70, 106; Novosel'skii, *Bor'ba*, 168–169.
54 Stashevskii, *Smolenskaia voina*, 1–8.
55 Nowak, "Polish Warfare Technique in the 17th Century," 30–31; Wimmer, "Piechota w wojsku polskim XV-XVIII w.," 169–170; Frost, *The Northern Wars*, 151.
56 Stashevskii, *Smolenskaia voina*, 75–78, 114–115, 120–121, 127, 130, 135; A. V. Malov, "Konnitsa novogo stroia v Russkoi armii," *Otechestvennaia istoriia* 1 (2006): 121; Hellie, *Enserfment*, 171–172; Chernov, *Vooruzhenye sily*, 134–136.
57 Kozliakov, *Mikhail Fedorovich*, 224.
58 These deliveries were recorded in *chetvert'* measure but without specifying whether these were 6-*pud* or 8-*pud chetverti*; hence the variation in total kilo yields. One *sokha* of inhabited taxbearing land was equivalent to 500–900 quarters of land per field in three-field tenure, depending on soil quality and the owner's social estate. One quarter in three fields equalled 1.5 *desiatiny* or 4 acres. Stashevskii, *Smolenskaia voina*, 195–216.
59 Hellie, *Enserfment*, 159; Lipiński, "Działania wojenne," 180–181.
60 Lipiński, "Działania wojenne," 185, 200; Stashevskii, *Smolenskaia voina*, 190, 211; Frost, *Northern Wars*, 144.
61 Fuller, Jr. *Strategy and Power in Russia*, 12–13; Lipiński, "Bój o Zaworonkowe wzgórza i osaczenie Szeina pod Smoleńskiem," 44, 51, 61, 69; Frost, *Northern Wars*, 145.

62 Hrushevsky, *History of Ukraine-Rus'*, VIII, 157–159; Novosel'skii, *Bor'ba*, 178–179, 209–221.

Chapter Three

1. Hrushevsky, *History of Ukraine-Rus'*, VIII, 179–180; Novosel'skii, *Bor'ba*, 245–248.
2. Novosel'skii, *Bor'ba*, 216–220; Smirnov, *Rossiia i Turtsiia* II, 38–40; Lunin, *Azovskaia epopeia, 1637–1641 gg.*, 28.
3. Beliaev, "O storozhevoi," 46.
4. Iakovlev, *Zasechnaia cherta*, 45–46, 57, 62–63; Iakovlev, *Prikaz sbora ratnykh liudei*, 120–121.
5. Hellie, *Enserfment*, 186; *RIB* XXXV, *Arkhiv P. M. Stroeva*, II, no. 477; Myshlaevskii, *Ofitserskii vopros*, 26–27; Iakovlev, *Zasechnaia cherta*, 274–278, 288.
6. *AAE* 3, no. 268; Zagorovskii, *Belgorodskaia cherta*, 17, 72–76.
7. As of August 1635 ten districts on the Nogai Front had 5,586 active duty servicemen and an additional 1,690 kinsmen and dependents not yet registered in service or on the tax rolls and therefore eligible for resettlement elsewhere. F. 210, Razriadnyi prikaz, Belgorodskii stol stolbets no. 210, ll. 14–21.
8. Davies, *State Power and Community*, 83, 90–91.
9. Ibid., 83–84.
10. *AMG* 2, no. 101; F. 210, Razriadnyi prikaz, Belgorodskii stol stolbets no. 92, ll. 330–331; Novosel'skii, *Bor'ba*, 303.
11. Davies, *State Power and Community*, 104, 121–133.
12. Ibid., 64–66, 71.
13. Zagorovskii, *Belgorodskaia cherta*, 93–94; Gulianitskii, *Gradostroitel'stvo Moskovskogo gosudarstva XVI-XVII vekov*, 75–76.
14. Fisher, "Azov in the Sixteenth and Seventeenth Centuries," 161–163, 169–170; Novosel'skii, *Bor'ba*, 257.
15. Zagorovskii, "Donskoe kazachestvo i razmery donskikh otpuskov," 142–144.
16. Riabov, *Voisko donskoe*, 22, 24; RGU, *Istoriia Dona*, 132–133; Lunin, *Azovskaia epopeia*, 29–32; Boeck, "Shifting Boundaries," 59.
17. Lunin, *Azovskaia epopeia*, 38–47, 56; RGU, *Istoriia Dona*, 134–135; Riabov, *Voisko donskoe*, 28–29.
18. Zagorovskii, "Sudostroenie na Donu i ispol'zovanie Rossieiu parusnogo-grebnogo flota protiv Krymskogo khanstva i Turtsii," 113.
19. Zagorovskii, "Obshchii ocherk istorii zaseleniia i khoziaistvennogo osvoeniia iuzhnykh okrain Rossii v epokhu zrelogo feodalizma," 11–13.
20. In winter the Great Corps was restationed at Livny, the Vanguard at Kursk, and the Rear Guard at Elets.
21. Vazhinskii, *Zemlevladenie*, 68; Glaz'ev, "Formirovanie Belgorodskogo razriada kak administrativno-territorial'noi edinitsy v seredine XVII v.," 116–117; Chernov, *Vooruzhennye sily*, 171. A different periodization is offered by Stevens, *Soldiers on the Steppe*, 37.
22. Chernov, *Vooruzhennye sily*, 187–188.
23. "Stat'i, kakoe opasenie i ratnykh liudei v ukrainykh gorodekh imet' ot Krymskago khana," *Zapiski Imperatorskago Russkago arkheologicheskago obshchestva* 2 (1861): 374–376.
24. A. A. Novosel'skii, "Dvortsovye krest'iane Komaritskoi volosti vo vtoroi polovine XVII veka," 66–68; Davies, "Village Into Garrison," 492–494.
25. *AMG* II, nos. 496 and 543; Zagorovskii, *Belgorodskaia cherta*, 145–147; Hellie, *Enserfment*, 193.
26. A roll from 1651 recorded 17,741 servicemen serving in twenty-two of the Line's garrison towns: 4,788 *deti boiarskie*, 4,021 cossacks, 3,432 musketeers, 2,942

dragoons, 975 Ukrainians, 513 gunners and sharpshooters, 1,055 *pomestnye atamany*, *belomestnye atamany*, and rangers, and 15 foreign mercenaries. Zagorovskii, *Belgorodskaia cherta*, 136–137, 141; Chernov, *Vooruzhennye sily*, 167.
27 Kochekaev, *Nogaisko-russkie otnosheniia*, 122–123; Ustiugov *et al.*, eds., *Ocherki istorii Kal'mytskoi ASSR. Do-oktiabr'skii period*, 106–108, 111–112; Khodarkovsky, *Where Two Worlds Met*, 83, 87–90.
28 Zagorovskii, "Donskoe kazachestvo i razmery donskikh otpuskov," 143.
29 Riabov, *Voisko donskoe*, 134; Zagorovskii, "Sudostroenie," 113–117, 130–141; Novosel'skii, *Bor'ba*, 373–385.
30 Zagorovskii, "Sudostroenie," 151–152; Riabov, *Voisko donskoe*, 33.
31 Hrushevsky, *History of Ukraine-Rus'*, VII, 263.
32 Ibid., 345, 364–374, 378–379; Podhorodecki, "Kampaniia Chocimska 1621 roku," 58–59.
33 Plokhy, *The Cossacks and Religion*, 113–115, 124.
34 Hrushevsky, *History of Ukraine-Rus'*, VII, 216, 427, 432.
35 Miklashevskii, *K istorii khoziaistvennago byta*, 126–127, 167–170; Ananovich, "Pereselenie ukraintsev v Rossiiu nakanune osvoboditel'noi voiny 1648–1654 gg.," 90–95; Vazhinskii, *Zemlevladenie*, 56.
36 F. 210, Razriadnyi prikaz, Vladimirskii stol stolbets no. 131, ll. 339–360, 451–453.
37 Trunov, "K materialam po istorii zaseleniia cherkasami voronezhskogo kraia," 110–112; Bagalei, *Istoriia slobodskoi ukraini*, 26–31; Zagorovskii, *Iziumskaia cherta*, 53–57; Hrushevsky, *History of Ukraine-Rus'*, VIII, 311–315.
38 For this reason the rebaptism of Ukrainian immigrants was often insisted upon. Plokhy, *The Cossacks and Religion*, 291, 293, 296, 297.
39 Hrushevsky, *History of Ukraine-Rus'*, VIII, 347.
40 Hrushevsky, VIII, 397; Zaborovskii, "Krymskii vopros," 265; Litavrin, ed., *Osmanskaia imperiia*, 192–196.
41 Hrushevsky, *History of Ukraine-Rus'*, VIII, 527, 538, 556–557, 579–614; *AIuZR* 3, nos. 195, 196, 224, 245, 256, 262.
42 Novosel'skii, "Bor'ba," 15; Litavrin, ed., *Osmanskaia imperiia*, 202–203, 206–207; *AIuZR* 3, nos. 282, 285, 305; Solov'ev, *Istoriia Rossii*, V, *tom* 10, 553–554, 571.
43 Litavrin, ed., *Osmanskaia imperiia*, 207; Slabeev *et al.*, eds, *Istoriia Ukrainskoi SSR. tom tretii*, 44–48; *AIuZR* 3, nos. 323, 328, 330.
44 Picheta, "Vneshniaia politika," 112, 117; Solov'ev, *Istoriia Rossii*, V, *tom* 10, 558–560, 581; Cherepnin, *Zemskie sobory*, 324–327; Sysyn, *Between Poland and Ukraine*, 182.
45 Picheta, "Vneshniaia politika," 113–116; Solov'ev, *Istoriia Rossii*, V, *tom* 10, 584–585.
46 *AIuZR* 3, no. 335, 487.
47 Plokhy, *The Cossacks and Religion*, 207–208, 212–220.
48 *AIuZR* VIII, no. 38, 364–365; Abetsedarskii, "Bor'ba," 181–183, 187–191, 203–206, 214–215.
49 Plokhy, *The Cossacks and Religion*, 316; Solov'ev, *Istoriia Rossii*, V, *tom* 10, 592–593; *AIuZR* III, no. 343, 501, 502; *AIuZR* VIII, no. 39, 371; Cherepnin, *Zemskie sobory*, 336.
50 On the administrative system of the Hetmanate at the time of the Pereiaslav Agreement, see: Magocsi, *A History of Ukraine*, 229–237; Schumann, "Der Hetmanstaat," 499–548.
51 Litavrin, ed., *Osmanskaia imperiia*, 213–217; Ignat'ev *et al.*, eds., *Istoriia vneshnei politiki Rossii. Konets XV-XVII vek*, 294–295; Novosel'skii, "Bor'ba," 17–22; Zaborovskii, "Krymskii vopros," 266–270; Sanin, *Otnoshenie Rossii i Ukrainy s Krymskim khanstvom v seredine XVII veka*, 232–235.
52 *AIuZR* X, no. 8, 432–452; Basarab, *Pereiaslav 1654*, 9, 219.

53 Plokhy, *The Cossacks and Religion*, 234, 257; Kohut, "Imagining Popular Rights and Liberties"; Davies, *God's Playground*, 322–323.
54 Picheta, "Vneshnaia politika," 121–122; Plokhy, *The Cossacks and Religion*, 325–326.
55 Kostomarov, "Getmanstvo Iuriia Khmel'nitskogo," 192; Sanin, "Antiosmanskie voiny v 70-e-90-e gody XVII veka i gosudarstvennost' Ukrainy v sostave Rossii i Rechi Pospolity," 65; Basarab, *Pereiaslav 1654*, 219.

Chapter Four

1 Sahanovich, *Neviadomaia vaina*, 10–11; Zamlinskii, *Bogdan Khmel'nitskii*, 301; Mal'tsev, *Rossiia i Belorussiia v seredine XVII veka*, 26–37.
2 Frost, *After the Deluge*, 33; Frost, *The Northern Wars*, 165; Brown, "Tsar Aleksei Mikhailovich," 123.
3 Novosel'skii, "Ocherk voennykh," 133.
4 According to Polish sources the Muscovites lost 7,000 dead and 15,000 wounded in their assaults on Smolensk. Reger, "In the Service of the Tsar," 87–92.
5 Longworth, *Alexis, Tsar of All the Russias*, 163; Andreev, *Aleksei Mikhailovich*, 265, 270–271; Brown, "Tsar Aleksei Mikhailovich," 128, 135–136; Novosel'skii, "Ocherk voennykh deistvii," 119–127.
6 Sahanovich, *Neviadomaia vaina*, 132–133; Brown, "Tsar Aleksei Mikhailovich," 124.
7 Solov'ev, *Istoriia Rossii*, V, *tom* 10, 628–633.
8 Sanin, *Otnosheniia*, 65–68; Ignat'ev et al., *Istoriia vneshnei politiki*, 301; Kostomarov, "Malorossiiskii getman Zinovii-Bogdan Khmel'nitskii," 277–278; Kubala, *Wojna Moskiewska*, 166–169.
9 Mal'tsev, "Boevoe," 272–273, 275–276; Sanin, *Otnosheniia*, 63–65; *AIuZR* XIV, no. 2, 67, 74.
10 Kubala, *Wojna Moskiewska*, 190; Sanin, *Otnosheniia*, 69, 86–88, 126, 133.
11 Sanin estimates total casualties on both sides exceeded 15,000, with Polish infantry taking especially heavy losses; Kubala thought the Muscovite–Ukrainian army was badly damaged, losing 9,000 men and 34 guns seized or spiked, whereas Polish cavalry lost only about 200 men and Polish infantry losses came more from the frost than from combat. Sanin, *Otnosheniia*, 134–136, 141–144; Zamlinskii, *Bogdan Khmel'nitskii*, 313–316, 335; Mal'tsev, "Boevoe," 278–282, 285; Kubala, *Wojna Moskiewska*, 195–199.
12 Sanin, *Otnosheniia*, 144–154; *AIuZR* XIV (1889), no. 19, 564.
13 Kargalov, *Moskovskie voevody*, 243–244; Mal'tsev, "Boevoe," 295–297, 299; Sanin, *Otnosheniia*, 169.
14 Sanin, *Otnosheniia*, 162, 164–165, 168; Novosel'skii, "Bor'ba," 26–27.
15 Longworth, *Tsar Alexis*, 105.
16 The *Sejm* did elect Tsar Aleksei as successor in 1658, but the election was immediately annulled upon the protest of the Polish bishops and the papal nuncio. Wójcik, "Russian Endeavors," 59–60; Ignat'ev et al., *Istoriia vneshnei politiki*, 304–306.
17 Novosel'skii, "Bor'ba," 29–30; Sanin, *Otnosheniia*, 179–180, 193–194, 205, 213.
18 Iavornitskii, *Istoriia zaporoz'kikh kozakiv*, II, 190.
19 When Bieniewski had first arrived at Chigirin in summer 1657 Vyhovs'kyi had reassured Moscow he understood he "has come for no other purpose than intrigue, so as to divide us." Plokhy, *The Cossacks and Religion*, 330–332; *AIuZR* XV (1892), no. 7, 324–325; Iavornitskii, *Istoriia zaporoz'skikh kozakiv*, II, 196; Litavrin, ed., *Osmanskaia imperiia*, 49–50, 52; Kostomarov, "Getmanstvo Vygovskogo," 59, 66–67.
20 Vyhovs'kyi, quoted in Iavornitskii, *Istoriia zaporoz'skikh kozakiv*, II, 197.

NOTES

21 Internal memoranda indicate the appointment of *voevody* and garrisons to these towns was motivated by defense concerns and that the Ambassadors' Chancellery had not yet worked out for itself what kind of administrative and fiscal authority the new *voevody* were to wield. Iavornitskii, *Istoriia zaporoz'skikh kozakiv*, II, 196; Litavrin, ed., *Osmanskaia imperiia*, 50–51; *AIuZR* XV (1892), no. 3.

22 *AIuZR* XV (1892), no. 7, 350; Litavrin, ed., *Osmanskaia imperiia*, 51–53.

23 *AIuZR* XV (1892), no. 4, 174, 176, 181, and no. 5, 215, 219, 221.

24 Ivan Vyhovs'kyi made a second unsuccessful attempt to seize Kiev on 26–30 October with 50,000 cossacks and 6,000 Tatars. *AIuZR* XV (1892), no. 6; Kostomarov, "Getmanstvo Vygovskogo," 107–108; Bul'vins'kii, "Ukrainsko-rosiis'ka viina," 179–180, 190.

25 Plokhy, *The Cossacks and Religion*, 62–64; Iakovleva, "Gadiachskii dogovor," 64, 68–69, 72, 75.

26 Romodanovskii's army – four corps under himself, F. F. Kurakin, S. R. Pozharskii, and S. P. L'vov – reportedly numbered about 15–20,000 men, the maximum that could have been spared at the time from the Belgorod Line, when it had entered Ukraine in November. A small corps of middle service class cavalrymen under A. V. Buturlin was also present. Trubetskoi had requested reinforcements of 2,000 men from Kiev, under Boriatinskii and Chaadaev, but they do not appear to have been sent. The number of cossacks under Bespalyi is not reported; he later testified to the Ambassadors' Chancellery that 2,000 of his men came to Trubetskoi's aid during the retreat from Konotop. Andrii Bul'vins'kii uses Trubetskoi's 200,000-ruble troop pay bill to argue Trubetskoi's corps must have numbered about 45,000 and the total Muscovite forces in the Konotop theater around 70,000. Korzon, *Dzieje wojen i wojskowości, Tom II*, 354; Litavrin, ed., *Osmanskaia imperiia*, 55; Grekov, "Iz istorii sovmestnoi bor'by Ukrainy i Rossii za osvobozhdenie Ukrainy i Belorussii (1654–1655 gg.)," 347; Novosel'skii, "Bor'ba," 65; *AIuZR* XV, no. 7, 356, and no. 8, 364–366; Kostomarov, "Getmanstvo Vygovskogo," 136–139, 147; Bul'vins'kii, "Ukrainsko-rosiis'ka viina," 204–205.

27 Some Polish and Ukrainian sources claim Pozharskii's and L'vov's force was ten times this size. Korzon, *Dzieje wojen i wojskowości, Tom II*, 354; Tys-Khrokhmaliuk, "The Victory at Konotop," 41; Bul'vins'kii, "Ukrainsko-rosiis'ka viina," 205–206.

28 In a letter to Warsaw Vyhovs'kyi claimed 17,000 Muscovites perished at Konotop; Pierre de Noyers, secretary to the Polish queen, accepted a figure of 8,000. The only estimate of Vyhovs'kyi's losses was given by an interpreter, Terentii Frolov, who did not actually see the battle: he told the Ambassadors' Chancellery about 3,000 cossacks and 500 Tatars were killed during the attacks on Trubetskoi's train. Novosel'skii, "Bor'ba," 65–70; Solov'ev, *Istoriia Rossii s drevneishikh vremen. Kniga VI, Tom 11*, 51; Bul'vins'kii, "Ukrainsko-rosiis'ka viina," 214–215.

29 Frost gives 36,000 men as the approximate total strength of the Polish royal army in 1659; Nagielski reports a total of 39,770 horse and foot. Frost, "The Polish-Lithuanian Commonwealth," 35; Nagielski, "Wysiłek mobilizacyny Rzeczpospolitej w latach 1656–1659," 176; Sikorski, ed., *Polskie tradycje wojskowe. Tom I*, 300.

30 F. 210, Razriadnyi prikaz, Belgorodskii stol stolbets no. 921, l. 517.

31 Chernov, *Vooruzhennye sily*, 144–145; Hellie, *Enserfment*, 195–196; Epifanov, "Voisko," 247.

32 Hellie, *Enserfment*, 196; Razin, *Istoriia voennogo iskusstva XVI–XVII vv.*, 223–224.

33 Malov, "Konnitsa," 121–126; Epifanov, "Voisko," 247; Chernov, *Vooruzhennye sily*, 140–141, 146–148.

34 Epifanov, "Voisko," 247, 251; Hellie, *Enserfment*, 269. For a breakdown of the military establishment and its wage bill in 1663, see Stashevskii, "Smeta voennykh sil Moskovskago gosudarstva na 1663 god," 15–42 and 5, 6: 55–88; Stashevskii, *Smeta voennykh sil Moskovskago gosudarstva v 1663 godu*.

35 Reger, "In the Service of the Tsar," 74; Epifanov, "Voisko," 254; Chernov, *Vooruzhennye sily*, 177. On ordnance types and production techniques, see Kolosov, "Razvitie artilleriiskogo vooruzheniia v Rossii vo vtoroi polovine XVII v.," 259–269; Epifanov, "Oruzhie," 275–280; Esper, "Military Self-Sufficiency and Weapons Technology in Muscovite Russia," 185–208; and Hellie, *Enserfment*, 184–185. On arms imports see Kotilaine, "In Defense of the Realm," 67–95.
36 Epifanov, "Voisko," 248; Hellie, *Enserfment*, 191, 227. On the foreign officers, see Reger, "In the Service of the Tsar"; Myshlaevskii, *Ofitserskii vopros*.
37 Epifanov, "'Uchenie i khitrost' ratnogo stroeniia pekhotnykh liudei' (Iz istroii russkoi armii XVII)," 77–98; Cracraft, *The Petrine Revolution in Russian Culture*, 106.
38 Baiov, *Kurs*, 142–146; Leonov and Ul'ianov, *Reguliarnaia pekhota*, 9; Cracraft, *The Petrine Revolution*, 108, 514.
39 Epifanov, "Voisko," 249; Bogoiavlenskii, "Vooruzhenie russkikh voisk v XVI-XVII vv.," 272; Chernov, *Vooruzhennye sily*, 152.
40 RGADA, F. 210, Razriadnyi prikaz, Prikaznyi stol stolbets no. 385, ll. 186–187, 279–280, 364–381; Sevskii stol stolbets no. 223, ll. 16–18; Chernov, *Vooruzhennye sily*, 142, 147.
41 Leach, ed., *Memoirs of the Polish Baroque*, 81–86.
42 Brown, "Early Modern Russian Bureaucracy," 419–421, 424–425, 458–460, 468; Brown, "Military Planning and High-level Decision-making in Seventeenth-century Russia," 79, 82–84; Golombievskii, "Stoly razriadnogo prikaza v 1668–1670 gg.," 2, 6, 7.
43 Stevens, *Soldiers on the Steppe*, 45–47, 57.
44 Stashevshii, "Biudzhet i armiia," 416.
45 Kotilaine, "In Defense of the Realm," 77; Bazilevich, "Elementy merkantilizma v ekonomicheskom politike pravitel'stva Alekseiia Mikhailovicha," 3–34.
46 Bazilevich, *Denezhnaia reforma Alekseiia Mikhailovicha i vosstanie v Moskve v 1662 g.*, 14, 26, 39–40; Botsianovskii, "Finansovyi krizis v Moskovskom gosudarstve XVII v.," 227, 231–234, 236.
47 Kostomarov, "Getmanstvo Iuriia Khmel'nitskogo," 245.
48 Kostomarov, "Getmanstvo Iuriia Khmel'nitskogo," 189–193.
49 Hniłko, *Wyprawa Cudnowska w 1660 roku*, 46–52, 96; Kostomarov, "Getmanstvo Iurii Khmel'nitskogo," 194–196; Baiov, *Kurs*, 153.
50 Kostomarov, "Getmanstvo Iuriia Khmel'nitskogo," 200–204.
51 Gordon, *Dnevnik 1659–1667*, 63–69.
52 Kostomarov, "Getmanstvo Iuriia Khmel'nitskogo," 215–218; Baiov, *Kurs*, 152–156; Gordon, *Dnevnik 1659–1667*, 73–77; *AIuZR* V, no. 21, ii, 38–39; *AIuZR* 5, no. 87, 201–202.
53 Kostomarov, "Getmanstvo Iuriia Khmel'nitskogo," 246, 252–261, 275, 282.
54 Kostomarov, *Ruina*, 10–23.
55 Frost, "The Polish-Lithuanian Commonwealth and the 'Military Revolution,'" 42–43; Stone, *The Polish-Lithuanian State*, 174–176.
56 Kostomarov, *Ruina*, 40, 44, 49; Bazilevich, *Denezhnaia reforma*, 78.
57 Sofronenko, "Malorossiiskii prikaz," 137; O'Brien, *Muscovy and the Ukraine*, 99, 104.
58 Litavrin, ed., *Osmanskaia imperiia*, 66–69; Kostomarov, *Ruina*, 53–54, 58, 74.
59 Ignat'ev et al., *Istoriia vneshnei politiki*, 322–325; Kostomarov, *Ruina*, 77, 91, 93–95.
60 Kostomarov, *Ruina*, 103–113.
61 Mikhnevich, ed., *Stoletie voennago ministerstva, tom IV. Glavnyi shtab. Chast' pervaia, kniga pervaia, otd. 1. Vooruzhennyia sily Rossii do tsarstvovaniia Imperatora Aleksandra I. Istoricheskii ocherk*, appendix 10, p. 11; Novosel'skii, "Bor'ba," 102.
62 Kostomarov, *Ruina*, 121, 124, 129.
63 Ibid., 161; Sofronenko, "Malorossiiskii prikaz," 137, 153; Ignat'ev et al., *Istoriia vneshnei politiki*, 133.

NOTES

Chapter Five

1. Galaktionov, "Rossiia i Pol'sha pered litsom turetsko-tatarskoi agressiii v 1667 g.," 383–384; Kostomarov, *Ruina*, 167, 174–175, 191; Smirnov, *Rossiia i Turtsiia*, II, 122–124.
2. Majewski, "Wojny polsko-tureckie," 362–363; Kołodziejcyk, *Podole pod panowaniem tureckim*, 50–55.
3. Majewski, "Wojny polsko-tureckie," 363–371, 376–385; Wimmer, *Historia piechoty Polskiej*, 246–248.
4. Kostomarov, *Ruina*, 259, 265, 270, 273–275, 279–287, 290–299.
5. Cossack scouts estimated the combined Ottoman and Tatar forces operating near Chyhyryn in late summer 1677 at 91,000 men. Ibraim Pasha had reportedly intended to strike first against Kiev, but Iurii Khmel'nyts'kyi and Selim Girei had urged that Chyhyryn be taken first. Zaruba, *Ukrainskoe kazatskoe voisko*, 35, 39; Smirnov, *Rossiia i Turtsiia*, II, 129–130, 133–134, 138.
6. Romodanovskii's corps numbered 11,135 infantry, 20,673 cavalry, and a train of 126 guns. Two-thirds of his troops were foreign formation. Zaruba, *Ukrainskoe kazatskoe voisko*, 37; Bogdanov, "Neizvestnaia voina Fedora Alekseevicha," 63.
7. Popov, "Turetskaia voina v tsarstvovanie Fedora Alekseevicha," 167–170; Zaruba, *Ukrainskoe kazatskoe voisko*, 46–50; Sedov, "Oborona Chigirina v 1677 g.," 496–498.
8. Colonel Patrick Gordon, Trauernicht's replacement as commandant of the Chyhyryn garrison, reported prisoner testimonies that Kara Mustafa's army consisted of 15,000 janissaries; 30,000 elite sipahis of the Porte; 32,000 pioneers, guards, and gunners; 10,000 Moldavians and Wallachians; 4 great siege guns, 135 field guns, and 15 mortars; and a train of 108,000 wagons, 5,000 camels, and 8,000 shepherds. He thought the Crimean Tatars under Khan Murat Girei numbered about 80,000, although they were more likely fewer than 30,000. Obolenskii and Possel't, "Dnevnik generala Patrika Gordona," 145; Gordon, *Dnevnik*, 54.
9. *AIuZR* XIII (St. Petersburg, 1884), nos. 83, 92, 93, 132; Obolenskii and Possel't, "Dnevnik generala Patrika Gordona," 115, 117, 118; Wojcik, *Rzeczpospolita*, 120.
10. Wójcik, *Rzeczpospolita*, 107–108, 123, 159; Smirnov, *Rossiia i Turtsiia*, II, 145–146.
11. *AIuZR* XIII, nos. 156, 132.
12. Smirnov, *Rossiia i Turtsiia*, II, 147–150.
13. *AIuZR* XIII, nos. 93, 102, 131; Obolenskii and Possel't, "Dnevnik generala Patrika Gordona," 143; Smirnov, *Rossiia i Turtsiia*, II, 150–151.
14. *AIuZR* XIII, nos. 95, 114, 115, 118, 120, 121, 128, 129, 132, 150, 152; Smirnov, *Rossiia i Turtsiia*, II, 150–151.
15. Smirnov, *Rossiia i Turtsiia*, II, 137–138.
16. *AIuZR* XIII, nos. 83, 92, 93, 120, 132; Smirnov, *Rossiia i Turtsiia*, II, 148–150.
17. Danilov, "V. V. Golicyn bis zum staatsreich vom Mai 1682," 13–24.
18. Zaruba, *Ukrainskoe kazatskoe voisko*, 72–73.
19. Vodarskii, "Mezhdunarodnoe polozhenie Russkogo gosudarstva i russko-turetskaia voina 1676–1681 gg.," 522; Mikhnevich, ed., *Stoletie voennago ministerstva, tom IV. Glavnyi shtab*, 69.
20. Obolenskii and Possel't, "Dnevnik generala Patrika Gordona," 108, 113, 114, 120, 139, 149, 151, 154, 171, 193; *AIuZR* XIII, no. 152; Zaruba, *Ukrainskoe kazatskoe voisko*, 72–73; Sedov, "Oborona Chigirina," 496.
21. Obolenskii and Possel't, "Dnevnik generala Patrika Gordona," 147; Sedov, "Oborona Chigirina," 492–494, 500–507.
22. On the 1677 campaign these two regiments were at full strength, whereas 16 percent of Romodanovskii's provincial foreign formation troops and 51 percent of his traditional formation cavalry had failed to appear for service. Zagorovskii, *Iziumskaia cherta*, 96; Sedov, "Oborona Chigirina," 491.

23 *AIuZR* XIII, nos. 80, 82, 88, 89; Obolenskii and Possel't, "Dnevnik generala Patrika Gordona," 105; Popov, "Turetskaia voina," VIII, 6: 167–169.
24 *AIuZR* XIII, no. 154, 673; Hajda, "Two Ottoman Gazanames Concerning the Chyhryn Campaign of 1678," 229–230; Popov, "Turetskaia voina," VIII, 7: 312–313; *Obolenskii*, 188–190.
25 *AIuZR* XIII, no. 150, 648.
26 *AIuZR* XIII, no. 154, 674, 679 and no. 156, 686–689; Smirnov, *Rossiia i Turtsiia*, II, 155–156.
27 Bogdanov, *V teni*, 141; *AIuZR* XIII, no. 132; *AIuZR* XII (1882), no. 183.
28 Smirnov, *Rossiia i Turtsiia*, II, 159–160; Zaruba, *Ukrainskoe kazatskoe voisko*, 69; *AIuZR* XIII, no. 157, 693.
29 Philipp, "Russia: The Beginning of Westernization," 576.
30 *AIuZR* XIII, no. 156.
31 *Letopis' samovidtsa*, 148, 150; Zaruba, *Ukrainskoe kazatskoe voisko*, 79–80; Mikhnevich, ed., *Stoletie*, 69; Bogdanov, *V teni*, 159; Novosel'skii, "Bor'ba," 112–114; Zagorovskii, *Iziumskaia cherta*, 132, 134–135, 138, 198–199; F. 210, Razriadnyi prikaz, Belgorodskii stol stolbets no. 1301, ll. 11–40 and Belgorodskii stol stolbets no. 994, ll. 13–14, 68–76, 99, 293–296.
32 Zaruba, *Ukrainskoe kazatskoe voisko*, 76–78; Kostomarov, *Ruina*, 352–355; Bagalei, *Ocherki iz istorii kolonizatsii*, 400; Baranovich, "Opustoshenie i vosstanovlenie pravoberezhnoi Ukrainy vo vtoroi polovine XVII i nachale XVIII v.," 148–150.
33 Kaminski, *Republic vs. Autocracy*, 188, 232; Babushkina, "Mezhdunarodnoe znachenie krymskikh pokhodov 1687 i 1689 gg.," 159.
34 Bagalei, *Ocherki iz istorii kolonizatsii*, 395, 397, 400–407; Sliusarskii, *Sotsial'no-ekonomicheskoe razvitie Slobozhanshchiny XVII-XVIII vv.*, 107–113; Zagorovskii, *Iziumskaia cherta*, 154–193.
35 *PSZ* 2, no. 744; Stevens, *Soldiers on the Steppe*, 82–83.
36 Stevens, *Soldiers on the Steppe*, 77–82; Zagorovskii, *Iziumskaia cherta*, 112–113; Epifanov, "Uchenie i khitrost'," 84.
37 *PSZ* 2, no. 812.
38 Chernov, *Vooruzhennye sily*, 187–189; F. 210, Razriadnyi prikaz, Belgorodskii stol stolbets no. 994, ll. 30–31, 78–83.
39 Miliukov, *Gosudarstvennoe khoziaistvo Rossii v pervoi chetverti XVIII stoletiia i reforma Petra Velikogo*, 61–66; Ustiugov, "Finansy," 421–423, 438; Sedov, "Rossiia na poroge novogo vremeni," 7–8.
40 Precedence suits had become rare by the 1670s, and it had long been the practice to appoint commanders on major military operations *bez mest*, that is, precluding precedence challenge to their appointments. Both Chyhyryn campaigns and the deployments of 1679–1681 had been conducted *bez mest*, and while there were still frequent quarrels among commanders with conflicting perceptions of the proper chain of command, not even the most acrimonious of them – the dispute between Romodanovskii and Golitsyn – had resulted in formal litigation. Markevich, *Istoriia mestnichestva*, 544–546, 548–549; Crummey, "Reflections on *Mestnichestvo* in the 17th Century," 271.
41 Man'kov, ed., *Rossiiskoe zakonodatel'stvo x-XX vekov. V desiati tomakh. Tom IV*, 35–36.
42 Das, "History Writing," 506–508.
43 Wójcik, *Rzeczpospolita*, 120–121, 133–135, 191, 196.
44 Kaminskii, *Republic vs. Autocracy*, 105.
45 Bogdanov, *Moskovskaia publitsistika poslednei chetvert XVII veka*, 117–119, 125; Chistiakova and Bogdanov, *"Da budet potomkam iavleno": Ocherki o russkikh istorikakh vtoroi polovine XVII veka i ikh trudakh*, 50–57, 120–124.
46 Hughes, *Sophia*, 187–188, 193; Wojcik, "King John III," 670.

47 Hughes, *Sophia*, 198.
48 Razin, *Istoriia voennogo iskusstva, XVI-XVII vv.*, 254.
49 Stevens, *Soldiers on the Steppe*, 113–116, 120.
50 Kostomarov, *Ruina*, 394–396; Iavornitskii, *Istoriia zaporoz'skikh kozakiv*, III, 22–26; Hughes, *Sophia*, 199.
51 Kostomarov, *Ruina*, 396–405.
52 Iavornitskii, *Istoriia zaporoz'skikh kozakiv*, III, 13–14, 25–26, 41–63.
53 Hughes, *Sophia*, 201–206; Artamonov, "Pozitsii getmanskoi vlasti i Rossii na Ukraine," 94; Kaminski, *Republic vs. Autocracy*, 216–217; Vozgrin, *Istoricheskie sud'by krymskikh tatar*, 230.
54 Fuller, *Strategy and Power*, 18–19; Stevens, *Russia's Wars of Emergence* (forthcoming); Kostomarov, *Ruina*, 424–425.
55 Razin, *Istoriia voennogo iskusstva, XVI-XVII vv.*, 258–260; Hughes, *Sophia*, 211–212; Fuller, *Strategy and Power*, 20; Kostomarov, *Ruina*, 425–426.
56 Paul Bushkovitch, *Peter the Great*, 155–169.
57 Bogoslovskii, *Petr I*, I: 208; Bagalei, *Istoriia slobodskoi ukraini*, 54; Porfir'ev, *Petr I*, 35–36.
58 Kostomarov, *Ruina*, 477–479, 485.
59 Bogoslovskii, *Petr I*, I: 211–233; Porfir'ev, *Petr I*, 38–39.
60 Bogoslovskii, *Petr I*, I: 233–267; Porfir'ev, *Petr I*, 39–41.
61 Bogoslovskii, *Petr I*, I: 271–332; Phillips, *The Founding of Russia's Navy*, 40; Porfir'ev, *Petr I*, 42–47.
62 Oreshkova, *Russko-turetskie otnosheniia v nachale XVIII v.*, 27–32; Bogoslovskii, *Petr I*, I: 336–337, 340, 356–365, 373–375; Kostomarov, *Ruina*, 490–505.

Chapter Six

1 Sikorski, *Polskie tradycje wojskowe*, I, 424–425; Stone, *The Polish-Lithuanian State, 1386–1795*, 241; Gierowski and Kaminski, "The Eclipse of Poland," 684.
2 Frost, *The Northern Wars*, 249, 250, 252, 256, 323.
3 Litavrin, ed., *Osmanskaia imperiia*, 304; Sikorski, *Polskie tradycje wojskowe*, I, 427.
4 Lukomski, *Liberty's Folly*, 7; Zgorniak, *Wojskowość polska w dobie wojen tureckich drugiej połowy XVII wieku*, 184.
5 Smirnov, *Krymskoe khanstvo*, 582, 590, 593–596, 608–609, 611, 613, 625, 634, 641, 665–666; Oreshkova and Ul'chenko, *Rossiia i Turtsiia*, 21–22.
6 Collins, "The Military Organization," 269–275.
7 *AIuZR* 5, no. 87, 201–202.
8 AN SSSR, Institut istorii, Kal'mytskii nauchno-issledovatel'skii institut iazyka, literatury, istorii *Ocherki istorii Kal'mytskoi ASSR. Dooktiabr'skii period* (Moscow, 1967), 151–155; Khodarkovsky, *Where Two Worlds Met*, 103–127; Kostomarov, *Ruina*, 10.
9 Fisher, "The Ottoman Crimea in the Mid-Seventeenth Century," pt. 1, 216–219, 223.
10 Smirnov, *Krymskoe khanstvo*, 573–575; Trepavlov, *Istoriia Nogaiskoi ordy*, 450–452; Abou-el-Haj, "The Formal Closure of the Ottoman Frontier in Europe," 471–474.
11 Khodyreva, "Rossiiskoe-turetskie peregovory 1681–1682 godov o ratifikatsii Bakhchisaraiskogo mirnogo dogovora," 160; Batiushkov, *Podoliia. Istoricheskoe opisanie*, 145–146.
12 Cited by Ostapchuk, "The Human Landscape," 32.
13 Agoston, *Guns for the Sultan*, 202.
14 Barkey, *Bandits and Bureaucrats*, 50–53; Faroqhi, "Crisis and Change, 1590–1699," 573.

15 Inalcik, "Military and Fiscal Transformation of the Ottoman Empire, 1600–1700," 288; Murphey, *Ottoman Warfare*, 51–52.
16 Murphey, *Ottoman Warfare*, 53.
17 After Mohacs (1526), the Ottomans had fought only two large field battles in Hungary (Mezokeresztes in 1596, and St. Gotthard in 1644).

> The situation crucially changed after 1683, when a new age of field battles started. Fifteen big battles took place between 1683 and 1697. The European field battle artillery taking part in these battles was extensively more mobile and thus regularly had an advantage over the Ottoman artillery.
> Agoston, *Guns for the Sultan*, 201.

18 Black, *European Warfare 1660–1815*, 12–13.
19 Parry, "La maniere de combattre," 232–237; Litavrin, ed., *Osmanskaia imperiia*, 240–242; Levy, "Military Reform and the Problem of Centralization in the Ottoman Empire in the Eighteenth Century," 230; Imber, *The Ottoman Empire, 1300–1650*, 284–286; Mears, "The Influence of the Turkish Wars in Hungary on the Military Theories of Count Raimondo Montecuccoli," 137–140.
20 Vodarskii, *Naselenie Rossii v kontse XVII-nachale XVIII veka*, 193.
21 Riabov, *Voisko donskoe*, 38–39, 45–46; Golobutskii, *Zaporozhskoe kazachestvo*, 322.
22 Boeck, "Shifting Boundaries on the Don Steppe Frontier," 319, 334, 374; Riabov, *Voisko donskoe*, 75.
23 Golobutskii, *Zaporozhskoe kazachestvo*, 305–306, 325.
24 Subtelny, *Ukraine: A History*, 159; Vodarskii, *Naselenie Rossii v kontse XVII-nachale XVIII veka*, 192.
25 Golobutskii, *Zaporozhskoe kazachestvo*, 324; Artamonov, "Pozitsii getmanskoi vlasti," 94.
26 For an opposing point of view – that Ordyn-Nashchokin laid the foundations for the emergence by 1700 of a Russian Grand Strategy – see LeDonne, *The Grand Strategy of the Russian Empire, 1650–1831*, 37.
27 Davies, "The Development of Russian Military Power, 1453–1815," 145–152; Stevens, *Russia's Wars of Emergence* (forthcoming).
28 Davies, *State Power and Community*, 22, 30–36, 70–74.
29 Vazhinskii, "Usilenie soldatskoi povinnosti v Rossii v XVII v (Po materialam iuzhnykh uezdov)," 53–54.
30 Vodarskii, *Naselenie Rossii v kontse XVII-nachale XVIII veka*, 153, 155, 167, 192.
31 Davies, "Service, Landholding, and Dependent Labour," 136–137, 151; Davies, *State Power and Community*, 245.
32 F. 210, Razriadnyi prikaz, Belgorodskii stol stolbets no. 921, ll. 492–495, 518–520.
33 Davies, "Service, Landholding, and Dependent Labour," 137–138.
34 Davies, *State Power and Community*, 247–248.

Bibliography

Abetsedarskii, L. S. "Bor'ba belorusskogo naroda za vossoedinenie s Rossieiu," in *Vossoedinenie Ukrainy s Rossiei. sbornik statei*, ed. A. I. Baranovich (Moscow: AN SSSR, 1954), 178–220.

Abou-el-Haj, Rifaat A. "The Formal Closure of the Ottoman Frontier in Europe: 1699–1703," *Journal of the American Oriental Society* 89 (1969): 467–475.

Abramovich, G. V. "Novgorodskoe pomest'e v gody ekonomicheskogo krizisa poslednei treti XVI v.," *Materialy po istoriisel'skogo khoziaistva i krest'ianstva SSSR. Sbornik* VIII (1974): 5–26.

Abramovich, Zigmunt "Staraia turetskaia karta Ukrainy s planom vzryva dneprovskikh porog i ataki turetskogo flota na Kiev," in *Vostochnye istochniki po istorii narodov iugovostochnoi i tsentral'noi Evropy, Tom II*, ed. A. S. Tveritinova (Moscow: Nauka, 1969), 76–97.

Agoston, Gabor "Ottoman Artillery and European Military Technology in the Fifteenth and Seventeenth Centuries," *Acta Orientalia Academiae Scientarum Hungarica* 48, 1–2 (1994): 15–48.

—— "Ottoman Warfare in Europe, 1453–1826," in *European Warfare, 1453–1815*, ed. Jeremy Black (Houndmills, Basingstoke: Macmillan, 1999), 118–144.

—— *Guns for the Sultan: Military Power and the Weapons Industry in the Ottoman Empire* (Cambridge: Cambridge University Press, 2005).

Akademiia Nauk SSSR *Vossoedinenie Ukrainy s Rossiei. Dokumenty i materialy v trekh tomakh. Tom tretii* (Moscow: AN SSSR, 1954).

Akademiia Nauk SSSR, Institut istorii, Kal'mytskii nauchno–issledovatel'skii institut iazyka, literatury, istorii *Ocherki istorii Kal'mytskoi ASSR. Dooktiabr'skii period* (Moscow: Nauka, 1967).

Aksan, Virginia "Locating the Ottomans among Early Modern Empires," *Journal of Early Modern History* 3, 2 (1999): 103–134.

—— "Ottoman War and Warfare, 1450–1812," in *War in the Early Modern World*, ed. Jeremy Black (London: University College London Press, 1999), 147–175.

Alef, Gustave "Muscovite Military Reforms in the Second Half of the Fifteenth Century," *Forschungen zur Osteuropäischen Geschichte* 18 (1973): 73–108.

Alekberli, M. A. *Bor'ba ukrainskogo naroda protiv turetsko-tatarskoi agressii vo vtoroi polovine XVI-pervoi polovine XVII vekov* (Saratov: Saratovskii Universitet, 1961).

Aleksandrov, A. V. "Streletskoe voisko na iuge Russkogo gosudarstva v XVII veka," Cand. diss., Moskovskii Gosudarstvennyi Universitet, 1947.

—— "Streletskoe naselenie iuzhnykh gorodov Rossii v XVII v.," in *Novoe o proshlom nashei strany: Pamiati akademika M. N. Tikhomirova*, Akademiia Nauk, Institut istorii, Arkheograficheskaia kommissiia (Moscow: Nauka, 1967), 235–250.
—— "Organizatsiia oborony iuzhnoi granitsy Russkogo gosudarstva vo vtoroi polovine XVI–XVII vv.," in *Rossiia, Pol'sha i Prichernomor'e v XV–XVIII vv.*, ed. B. A. Rybakov (Moscow: Nauka, 1979), 159–173.
Alekseev, Iu. G. *Osvobozhdenie Rusi ot ordynskogo iga* (Leningrad: Nauka, 1989).
Ananovich, E. M. "Pereselenie ukraintsev v Rossiiu nakanune osvoboditel'noi voiny 1648–1654 gg.," in *Vossoedinenie Ukrainy s Rossiei, 1654–1954. Sbornik statei*, ed. A. N. Baranovich (Moscow: AN SSSR, 1954), 78–104.
Andreev, A. R. *Neizvestnoe Borodino: Molodinskaia bitva 1572 g.* (Moscow: Izd. Mezhregional'nyi tsentr otraslevoi informatiki Gosatomnadzora Rossii, 1997).
Andreev, Igor *Aleksei Mikhailovich* (Moscow: Molodaia gvardiia, 2003).
Artamonov, V. A. "Pozitsii getmanskoi vlasti i Rossii na Ukraine," in *Rossiia-Ukraina: Istoriia vzaimootnoshenii*, ed. A. I. Miller, V. F. Reprintsev, and B. N. Floria (Moscow: Iazyki russkoi kul'tury, 1997), 89–100.
—— "Ochagi voennoi sily Ukrainskogo naroda v kontse XVI–nachale XVIII v.," in *Belorussiia i Ukraina. Istoriia i kul'tura. Ezhegodnik 2003* (Moscow: Nauka, 2003), 41–58.
Babushkina, G. K. "Mezhdunarodnoe znachenie krymskikh pokhodov 1687 i 1689 gg.," *Istoricheskie zapiski* 33 (1950): 158–177.
Bachinskii, A. D. and Dobroliubskii, A. O. "Budzhakskaia orda v XVI–XVII vv.," in *Sotsial'no-ekonomicheskaia i politicheskaia istoriia Moldavii perioda feodalizma*, ed. P. V. Sovetov (Kishinev: Shtinitsa, 1988), 82–94.
Bagalei [Bagalii], D. I. *Materialy dlia istorii kolonizatsii i byta stepnoi okrainy Moskovskago gosudarstva* (Khar'kov, 1886).
—— *Ocherki iz istorii kolonizatsii stepnoi okrainy Moskovskago gosudarstva* (Moscow, 1887).
—— *Istoriia slobodskoi ukrainy* (Kharkov, 1918).
Baiov, A. *Kurs istorii russkago voennago iskusstva. Vypusk pervyi* (St. Petersburg, 1909).
Baranovich, A. I. "Opustoshenie i vosstanovlenie pravoberezhnoi Ukrainy vo vtoroi polovine XVII i nachale XVIII v.," *Istoriia SSSR* 5 (1960): 145–158.
Baranowski, Bohdan "Organizacja i skład społeczny wojska polskiego w połowie XVII w.," in *Polska w okresie drugiej wojny północnej, 1655–1660. Tom drugi*, Polska Akademia Nauk, Instytut historii (Warsaw: Państwowe Wyd. Naukowe, 1957), 7–46.
Bardach, Juliusz, Bogusław Lesnodorski, and Michał Pietrzak, eds. *Historia ustroju i prawa polskiego* (Warsaw: Wyd. Naukowe PAN, 1994).
Barkey, Karen *Bandits and Bureaucrats: The Ottoman Route to State Centralization* (Ithaca, NY: Cornell University Press, 1994).
Bartusis, Mark *The Late Byzantine Army. Arms and Society, 1204–1453* (Philadelphia: University of Pennnsylvania Press, 1992).
Basarab, John *Pereiaslav 1654: A Historiographical Study* (Edmonton: Canadian Institute of Ukrainian Studies, 1982).
Batiushkov, P. N. *Podoliia. Istoricheskoe opisanie* (St. Petersburg, 1891).
Batmaev, M. M. "Vnutrennaia obstanovka v kal'mytskom khanstve v kontse XVII

v." in *Iz istorii dokapitalisticheskikh i kapitalisticheskikh otnoshenii v Kal'mykii*, Kal'mytskii Nauchno-issledovatel'skii institut iazyka, literatury i istorii (Elista: Kal'mytskii Nauchno-issledovatel'skii institut, 1977), 34–53.

Bazilevich, K. V. *Denezhnaia reforma Alekseiia Mikhailovicha i vosstanie v Moskve v 1662 g.* (Moscow: AN SSSR, 1936).

—— "Elementy merkantilizma v ekonomicheskom politike pravitel'stva Alekseiia Mikhailovicha," *Uchenye zapiski MGU. Istoriia*, 41 (1940): 3–34.

Bazylev, L. "Pol'sko-turetskie diplomaticheskie sviazi v XVI v.," in *Rossiia, Pol'sha i Prichernomor'e v XV–XVIII vv.*, ed. B. A. Rybakov (Moscow: Nauka, 1979), 12–28.

Bel'iaev, I. D. *O russkom voiske v tsarstvovanie Mikhaila Fedorovicha i posle ego, do preobrazovanii sdelannykh Petrom Velikom* (Moscow, 1846).

—— "O storozhevoi, stanichnoi, i polevoi sluzhbe na pol'skoi ukraine Moskovskogo gosudarstve do tsariia Alekseiia Mikhailovicha," 2 parts, *ChOIDR* 4 (1846): 1–60 + 1–86.

Belotserkovskii, G. M. *Tula i Tul'skii uezd v XVI i XVII vv.* (Kiev, 1914).

Berelowitch, Andre "La noblesse moscovite et la modernisation de l'armee (1613–1682)," in *Guerre et pouvoir en Europe au XVIIe siecle*, ed. V. Barrie-Curien (Paris: Henri Veyrier, 1991), 35–55.

Berezhkov, M. N. "Russkie plenniki i nevol'niki v Krymu," *Trudy VI-ogo arkheologicheskogo s'ezda v Odesse* 2 (1884): 342–272.

—— "Plan zavoevaniia Kryma, sostavlennyi Iuriem Krizhanichem," 2 parts, *Zhurnal Ministerstva narodnago prosveshcheniia* 278, 10 (1891): 483–517 and 11 (1891): 65–119.

Bibikov, G. I. "Opyt voennoi reform 1609–1610 gg.," *Istoricheskie zapiski* 19 (1946): 1–16.

Black, Jeremy *European Warfare 1660–1815* (New Haven, CT: Yale University Press, 1994).

Bobylev, V. S. *Vneshniaia politika Rossii epokhi Petra I* (Moscow: Universitet druzhby narodov, 1990).

Boeck, Brian "Shifting Boundaries on the Don Steppe Frontier: Cossacks, Empires and Nomads to 1779," Doctoral dissertation, Harvard University, 2002.

Bogdanov, A. P. "Neizvestnaia voina Fedora Alekseevicha," *Voenno-istoricheskii zhurnal* 6 (1997): 61–70.

—— "Pochemu tsar Fedor Alekseevich prikazal sdat' Chigirin," *Voenno-istoricheskii zhurnal* 1 (1998): 38–45.

—— *V teni velikogo Petra* (Moscow: Armada, 1998).

—— *Moskovskaia publitsistika poslednei chetvert XVII veka* (Moscow: Institut rossiiskoi istorii RAN, 2001).

Bogoiavlenskii, S. K. "Vooruzhenie russkikh voisk v XVI–XVII vv.," *Istoricheskie zapiski* 4 (1938): 258–283.

—— "Materialy po istorii kalmykov v pervoi polovine XVII v.," *Istoricheskie zapiski* 5 (1939): 48–101.

Bogoslovskii, M. M. *Petr I: Materialy dlia biografii. Tom pervyi* (Moscow: OGIZ, 1940).

Botsianovskii, V. "Finansovyi krizis v Moskovskom gosudarstve XVII v.," *Russkaia starina* 80 (1893): 225–242.

BIBLIOGRAPHY

Braudel, Fernand *The Mediterranean and the Mediterranean World in the Age of Philip II. Volume One* (New York: Harper and Row, 1976).
Brown, Peter B. "Early Modern Russian Bureaucracy: The Evolution of the Chancellery System from Ivan III to Peter the Great," Doctoral dissertation, University of Chicago, 1978.
—— "Muscovy, Poland and the Seventeenth-century Crisis," *The Polish Review* 28, 3–4 (1982): 55–69.
—— "Muscovite Government Bureaus," *Russian History/Histoire Russe* 3 (1983): 269–330.
—— "The Pre-1700 Origins of Peter the Great's Provincial Administrative (Guberniia) Reform: The Significance of the Frontier," unpublished paper, 1992.
—— "With All Deliberate Speed: The Officialdom and Departments of the Seventeenth-century Muscovite Military Chancellery (Razriad)," *Russian History/Histoire Russe* 28, 1–4 (2001): 137–152.
—— "Military Planning and High-level Decision-making in Seventeenth-century Russia: The Roles of the Military Chancellery (Razriad) and the Boyar Duma," *Forschungen zur Osteuropaischen Geschichte* 58 (2001–2002): 79–89.
—— "Tsar Aleksei Mikhailovich: Command Style and Legacy," in *The Military and Society in Russia, 1450–1917*, ed. Eric Lohr and Marshall Poe (Leiden: E. J. Brill, 2002), 119–146.
Bruckner (Brikner), Alexander *Patrik Gordon i ego dnevnik* (St. Petersburg, 1878).
Buganov, V. I. "Gramota livenskomu voevode Ivanu Osipovichu Polevu 1595 g.," *Zapiski otdela rukopisei gos. biblioteka SSSR imeni V.I. Lenina* 20 (1958): 177–185.
Bul'vins'kii, Andrii "Ukrainsko-rosiis'ka viina 1658–1659 rr.: osnovni bitvi, strategiia, chisel'nist' ta slkad viisk," in *Ukraina ta Rosiia: Problemi politichnikh i sotsiokul'turnikh vidnosin*, ed. V. A. Smolii, V. M. Gorobets, and O. I. Gurzhy (Kiev: Institut istorii Ukrainy NAN Ukrainy, 2003): 174–218.
Burdei, G. D. *Russko-turetskaia voina 1569 goda* (Saratov: Izd. Saratovskogo Universiteta, 1962).
Bushkovitch, Paul *The Merchants of Moscow, 1580–1650* (Cambridge: Cambridge University Press, 1980).
—— "Cultural Change among the Russian Boyars, 1650–1680: New Sources and Old Problems," *Forschungen zur Osteuropaischen Geschichte* 56 (2000): 91–111.
—— *Peter the Great: The Struggle for Power, 1671–1725* (Cambridge: Cambridge University Press, 2001).
Butterwick, Richard *The Polish-Lithuanian Monarchy in European Context, c. 1500–1700* (Houndmills, Basingstoke: Palgrave Macmillan, 2001).
Bystron, Jan Stanislaw *Dzieje obyczajow w dawnej Polsce wiek XVI–XVIII* 2 vols. (Warsaw: Panstwowy Instytut Wydawniczy, 1994).
Çelebi, Evliya *Kniga puteshestviia (Izvlechenii iz sochinenii turetskogo puteshestvennika XVII veka. Perevod i kommentarii) Vypusk 1. Zemli Moldavii i Ukrainy* (Moscow: Izd. Vostochnoi literatury, 1961).
—— *Kniga puteshestvii Evlii Chelebi. Pokhody s tatarami i puteshestviia po Krymu (1641–1667)*, ed. and trans. M. B. Kizilov (Simferopol': Tavriia, 1996).
Chandler, David *The Art of Warfare in the Age of Marlborough* (New York: Sarpedon, 1994).

Chase, Kenneth *Firearms: A Global History to 1700* (Cambridge: Cambridge University Press, 2003).
Cherepnin, L. V. *Obrazovanie Russkogo tsentralizovannogo gosudarstva v XIV–XV vekakh* (Moscow: Izd. Sotsial'no-ekonomicheskoi literatury, 1960).
—— *Zemskie sobory Russkogo gosudarstva v XVI–XVII vv.* (Moscow: Nauka, 1978).
—— "Sobor 1642 po voprosu ob Azove," in *Rossiia, Pol'sha i Prichernomor'e v XV–XVIII vv.*, ed. B. A. Rybakov (Moscow: Nauka, 1979), 211–222.
Chermenskii, P. N. *Ocherki po sitorii kolonizatsii tambovskago kraia* (Tambov, 1911).
Chernov, A. V. "Tsentral'nyi gosudarstvennyi arkhiv drevnikh aktov, kak istochnik po voennoi istorii Russkogo gosudarstva do XVII v.," *Trudy Moskovskogo gosudarstvennogo istoriko-arkhivnogo instituta* 4 (1948), 115–157.
—— "Obrazovanie streletskogo voiska," *Istoricheskie zapiski* 38 (1951): 281–290.
—— *Vooruzhennye sily Russkogo gosudarstva v XV–XVII vv.* (Moscow: Ministerstvo Oborony SSSR, 1954).
Chicherin, B. N. *Oblastnyia uchrezhdeniia Rossii v XVII st.* (Moscow, 1856).
Childs, John *The Military Use of Land: A History of the Defence Estate* (Bern: Peter Lang, 1998).
Chirot, Daniel, ed. *The Origins of Backwardness in Eastern Europe. Economics and Politics from the Middle Ages until the Twentieth Century* (Berkeley: University of California Press, 1989).
Chistiakova, E. D. "Ideia sovmestnoi oborony iuzhnykh granits Rossii i Pol'shi v russkoi publisistike vtoroi poloviny XVII v.," in *Rossiia, Pol'sha i Prichernomor'e v XV–XVIII vv.*, ed. B. A. Rybakov (Moscow: Nauka, 1979), 287–298.
Chistiakova, E. D. and Bogdanov, A. P. *"Da budet potomkam iavleno": Ocherki o russkikh istorikakh vtoroi polovine XVII veka i ikh trudakh* (Moscow: Universitet Druzhby Narodov, 1988).
Chowaniec, Czesław "Sobieski wobec tatarszczyzny 1683–1685," *Kwartalnik Historyczny* 42 (1928): 52–66.
Collins, L. J. D. "The Military Organization and Tactics of the Crimean Tatars, 16th–17th Centuries," in *War, Technology, and Society in the Middle East*, ed. V. J. Perry and M. E. Yapp (London: Oxford University Press, 1975), 257–276.
Cracraft, James *The Petrine Revolution in Russian Culture* (Cambridge, MA: Harvard University Press, 2004).
Crummey, Robert O. "Reflections on *Mestnichestvo* in the 17th Century," *Forschungen zur Osteuropaischen Geschichte* 27 (1980): 269–281.
Czapliński, Władysław "Sprawa najazdów tatarskich na Polske w pierwszej połowie XVII v.," *Kwartalnik Historyczny* 70, 3 (1963): 713–720.
Danilov, N. N. "V. V. Golicyn bis zum staatsreich vom Mai 1682," *Jahrbucher fur Geschichte Osteuropas* 1 (1936): 1–33.
Das, David "History Writing and the Quest for Fame in Late Muscovy: Andrei Lyzlov's History of the Scythians," *Russian Review*, 51, 4 (Oct. 1992): 502–509.
Davies, Brian L. "The Town Governors in the Reign of Ivan IV," *Russian History/Histoire Russe* 14, 1–4 (1987): 77–144.
—— "Village Into Garrison: The Militarized Peasant Communities of Southern Muscovy," *Russian Review* 4 (1992): 481–501.
—— "Service, Landholding, and Dependent Labour in Kozlov District, 1675," *New Perspectives on Muscovite History*, ed. Lindsey Hughes (New York: St. Martin's, 1993), 129–155.

―――"The Development of Russian Military Power, 1453–1815," *European Warfare, 1453–1815*, ed. Jeremy Black (Houndmills, Basingstoke: Macmillan, 1999), 145–179.

―――"The Foundations of Muscovite Military Power, 1453–1613," in *The Military History of Tsarist Russia*, ed. Frederick Kagan and Robin Higham (Houndmills, Basingstoke: Palgrave Macmillan, 2002), 11–30.

―――*State Power and Community in Early Modern Russia: The Case of Kozlov, 1635–1649* (Houndmills, Basingstoke: Palgrave Macmillan, 2004).

Davies, Norman *God's Playground. A History of Poland. Volume One: The Origins to 1795* (New York: Columbia University Press, 1984).

de Beauplan, Sieur (Guillaume Le Vasseur), *A Description of Ukraine*, trans. and ed. Andrew Pernal and Dennis Essar (Cambridge, MA: Harvard Ukrainian Research Institute, 1993).

de Liuk, Zhan "Opisanie perekopskikh i nogaiskikh tatar ... Zhana de Liuka, monakha dominikanskago ordena, 1625," *Zapiski Imperatorskago odesskago obshchestva istorii i drevnostei* 11 (1879): 473–493.

Demidova, N. F. *Sluzhilaia biurokratiia v Rossii XVII veka i ee rol' v formirovanii absoliutizma* (Moscow: Nauka, 1987).

Denisova, M. M. "Pomestnaia konnitsa i ee vooruzhenie v XVI–XVII vv.," *Trudy Gosudarstvennoi istoricheskoi muzei* 20 (1948): 29–46.

Downing, Brian *The Military Revolution and Political Change. Origins of Democracy and Autocracy in Early Modern Europe* (Princeton, NJ: Princeton University Press, 1992).

Druzhinin, V. "Pervaia chernomorskaia flotilliia Moskovskogo gosudarstva postroennaia pod rukovodtsvom donskikh kazakov," *Zhurnal Ministerstva narodnago prosveshcheniia* 2 (1917): 224–240.

Duffy, Christopher *Siege Warfare: The Fortress in the Early Modern World* (New York: Barnes and Noble, 1979).

Dulov, A. V. *Geograficheskaia sreda i istoriia Rossii konets XV–seredina XIX v.* (Moscow: Nauka, 1983).

Dunning, Chester S. "Cossacks and the Southern Frontier in the 17th Century," *Russian History/Histoire Russe* 19, 1–4 (1992): 57–74.

Epifanov, P. P. "'Uchenie i khitrost' ratnogo stroeniia pekhotnykh liudei' (Iz istorii russkoi armii XVII)," *Uchenye zapiski Moskovskogo gosudarstvennogo universiteta, kafedry istorii SSSR* 167 (1954): 77–98.

―――"Voisko i voennaia organizatsiia," in *Ocherki russkoi kul'tury XVI veka. Chast' pervaia*, ed. A. V. Artsikhovskii (Moscow: Moskovskii Gosudarstvennyi Universitet, 1976), 336–380.

―――"Voisko," in *Ocherki russkoi kul'tury XVII veka. Chast' pervaia*, ed. A. V. Artsikhovskii (Moscow: Moskovskii Gosudarstvennyi Universitet, 1979), 234–264.

―――"Oruzhie," in *Ocherki russkoi kul'tury XVII veka. Chast' pervaia*, ed. A. V. Artsikhovskii (Moscow: Moskovskii Gosudarstvennyi Universitet, 1979), 265–283.

Ermolaev, I. P. *Kazanskii krai vo vtoroi polovine XVI–XVII vv.* (Kazan': Kazanskii Universitet, 1980).

―――*Srednee Povol'zhe vo vtoroi polovine XVI–XVII vv.* (Kazan': Kazanskii Universitet, 1982).

Ernst, N. L. and Beliavskii, S. L., trans. and ed. *Tumann, Krymskoe khanstvo* (Simferopol': Tavriia, 1991).
Esper, Thomas "Military Self-Sufficiency and Weapons Technology in Muscovite Russia," *Slavic Review* 28, 2 (1969): 185–208.
Faroqhi, Suraiya "Crisis and Change, 1590–1699," in *An Economic and Social History of the Ottoman Empire, 1300–1914*, ed. Halil Inalcik and Donald Quataert (Cambridge: Cambridge University Press, 1994), 411–636.
Fennell, J. L. I. *Ivan the Great of Moscow* (London: MacMillan, 1963).
——, ed. *Kurbskii's History of Ivan IV* (Cambridge: Cambridge University Press, 1965).
Finkel, Caroline *The Administration of Warfare: The Ottoman Military Campaigns in Hungary, 1593–1606* (Vienna: JWGO, 1988).
—— "The Costs of Ottoman Warfare and Defence," *Byzantinische Forschungen* 16 (1991): 91–103.
Fisher, Alan "Muscovy and the Black Sea Slave Trade," *Canadian-American Slavic Studies* 6, 4 (1972): 575–594.
—— "Azov in the Sixteenth and Seventeenth Centuries," *Jahrbucher fur Geschichte Osteuropas* 21, 2 (1973): 161–173.
—— "Muscovite–Ottoman Relations in the Sixteenth and Seventeenth Centuries," *Humaniora Islamica* 1 (1973): 207–217.
—— "Crimean Separatism in the Ottoman Empire," in *Nationalism in a Non-National State: The Dissolution of the Ottoman Empire* (Columbus: Ohio State University Press, 1977), 57–76.
—— *The Crimean Tatars* (Stanford, CT: Hoover Institution Press, 1978).
—— "The Ottoman Crimea in the Mid-Seventeenth Century: Some Problems and Preliminary Considerations," *Harvard Ukrainian Studies* III/IV (1979–1980), part 1, 215–226.
Fletcher, Giles "Of the Russe Commonwealth," in *Rude and Barbarous Kingdom: Russia in the Accounts of Sixteenth-Century English Voyagers*, ed. Lloyd Berry and Robert Crummey (Madison: University of Wisconsin Press, 1968), 109–246.
Floria, B. N. "Proekt antituretskoi koalitsii serediny XVI v.," in *Rossiia, Pol'sha, i Prichernomor'e v XV–XVIII vv.*, ed. B. A. Rybakov (Moscow: Nauka, 1979), 71–86.
—— "Zaporozhskoe kazachestvo i Krym pered vosstaniem Khmel'nitskogo," in *Issledovaniia po istorii Ukrainy i Belorussii. Vypusk 1* (Moscow: Moskovskii Gosudarstvennyi Universitet, 1995), 51–61.
—— "Spornye voprosy russko-ukrainskikh otnoshenii v pervoi polovine i seredine XVII v.," in *Belorussiia i Ukraina. Istoriia i kul'tura. Ezhegodnik 2003*, ed. B. N. Floria (Moscow: Nauka, 2003), 29–40.
—— *Pol'sko-litovskaia interventsiia v Rossii i russkoe obshchestvo* (Moscow: Indrik, 2005).
Frost, Robert I. *After the Deluge. Poland-Lithuania and the Second Northern War* (Cambridge: Cambridge University Press, 1993).
—— "The Polish-Lithuanian Commonwealth and the 'Military Revolution,'" in *Poland and Europe: Historical Dimensions. Volume One*, ed. M. B. Biskupski and James Pula (New York: Columbia University Press, 1993), 19–47.
—— "Potop a teorii rewolucji militarnej," in *Rzeczpospolita w latach Potopu*, ed.

Jadwiga Muszyńska and Jacek Wijacki (Kielce: Wyzsa szkola pedagogiczna imieni Jana Kochanowskiego, 1996), 147–165.

—— *The Northern Wars, 1558–1721* (London: Longman, 2000).

—— "Scottish Soldiers, Poland-Lithuania, and the Thirty Years' War, 1618–1648," in *Scotland and the Thirty Years' War, 1618–1648*, ed. Steve Murdoch (Leiden: E. J. Brill, 2001), 191–212.

Fuller, William C., Jr. *Strategy and Power in Russia, 1600–1914* (New York: Free Press, 1992).

Gajecki, George *The Cossack Administration of the Hetmanate* 2 vols. (Cambridge, MA: Harvard Ukrainian Research Institute, 1978).

Galaktionov, I. V. "Andrusovskii dogovor 1667 goda i problema russko-pol'skogo soiuza," *Slavianskii sbornik* 2 (1978): 71–120.

—— "Rossiia i Pol'sha pered litsom turetsko-tatarskoi agressiii v 1667 g.," in *Rossiia, Pol'sha i Prichernomor'e*, ed. B. A. Rybakov (Moscow: Nauka, 1979), 382–389.

Gebei, Sandor "Rol' Rossii v antituretskoi voine Sviashchennoi Ligi (1687–1700)," in *Mesto Rossii v Evrope. The Place of Russia in Europe*, ed. Gyula Szvak (Budapest: Magyar Ruszisztikai Intezet, 1999), 198–210.

—— "Russko-turetskie peregovory v Karlovitsakh i Konstantinopole (1699–1700)," in *Mesto Rossii v Evrazii. The Place of Russia in Eurasia*, ed. Gyula Szvak (Budapest: Magyar Ruszisztikai Intezet, 2001), 214–220.

Geraklitov, A. A. *Istoriia saratovskogo kraia v XVI–XVIII vv.* (Saratov: Drukar', 1923).

Gierowski, Jozef and Kaminski, Andrzej "The Eclipse of Poland," in *The New Cambridge Modern History. Volume VI. The Rise of Great Britain and Russia, 1688–1715/25* (Cambridge: Cambridge University Press, 1970), 681–715.

Giertyzh, Jedrzej, ed. *Expedition to Moscow: A Memoir by Hetman Stanislas Zolkiewski* (London: Polonica Publications, 1959).

Glaz'ev, V. N. "Formirovanie Belgorodskogo razriada kak administrativno-territorial'noi edinitsy v seredine XVII v.," in *Naselenie i territoriia tsentral'nogo chernozem'ia i zapada Rossii v proshlom i nastoiashchem*, ed. A. N. Akinshin (Voronezh: Voronezhskii Gosudarstvennyi Universitet, 2000), 116–119.

Glete, Jan *War and the State in Early Modern Europe: Spain, the Dutch Republic, and Sweden as Fiscal-Military States, 1500–1660* (London: Routledge, 2002).

Gokbilgin, Tayyib "L'Expedition Ottomane contre Astrakhan en 1569," *Cahiers du monde russe et sovietique* 2, 1 (1970): 118–123.

Golobutskii, V. A. *Zaporozhskoe kazachestvo* (Kiev: Gosudarstvennoe Izd. politicheskoi literatury USSR, 1957).

Golombievskii, A. A. "Stoly razriadnogo prikaza v 1668–1670 gg.," *Zhurnal Ministerstva narodnago prosveshcheniia* 270 (1890): 1–16.

Gordon, Linda *Cossack Rebellions: Social Turmoil in the Sixteenth-century Ukraine* (Albany: State University of New York Press, 1983).

Gordon, Patrick *Patrik Gordon. Dnevnik 1659–1667*, trans. V. G. Fedosov (Moscow: Nauka, 2002).

—— *Patrik Gordon. Dnevnik, 1677–1678*, trans. D. G. Fedosov (Moscow: Nauka, 2005).

Gorobets, Viktor "Ukrainsko-rossiiskie otnosheniia i politiko-pravovoi status getmanshchiny (vtoraia polovina XVII–pervaia chetvert' XVIII veka)," in *Rossiia-Ukraina. Istoriia vzaimotnosheniia*, ed. A. I. Miller, V. F. Reprintsev, and B. N. Floria (Moscow: Iazyki russkoi kul'tury, 1997), 77–87.

Gorskaia, N. A. *Istoricheskaia demografiia Rossii epokhi feodalizma* (Moscow: Nauka, 1994).
Gradovskii, A. D. "Istoriia mestnago upravlenii v Rossii," *Sobranie sochinenii A. D. Gradovskago. Tom vtoroi* (St. Petersburg, 1899), 3–492.
Grala, N. et al., eds. *Pamiatniki istorii vostochnoi Evropy. Tom III, Dokumenty Livonskoi voiny* (Moscow: Arkheograficheskii tsentr, 1998).
Grant, Jonathan "Rethinking the Ottoman 'Decline': Military Technology Diffusion in the Ottoman Empire, Fifteenth to Eighteenth Centuries," *Journal of World History* 10, 1 (1999): 178–201.
Grekov, I. B. "Iz istorii sovmestnoi bor'by Ukrainy i Rossii za osvobozhdenie Ukrainy i Belorussii (1654–1655 gg.)," in *Vossoedinenie Ukrainy s Rossiei, 1654–1954. Sbornik statei*, ed. A. N. Baranovich (Moscow: AN SSSR, 1954), 307–356.
——— "K voprosu o kharakhtere politicheskogo sotrudnichestva Osmanskoi imperii i Krymskogo khanstva v vostochnoi Evrope v XVI–XVII vv.," in *Rossiia, Pol'sha i Prichernomor'e v XV–XVIII vv.*, ed. B. A. Rybakov (Moscow: Nauka, 1979), 299–314.
———, ed. *Osmanskaia imperiia i strany tsentral'noi, vostochnoi, i iugovostochnoi Evropy v XV–XVI vv.* (Moscow: Nauka, 1984).
Grzybowski, Stanislaw "The Gentry and the Beginnings of Colonization," in *Poland at the Fourteenth International Congress of Historical Sciences in San Francisco*, Polish Academy of Sciences, Institute of History (Wrocław: Wyd. Polskiej Akademii Nauk, 1975), 23–43.
Gulianitskii, N. F. *Gradostroitel'stvo Moskovskogo gosudarstva XVI–XVII vekov* (Moscow: Stroizdat, 1994).
Hajda, Lubomyr "Two Ottoman Gazanames Concerning the Chyhryn Campaign of 1678," Doctoral dissertation, Harvard University, 1984.
Hall, Bert S. *Weapons and Warfare in Renaissance Europe: Gunpowder, Technology, and Tactics* (Baltimore, MD: Johns Hopkins University press, 1997).
Hellie, Richard *Enserfment and Military Change in Muscovy* (Chicago, IL: University of Chicago Press, 1971).
——— "The Costs of Muscovite Military Defense and Expansion," in *The Military and Society in Russia, 1450–1917*, ed. Eric Lohr and Marshall Poe (Leiden: E. J. Brill, 2002), 41–66.
Hniłko, Antoni *Wyprawa Cudnowska w 1660 roku* (Warsaw: Wojskowy Instytut Naukowo-Wydawniczy, 1931).
Horak, Stephen M. "Russian Expansion and Policy in Ukraine, 1648–1791," in *Russian Colonial Expansion to 1917*, ed. Michael Rywkin (London: Mansell, 1988), 103–122.
Horn, Maurycy "Chronologia i zasięg najazdów tatarskich na ziemie Rzeczpospolitej Polskiej w latach 1600–1647," *Studia i Materiały do Historii Wojskowości* 8, 1 (1962): 3–71.
Hrushevsky, Michael (Mykhailo), *A History of Ukraine*, ed. O. J. Frederikson (New Haven, CT: Yale University Press, 1941).
——— *History of Ukraine-Rus'. Volume Seven: The Cossack Age to 1625*, trans. Bohdan Struminski (Edmonton: Canadian Institute of Ukrainian Studies Press, 1999).
——— *History of Ukraine-Rus'. Volume Eight: The Cossack Age, 1626–1650*, trans. Marta Olynyk (Edmonton: Canadian Institute of Ukrainian Studies, 2002).

Hughes, B. P. *Firepower. Weapons Effectiveness on the Battlefield, 1630–1850* (New York: Sarpedon, 1974).
Hughes, Lindsey *Sophia, Regent of Russia, 1657–1704* (New Haven, CT: Yale University Press, 1990).
Huttenbach, Henry "Muscovy's Conquest of Muslim Kazan and Astrakhan, 1552–1556," in *Russian Colonial Expansion to 1917*, ed. Michael Rywkin (London: Mansell, 1988), 45–69.
Iakovlev, A. I. *Zasechnaia cherta Moskovskogo gosudarstva v XVII veke. Ocherki iz istorii oborony ouzhnoi okrainy Moskovskogo gosudarstva* (Moscow, 1916).
—— *Prikaz sbora ratnykh liudei 1637–1653 gg.* (Moscow, 1917).
Iakovleva, T. G. "Gadiachskii dogovor – legenda i real'nost'," in *Issledovanie po istorii Ukrainy i Belorussii, Vyp. 1*, ed. M. V. Dmitriev (Moscow: MGU 1995), 62–78.
—— "Problemy vzaimootnoshenii Ukrainy i Rossii 1654–1667 gg.," in *Belorussiia i Ukrainy. Istoriia i kul'tura. Ezhegodnik 2003*, ed. B. N. Floria (Moscow: Nauka, 2003), 41–58.
Ianchevskii, N. *Kolonial'naia politika na Donu torgovogo kapitala Moskovskogo gosudarstva v XVI–XVII vv.* (Rostov: Severnyi Kavkaz, 1930).
Iashchurzhinskii, Khr. "Iuzhno-russkie plenniki v Krymu," *Izvestiia Tavricheskoi uchenoi arkhivnoi komissii* 47 (1912): 158–166.
Iavornitskii, D. I. *Istoriia zaporoz'kikh kozakiv* 3 vols. (Kiev; Naukova dumka, 1990).
Ibragimbeili, Kh. M. and Rashba, N. S., eds. *Osmanskaia imperiia v pervoi chetverti XVII veka. Sbornik dokumentov i materialov* (Moscow: Nauka, 1984).
Ignat'ev, A. V., V. B. Mikhailov, A. A. Preobrazhenskii, and G. A. Sanin, eds. *Istoriia vneshnei politiki Rossii. Konets XV–XVII vek* (Moscow: Mezhdunarodnye otnosheniia, 1999).
Imber, Colin *The Ottoman Empire, 1300–1650: The Structure of Power* (Houndmills, Basingstoke: Palgrave MacMillan, 2002).
Inalcik, Halil "The Origin of the Ottoman–Russian Rivalry and the Don-Volga Canal (1569)," *Annals of the University of Ankara* 1 (1946–1947): 47–106.
—— "The Sociopolitical Effects of the Diffusion of Firearms in the Middle East," in *War, Technology and Society in the Middle East*, ed. V. J. Parry and M. E. Yapp (London: Oxford University Press, 1975), 195–217.
—— "Centralization and Decentralization in Ottoman Administration," in *Studies in Eighteenth-century Islamic History*, ed. T. Neff and R. Owen (Carbondale: University of Northern Illinois Press, 1977), 27–52.
—— "Servile Labor in the Ottoman Empire," in *Mutual Effects of the Islamic and Judeo-Christian Worlds: The East European World*, ed. A. Ascher, T. Halasi-Kun, and B. Kiralyi (Brooklyn, NY: Brooklyn College Press, 1979), 25–52.
—— "The Khan and the Tribal Aristocracy: The Crimean Khanate Under Sahib Giray I," *Harvard Ukrainian Studies* 3, 4 (1979–1980): 445–466.
—— "Military and Fiscal Transformation of the Ottoman Empire, 1600–1700," *Archivum Ottomanicum* 6 (1980): 283–337.
—— "The Ottoman State; Economy and Society, 1300–1600," in *An Economic and Social History of the Ottoman Empire*, ed. Halil Inalcik and Donald Quataert (Cambridge: Cambridge University Press, 1994), 9–409.
—— *The Ottoman Empire: The Classical Age, 1300–1600* (London: Phoenix Press, 2000).

Issawi, Charles "The Ottoman-Habsburg Balance of Forces," in *Suleiman the Second and His Time*, ed. Halil Inalcik and Cemal Kefadar (Istanbul: Isis Press, 1993), 145–151.
Ivanios, Maria "Uchastie kazach'ikh otriadov v avstro-turetskoi voine 1593–1606 gg.," in *Mesto Rossii v Evrope. The Place of Russia in Europe*, ed. Gyula Szvak (Budapest: Magyar Ruszisztika Intezet, 1999), 161–165.
Ivanov, P. *Opisanie gosudarstvennago razriadnago arkhiva* (Moscow, 1842).
Jackson, Peter *The Mongols and the West, 1221–1410* (London: Longman, 2005).
Kaldy-Nagy, Gyula "The First Centuries of the Ottoman Military Organization," *Acta Orientalia Scientarum Hungaricae* 31, 2 (1977): 147–183.
Kalinychev, F. I. *Pravovye voprosy voennoi organizatsii Russkogo gosduarstva vtoroi poloviny XVII veka* (Moscow: Gosiurizdat, 1954).
Kaminski, Andrzej Sulima *Republic vs. Autocracy: Poland-Lithuania and Russia, 1686–1697* (Cambridge, MA: Harvard Ukrainian Research Institute, 1993).
Kappeler, Andreas *Russlands Erste Nationalitaten. Das Zarenreich und die Volker der Mittleren Wolga vom 16. bis 19. Jahrhundert* (Cologne: Bohlau Verlag, 1982).
Kargalov, V. V. *Na stepnoi granitse. Oborona "krymskoi ukrainy" Russkogo gosudarstva v pervoi polovine XVI stoletiia* (Moscow: Nauka, 1974).
—— *Konets ordynskogo iga* (Moscow: Nauka, 1980).
—— *Polkovodtsy X–XVI vv.* (Moscow: Nauchno-khudozhestvennaia literatura, 1989).
—— *Moskovskie voevody XVI–XVII vv.* (Moscow: Russkoe slovo, 2002).
Karpov, G. "Malorossiiskie goroda v epokhu soednieniia Malorosii s Velikoiu Rossiei," *Letopis' zaniatii Arkheograficheskoi kommissii, 1872–1875* 6 (1877), part 1, 1–43.
Kazakov, A. V. *Terminy i poniatii voennoi istorii Rusi, Rossii* (St. Petersburg: Nestor, 1998).
Keep, J. L. H. *Soldiers of the Tsar: Army and Society in Russia, 1462–1874* (Oxford: Clarendon, 1985).
Kelenik, Jozsef "The Military Revolution in Hungary," in *Ottomans, Hungarians, and Habsburgs in Central Europe. The Military Confines in the Era of Ottoman Conquest*, ed. Geza David and Pal Fodor (Leiden: E. J. Brill, 2000), 117–159.
Kessel'brenner, G. L. *Krym: Stranitsy istorii* (Moscow: SVR-Argus, 1994).
Khazin, O. A. *Trudnyi put' k Poltave* (Moscow: Institut naslediia, 2001).
Khenzel', V. "Problem iasyria v pol'sko-turetskikh otnosheniiakh XVI–XVII vv.," in *Rossiia, Pol'sha i Prichernomor'e v XV–XVIII vv.*, ed. B. A. Rybakov (Moscow: Nauka, 1979), 147–158.
Khodarkovsky, Michael *Where Two Worlds Met: The Russian State and the Kalmyk Nomads, 1600–1771* (Ithaca, NY: Cornell University Press, 1992).
—— "Taming the Wild Steppe: Muscovy's Southern Frontier, 1480–1600," *Russian History/Histoire Russe* 26, 3 (1999): 241–297.
—— *Russia's Steppe Frontier: The Making of a Colonial Empire, 1500–1800* (Bloomington: Indiana University Press, 2002).
Khodyreva, G. V. "Rossiiskoe-turetskie peregovory 1681–1682 godov o ratifikatsii Bakhchisaraiskogo mirnogo dogovora," *Otechestvennaia istoriia* 2 (2003): 151–162.
Khoroshkevich, A. L. *Rus' i Krym. Ot soiuza k protivostoianiiu* (Moscow: Editorial URSS, 2001).

Kichikov, M. *Istoricheskie korni druzhby russkogo i kal'mytskogo narodov, Obrazovanie kal'mytskogo gosudarstva v sostave Rossii* (Elista: Kal'mytskoe knizhnoe izdatel'stvo, 1966).

King, Charles *The Black Sea: A History* (Oxford: Oxford University Press, 2004).

Kirpichnikov, A. V. "Oborona Pskova v 1615 g. (po novym russkim i shvedskim materialam)," in *Srednevekovaia i novaia Rossiia. Sbornk nauchnykh statei*, ed. Iu. G. Alekseev (St. Petersburg: Sankt-Peterburgskii Universitet, 1996), 424–450.

Kleimola, Ann "Holding on in the Stamped-Over District – The Survival of a Political Elite: Riazan' Landholders in the Sixteenth Century," *Russian History/ Histoire Russe* 19, 1–4 (1992): 129–142.

Kobrin, V. B. "Stanovlenie pomestnoi sistemy," *Istoricheskie zapiski* 105 (1980): 150–195.

Kochekaev, B-A. B. *Nogaisko-russkie otnosheniia v XV–XVIII vv.* (Alma-Ata: Nauka, 1988).

Kohut, Zenon E. "Origins of the Unity Paradigm: Ukraine and the Construction of Russian National History (1620–1860)," *Eighteenth-century Studies* 35, 1 (2001): 70–76.

—— "Imagining Popular Rights and Liberties: Representation of the Pereiaslav Agreement in the Cossack Chronicles," unpublished paper, Natl. Convention of the AAASS, Boston MA, 5 December 2004.

Kolankowski, Ludwik "Problem Krymu w dziejach Jagiełłonskich," *Kwartalnik Historyczny* 49 (1935): 279–300.

Kolodziejczyk, Dariusz "Ottoman Podillja: The Eyalet of Kam'janec, 1672–1699," *Harvard Ukrainian Studies* 16, 1–2 (1992): 87–101.

—— *Podole pod panowaniem tureckim. Ejalet Kamieniecki, 1672–1699* (Warsaw: Polczek, 1994).

—— "Stosunki Polsko-Tureckie w polowie XVII wieku," in *Rzeczpospolita w latach Potopu*, ed. Jadwiga Muszynska and Jecek Wijacki (Kielce: Wyzsa szkola pedagogiczna imieni Jana Kochanowskiego, 1996), 41–48.

Kolosov, E. E. "Razvitie artilleriiskogo vooruzheniia v Rossii vo vtoroi polovine XVII v.," *Istoricheskie zapiski* 71 (1962): 259–269.

Konopczynski, Wladyslaw *Polska a Turcja, 1683–1792* (Warsaw: Nakladem Instytuta Wschodniego, 1936).

Koroliuk, V. D. *Livonskaia voina. Iz istorii vneshnei politiki Russkogo tsentralizovannogo gosudarstva vo vtoroi polovine XVI v.* (Moscow: AN SSSR, 1954).

Kortepeter, Carl Max "Ottoman Imperial Policy and the Economy of the Black Sea Region in the Sixteenth Century," *Journal of the American Oriental Society* 86 (1966): 86–113.

—— *Ottoman Imperialism During the Reformation: Europe and the Caucasus* (New York: New York University Press, 1972).

Korzon, Tadeusz *Dzieje wojen i wojskowości w Polsce. Tom II. Epoka Przedrozbiorowa* (Lwow: Wyd. Zakladu Narodowej imienia Ossolonskich, 1923).

Kostomarov, N. I. "Malorossiiskii getman Zinovii-Bogdan Khmel'nitskii," *Russkaia istoriia v zhizneopisaniiaiakh ee glavneshikh deiatelei. Vtoroi otdel, vyp. 5. XVII stoletie* (St. Petersburg, 1874), 221–286.

—— *Smutnoe vremia Moskovskogo gosudarstva v nachale XVII stoletiia. 1604–1613* (Moscow: Charli, 1994).

——"Getmanstvo Iuriia Khmel'nitskogo," *Kazaki. Istoricheskie monografii i issledovaniia* (Moscow: Charli, 1995), 168–286.
——"Getmanstvo Vygovskogo," *Kazaki. Istoricheskie monografii i issledovaniia* (Moscow: Charli, 1995), 46–167,
——*Ruina. Mazepa. Mazepintsy* (Moscow: Charli, 1995).
Kotarski, Henryk "Wojskowość Polsko-Litewska doby Batorianskiej (1576–1586)," in *Historia wojskowości Polskiej*, ed. Witold Bieganski (Warsaw: Ministerstwa Obrony Narodowej, 1972): 136–160.
Kotilaine, J. L. "In Defense of the Realm: Russian Arms Trade and Production in the Seventeenth and Eighteenth Centuries," in *The Military and Society in Russia, 1450–1917*, ed. Eric Lohr and Marshall Poe (Leiden: E. J. Brill, 2002): 67–95.
Kozliakov, V. N. *Sluzhilyi "gorod" Moskovskogo gosudarstva XVII veka (ot smuty do sobornogo ulozheniia)* (Iaroslavl': Izd. Iaroslavskogo gosudarstvennogo pedagogicheskogo universiteta, 2000).
——*Mikhail Fedorovich* (Moscow: Molodaia gvardiia, 2004).
Kriedte, Peter *Peasants, Landlords, and Merchant Capitalists: Europe and the World Economy, 1500–1800* (Cambridge: Cambridge University Press, 1983).
Kubala, Ludwik *Wojna Moskiewska r. 1654–1655* (Warsaw, 1910).
Kurat, A. N. "The Turkish Expedition to Astrakhan' in 1569 and the Problem of the Don-Volga Canal," *Slavonic and East European Review* 40 (1961): 7–23.
Kuznetsov, A. B. "Rossiia i politika Kryma v vostochnoi Evrope v pervoi treti XVI v.," in *Rossiia, Pol'sha i Prichernomor'e v XV–XVIII vv.*, ed. B. A. Rybakov (Moscow: Nauka, 1979), 62–70.
——*Diplomaticheskaia bor'ba Rossii za bezopasnost' iuzhnykh granits (pervaia polovina XVI v.)* (Minsk: Izd. Universitetskoe, 1986).
Lapteva, T. A. "Dokumenty Inozemnagoo prikaza kak istochnik po istorii Rossii XVII veka," *Arkhiv russkoi istorii* 5 (1994): 109–127.
Lashkov, F. *Pamiatniki diplomaticheskikh snoshenii Krymskago khanstva s Moskovskim gosudarstvom v XVI i XVV vv.* (Simferopol', 1891).
Lavrov, A. S. "Novyi istochnik o pervom krymskom pokhode," *Vestnik Sankt-Peterburgskogo universiteta. Serria vtoraia* 4 (1994): 14–19.
——*Regenstvo tsarevny Sof'i Alekseevny* (Moscow: Arkheograficheskii tsentr, 1999).
Lazar'ev, M. S. and Khalfin, N. A., eds. *Russkii posol v Stambule (Petr Andreevich Tol'stoi i ego opisanie Osmanskoi imperii nachala XVIII v.)* (Moscow: Nauka, 1985).
Leach, Catherine S., ed. *Memoirs of the Polish Baroque: The Writings of Jan Chryzostom Pasek, A Squire of the Commonwealth of Poland and Lithuania* (Berkeley: University of California Press, 1976).
LeDonne, John P. *The Grand Strategy of the Russian Empire, 1650–1831* (Oxford: Oxford University Press, 2004).
Leonov, O. and Ul'ianov, I. *Reguliarnaia pekhota 1698–1801* (Moscow: AST, 1995).
Letopis' samovidtsa: The Eyewitness Chronicle, Harvard Series in Ukrainian Studies 7, 1 (Munich: Wilhelm Fink Verlag, 1972).
Levy, Avigdor "Military Reform and the Problem of Centralization in the Ottoman Empire in the Eighteenth Century," *Middle Eastern Studies* 18, 3 (1982): 227–249.
Lipiński, Wacław "Działania wojenne Polsko-Rosyjskie pod Smoleńskiem od października 1632 do września 1633 r.," *Przegląd Historyczno-Wojskowy* 5, 2 (1932): 165–206.

—— "Bój o Zaworonkowe wzgórza i osaczenie Szeina pod Smoleńskiem (16–30 październik 1633 r.)," *Przegląd Historyczno-Wojskowy* 7, 1 (1934): 39–74.

Liseitsev, D. V. "Russko-turetskie otnosheniia v nachale XVII veka: ot konfrontatsii k sblizheniiu," *Otechestvennaia istoriia* 5 (2002): 169–177.

Litavrin, G. G., ed. *Osmanskaia imperiia i strany tsentral'noi, vostochnoi, i iugo-vostochnoi Evropy v XVII v.* (Moscow: Pamiatniki istoricheskoi mysli, 2001).

Litvin, Mikhalon *O nravakh tatar, litovstev i moskvitian* (Moscow: Moskovskii Universitet, 1994).

Liubavskii, M. K. *Obzor istorii russkoi kolonizatsii* (Moscow: Moskovskii Universitet, 1996).

—— *Istoricheskaia geografiia Rossii v sviazi s kolonizatsiei* (St. Petersburg: Lan', 2000).

Longworth, Philip "Transformations in Cossackdom: Technological and Organizational Aspects of Military Change, 1650–1850," in *East Central European Society and War in the Pre-Revolutionary Eighteenth Century*, ed. Gunther Rothernburg, Bela Kiraly, and Peter Sugar (New York: Columbia University Press, 1982), 451–469.

—— *Alexis, Tsar of All the Russias* (New York: Franklin Watts, 1984).

—— "Muscovy and the Antemuriale Christianitatis," in *Mesto Rossii v Evrope. The Place of Russia in Europe*, ed. Gyula Szvak (Budapest: Magyar Ruszisztikai Intezet, 1999), 82–87.

Lukomski, Jerzy *Liberty's Folly: The Polish-Lithuanian Commonwealth in the Eighteenth Century, 1697–1795* (London: Routledge, 1991).

Lund, Erik A. *War for the Every Day: Generals, Knowledge and Warfare in Early Modern Europe* (Westport, CT: Greenwood Press, 1999).

Lunin, B. V. *Azovskaia epopeia, 1637–1641 gg.* (Rostov-na-Donu: Rostovskoe knizhnoe izd., 1988).

Lynn, John A. *Giant of the Grand Siecle: The French Army, 1610–1715* (Cambridge: Cambridge University Press, 1997).

McNeill, William H. *Europe's Steppe Frontier, 1500–1800* (Chicago, IL: University of Chicago Press, 1964).

Magocsi, Robert Paul *A History of Ukraine* (Seattle: University of Washington Press, 1997).

Majer, Hans George "The Ottoman State on the Eve of Lepanto, 1571," *Byzantinische Forschungen* 16 (1991): 53–73.

Majewski, Wieslaw "The Polish Art of War in the Sixteenth and Seventeenth Centuries," in *A Republic of Nobles. Studies in Polish History to 1864*, ed. J. K. Fedorowicz (Cambridge: Cambridge University Press, 1982), 179–197.

—— "Wojny polsko-tureckie 1672–1699," in *Polskie tradycje wojskowe. Tom I: Tradycje walk obronnych z njazdami niemców, krzyżaków, szwedów, turków i tatarów*, ed. Janusz Sikorski (Warsaw: Wyd. Ministerstwa Obrony Narodowej, 1990), 362–428.

—— "Wojny polsko-tureckie w pierwszej połowie XVII w.," in *Polskie tradycje wojskowe. Tom I: Tradycje walk obronnych z najazdami niemców, krzyżaków, szwedów, turków i tatarów*, ed. Janusz Sikorski (Warsaw: Wyd. Ministerstwa Obrony Narodowej, 1990), 264–295.

Malov, A. V. "Konnitsa novogo stroia v Russkoi armii," *Otechestvennaia istoriia* 1 (2006): 118–131.

Mal'tsev, A. N. "Voina za Belorussiiu i osvobozhdenie Smolenska v 1654 g.," *Istoricheskie zapiski* 37 (1951): 125–143.
—— "Boevoe sodruzhestvo russkogo, ukrainskogo i belorusskogo narodov v bor'be za osvobozhdenie Ukrainy i Belorussii (1654–1655)," in *Vossoedinenie Ukrainy s Rossiei, 1654–1954. Sbornik statei*, ed. A. N. Baranovich (Moscow: AN SSSR, 1954), 264–306.
—— *Rossiia i Belorussiia v seredine XVII veka* (Moscow: Moskovskii Gosudarstvennyi Universitet, 1974).
Man'kov, A. G., ed. *Rossiiskoe zakonodatel'stvo X–XX vekov. V desiati tomakh. Tom IV: Zakonodatel'stvo perioda stanovleniia absoliutizma* (Moscow: Iuridicheskaia literatura, 1986).
Margeret, Jacques *The Russian Empire and the Grand Duchy of Muscovy: A Seventeenth-century French Account*, trans. and ed. Chester Dunning (Pittsburgh, PA: University of Pittsburgh Press, 1983).
Margolin, S. L. "Oborona Russkogo gosudarstva ot tatarskikh nabegov v kontse XVI veka: Storozhevaia i stanichnaia sluzhba i zasechnaia cherta," *Trudy gosudarstvennogo istoricheskogo muzeiia. Voenno-istoricheskii sbornik* 20 (1948), 3–28.
—— "Vooruzhenie streletskogo voiska," *Trudy Gosudarstvennoi istoricheskoi muzei* 20 (1948): 85–102.
Markevich, A. I. *Istoriia mestnichestva v Moskovskom gosudarstve v XV–XVII v.* (Odessa, 1888).
Markhotskii, N. *Istoriia moskovskoi voiny* (Moscow: ROSSPEN, 2000).
Martin, Janet "Muscovite Frontier Policy: The Case of the Khanate of Kasimov," *Russian History/Histoire Russe* 19, 1–4 (1992): 169–179.
—— "Tatars in the Muscovite Army During the Livonian War," in *The Military and Society in Russia, 1450–1917*, ed. Eric Lohr and Marshall Poe (Leiden: E. J. Brill, 2002), 365–387.
Maskiewicz, S. *Pamiętniki Samuela i Bogusława Kazimierza Maskiewiczów (wiek XVII)*, ed. A Sajkowski and Wł. Czapliński (Wrocław: Zakład Narodowy imieni Ossolińskich, 1961).
Maslovskii, D. F. "Pomestnyia voiska russkoi armii v XVII stoletii," *Voennyi sbornik* 195, 8 (1890): 5–36.
Massa, Isaac *Massa's Short History of the Muscovite Wars*, trans. and ed. G. Edward Orchard (Toronto: University of Toronto Press, 1982).
Mears, John A. "The Influence of the Turkish Wars in Hungary on the Military Theories of Count Raimondo Montecuccoli," in *Asia and the West: Encounters and Exchanges from the Age of Explorations*, ed. Cyriac Pullapilly (Notre Dame, IN: Cross Roads Books, 1986), 129–145.
Meier, M. S. "Novye iavleniia v sotsial'no-politicheskoi zhizni Osmanskoi imperii vo vtoroi polovine XVII–XVIII vv.," in *Osmanskaia imperiia: gosudarstvennost', vlast', i sotsial'no-politicheskaia struktura*, ed. S. F. Oreshkova (Moscow: Nauka, 1990), 155–185.
—— "Osnovnye etapi rannei istorii russko-turetskikh otnoshenii," in *Osmanskaia imperiia: Problemy vneshnei politiki a otnoshenii s Rossiei*, cd. S. F. Oreshkova (Moscow: RAN, Institut vostokovedeniia, 1996), 47–116.
Mert, Ozcam "The Age of Ayans in the History of the Ottoman State," in *The Great Ottoman-Turkish Civilization. Volume Three*, ed. Halil Inalcik, Kemal Cicek, Nejat Goyunc, and Ilber Ortayli (Ankara: Yeni Turkiye, 2000), 563–570.

Miakotin, V. A. *Ocherki sotsial'noi istorii Ukrainy v XVII–XVIII vv. Tom pervyi, vypuski 1–3* (Prague: Vataga i plamia, 1924–1926).
Mihneva, Roumiana "The Muscovite Tsardom, the Ottoman Empire, and European Diplomacy (mid-sixteenth–end of seventeenth century)," 2 parts, *Etudes Balkaniques* 3–4 (1998): 98–129 and 3 (2000): 41–54.
Mikhailova, A. I. "Sluzhba donskikh kazakov po okhrane iuzhnykh granits Russkogo gosudarstva v XVII veke," *Vestnik Moskovskogo universiteta* 2 (1956): 141–156.
Mikhnevich, N. P., ed. *Stoletie voennago ministerstva, tom IV. Glavnyi shtab. Chast' pervaia, kniga pervaia, otd. 1. Vooruzhennyia sily Rossii do tsarstvovaniia Imperatora Aleksandra I. Istoricheskii ocherk* (St. Petersburg, 1902).
Miklashevskii, I. N. *K istorii khoziaistvennago byta Moskovskago gosudarstva. Chast' pervaia. Zaselenie i sel'skoe khoziaistvo iuzhnoi okrainy XVII veka* (Moscow, 1874).
Miliukov, P. M. *Gosudarstvennoe khoziaistvo Rossii v pervoi chetverti XVIII stoletiia i reforma Petra Velikogo* (St. Petersburg, 2nd ed., 1905).
Miller, G. G. *Istoriia Sibiri. Tom pervyi* (Moscow: AN SSSR, 1937–1941).
Molchanov, N. N. *Diplomatiia Petra Pervogo* (Moscow: Mezhdunarodnye otnosheniia, 1984).
Moon, David "Peasant Migration and the Settlement of Russia's Frontiers, 1550–1897," *The Historical Journal* 40, 4 (1997): 859–893.
Murphey, Rhoads *Ottoman Warfare, 1500–1700* (London: University College London Press, 1999).
Myshlaevskii, A. Z. *Ofitserskii vopros v XVII veke (ocherk iz istorii voennogo dela v Rossii)* (St. Petersburg, 1899).
Myzik, Iu. A. "Moskovskie voiska i kazaki zadneprovskie stiagivaiutsia pod Romny," *Istoricheskii arkhiv* 4 (2002): 204–219.
Myzis, Iu. A. "Donskaia torgovlia v XVII–Nachale XVIII vv.," in *Problemy izucheniia istorii tsentral'nogo chernozem'ia*, ed. A. N. Akinshin and V. P. Zagorovskii (Voronezh: Tsentr dukhovnogo vozrozhdeniia chernozemnogo kraia, 2000), 131–145.
Nagielski, Mirosław "Wysiłek mobilizacyny Rzeczpospolitej w latach 1656–1659," in *Rzeczpospolita w latach potopu*, ed. Jadwiga Muszynska and Jacek Wijacki (Kielce: Wyzsa Szhola Pedagogizcna im. Jana Kochanowskiego, 1996), 167–178.
"Nakaz voevode kniaziu Ivanu Kugushevu o prieme goroda Insary," *Vremennik* 14 (1852): 1–9.
Nasonov, A. N. and Cherepnin, L. V., eds. *Ocherki istorii SSSR. Period foedalizma, konets XV–nachala XVII vv.* (Moscow: AN SSSR, 1955).
Nefedov, S. A. "Reformy Ivana III i Ivana IV: Osmanskoe vliianie," *Voposy istorii* 11 (2002): 30–53.
Nekrasov, A. M. "Voznikovenie i evoliutsiia krymskogo gosudarstva v XV–XVI vekakh," *Otechestvennaia istoriia* 2 (1999): 48–58.
Nikitin, A. V. "Oboronitel'nye sooruzheniia zasechnoi cherty XVI–XVII vv.," *Materialy i issledovaniia po arkheologii SSSR* 44 (1955): 116–213.
Nikitin, N. I. "K voprosu o sotsial'noi prirode kazach'ikh obshchestv v XVI–pervoi polovine XVII v.," in *Feodalizm v Rossii. Iubileinye chteniia, posviashchennye 80-letiiu so dnia rozhdeniia akademika L'va Vladimirovicha Cherepnina. Tezisy, doklady, i soobshcheniia*, ed. AN SSSR, Otdelenie istorii, Istoricheskii fakul'tet Moskovskogo gosudarstvennogo universiteta (Moscow: AN SSSR, 1985), 99–102.

Novokhvatko, O. V. *Zapisnye knigi moskovskogo stola razriadnogo prikaza XVII veka* (Moscow: Pamiatniki istoricheskoi mysli, 2001).

Novosel'skii, A. A. "Zemskii sobor 1639 g.," *Istoricheskie zapiski* 24 (1947): 14–29.

—— *Bor'ba Moskovskogo gosudarstva s tatarami v pervoi polovine XVII v.* (Moscow: AN SSSR, 1948).

—— "Iz istorii donskoi torgovli v XVII veke," *Istoricheskie zapiski* 26 (1948): 198–216.

—— "Dvortsovye krest'iane Komaritskoi volosti vo vtoroi polovine XVII veka," in *Voprosy istorii sel'skogo khoziaistva, krest'ianstva, i revoliutsionnogo dvizheniia v Rossii. Sbornik statei*, AN SSSR, Institut istorii (Moscow: AN SSSR, 1961), 65–80.

—— "Bor'ba Moskovskogo gosudarstva s tatarami vo vtoroi polovine XVII veka," in *Issledovaniia po istorii epokhi feodalizma* (Moscow: Nauka, 1994), 13–115.

—— "Ocherk voennykh deistvii boiarina Vasiliia Petrovich Sheremeteva v 1654 na Novgorodskom fronte," in *Issledovaniia po istorii epokhi feodalizma* (Moscow: Nauka, 1994), 117–135.

Nowak, Tadeusz Marian "Polish Warfare Technique in the 17th Century: Theoretical Conceptions and Their Practical Applications," in *Military Technique, Policy, and Strategy in History*, ed. Witold Bieganski (Warsaw: Ministry of Defense Publishing House, 1976), 11–94.

—— "Walki obronne z najazdami tatarów i turków w XIII–XVI w.," in *Polskie tradycjye woskowe. Tom I. Tradycje walk obronnych z najazdami niemców, krzyżaków, szwedów, turków i tatarów*, ed. Janusz Sikorski (Warsaw: Wyd. Ministerstwa Obrony Narodowej, 1990), 136–167.

Obolenskii, M. A. and Possel't, M. E., eds. "Dnevnik generala Patrika Gordona. Chast' vtoraia (1661–1684 gg.)," *Chteniia v Obshchestve istorii i drevnostei rossiiskikh pri Moskovskom universitete* 162, 3 (1892), part 3, 1–194.

O'Brien, C. Bickford "Russia and Turkey, 1677–1681: The Treaty of Bakhchisarai," *Russian Review* 12, 4 (1953): 259–268.

—— *Muscovy and the Ukraine from the Pereiaslavl' Agreement to the Truce of Andrusovo, 1654–1667* (Berkeley: University of California Press, 1963).

Ochmański, Jerzy "Organizacja obrony w Wielkim Księstwie Litewskim przed napadami tatarów krymskich w XV–XV wieku," *Studia i materiały do historii wojskowości* 5 (1960): 349–398.

Oreshkova, S. F. *Russko-turetskie otnosheniia v nachale XVIII v.* (Moscow: Nauka, 1971).

Oreshkova, S. F. and Ul'chenko, N. Iu. *Rossiia i Turtsiia (problemy formirovaniia granits)* (Moscow: IV RAN, 1999).

Ortayli, Ilber "Suleyman and Ivan: Two Autocrats of Eastern Europe," in *Suleyman the Second and His Time*, ed. Halil Inalcik and Cemal Kefadar (Istanbul: Isis Press, 1993), 203–210.

Ossoliński, Lukasz "Kampania na Ukrainie w 1660 roku," Dyplomowaja praca, Institut Historyczny, Uniwersytet Warszawskiego, 1995.

Ostapchuk, Victor "The Chronicle of Remmel Khoja *The History of Sahi Gerey Khan* as a Source on Crimean Tatar Campaigns," unpublished paper.

—— "The Ottoman Black Sea Frontier and the Relations of the Porte with the Polish-Lithuanian Commonwealth and Muscovy, 1622–1628," Doctoral dissertation, Harvard University, 1989.

—— "The Human Landscape of the Ottoman Black Sea in the Face of the Cossack Naval Raids," *Oriente Moderno* 20, 8 (2001): 23–95.

Ostrowski, Donald "The Military Land Grant Along the Muslim–Chinese Frontier," *Russian History/Histoire Russe* 19, 1–4 (1992): 327–359.

—— "Troop Mobilization by the Muscovite Grand Princes (1313–1533)," in *The Military and Society in Russia, 1450–1917*, ed. Eric Lohr and Marshall Poe (Leiden: E. J. Brill, 2002), 19–40.

Ozkaya, Yucel "The Consequences of the Weakening of Centralized State Structure: Ayanlik System and Great Dynasties," in *The Great Ottoman-Turkish Civilization. Volume Three*, ed. Halil Inalcik (Ankara: Yeni Turkiye, 2000), 554–570.

Pallot, Judith and Shaw, Dennis J. B. *Landscape and Settlement in Romanov Russia, 1613–1917* (Oxford: Clarendon Press, 1990).

Parrott, David "Strategy and Tactics in the Thirty Years' War: 'The Military Revolution,'" *Militärgeschichte Mitteilungen* 38 (1985): 7–26.

Parry, V. J. "La maniere de combattre," *War, Technology and Society in the Middle East*, ed. V. J. Parry and M. E. Yapp (London: Oxford University Press, 1975), 218–256.

Paul, Michael C. "The Military Revolution in Russia, 1550–1682," *Journal of Military History* 68, 1 (2004): 9–45.

Pavlov-Sil'vanskii, N. P. *Gosudarevy sluzhilye liudi* (Moscow: Kraft, 2001).

Pelenski, Jaroslaw *Russia and Kazan: Conquest and Imperial Ideology (1438–1560s)* (Hague: Mouton, 1974).

Penskoi, V. V. "Popytka voennykh reform v Rossii nachale XVII veka," *Voprosy istorii* 11 (2003): 127–138.

Peresvetov, Ivan "Sochineniia Ivana Semenovicha Peresvetova: Malaia chelobitnaia. Bol'shaia chelobitnaia," in *Pamiatniki literatury drevnei Rusi. Konets XV–pervaia polovina XVI veka*, ed. L. A. Dmitriev and D. S. Likhachev (Moscow: Khudozhestvennaia literatura, 1984), 596–625 + 756–763.

Perjes, G. "Army Provisioning, Logistics, and Strategy in the Second Half of the Seventeenth Century," *Acta Historica Academiae Scientarum Hungaricae* 16 (1970): 1–51.

Petros'ian, Iu. A. *Osmanskaia imperiia. Mogushchestvo i gibel'* (Moscow: Nauka, 1990).

Petrosyan, Irina "The Janissary Corps in the Late Sixteenth and Early Seventeenth Century: The First Attempt at Military Reform in the Ottoman Empire," in *The Great Ottoman-Turkish Civilization. Volume Three*, ed. Halil Inalcik, Kemal Cicek, Nejat Goyunc, and Ilber Ortayli (Ankara: Yeni Turkiye, 2000), 750–760.

Philipp, Werner "Russia: The Beginning of Westernization," in *The New Cambridge Modern History, Volume Five: The Ascendancy of France, 1648–1688*, ed. F. L. Carsten (Cambridge: Cambridge University Press, 1969).

Phillips, Edward J. *The Founding of Russia's Navy: Peter the Great and the Azov Fleet, 1688–1714* (Westport, CT: Greenwood Press, 1996).

Picheta, V. I. "Vneshniaia politika Rossii pri tsare Aleksee Mikhailoviche," in *Tri veka. Rossiia ot Smuty do nashego vremeni. Tom II. XVII veka. Vtoraia polovina*, ed. V. V. Kallash (Moscow: GIS, reprint ed., 1991), 106–139.

Pirog, P. V. "K voprosu o russkikh voevodakh na Ukraine vo vtoroi polovine XVII veka," *Otechestvennaia istoriia* 2 (2003): 162–168.

Piskarev, P. I. *Sobranie materialov dlia istorii zapadnago kraia Tambovskoi gubernii i eparkhii* (Tambov, 1878).
Pitcher, Donald Edgar *An Historical Geography of the Ottoman Empire, from Earliest Times to the End of the Sixteenth Century* (Leiden: E. J. Brill, 1972).
Platonov, S. F. *Ocherki po istorii smuty v Moskovskom gosudarstve XVI–XVII vv.* (Moscow: Sotsekgiz, 1937).
Plewczyński, Marek *Ludzie Wschodu w wojsku ostatnich Jagiełłonów* (Warsaw: Bellona, 1995).
Plokhy, Serhii *The Cossacks and Religion in Early Modern Ukraine* (Oxford: Oxford University Press, 2001).
—— "The Ghosts of Pereiaslav: Russo-Ukrainian Historical Debates in the Post-Soviet Era," *Europe-Asia Studies* 53, 3 (2001): 489–505.
Podhorodecki, Leszek "Kampaniia Chocimska 1621 roku," 2 parts, *Studia i materiały do Historii Wojskowości* 10 (1964): 88–143 and 11 (1965): 37–68.
—— *Chocim, 1621* (Warsaw: Wyd. Ministerstwa Obrony narodoowej, 1988).
Poe, Marshall "The Consequences of the Military Revolution in Muscovite Society: A Comparative Perspective," *Comparative Studies in Society and History* 38, 4 (1996): 603–618.
—— "Muscovite Personnel Records: New Light on the Early Evolution of Russian Bureaucracy," *Jahrbucher fur Geschichte Osteuropas* 45 (1997): 361–378.
—— "The Military Revolution, Administrative Development, and Cultural Change in Early Modern Russia," *Journal of Early Modern History* 2, 2 (1998): 156–180.
Pokhlebkin, V. V. *Tatary i Rus': 360 let otnoshenii, 1238–1598. Spravochnik* (Moscow: Mezhdunarodnye otnoshenii, 2000).
Popov, A. N. "Turetskaia voina v tsarstvovanie Fedora Alekseevicha," 2 parts, *Russkii vestnik* 8, 2 (1857): 143–180 and 8, 2 [sic] (1857): 285–328.
Porfir'ev, E. I. *Petr I. Osnovopolozhnik voennogo iskusstva russkoi reguliarnoi armii i flota* (Moscow: Voennoe ministerstvo SSSR, 1952).
Porshnev, B. F. *Muscovy and Sweden in the Thirty Years' War*, ed. Paul Dukes, trans. Brian Pearce (Cambridge: Cambridge University Press, 1995).
Priakhin, A. D. and Glaz'ev, V. N., eds. *Rossiiskaia krepost' na iuzhnykh rubezhakh. Dokumenty o stroitel'stve El'tsa, zaselenii goroda i okrestnostei v 1592–1594 gg.* (Elets: Eletskii Gosuniversitet, 2001).
Pronshtein, A. P. "K istorii voznikoveniia kazach'ikh poselenii i obrazovaniia sosloviia kazakov na Donu," in *Novoe o proshlom nashei strany. Pamiati akademika M. N. Tikhomirova*, ed. AN SSSR, Otdelenie istorii, Arkheograficheskaia komissiia (Moscow: Nauka, 1967), 158–173.
Pushkarev, L. N. *Obshchestvenno-politicheskaia mysl' Rossii, vtoraia polovina XVII veka* (Moscow: Nauka, 1982).
Rabinovich, M. D. "Sud'ba sluzhilykh liudei starykh sluzhb i odnodvortsev v period oformleniia reguliarnoi russkoi armii v nachale XVIII veke," Cand. diss., Moskovskii Gosudarstvennyi Universitet, 1953.
—— *Polki Petrovskoi armii, 1698–1725. Kratkii spavochnik* (Moscow: Sovetskaia Rossiia, 1977).
Ralston, David B. *Importing the European Army. The Introduction of European Military Techniques and Institutions in the Extra-European World, 1600–1914* (Chicago, IL: University of Chicago Press, 1990).

Razin, E. A. *Istoriia voennogo iskusstva XVI–XVII vv.* (St. Petersburg: Poligon, 1994).

Reger, William H. IV "In the Service of the Tsar: European Mercenary Officers and the Reception of Military Reform in Russia, 1654–1667," Doctoral dissertation, University of Illinois at Urbana-Champaign, 1997.

——"Baptizing Mars: The Conversion to Russian Orthodoxy of European Mercenaries During the Mid-seventeenth Century," in *The Military and Society in Russia, 1450–1917*, ed. Eric Lohr and Marshall Poe (Leiden: E. J. Brill, 2002), 389–412.

Riabov, S. I. *Voisko Donskoe i rossiiskoe samoderzhavie (1613–1725)* (Volgograd: Peremena, 1993).

Roberts, Michael *The Early Vasas: A History of Sweden, 1523–1611* (Cambridge: Cambridge University Press, 1968).

Rogers, Clifford, ed. *The Military Revolution Debate. Readings on the Military Transformation of Early Modern Europe* (Boulder, CO: Westview Press, 1995).

Rostovskii Gosudarstvennyi Universitet, *Istoriia Dona s drevneishikh vremen do velikoi oktiabr'skoi sotsialisticheskoi revoliutsii* (Rostov-na-Donu: Rostovskii Universitet, 1965).

Rothenburg, Gunther "The Austrian Military Border in Croatia, 1522–1747," in *Illinois Studies in the Social Sciences. Volume 48* (Urbana: University of Illinois, 1960).

——"Aventinus and the Defense of the Empire Against the Turks," *Studies in the Renaissance* 10 (1963): 60–67.

Rybakov, B. A., ed. *Istoriia SSSR s drevneishikh vremen do kontsa XVIII veka* (Moscow: Vysshaia shkola, 1975).

Sadikov, P. A. "Pokhod tatar i turok na Astrakhan' v 1569 g.," *Istoricheskie zapiski* 2 (1947): 132–166.

Sahanovich, Genadz *Neviadomaia vaina 1654–1667* (Minsk: Navuka i tekhnika, 1995).

Sanin, G. A. "Russko-pol'skie otnosheniia 1667–1672 gg. i krymsko-turetskaia politika v vostochnoi Evrope," in *Rossiia, Pol'sha i Prichernomor'e v XV–XVIII vv.*, ed. B. A. Rybakov (Moscow: Nauka, 1979), 276–286.

—— *Otnosheniia Rossii i Ukrainy s Krymskim khanstvom v seredine XVII veka* (Moscow: Nauka, 1987).

——"Iuzhnaia granitsa Rossii vo vtoroi polovine XVII–pervoi polovine XVIII vv.," *Russian History/Histoire Russe* 19, 1–4 (1992): 433–457.

——"Antiosmanskie voiny v 70-e-90-e gody XVII veka i gosudarstvennost' Ukrainy v sostave Rossii i Rechi Pospolity," in *Rossiia-Ukraina: Istoriia vzaimootnosheniia*, ed. A. I. Miller, V. F. Reprintsev, and B. N. Floria (Moscow: Iazyki russkoi kul'tury, 1997), 61–75.

Saveleva, A. "O storozhevykh zasechnykh liniiakh na iuge v drevnei Rossii," *Trudy vtorogo arkheologicheskogo s'ezda* (1876): 109–114.

Schumann, Hans "Der Hetmanstaat (1654–1764)," *Jahrbucher fur Geschichte Osteuropas* 1, 1 (1936): 499–548.

Schutz, E. *An Armeno-Kipchak Chronicle on the Polish–Turkish Wars in 1620–1621* (Budapest: Akademiai Kiado, 1968).

Schwarz, Iskra "Iz istorii avstro-russkikh diplomaticheskikh otnoshenii v seredine XVII veka," in *Mesto Rossii v Evrazii. The Place of Russia in Eurasia*, ed. Gyula Szvak (Budapest: Magyar Ruszisztikai Intezet, 2001), 163–172.

Sedov, P. V. "Rossiia na poroge novogo vremeni: Reformy tsaria Fedora Alekseevicha," *Forschungen zur Osteuropiaschen Geschichte* 56 (2000): 291–301.

—— "Oborona Chigirina v 1677 g.," in *Rossiiskoe gosudarstvo v XIV–XVII vv. Sbornik statei, posviashchennyi 75-letiiu so dnia rozhdeniia Iu. G. Alekseeva*, ed. A. G. Mankov and A. P. Pavlov (St. Petersburg: Dmitrii Bulianian, 2002): 484–508.

Serczyk, Wladyslaw "Rech' Pospolitaia i kazachestvo v pervoi chetverti XVII v.," in *Rossiia, Pol'sha i Prichernomor'e v XV–XVIII vv.*, ed. B. A. Rybakov (Moscow: Nauka, 1979): 174–193.

Sergienko, G. Ia., V. I. Borisenko, V. A. Markina, and L. G. Mel'nik, eds. *Istoriia Ukrainskoi SSR. V desiati tomakh. Tom tretii* (Kiev: Naukova dumka, 1983).

Shaw, Denis J. B. "Southern Frontiers of Muscovy," in *Studies in Russian Historical Geography. Volume One*, ed. J. H. Bater and R. A. French (New York: Academic Press, 1983), 118–142.

Shaw, Stanford *History of the Ottoman Empire and Modern Turkey. Volume One: Empire of the Gazis: The Rise and Decline of the Ottoman Empire, 1280–1808* (Cambridge: Cambridge University Press, 1976).

Shcherbin, V. I. "Kievskie voevody, gubernatory i general-gubernatory ot 1654 do 1775 g.," *Chteniia v istoricheskom obshchestve Nestora letopistsa* 6, 2 (1892): 123–145.

Shirokorad, A. B. *Russko-turetskie voiny 1676–1918 gg.* (Minsk: Kharvest, ACT 2000).

Shmidt, S. O. "Russkie polonianiki v Krymu i sistema ikh vykupka v seredine XVI v.," in *Voprosy sotsial'no-ekonomicheskoi istorii i istochnikovedenie perioda feodalizma v Rossii*, AN SSSR, Institut istorii (Moscow: Nauka, 1961), 30–34.

—— "Mestnichestvo i absoliutizma," in *Absoliutizm v Rossii (XVII–XVIII vv.)*, ed. N. M. Druzhinin and V. V. Kafengauz (Moscow: Nauka, 1964), 168–205.

Sikorski, Janusz, ed. *Polskie tradycje wojskowe. Tom I. Tradycje walk obronnych z najazdami niemców, krzyżaków, szwedów, turków i tatarów* (Warsaw: Wyd. Ministerstwa Obrony Narodowej, 1990).

Skalon, D. A., ed. *Stoletie Voennago ministerstva, 1802–1902. Glavnyi shtab. Tom 4, chast' 1, nomer 1, otd. 2. Kratkii istoricheskii ocherk voznikoveniia i razvitiia General'nago shtaba v Rossii do XVIII-go stoletiia vkliuchitel'no* (St. Petersburg, 1902), 3–168.

Skobel'kin, O. V. "Voronezh i vykhodtsy iz tatarskogo plena (konets 20-kh gg. XVII v.)," in *Problemy izucheniia istorii tsentral'nogo chernozem'ia*, ed. A. N. Akinshin and V. P. Zagorovskii (Voronezh: Tsentr dukhovnogo vozrozhdeniia chernozemnogo kraia, 2000), 94–103.

Skrynnikov, R. G. *Ivan the Terrible* (Gulf Breeze, FL: Academic International Press, 1981).

—— *Sibirskaia ekspeditsiia Ermaka* (Novosibirsk: Nauka, 1982).

—— *Rossiia nakanune "smutnogo vremeni"* (Moscow: Mysl', 1985, 2nd ed.).

—— *Sotsial'no-politicheskaia bor'ba v Russkom gosudarstve v nachale XVII veka* (Leningrad: Leningradskii Gos. Universitet, 1985).

Slabeev, I. S. and Iu. Kondufor, eds. *Istoriia Ukrainskoi SSR. V desiati tomakh. Tom vtoroi: Razvitie feodalizma. Narastanie antifeodal'noi i osvoboditel'noi bor'by (vtoraia polovina XIII–pervaia polovina XVIII v)*. (Kiev: Naukova dumka, 1982).

Sliusarskii, A. G. *Sotsial'no-ekonomicheskoe razvitie Slobozhanshchiny XVII–XVIII vv.* (Khar'kov: Kharkovskoe knizhnoe izd., 1964).

"Smetnyi spisok 7139 g.," *Vremennik* 4 (1849): 19–27.

Smirnov, I. I. "Vostochnaia politika Vasiliia III," *Istoricheskie zapiski* 27 (1948): 18–66.

Smirnov, N. A. *Rossiia i Turtsiia v XVI–XVII vv.* (2 parts) *Uchenye zapiski Moskovskogo gosudarstvennogo uniersiteta*, 94 (Moscow: Moskovskii Universitet, 1946).

—— "Bor'ba russkogo i ukrainskogo narodov protiv agressii sultanskoi Turtsii v XVII–XVIII vv.," in *Vossoedinenie Ukrainy s Rossiei, 1654–1954. Sbornik statei*, ed. A. I. Baranovich (Moscow: AN SSSR, 1954), 357–394.

Smirnov, V. D. *Krymskoe khanstvo pod verkhoventsvom Otomanskoi Porty do nachala XVIII veka* (St. Petersburg, 1887).

Smith, Abby "The Brilliant Career of Prince Golitsyn," *Harvard Ukrainian Studies* 29 (1995): 639–654.

Smith, Dianne L. "Muscovite Logistics, 1462–1598," *Slavonic and East European Review* 71, 1 (1993): 35–65.

Smoliy, V., V. Matiakh, V. Gorobets, and Iu. Mitsik, eds. *Pereiaslavs'ka rada ta Ukrains'ko-Rosiis'ka ugoda 1654 roku: Istoriia, istoriografiia, ideologiia* (Kiev: Institut istorii Ukrainy NAN Ukrainy, 2005).

Sofronenko, K. A. "Malorossiiskii prikaz Russkogo gosdudarstva vtoroi poloviny XVII i nachala XVIII veka," Ph.D. diss., Moskovskii Iuridicheskii Institut, 1960.

Solodkin, Ia. G. "Nekotorye spornye voprosy istorii voronezhskogo kraia nachala XVII veka," in *Voronezhskii krai na iuzhnykh rubezhakh Rossii (XVII–XVIII vv.)*, ed. V. P. Zagorovskii (Voronezh: Voronezhskii Gosudarstvennyi Universitet, 1981), 5–20.

—— "Iz rannei istorii Tsareva-Borisova," in *Problemy izucheniia istorii tsentral'nogo chernozem'ia*, ed. A. N. Akinshin and V. P. Zagorovskii (Voronezh: Tsentr dukhovnogo vozrozhdeniia chernozemnogo kraia, 2000), 81–93.

Solov'ev, S. M. *Istoriia Rossii s drevneishikh vremen. Kniga piataia, tom deviatyi* (Moscow: Izd. Sotsial'no-ekonomicheskoi literatury, 1961).

—— *Istoriia Rossii s drevneishikh vremen. Kniga shestaia, tom odinnadtsatyi* (Moscow: Izd. Sotsial'no-ekonomicheskoi literatury, 1961).

Solov'ev, V. M. "Goroda belgorodskoi cherty nakanune krest'ianskoi voiny 1670–1671 gg. v Rossii," *Problemy istorii SSSR. Istoricheskii fakul'tet, Moskovskii gosudarstvennyi universitet* 9 (1979): 42–59.

Sorokoletov, S. F. *Istoriia voennoi leksiki v russkom iazyke* (Leningrad: Nauka, 1970).

Stanislavskii, A. L. *Grazhdanskaia voina v Rossii XVII v.* (Moscow: Mysl', 1990).

Stashevshii, E. D. "Stat'i, kakoe opasenie i ratnykh liudei v ukrainykh gorodekh imet' ot Krymskago khana," *Zapiski Imperatorskago Russkago arkheologicheskago obshchestva* 2 (1861): 374–376.

—— "Smeta voennykh sil Moskovskago gosudarstva na 1663 god," *Voenno-istoricheskii vestnik* 7, 8 (1909): 15–42 and 5, 6 (1910): 55–88.

—— *Smeta voennykh sil Moskovskago gosudarstva v 1663 godu* (Kiev, 1910).

—— "Biudzhet i armiia v Moskovskom gosudarstve," in *Russkaia istoriia v ocherkakh i statiakh. Tom tretii*, ed. M. V. Dovnar-Zapol'skii (Kiev, 1912), 411–417.

—— "K istorii kolonizatsii iuga (Velikii boiarin Ivan Nikitich Romanov i ego slobody v Eletskom uezde)," *Drevnosti. Trudy arkheograficheskoi kommissii Imp. Moskovskago arkheologicheskago obshchestva* 3 (1913): 239–294.

—— *Ocherki po istorii tsarstvovaniia Mikhaila Fedorovicha do epokhi Smolenskoi voiny* (Kiev, 1913).

―― *Smolenskaia voina 1632–1634 gg. Organizatsiia i sostoianie moskovskoi armii* (Kiev, 1919).
Stelletskii, Boris "Pol'sko-kazatskaia voina s Turtsiei 1621 goda," 4 parts, *Voenno-istoricheskii sbornik* 5–6 (1909): 11–53; 7–8 (1909): 1–14; 1–2 (1910): 39–51; 3–4 (1910): 131–147.
Stevens, Carol Belkin "Why Seventeenth-century Muscovite Campaigns Against Crimea Fell Short of What Counted," *Russian History/Histoire Russe* 19, 1–4 (1992): 487–504.
―― *Soldiers on the Steppe: Army Reform and Social Change in Early Modern Russia* (De Kalb: Northern Illinois University Press, 1995).
―― *Russia's Wars of Emergence* (New York: Longman, forthcoming 2007).
Stolz, Benjamin, trans. *Konstantin Mihailovic. Memoirs of a Janissary* (Ann Arbor: University of Michigan Press, 1975).
Stone, Daniel *The Polish-Lithuanian State, 1386–1795. A History of East Central Europe, Volume IV* (Seattle: University of Washington Press, 2001).
Subtelny, Orest *Ukraine: A History* (Toronto: University of Toronto Press, 1988).
Sunderland, Willard *Taming the Wild Field: Colonization and Empire on the Russian Steppe* (Ithaca, NY: Cornell University Press, 2004).
Svatikov, S. G. *Rossiia i Don (1549–1917)* (Rostov-na-Donu: Donskaia istoricheskaia komissiia, 1924).
Svechin, Aleksandr *Evoliutsiia voennogo iskusstva* (Moscow: Akademicheskii proekt, 2002).
Sysyn, Frank E. *Between Poland and Ukraine: The Dilemma of Adam Kysil, 1600–1653* (Cambridge, MA: Harvard Ukrainian Research Institute, 1985).
―― "Ukrainian Social Tensions Before the Khmel'nyts'kyi Uprising," in *Religion and Culture in Early Modern Russia and Ukraine*, ed. Samuel Baron and Nancy Shields Kollmann (De Kalb: Northern Illinois University Press, 1997), 52–70.
Tan'kov, A., ed. *Istoricheskaia letopis' kurskago dvorianstva. Tom pervyi* (Moscow, 1913).
Teodorczyk, Jerzy "Wojskowość Polska w pierwszej połowie XVII wieku," in *Historia wojskowości Polskiej*, ed. Witold Bieganski (Warsaw: Wyd. Ministerstwa Obrony Narodowej, 1972), 177–193.
Tikhomirov, M. N. *Rossiia v XVI stoletii* (Moscow: AN SSSR, 1962).
Tolmacheva, Marina "The Cossacks at Sea: Pirate Tactics in the Frontier Environment," *East European Quarterly* 24, 4 (1991): 483–512.
Trepavlov, V. V. *Istoriia Nogaiskoi ordy* (Moscow: Vostochnaia literaura, RAN, 2001).
Trunov, M. "K materialam po istorii zaseleniia cherkasami voronezhskogo kraia," *Pamiatnaia knizhka voronezhskoi gubernii* (1916): 110–112.
Tushin, Iu. P. *Russkoe moreplavanie na Kaspiiskom, Azovskom, i Chernom moriakh* (Moscow: Nauka, 1978).
Tys-Khrokhmaliuk, Yuriy "The Victory at Konotop," *The Ukrainian Review* 6, 3 (1959): 34–45.
Ustiugov, N. V. "Finansy," in *Ocherki istorii SSSR. Period feodalizma, XVII v.*, ed. A. A. Novosel'skii and N. V. Ustiugov (Moscow: AN SSSR, 1955), 411–439.
―― ed. *Ocherki istorii Kal'mytskoi ASSR. Do-oktiabr'skii period* (Moscow: Nauka, 1967).
van der Hoeven, Marco *Exercise of Arms: Warfare in the Netherlands (1568–1648)* (Leiden: E. J. Brill, 1997).

Vazhinskii, V. M. "Razvitie rynochnykh sviazei v iuzhnykh russkikh gorodakh vo vtoroi polovine XVII veka," *Uchenye zapiski Kemerovskogo pedagogicheskogo instituta* 5 (1963): 102–141.

——*Zemlevladenie i skladyvanie obshchiny odnodvortsev v XVII v.* (Voronezh: Voronezhskii gos. pedagogicheskii institut, 1974).

——"Sbory zaprosnogo khleba v kontse XVII v. dlia obespecheniia krymskikh i azovskikh pokhodov," *Izvestiia Voronezhskogo gosudarstvennogo pedagogicheskogo instituta* 153 (1975): 23–46.

——"Usilenie soldatskoi povinnosti v Rossii v XVII v (Po materialam iuzhnykh uezdov)," *Izvestiia Voronezhskogo pedagogicheskogo instituta* 157 (1976).

——*Sel'skoe khoziaistvo v chernozemnom tsentre Rossii v XVII veke* (Voronezh: Voronezhskii gos. pedagogicheskii instituta, 1983).

Vernadsky, George *A History of Russia. Volume Three: The Mongols and Russia* (New Haven, CT: Yale University Press, 1953).

——*A History of Russia. Volume Five: The Tsardom of Muscovy, 1547–1682, Part One* (New Haven, CT: Yale University Press, 1969).

Veselovskii, S. B. "Smety voennykh sil Moskovskago gosudarstva, 1661–1663 gg.," *ChOIDR* 3 (1911): 1–60.

Vinogradov, A. V. "Krymskie khany v XVI veke," *Otechestvennaia istoriia* 2 (1999): 58–69.

Vodarskii, Ia. E. "Mezhdunarodnoe polozhenie Russkogo gosudarstva i russko-turetskaia voina 1676–1681 gg.," *Ocherki istorii SSSR. Period feodalizma XVII v.*, ed. A. A. Novosel'skii and N. V. Ustiugov (Moscow: AN SSSR, 1955), 518–531.

——*Naselenie Rossii za 400 let (XVI–nachalo XX vv.)* (Moscow: Prosveshchenie, 1973).

——*Naselenie Rossii v kontse XVII–nachale XVIII veka* (Moscow: Nauka, 1977).

Volkov, V. *Voiny i voiska Moskovskogo gosudarstva* (Moscow: Algoritm, 2004).

Vorob'ev, V. M. "Konnost', liudnost', oruzhnost' i sbruinost' sluzhilykh gorodov pri pervykh Romanovykh," in *Dom Romanovykh v istorii Rossii*, ed. Iu. G. Alekseev and I. Ia. Froianov (St. Petersburg: Sankt-Peterburgskii Universitet, 1995), 93–108.

——"Kak s chego sluzhili na Rusi v XVII v.," in *Srednevekovaia i novaia Rossiia. Sbornik nauchnykh statei*, ed. Iu. G. Alekseev and I. Ia. Froianov (St. Petersburg: Sankt-Peterburgskii Universitet, 1996), 451–462.

Vorob'ev, V. M. and Degtiarev, A. Ia. *Russkoe feodal'noe zemlevladenie ot "smutnogo vremeni" do kanune petrovskikh reform* (Leningrad: Leningradskii Gos. Universitet, 1986).

Vozgrin, V. E. *Istoricheskie sud'by krymskikh tatar* (Moscow: Mysl', 1992).

Vtorov, N. and Aleksandrov-Dol'nik, K. *Drevniia gramoty i drugie pis'mennye pamiatniki, kasaiushchiesia Voronezhskoi gubernii i chastiiu Azova, vyp. 2* (Voronezh, 1851–1853).

Wandycz, Piotr *The Price of Freedom: A History of East Central Europe from the Middle Ages to the Present* (London: Routledge, 1992).

Wilson, Peter H. *German Armies: War and German Politics, 1648–1806* (London: Routledge, 1998).

Wimmer, Jan "Piechota w wojsku polskim XV–XVIII w.," in *Historia wojskowości polskiej*, ed. Witold Bieganski (Warsaw: Wyd. Ministerstwa Obrony Narodowej, 1972), 161–176.

——"Jan Sobieski's Art of War," in *Historia Militaris Polonica*, ed. Witold Bieganski et al. (Warsaw: Ministry of Defense Publishing House, 1977), 19–37.
——*Historia piechoty Polskiej do roku 1864* (Warsaw: Wyd. Ministerstwa Obrony Narodowej, 1978).
Wisner, Henryk *Władysław IV Waza* (Wrocław: Zakład Narodowy imienia Ossolińskich, 1995).
Wojcik, Zbigniew *Traktat Andruszowski 1667 roku i jego geneza* (Warsaw: Panstwowe Wyd. Naukowe, 1959).
——"Some Problems of Polish–Tatar Relations in the Seventeenth Century. The Financial Aspects of the Polish–Tatar Alliance in the Years 1654–1666," *Acta Poloniae Historica* 13 (1966): 87–102.
——"Poland and Russia in the 17th Century: Problems of Internal Development," in *Poland at the Fourteenth International Congress of Historical Sciences in San Francisco*, Polish Academy of Sciences, Institute of History (Wroclaw: Wyd. Polskiej Akademii Nauk, 1975), 113–133.
——*Rzeczpospolita wobec Turcji i Rosji 1674–1679* (Wroclaw: Wyd. Polskiej Akademii Nauk, 1976).
——"King John III of Poland and the Turkish Aspects of His Foreign Policy," *Turk Tarih Kurumu: Belleten* XLIV, 176 (1980): 659–673.
——"Russian Endeavors for the Polish Crown in the Seventeenth Century," *Slavic Review* XLI, 1 (1982): 59–72.
Wolinski, Janusz *Z dziejów wojen polsko-tureckich* (Warsaw: Wyd. Ministerstwa Obrony Narodowej, 1983).
Zaborovskii, L. V. "Krymskii vopros vo vneshnei politike Rossii i Rechi Pospolitoi v 40-kh-seredine 50-kh godov XVII v.," in *Rossiia, Pol'sha i Prichernomor'e v XV–nachale XVIII v.*, ed. B. A. Rybakov (Moscow: Nauka, 1979), 263–275.
——*Rossiia, Rech' Pospolitaia i Shvetsiia v seredine XVII v.* (Moscow: Nauka, 1981).
——*Velikoe kniazhestvo Litovskoe i Rossiia vo vremia pol'skogo potopa* (Moscow: Nauka, 1994).
Zagorovskii, V. P. "Donskoe kazachestvo i razmery donskikh otpuskov v XVII veke," *Trudy Voronezhskogo universiteta* 53 (1960): 131–147.
——"Vopros o russkom morskom flote na Donu do Petra I," *Trudy Voronezhskogo universiteta* 53, 1 (1960): 149–166.
——"Sudostroenie na Donu i ispol'zovanie Rossieiu parusnogo-grebnogo flota v bor'be protiv Krymskogo khanstva i Turtsii," Cand. diss., Voronezhskii Gosudarstvennyi Universitet, 1961.
——"Iz istorii gorodov na belgorodskoi cherte," *Trudy Voronezhskogo universiteta* 64 (1966): 3–33.
——*Belgorodskaia cherta* (Voronezh: Voronezhskii Gosudarstvennyi Universitet, 1969).
——"Nekotorye osobennosti kolonizatsionnogo protsessa iuzhnoi okrainy Rossii v XVII veke i ego periodizatsiia," *Iz istorii voronezhskogo kraia* 3 (1969): 83–93.
——"Nekotorye voprosy rannei narodnoi kolonizatsii polevoi okrainy Rossii," *Ezhegodnik po agrarnoi istorii vostochnoi Evropy 1968 g.* (1972): 37–40.
——"Soldatskie sela i soldatskoe zemlevladenie v voronezhskom krae XVII veka," *Iz istorii voronezhskogo kraia* 4 (1972): 90–97.
——*Iziumskaia cherta* (Voronezh: Voronezhskii Gosudarstvennyi Universitet, 1980).

—— "Obshchii ocherk istorii zaseleniia i khoziaistvennogo osvoeniia iuzhnykh okrain Rossii v epokhu zrelogo feodalizma," in *Istoriia zaseleniia i khoziaistvennogo osvoeniia voronezhskogo kraia v epokhu feodalizma*, Voronezhskii Gosudarstvennyi Universitet (Voronezh: Voronezhskii Gosudarstvennyi Universitet, 1987), 3–23.

—— *Istorii vkhozhdeniia tsentral'nogo chernozem'ia v sostav Rossiiskogo gosudarstva v XVI veke* (Voronezh: Voronezhskii Gosudarstvennyi Universitet, 1991).

Zaitsev, I. V. *Astrakhanskoe khanstvo* (Moscow: Izd. "Vostochnaia literatura" RAN, 2004).

Zamlinskii, Vladimir *Bogdan Khmel'nitskii* (Moscow: Molodaia gvardiia, 1989).

Zaozerskii, A. I. *Feld'marshal B. P. Sheremetev* (Moscow: Nauka, 1989).

Zaruba, V. N. *Ukrainskoe kazatskoe voisko v bor'be s turetsko-tatarskoi agressiei (poslednaia chetvert' XVII v.)* (Khar'kov: Osnova, 1993).

Zernack, Klaus *Polen und Russland. Zwei Wege in der Europaischen Geschichte* (Berlin: Propylaen Verlag, 1994).

Zgorniak, Marian *Wojskowość polska w dobie wojen tureckich drugiej połowy XVII wieku* (Wrocław: Zakład Narodowy im. Ossolińskich, 1985).

Zhigarev, Sergei *Russkaia politika v vostochnom voprose* (Moscow, 1896).

Zimin, A. A. "K istorii voennykh reform 50-kh godov," *Istoricheskie zapiski* LV (1956): 344–359.

—— *I. S. Peresvetov i ego sovremenniki* (Moscow: AN SSSR, 1958).

Zimin, A. A. and Khoroshkevich, A. L. *Rossiia vremen Ivana Groznogo* (Moscow: Nauka, 1982).

Zolotarev, V. A., ed. *Voennaia istoriia otechestva s drevnikh vremen do nashikh dnei. Tom pervyi* (Moscow: Mosgorarkhiv, 1995).

—— *Istoriia voennoi strategii Rossii* (Moscow: Kulikovo pole, 2000).

Index

Aadil Girei, Crimean Khan 190
Adashev, Danilo 56–7
Agoston, Gabor 196
Aiuki, Kalmyk Taishi 192
Akhmet, Khan of the Great Horde 5, 9
Akhtyrka 91, 178–9
Akkerman 7, 23, 78, 195
Aleksei Mikhailovich, Tsar of Muscovy 106–17, 124–7, 131–2, 137, 159, 202–4
Aleksin 46, 54, 65
Algirdas, Grand Duke of Lithuania 2
Almazov, Semen 162
Ambassadors' Chancellery (*Posol'skii prikaz*) 29–30, 59, 61, 75, 108, 131, 140, 164, 217
Andrusovo Treaty 150, 155, 157–8, 162, 176, 200, 203
Artopolot' River 160, 163
Assembly of the Realm (*Zemskii sobor*) 90, 107
Astrakhan 8, 12; annexed by Muscovy 12; as Muscovite garrison town 12–13, 15, 23, 27–8, 78, 95
Azov 2, 5–8, 11–13, 23, 26, 30–1, 58–9, 77, 79–80, 88–91, 96, 170, 183–7, 192, 194, 199, 201

Bagadur Girei, Crimean Khan 90–1
Bakhchisarai 6, 20, 25, 111, 155, 159; Treaty of 170–2, 176, 180, 190, 193–4
Bar 4, 19, 119, 147, 155–6, 158
Barabash, Iakov 127–8
Baranowski, Bohdan 25
Bashmakov, Dementii 140
Baturin 132, 148, 150, 163–4
Bayezit II, Ottoman Sultan 9
Beauplan, Guillaume le Vasseur, Sieur de 18, 20–1, 38
Belarus' 9, 109–10, 114–17, 121, 142, 151
Belgorod 18–19, 61, 67, 76, 85, 88, 92–4, 118–19, 128, 138, 153, 170, 206; Army Group and territorial military administration 92, 160, 162–3, 165, 171–3, 178–9, 183, 204–5

Bendery 10, 23, 78, 195
Berestechko, battle of 106
Bespalyi, Ivan 130
Bieniewski, Stanisław 127, 129, 142
Bila Tserkva 4, 35, 38, 106–9, 118–21, 123, 128, 138, 147, 150
Black Sea 1–2, 4–5, 7, 24, 98, 100, 203, 206; *see also* Crimean Khanate; naval and riverine warfare
Bogdanov, A. P. 168–9
Bohun, Ivan 120, 131, 148
Boretsky, Iov, Metropolitan of Kiev 99, 102
Boris Godunov, Tsar of Muscovy 40, 58
Botero, Giovanni 24, 177
Boyar Duma (*Boiarskaia duma*) 49, 75–6, 79–80, 88, 110, 162, 174–5
Bratslav 4, 19, 35, 106, 110, 120–1, 126, 129, 142, 150, 155, 171
Brest 109, 122
Briansk 46, 119, 163, 179
Briukhovets'kyi, Ivan 147–50, 152–4
Brown, Peter 140–1
Bucak Horde (Belgorod Horde) 8, 77–8, 123, 132, 183, 193
Buchach, Treaty of 156, 175
Bug River 2, 8, 19, 104, 119–20, 143, 157–8, 171–2, 183, 190, 197
Buturlin, Andrei Vasil'evich 118–19, 121, 123, 128, 132
Buturlin, Fedor Vasil'evich 118–19, 121
Buturlin, Vasilii Vasil'evich 110, 113, 120–4
Buzhin 160, 162–3

Cantacuzene, Foma 89–90
Cecora 99, 157, 193
Çelebi, Evliya 15, 25–6, 192, 194–5
chancelleries (*prikazy*) 40, 43, 45, 49, 60, 66, 69, 71, 73, 79–81, 140–2, 165, 172, 205; and Privy Chancellery 116, 140, 204; secretaries and clerks 30, 48, 80–1, 103, 140; *see also* Ambassadors' Chancellery;

INDEX

field army, Muscovite; garrisons, Muscovite; Military Chancellery
Cherkasskii, Iakov Kudenetovich 115, 148
Cherkasskii, Ivan Borisovich 69, 71, 79–81, 85, 97, 103
Cherkasy 4, 32, 35, 38, 56, 158, 169, 171
Chernigov 2, 4–5, 76, 102, 106, 113, 120, 126, 128–9, 132, 142, 149, 151, 132, 177, 184
Chodkiewicz, Stanisław 66, 99
Chudnovo, battle of 144–6, 197
Chuguev 82, 102
Chyhyryn 19, 38, 103, 110, 113, 125, 128, 130, 132, 146, 150, 152, 158–70, 172, 179, 190–1, 196
Collins, L. J. D. 21
Commonwealth, Polish-Lithuanian 4, 9–11, 13, 113 *passim*; Grand Duchy of Lithuania 1–5, 9, 13–14, 34, 109–11, 115–17, 133, 203–4; Kingdom of Poland 2, 7, 9, 13–14, 133; monarchy and estates 3–4, 9–10, 33–5, 38, 70, 73–4, 98–9, 106–9, 113, 116, 129, 133, 149–50, 156–7, 162, 175–6, 178, 188–9, 216; *see also* Crimean Khanate; Muscovy, Tsardom of; Ottoman Empire; Polish-Lithuanian army; Ukraine
Constantinople, Treaty of 188, 199
Court (*Dvor*) 41, 80, 165, 177–8, 186, 203; and precedence (*mestnichestvo*) 47, 80, 116, 174–5, 203, 220–1
Coyet, Julius 71
Cracow 9, 20, 143
Crawford, Alexander 94, 134, 137
Crimean Khanate: beys and mirzas of 6–8, 16, 22, 77–8, 90–1, 101, 111, 125, 181, 202; economy and population of 6, 23–5, 192; founding of 6; Girei khans and their territorial claims 5–7, 9, 11–12, 14–15; Girei khans in vassalage to Ottoman sultans 6–10, 15–17, 70, 78–9, 88–9, 91, 104, 111, 125, 155–7, 159–62, 167, 178, 182, 187, 190–1, 193–4; in alliance with Doroshenko 152–9; in Russo-Turkish War 159–62, 167–72, 175; in Thirteen Years' War 111, 119–21, 123, 126–31, 133, 143–8, 150, 152; raids and invasions in fifteenth–sixteenth centuries 1, 7–9, 14–18, 23, 27, 33–4, 42, 45–7, 49, 53 *passim*; relations with Don Cossacks 29–31, 58, 78–9, 88–90 *passim*; relations with Hetmanate of Khmel'nits'kyi 97, 104–5, 107, 111–12, 125, 127–30, 150, 153, 199–200; relations with Muscovy 11–29 *passim*; relations with Nogai hordes 8, 12, 15–16, 22, 27–9, 57, 77–8, 95, 97, 192–3; relations with Poland-Lithuania 9, 6–18, 98, 106, 111, 126, 133, 143, 146–7, 190; relations with Zaporozhian Sich 32–3,

37–9, 56–7, 100, 103, 123, 157, 179–80, 182–3, 192, 199; slaveraiding and the slave trade 17, 21–7, 66, 76–7
Crimean Tatar army 11, 18, 20–2, 37, 64, 138, 191; *see also* Crimean Khanate; trails
Czarniecki, Stefan 108, 138–9, 146–8

Daichin, Kalmyk Taishi 28, 95, 192
Dam, Heinrich von 71
Dankov 60, 66–7
Danube River 1, 2, 7–9, 24, 98, 151, 157, 159, 193–5
Daudov, Vasilii 158
Dedilov 46, 60, 67–8
defense lines: Abatis Line 22, 44–7, 59–60, 65, 67, 76, 79–82, 89, 91, 204; Bank 42–5, 47, 60; Belgorod Line 79, 84, 88–94, 96, 101–2, 105–6, 111, 146, 153, 171, 182, 191, 205; Izium Line 170–2, 182, 191
Deulino, Treaty of 66
Devlet Girei I, Crimean Khan 12, 16–18, 49, 54–5
diplomacy, conduct of 1, 11, 13, 28, 113, 127, 159, 176–7, 201–3; *see also* Ambassadors' Chancellery; tribute, gifts, and contributions
Dmitrii Donskoi, Grand Prince of Moscow 4, 177
Dnepr River 1, 8, 56, 67, 74 *passim*
Dnestr River 7, 8, 19, 157, 161, 183
Dobruja 24, 39, 193
Dobryi 91, 186
Dobrynichi, battle of 52
Dolgorukii, Iurii Alekseevich 139, 163
Don Cossack Host: colonization and formation of 28–30, 58; independent military action by 12, 17, 26–7, 29, 31, 59, 78–80, 89, 91 95, 104–5, 111, 193, 199; and Muscovite Don Shipments 28, 58–9, 79, 95–6, 198–9; and Muscovite expeditionary forces on Don 95–7, 185–6; political organization and social order 31, 59, 198–9; role in Muscovite frontier defense 26, 29, 56, 58–9, 118–19, 121–2, 146, 157, 163, 179; *see also* Azov; Crimean Khanate; Don River; field army, Muscovite; garrisons, Muscovite; naval and riverine operations; Zaporozhian Sich
Don River 5, 17–8, 23, 27, 67, 84, 192–3, 201; settlements of Lower Reaches 30–2, 79, 89–91, 97, 183, 185–6, 198–9, 206; settlements of Upper Reaches 30, 40, 65; *see also* Don Cossack Host
Dorogobuzh 72, 73, 75, 115
Doroshenko, Petro 150–8
Drizhipol'e, battle of 120–1, 138
Drummond, William 13
Duca, Gheorge, Hospodar of Moldavia 156, 171, 194

250

INDEX

Dzhemboiluk Horde 57, 95, 183
Dzikovsky, Ivan 102

Edigei, Khan of the Great Horde 2, 4
Edisan Horde 8, 95, 183
Efremov 82, 173
Elets 46, 61, 65–6, 83–4, 92, 173
Epifan' 60, 65
Eternal Peace, Treaty of 178
ethnic cleansing and herding 57, 96, 97, 117, 120, 131, 142, 146, 158, 170–2, 190, 192, 200; *see also* Crimean Khanate, slave-raiding and the slave trade

Fedor Alekseevich, Tsar of Muscovy 162
Fedor Ivanovich, Tsar of Muscovy 40
Fetih Girei, Crimean kalga 120
field army, Muscovite: armament 41, 50, 52, 60, 71, 128, 134–5, 137, 203; artillery 43, 53–4, 74–5, 115, 130–1, 135, 138, 143–4, 181–3, 196, 203; cavalry, foreign formation 71–2, 80, 84, 93–4, 115, 119, 128, 131, 134, 143, 160–1, 166, 172, 179, 205; cavalry, traditional formation 41–2, 50, 72, 81, 85, 94, 115, 118, 131, 134–5, 137–8, 163, 203; corps, arrays, army groups, and territorial military administrations 41–2, 46–7, 49–53, 68, 70, 72–3, 79–81, 92, 94–5, 115–16, 118–21, 129–30, 133, 143, 146, 153, 160, 162–3, 170, 172, 179, 181, 183, 185, 203, 206; financing 40, 60, 64, 66, 73, 141–2, 149, 174, 179, 206; infantry, foreign formation 71, 74, 87, 92–4, 97, 118–19, 127–8, 133–7, 143, 160, 166, 167, 173, 179, 204–5; infantry, musketeer 43–4, 130, 135, 160, 162–3, 173–4, 203; logistics 51–2, 72–3, 74–6, 93, 96–7, 116, 119, 126, 128, 138, 141, 143, 163, 179–81, 184–6, 197, 206; losses 75, 131, 133, 142, 146, 149, 161, 166, 169, 182, 205; mobilizations and force strengths 42, 47, 49–52, 70, 72, 79–81, 94–5, 115–16, 118–21, 129–30, 133, 143, 146, 153, 160, 162–3, 170, 172, 179, 181, 183, 185, 203, 206; officers and command-and-control 40, 42–5, 47–9, 53–4, 60, 66, 71, 80, 88, 91–3, 116–17, 135, 140–1, 163, 165–6, 174–5, 204–5; pay 71–2, 81, 94, 133–5, 141, 163, 185, 204; tactics 52–6, 73–6, 116–17, 124, 130–1, 136, 166–8, 184–6, 196, 203–4; training 133–8, 166, 173; *wagenburg*, *tabor*, and *guliai-gorod* 52, 54–5, 120, 123, 131, 135–40, 144–5, 160, 180, 182, 191, 197, 204; *see also* defense lines; garrisons, Muscovite; Military Chancellery
Filaret, Patriarch of Moscow (Fedor Nikitich Romanov) 59, 66, 69–71, 79, 97

Fisher, Alan 24
Fletcher, Giles 52
Frantsbek, Iurii 53, 55
Frost, Robert I. 36

Galicia 2, 4, 9, 25, 129
garrisons, Muscovite: construction and settlement of 13, 17–19, 29–31, 39–40, 46–7, 59–70, 77, 79, 97, 101, 105–6, 172, 198; established in Ukraine 113, 128, 140, 142–3, 146–51, 153–4, 161, 165, 171, 201, 205, 217; and network relations with other towns and corps 40, 42, 49–51, 53–4, 67, 92–3, 140; running steppe reconnaissance 46–7, 60, 63 67; under siege alert 21, 40, 63–4, 67; *see also* defense lines; field army, Muscovite; migration and settlement; Military Chancellery; military service; town governors
Gavrenev, Ivan 80, 140–1
Gazy Girei I, Crimean Khan 15
Gazy Girei II, Crimean Khan 17, 57
Gazy Girei, Crimean nuraddin 130, 143–4
Genoese 2, 6–7
Germanovka 132
Glukhov 132, 142, 147, 150, 153; Treaty of 154, 158, 200
Gniński, Jan 175–6
Golitsyn, Vasilii Vasil'evich 160, 163–5, 169–70, 174–182, 191, 205
Golovin, Avtomon Mikhailovich 183–4, 186
Gordon, Patrick 136, 145, 166–7, 169, 177, 180, 183–6
Gosiewski, Vincenty 116, 133
Great Horde 2, 4–6, 9, 11, 14
Great Nogai Horde 8, 12, 14–15, 17, 27–9, 32, 57–8, 77–8, 95–7, 202
Gustavus II Adolphus, King of Sweden 70–1, 76, 136
Gyorgy II Rakoczy, Prince of Transylvania 108, 121

Hadiach, Articles of 129, 132, 145, 146, 150, 153
Haji Girei I, Crimean Khan 6–7
Haji Girei II, Crimean Khan 191
Henri de Valois, King of Poland 10
Holy League, War of the 176–83, 189, 191, 194, 196
Holy Roman Empire 2, 151, 176–8, 182–3, 187, 190, 196–7
Hrushevsky, Mykhailo 39–40
Hungary 2, 9–10, 17, 89, 194, 197
Hussein Deli 90
Hussein Pasha 157, 196

Iablonov 82, 84, 88, 92, 94
Iaik River 28, 95

251

INDEX

Ibrahim I, Ottoman Sultan 25, 90–1
Ibrahim Shaitan Pasha 157, 160–1
Inaet Girei, Crimean Khan 78–9
Ishterek, Nogai Bey 27, 57
Islam Girei I, Crimean Khan 15
Islam Girei II, Crimean Khan 16
Islam Girei III, Crimean Khan 91, 97, 109, 111
Islam-Kermen 56
Ismail, Nogai Bey 12, 27, 57
Iur'ev, Nikita Romanovich 60
Ivan III, Grand Prince of Moscow 4, 5, 9, 13–14, 202
Ivan IV, Tsar of Muscovy 12, 15–16, 40, 42, 47, 49, 51, 56–7, 60, 202
Izium 102, 163, 171; *see also* defense lines
Izmailov, Artemii Vasil'evich 73

Jan Kazimierz, King of Poland 106–7, 109, 111, 116, 119, 121–4, 129, 133, 147–9, 150–1, 188–9
Janibek Girei, Crimean Khan 18, 70, 77–8
Jaruga, Treaty of 11
Jogaila, Grand Duke of Lithuania 2

Kaffa 6–7, 11, 16–17, 20, 23–5, 98, 121
Kalmyks 27–9, 78, 95, 123, 125, 192
Kaluga 42, 46, 53–4, 75
Kamianets-Podol'sk 4, 35, 118, 120, 152, 156–7, 175, 194
Kamil Mehmet Girei, Crimean Khan 91, 111, 123, 125, 130–1
Kammambet, Crimean Mirza 119–20, 150
Kanev 35, 38, 56, 169, 171
Kaplan Pasha 157–8
Kara Mustafa Pasha 159, 161, 168–9, 172, 176
Karachev 46
Karl X Gustavus, King of Sweden 121, 123, 124, 126, 132
Karl XI, King of Sweden 132, 176
Karlowitz, Treaty of 187, 191, 199
Karpov 91–2, 94, 118–19
Kashira 16–17, 46, 53–4, 77, 135
Kasim Pasha 12–13
Kasimov Khanate 5, 27
Katorzhnyi, Ivan 89–90
Kazan' 2, 5, 8, 12, 14–15; under Muscovite sovereignty 16–17, 23, 44, 93, 116, 173, 175, 178
Kazimierz III, King of Poland 3
Kazimierz IV, King of Poland 5, 9
Kazy-Kermen 180, 183
Kerch 23, 56, 121, 186–7, 194
Khantimur 78, 89
Kharkov 102, 171
Khmel'nyts'kyi, Bohdan 95, 102–16, 118, 121–7, 132, 154, 192, 199, 200
Khmel'nyts'kyi, Iurii 125, 127, 132, 143–6, 159–62, 169–71, 193–4

Khotyn 18, 38, 99, 157, 191, 193, 196
Khovanskii, Semen Andreevich 153, 163
Khrushchev, Petr 30

Kiev 2–4, 9, 32, 35, 99, 106, 108, 110, 112, 113, 118, 126, 129; Muscovite garrison at 118–20, 123, 128–32, 142–5, 149–50, 152, 155, 158–65, 168, 170–1, 176–9
Kilia 7, 9–10, 195
Kipchak Horde (Golden Horde) 1–2, 5–6
Kodak 100, 123, 150, 170, 179, 181, 197
Kolomna 42, 46, 51, 53–4, 61, 77
Komaritskaia canton 94, 153
Kondyrev, Zhdan 96
Koniecpolski, Stanisław 99–100
Konotop, battle of 128, 130–2, 138, 158
Konskie Vody 179–80
Köprülü viziers 125, 156, 191
Kopynsky, Isaia 102–3
Korocha 83, 88, 101
Korotoiak 91, 185
Korsak, Rafael 118, 122, 128
Korsun' 3, 104, 128, 150, 155, 158, 169, 176
Korzon, Tadeusz 130
Kosagov, Grigorii Ivanovich 146, 149, 170, 179–80, 198
Kozlov 75, 82–4, 88, 91, 94, 101, 133, 137, 170, 186, 206
Kozlovskii, Grigorii Afanas'evich 114, 143
Krapivna 45–6, 60, 65, 68
Kravkov, Matvei Osipovich 135, 137, 167
Kremenchug 148, 150
Kunitskyi, Stepan 171, 178
Kurakin, Fedor Semenovich 118–19, 148
Kurakin, Grigorii Semenovich 153
Kursk 25, 46, 61, 160, 162, 164
Kurukove, Treaty of 100
Kysil, Adam 76, 105, 108, 113

Lanckoroński, Stanisław 119–21, 143
Lazar'ev, Andrei 97
Lebedian' 19, 66–7, 84, 88, 173
Lefort, Franz 182–6
Leopold I, Holy Roman Emperor 156, 176–7, 183, 187
Leslie, Alexander 71, 74
Lesser Nogai Horde (Kazyev ulus) 8, 12, 16, 28, 31, 57, 77–9, 106, 111, 183, 191–3
Lisnytski, Grygori 122, 126–8
Lithuania, Grand Duchy of *see* Commonwealth, Polish-Lithuanian
Litvin, Mikhalon 24–5
Liutik 183, 185
Livny 18, 46, 61, 67, 76, 92, 173
Livonia 1, 35, 64, 121, 124, 132
Livonian War (1558–1583) 22, 44, 47, 51, 59, 64
Lokhvitsa 129–30, 168

252

lower service class 45, 85, 186; gunners 49, 51, 53, 60, 65, 135, 162–3, 166, 215; musketeers *see* field army, Muscovite: infantry, musketeer; service Cossacks 31, 40, 50, 60, 62–5, 67, 71–2, 79, 81–3, 85–6, 101–2, 118, 153, 173, 182; *see also* field army, Muscovite; garrisons, Muscovite; military service
Lubar 143–4, 146
Lublin 9, 19, 122
Lubny 38, 150, 163
Lubomirski, Jerzy 99, 143–5, 149–50
L'viv 104, 120, 122, 138, 157–8, 190
L'vov, Semen Petrovich 131
Lyzlov, Andrei 177

Małopolska 9, 20, 124, 155
Mamai 2
Massa, Isaak 24, 53
Matveev, Artemon Sergeevich 122, 159
Maurice of Nassau 52, 70, 136
Mazepa, Ivan 165–6, 180–1, 183, 187, 200–1
Mehmet Girei I, Crimean Khan 11, 14, 15
Mehmet Girei II, Crimean Khan 16
Mehmet III, Ottoman Sultan 11, 17
Mehmet IV, Ottoman Sultan 104, 109, 152, 155, 172, 175–6, 193
Mengli Girei I, Crimean Khan 5, 13–14, 23
Meshchera 44, 54
Mezhibozh'e 143, 156, 158
middle service class (*dvoriane* and *deti boiarskie*) 41–4, 50–1, 59–60, 62–5, 67–72, 79, 83, 85, 87, 116, 131, 134–5, 137; *see also* field army, Muscovite: cavalry, traditional formation; military service
migration and settlement: of Commonwealth Ukraine 2–3, 5, 33, 35, 38, 97–8; of Sloboda Ukraine and southern Muscovy, by Ukrainian immigrants 84, 101–2, 171–2, 205–6; of southern Muscovite frontier, by private voluntary initiative 4–6, 19, 25, 64, 66–7, 83–4, 96, 100–1; of southern Muscovite frontier, by state-directed military colonization 40, 46, 59–61, 64–6, 79, 81–7, 91–2, 94, 205; *see also* garrisons, Muscovite
Mikhail Fedorovich, Tsar of Muscovy 58–9, 66–7, 89–90
Mikhailov 46, 60, 69
Military Chancellery (*Razriadnyi prikaz*) 25, 42–3, 46–54, 59, 62–73, 80–108, 119, 134, 140–2, 153, 163, 165, 168, 170, 173, 179–80, 204–5
military service (*sluzhba*), 29, 40, 43, 45, 64, 66, 85, 186, 203, 206–7; and allodial estates of court nobility 41–3; and allotments (*nadely*) of registered cossacks, gunners, and musketeers 45; assignment to locus of service (bank service, corps service, distant campaign service, town service) 30, 43, 50–1, 59, 60, 65–6, 69, 85, 173, 186, 203, 206; Decree on Service (1556) 42–3, 50, 60, 69, 85, 204; eligibility for service 65, 81–5, 94, 101, 173; enserfment of peasant tenants in support of servicemen 69–70, 82, 85; remuneration entitlements 48, 50, 65, 68; service-conditional estates (*pomest'ia*) of the traditional formation cavalry 40–2, 45, 50, 59, 65–6, 68–9, 82, 85–6, 87, 94, 101, 134, 141, 172, 203–4, 206; yeomen (*odnodvortsy*) 85–7, 137, 186, 206–7; *see also* Court; field army, Muscovite; garrisons, Muscovite; lower service class; middle service class; Military Chancellery
Miloslavskii clan 169, 174, 176
Mirgorod 128, 130, 146, 150, 155
Mius' River 105, 198, 201
Mnogogreshnyi, Demian 154–5, 200
Mogilev 109, 115
Mohacs, battle of 10
Mohyla, Petro 103
Moldavia 2, 7, 9–11, 98–9, 108–9, 111, 118–19, 156, 178, 188–90, 193
Molodi, battle of 16, 52–5
Montecuccoli, Raimondo 197
Moscow 4–5, 14–18 *passim*; Grand Principality of 1, 2, 4–5 *passim*; *see also* Muscovy, Tsardom of
Mozhaisk 72, 75
Mstislavl' 115, 117
Mtsensk 46, 68, 76, 92
Mubarek Girei 77
Murat III, Ottoman Sultan 17
Murat IV, Ottoman Sultan 70, 76, 78–9, 89–90
Murat Girei, Crimean Khan 161–2, 167, 170–2, 190–2
Murphey, Rhoads 196
Muscovy, Tsardom of 1, 4–5, 6, 8, 11–18 *passim*; *see also* defense lines; diplomacy, conduct of; field army, Muscovite; garrisons, Muscovite; migration and settlement; Moscow, Grand Principality of
Muzhilovsky, Syluian 105

Naryshkin clan, 182, 198
naval and riverine warfare 32–3, 38–9, 53, 56, 58, 66, 78, 89, 100, 103, 121, 160, 163, 167, 179, 184–6, 193–4, 199, 211
Nepliuev, Leontii Romanovich 171, 178, 180
Nezhin 128, 132, 142, 146, 148–50, 154
Niemiez, Armistice of 124, 126
Nikon, Patriarch of Moscow 108
Nizhnii-Novgorod 42, 44

INDEX

Northern Donets River 18, 88, 107, 171–2, 201
Novgorod 4–5, 93, 118–19, 124, 173, 175
Novgorod-Severskii 2, 4–5, 14, 61, 73, 126, 132, 142, 148, 150, 177
Novobogoroditskoe 180–1, 199
Novosergeevsk 181, 199
Novosil' 5, 18, 60, 65, 68, 76, 92
Novyi Oskol' 88, 91–2

Ochakov 32, 56, 70, 78, 126, 159, 184, 195
Odoevskii, Nikita Iakovlevich 53–4
Odoevskii, Nikita Ivanovich 115
Oka River 4, 5, 14, 17, 23, 41–2, 47, 53–4, 60, 68, 76, 81
Okhmativ 119–20
Olearius, Adam 6
Oliva, Treaty of 132, 143
Ol'shansk 91
Oprichnina Terror (1565–1672) 47, 49
Ordyn-Nashchokin, Afanasii Lavrent'evich 123–4, 151, 155, 202–3
Orel 82, 92–3
Orthodox Church 3, 13, 29, 66, 98–104, 105–10, 112–13, 117, 125, 129, 135, 177, 199
Oskol' River 65, 171
Osman II, Ottoman Sultan 99, 193
Ossoliński, Jerzy 108
Oster 35, 147–8, 150, 154
Ostrianyn, Iatsko 102
Ostrogozhsk 102
Ostroz'kyi, Kostiantyn 3
Ottoman army 34, 37, 44, 67, 196–8, 204; and *timar* system 43, 69, 195
Ottoman Empire: Crimean, Black Sea, and Ukrainian interests 1, 2, 6–13, 17, 23–6, 28, 31, 39, 57, 66, 70, 76, 78–80, 89–91, 96–8, 100, 104, 109, 155–72, 192–3, 199, 201, 204–6; Danubian interests 9, 11, 17, 99, 113, 189, 191, 193–4; and Hetmanate 107, 109, 125, 150–3; and Holy League 175–87, 194; internal crises and reconfiguration of political system 195–6; and treaties of Karlowitz and Constantinople 157, 187–8, 191, 193–5, 199; Volga interests 15–16, 47, 61; *see also* Commonwealth, Polish-Lithuanian; Crimean Khanate; Holy Roman Empire; Moldavia; Muscovy, Tsardom of; Podolia; Polish-Ottoman Wars; Russo-Turkish War
Ozernaia, battle of 123, 125

Pac, Michal 147, 161, 189
Palyi, Semen 178
Panshin 184–5
Pasek, Jan 138–40

Pereiaslav 2, 38, 126, 132, 146, 149–51, 169; Agreement of 110–14, 128–30, 142, 154, 215–16
Pereiaslavl'-Riazan' 46, 69
Perekop 6, 18, 20, 56, 58, 77, 96, 120, 148, 151–2, 178, 180–3, 187, 191, 201
Peresvetov, Ivan 44, 52
Perevolok Expedition (1569) 12–13, 17, 47
Perfil'ev, Tomilo 116
Persia 11, 12, 59, 151
Peter I, Tsar of Muscovy and Emperor of Russia 1, 93, 136–7, 182–7, 194–5, 197, 203, 206
Petrik 200
Podolia 2, 4, 9, 25, 33 109, 120–1, 129, 152, 156, 178, 188–90, 193–4
Poland, Kingdom of *see* Commonwealth, Polish-Lithuanian
Polianovka, Treaty of 76, 106–7, 110
Polish-Lithuanian army: artillery 35, 70, 73–5, 191; castles and garrisons in Ukraine 35, 100, 156, 197; cavalry 34–5, 70, 73–4, 115, 133, 156, 191; cossacks as auxiliaries 11, 32–3, 37–9, 76, 98–9; finance and logistics 10, 33–4, 143, 148–9, 157, 178, 189–90, 204; foreign formation troops 70, 133, 204; frontier defense and Quarter Army 10, 18–20, 98; infantry 34–5, 70, 133, 188–9; mobilizations and force strengths 33–4, 70, 74, 106, 109, 115, 118–20, 122–3, 133, 143, 147, 156–7, 188–9; private forces 4, 9, 11, 32, 98, 156; tactics 35–8, 122, 138–40, 144–5, 147, 157, 188, 191; *see also* Commonwealth, Polish-Lithuanian
Polish-Ottoman War (1620–1621) 99, 193
Polish-Ottoman War (1672–1676) 155–7, 159, 175, 196, 200
Polish-Swedish War (1655–1660) 121, 123–4, 132–3
Polotsk 44, 51, 73, 115–16, 123
Poltava 127–8, 130, 146, 149, 155, 172
Potemkin, Petr Ivanovich 122
Potocki, Andrzej 128, 130
Potocki, Stanisław 118–20, 122, 143–5, 147
Pozharskii, Semen Romanovich 96, 131, 217
Pronsk 46, 51, 69
propaganda 13, 24, 99–100, 104, 106, 108, 126–7, 150, 175, 177–8
Prozorovskii, Semen Vasil'evich 73–6
Pruth River 10, 19, 197
Pskov 5, 118–19, 124
Pushkar, Martyn 127–8, 200
Putivl' 5, 14, 18–20, 46, 61, 67, 69, 76, 101, 130–1, 143, 145, 160, 163–5, 170, 175, 205
Pyliavtsi, battle of 33, 104

Radziwiłł, Janusz 106, 109, 115–16, 118, 121, 123

254

Radziwiłł, Krzysztof 73–4
Rares, Petru, Moldavian Voivode 10
Repnin, Boris Aleksandrovich 108–9
Riazan' 5–6, 14, 19, 29, 42, 44, 45, 47, 50, 54, 66, 69, 77, 88, 93, 173, 178
Riazhsk, 19, 45, 60, 66, 67, 69, 86, 88
Riga 123–4
Rodenburg, Jan Cornelius van 74, 80, 88
Romanov, Ivan Nikitich 67
Romodanovskii, Grigorii Grigor'evich 121–3, 126–7, 129–31, 137, 146–8, 153–4, 158–68, 174, 205
Romodanovskii, Ivan Ivanovich 118
Rosworm, Eremei 71, 74, 80
Rus' Czerwona 3–4, 9, 19, 33, 125
Russo-Lithuanian Wars (1470s–1530s) 4–5, 9, 13–14, 202
Russo-Turkish War (1676–1681) 13, 159–72, 174, 190, 193, 196, 204–5
Ryl'sk 5, 14, 18, 61, 69, 118, 130, 163–4, 168

Saadet Girei I, Crimean Khan 11, 15
Saadet Girei II, Crimean Khan 191
Safa Girei I, Crimean Khan 191
Sagaidachnyi, Petro 68, 98–9
Sahib Girei I, Crimean Khan 12, 14–16, 61
Samara River 179–81
Samoilovich, Ivan 159–70, 176, 179–80, 201
Sapieha, Pawel 116, 133, 147
Sefer Gazy Aga 119
Selim I, Ottoman Sultan 7, 9
Selim II, Ottoman Sultan 12–13
Selim Girei I, Crimean Khan 157, 159, 161, 181, 184, 187, 191–2, 200; as *nuraddin* 129–30
Serebrianyi, Petr Semenovich 12
Serpukhov 17–8, 46, 54–5, 66, 77
Seversk Land 6, 18, 42, 66, 70, 73, 76, 106, 110, 151
Sevsk 18, 76, 116, 131; Army Group and territorial military administration 93–4, 130, 141, 153, 160, 162, 170, 171, 173, 178–9, 183, 204–6
Shatsk 19, 44–6, 60, 66–7, 84, 88
Shcherbatov, Konstantin Osipovich 168, 170
Shcherbatov, Osip Ivanovich 143
Shein, Aleksei Semenovich 178, 181, 186
Shein, Mikhail Borisovich 73–6
Shepelev, Agei Alekseevich 128, 167
Shepeleviche, battle of 116
Sheremetev, Boris Petrovich 183–4, 205
Sheremetev, Ivan Petrovich 81
Sheremetev, Vasilii Borisovich 26, 118–19, 121, 128 30, 132, 143 6, 197
Sheremetev, Vasilii Petrovich 115, 117
Shuiskii, Ivan Petrovich 53–4
Silistria 7, 10
Simbirsk 91

Sirko, Ivan 26, 33, 132, 146, 148, 151, 158, 160, 169, 192
Sloboda Ukraine 102, 148, 153, 170–1, 177, 179, 181, 193, 198, 200–1, 205–6
Slobodishche, battle of 143–5
Smirnov, N. A. 163–4
Smolensk 4–5, 9, 14, 17, 22, 66, 70–7, 92, 103, 106, 109–10, 115–17, 123, 159, 162, 173, 177
Smolensk War (1632–1634) 22, 68, 70–9, 81, 88, 202
Sobieski, Jan 152, 155–7; as King of Poland 22, 157–9, 161–2, 175–6, 178, 183, 188–91
Sokol'sk 91, 186
Solonoi Gorodok, battle of 122
Somko, Ivan 146–7
Staden, Heinrich von 53
Starodub 5, 14, 73, 110, 118, 126, 142, 153
Staryi Bykhov 109, 116–17, 126
Stavishche 148–9
Stefan (Istvan) Bathory, Prince of Transylvania and King of Poland 10, 32, 34–5
Stefan the Great, Moldavian Voivode 7, 9
Strel'nikov Hill, battle of 167–8
Sukhotin, Fedor 82, 88
Suleiman I, Ottoman Sultan 7, 10–11, 16
Sumy 102, 148, 178, 181
Sweden 1, 111, 114, 123–5, 132, 189, 201, 203
Szalankemen, battle of 196

Tagenrog 186–7, 194, 199
Tambov 79, 82–4, 91, 93, 170, 173, 183
Tarusa 6, 53–4
Tatarinov, Mikhail 89–90
tax-bearing obligations (*tiaglo*) 29, 40, 45–6, 51, 66, 73, 81–2, 84, 133–4, 141, 174, 186, 203, 206, 213
Temkin-Rostovskii, Mikhail Mikhailovich 115
Terek River 12–13
Teteria, Pavlo 146–7, 150
Theophanes III, Patriarch of Jerusalem 99
Thirteen Years' War (1654–1667) 48, 93, 102, 107–11, 113–14, 115–51, 192, 200, 202–5
Tiapkin, Vasilii 152
Tias'min River 161, 168
Time of Troubles (1598–1613) 8, 53, 59, 65–6, 68, 98, 102–3
Timur Leng (Tamerlane) 2, 4
Tinekhmat, Nogai Bey 12, 27, 57
Tokhtamysh 2, 4
town governors (*gorodovye voevody*) 27–28, 31–2, 40, 45, 48–50 *passim*; *see also* field army, Muscovite; garrisons, Muscovite; Ukraine

INDEX

trails: Czarny 19; Iziuma 18, 82, 88; Kal'miuss 18, 31, 82, 88, 91; Kuczman 19; Murava 18, 88, 91, 170; Nogai 18–19, 31, 79, 88, 91; Woloski 19
Transylvania 10, 108, 121, 125, 156
Trauernicht, Afanasii 160, 166
tribute, gifts, and contributions 7–9, 17–18, 22, 27, 51, 72, 122, 192, 199; *see also* Don Cossack Host, and Muscovite Don Shipments
Trubetskoi, Aleksei Nikitich 112, 115, 117, 119, 122, 126–7, 130–2, 142
Tsarev-Borisov 18, 58, 61, 67, 102, 171–2
Tsaritsyn' 17, 19, 57, 184–5
Tsetsura, Tymofei 132, 143, 145, 147
Tugai Shirin, Crimean Bey 97, 104
Tula 14, 16, 18, 42, 45–6, 51, 54, 64–5, 80–1, 85, 92, 118, 135, 173
Tyszkiewicz, Krzysztof 120

Ugra River 5, 41–2, 44, 54
Ukraine: in Grand Duchy of Lithuania 3, 5, 32, 34, 37; Left Bank 33, 35, 40, 98–100, 133, 140, 145, 147–53, 155–6, 158, 160–1, 165, 170, 172, 188, 193, 200–1, 203, 205; in Polish-Lithuanian Commonwealth 1, 4, 9–10; Right Bank 110, 146–8, 151, 153–9, 161, 165, 169–72, 176, 178, 188, 194, 200–1; Settled Lands 38–9, 98, 100, 104, 200; under Muscovite protectorate, 110–14 *passim*; unified Hetmanate of 104–14, 153–4, 158, 162, 200, 202; *see also* Thirteen Years' War; Zaporozhian Sich
Uman' 118–19, 126, 130, 142–3
Userdsk 67, 82–3, 88, 94, 170
Usman' 91, 131, 170

Vallisaari, Armistice of 132–3
Valuiki 18–19, 61, 67, 76, 88, 101
Vasilii III, Grand Prince of Moscow 1, 4–5, 14, 42, 201–2
Velikie Luki 115–16
Viaz'ma 72, 75
Vienna, siege of 176, 191, 196
Vilnius 9, 20, 109, 114, 115, 122, 133
Vinnitsa 4, 126
Vitebsk 20, 115, 123, 151
Vladimir 15, 54, 93, 173
Volga River 1, 4, 6, 8, 27–9, 42, 45, 91, 95, 121, 175, 192, 201
Volhynia 3, 9, 25, 106, 110, 125, 129, 143, 147

Voronezh 19, 26, 51, 61, 83–5, 91, 101–2, 131, 184, 186
Voronezh River 5, 17, 19, 23, 32, 40, 65, 79, 91
Vorotynskii, Mikhail Ivanovich 53–5, 61–2
Vyhov'skyi, Danilo 129
Vyhov'skyi, Dymitro 122
Vyhov'skyi, Ivan 107–8, 110–11, 113–14, 125–32, 142, 150, 154, 200
Vyshnevets'kyi (Wisniowiecki), Dymitro 32, 37, 56–7, 96

Wallachia 2, 11, 98, 108–9, 111, 118, 150, 191, 193
Wallhausen, Johann von 136
Warki, battle of 133
Warsaw 121–2, 124, 176–7
Western Dvina River 14, 116, 123
Wiełkopolska 124
Wisniowiecki, Jeremi 76, 101, 103–4, 106
Wiśniowiecki, Michał Korybut, King of Poland 155–7
Władysław II, King of Poland 9; *see also* Jogaila
Władysław IV Waza, King of Poland 66, 70, 74–6, 98–9, 103, 105, 117, 188
Wolf, Franz 166

Zahlen, Nicholas von 160
Zahlen, Wilhelm von 181
Zalozhitsy 123, 138
Zamoyski, Jan 10, 34
Zapolyai, Janos, King of Hungary 10
Zaporozhian Sich 32–3, 37–9, 98, 100, 103, 107–8, 111, 125–7, 130, 132, 140, 148, 150–3, 159, 170–1, 177–81, 183–4, 187, 191, 199–200
Zbarazh 105, 191
Zboriv, Treaty of 105–6, 109, 129
Zenta, battle of 196
Zhevty Vody, battle of 104
Zhizdra River 44–5, 54
Zhvanets 111, 156
Żółkiewski, Stanisław 98–9
Zolotarenko, Ivan 115, 117–18
Zolotarenko, Vasilii 132, 146–7
Żórawno, Treaty of 157, 159, 161, 175
Zygmunt I, King of Poland 9, 14, 33, 37
Zygmunt II Avgust, King of Poland 10, 37, 56
Zygmunt III Waza, King of Poland 10, 73, 98–100